A.C.S. Peacock is Reader in Middle Eastern Studies at the University of St Andrews, and holds a PhD from the University of Cambridge. His publications include *Early Seljuq History: A New Interpretation* (2010) and *The Great Seljuk Empire* (2015).

Sara Nur Yıldız is Research Fellow at the University of St Andrews, affiliated with the Orient-Institut, Istanbul. She earned her PhD from the University of Chicago in 2006 with a thesis entitled *Mongol Rule in Thirteenth-century Seljuk Anatolia: the Politics of Conquest and History Writing, 1243–1282*, and has taught at the universities of Manchester and Istanbul Bilgi.

THE SELJUKS OF ANATOLIA

Court and Society in the Medieval Middle East

Edited by
A.C.S. Peacock and Sara Nur Yıldız

I.B. TAURIS
LONDON · NEW YORK

New paperback edition published in 2015 by
I.B.Tauris & Co Ltd
London • New York
www.ibtauris.com

First published in hardback in 2013 by I.B.Tauris & Co Ltd

Copyright © 2013, 2015 A.C.S. Peacock and Sara Nur Yıldız

The right of A.C.S. Peacock and Sara Nur Yıldız to be identified as the author of this work has been asserted by the author in accordance with the Copyright, Designs and Patents Act 1988.

All rights reserved. Except for brief quotations in a review, this book, or any part thereof, may not be reproduced, stored in or introduced into a retrieval system, or transmitted, in any form or by any means, electronic, mechanical, photocopying, recording or otherwise, without the prior written permission of the publisher.

Every attempt has been made to gain permission for the use of the images in this book. Any omissions will be rectified in future editions.

References to websites were correct at the time of writing.

ISBN: 978 1 78453 165 2
eISBN: 978 0 85773 346 7

A full CIP record for this book is available from the British Library
A full CIP record is available from the Library of Congress

Library of Congress Catalog Card Number: available

Typeset by Newgen Publishers, Chennai
Printed and bound by CPI Group (UK) Ltd, Croydon, CR0 4YY

FSC www.fsc.org MIX Paper from responsible sources FSC® C013604

CONTENTS

LIST OF ILLUSTRATIONS

ACKNOWLEDGEMENTS

The ideas for the chapters in this volume derive from debates which arose during a workshop entitled 'Court and Society in Seljuk Anatolia' held at the German Orient-Institut in Istanbul in October 2009. The workshop was supported by the Gerda Henkel Stiftung, whose financial contribution is gratefully acknowledged. We would also like to thank the other workshop participants, whose contributions helped shape our thinking on Seljuk Anatolia but whose papers, for reasons of space, it is unfortunately impossible to include. We are also very grateful for the assistance of our editor at I.B.Tauris, Maria Marsh, and our copyeditor Ian McDonald. The publication of this volume was made possible by a contribution from the Gerda Henkel Stiftung towards production costs.

A NOTE ON USAGE AND TRANSLITERATION

Anglicised Words

Common words, titles and names of Arabic, Persian or Turkish origin such as qadi, madrasa and caravanserai have been rendered according to their usage in English. Dynastic names with the suffix '-id' and words assimilated to English are not transliterated, e.g., Khan instead of Khān, Ilkhanid instead of Īl-khānid, Qur'an instead of Qur'ān, Karamanid rather than Qarāmanid and Abbasid rather than 'Abbāsid. We have made use of the *International Journal of Middle East Studies (IJMES)* standards to determine which terms and names are Anglicised.

Place Names

Place names have been given their modern form whenever possible (Konya, Aksaray, Kayseri, Beyşehir, Erzurum, Maraş, Erzincan, Malatya, Bukhara, Samarqand, Khurasan, Herat, Iran). Variants are provided in parentheses when appropriate. Well-known place names are given their accepted English forms, such as Damascus, Aleppo, Tabriz, Mosul and Qipchaq steppe. Lesser-known names will be rendered in their medieval as well as their modern form.

Transliteration

Persian and Arabic names of texts and individuals have been transliterated according to the system used by the Library of Congress. The vowels of Turkic and Mongolian names and words have not been rendered long even if in the Arabic script they have been written so. Hence Balasaghun, rather than Balāsāghūn, Arslan rather than Arslān. With the exception of standard forms such as Chinggis Khan, Mongolian names, place names and terms have been rendered according to Igor de Rachewiltz's *Index to the Secret History of the Mongols* (Bloomington, Indiana: Indiana University, 1972). We however have modified this system slightly by rendering Rachewiltz's use of /c/ as /ch/ to reflect a more common pronunciation in English. We have followed the standard practice in Byzantine studies of transcribing Byzantine names rather than Latinising them, using as a model the works of Paul Magdalino and Dimiter Angelov. Thus we render Palaiologos, not Palaeologus. We, however, retain the common English forms of names such as Constantine, Theodore and Anna Comnena.

The transliterations of original passages have been italicised.

LIST OF CONTRIBUTORS

Rachel Goshgarian is Assistant Professor of History at Lafayette College, Pennsylvania. She received her PhD from Harvard University in 2008 and formerly directed the Krikor and Clara Zohrab Information Center. She was a Senior Fellow at Koç University's Research Center for Anatolian Civilizations in Istanbul in 2010–11.

Dimitri Korobeinikov is Assistant Professor, Department of History, University at Albany, SUNY, New York, and Senior Research Fellow, Centre for Byzantine and Eastern Christian Studies, Institute of General History, Russian Academy of Sciences, Moscow. His book *Byzantium and the Turks in the Thirteenth Century* was published by Oxford University Press in 2014.

Gary Leiser is a retired civil servant. He completed a doctorate in Middle Eastern history at the University of Pennsylvania under George Makdisi in 1976. His primary area of interest is the eastern Mediterranean world in the twelfth to the thirteenth centuries. He has translated from Turkish the most important historical works of M.F. Köprülü.

Oya Pancaroğlu's research interests are piqued by the medieval visual and literary heritage of the lands between Anatolia and Central Asia.

She is captivated in equal measure by the pre- and post-Mongol architecture of Anatolia, the dissemination of Abbasid material culture, the appearance and development of inscriptions on the ceramics of Iran and the trajectory of ancient cults and rituals in medieval architecture and arts. Issues of methodology are a recurrent preoccupation and frequently infiltrate her teaching at the History Department of Boğaziçi University, Istanbul. The experience of researching and writing her chapter for this volume has left her with a new fascination for the political and artistic landscapes of the 1190s.

A.C.S. Peacock is Reader in Middle Eastern Studies in the School of History, University of St Andrews, and holds a PhD from the University of Cambridge. His publications include *Mediaeval Islamic Historiography and Political Legitimacy* (London: Routledge, 2007), *Early Seljuq History* (London: Routledge, 2010) and *The Great Seljuk Empire* (Edinburgh: Edinburgh University Press, 2015) in addition to numerous articles on medieval Islamic history, especially with reference to Anatolia.

Scott Redford is Nasser D. Khalili Professor of Islamic Art and Archaeology at the School of Oriental and African Studies, University of London. He is the author of four books and many articles on the art, architecture and archaeology of medieval Anatolia and the eastern Mediterranean. His *Legends of Authority: The 1215 Seljuk Inscriptions of Sinop Citadel, Turkey* was published in 2014 by Koc University Press in Istanbul.

Haşim Şahin, a specialist in the religious history of late medieval Anatolia, is a Lecturer at the Department of History, Sakarya University, Turkey, and holds a doctorate from Marmara University, Istanbul. He is the author of a collection of essays, *Orta Zaman Türkleri: Orta Çağ İslâm ve Türk Tarihine Dair Yazılar* (Istanbul: Yeditepe Yayınevi, 2011).

Rustam Shukurov is a docent in Byzantine and Oriental Studies at Moscow State University. His scholarly interest covers the relations between the Byzantine world and the Orient during the late Byzantine period. He is the author of the monograph *The Grand Komnenoi and the Orient, 1204–1461* (St Petersburg: Alateia, 2001) (in Russian).

Sara Nur Yıldız is Research Fellow at the University of St Andrews, affiliated with the Orient-Institut, Istanbul. She earned her PhD from the University of Chicago in 2006 with a thesis entitled *Mongol Rule in Thirteenth-century Seljuk Anatolia: the Politics of Conquest and History Writing, 1243–1282*, and has taught at the universities of Manchester and Istanbul Bilgi.

CHAPTER ONE

INTRODUCTION

A.C.S. Peacock and Sara Nur Yıldız

The kingdom of Turkey was very famous and very rich ...[1] [There were] almost a hundred cities there, quite apart from castles, towns, and estates. There was such an abundance of riches there that one amir, no matter what the winter, used to feed 10,000 rams on barley, quite apart from those which were in his pastures. This same amir also used to feed 10,000 horses on barley, quite apart from those which were in his pastures and stud-[farms]. Moreover, on his land the sultan used to have six – or, according to certain people – ten silver [mines], one of which was worth 10,000 soldani per day. The silver [mine] in Lebena, it is said, is worth three rotas of purified silver per day. This is worth 3,000 soldani once the workers have been paid. So the sultan's land was worth 4,000 hyperberi to him per day – i.e. 57,000 silver marks. What is more, there are three copper mines there and even more iron mines. There is also an alum mine very near Sivas, which is worth one silver [mine][2] ... In the land of Konya a mine of lapis lazuli has been discovered, but it has been completely covered by the earth which collects over it. There, too, in addition to sheep's wool, they have the best goat's wool from which are made bonnets which are sent to

> be sold in France and England. Therefore, the sultan of Turkey was well able to pay each one of his 50,000 soldiers a thousand byzantici every year ... One of the sultan's treasurers has also said that there were three houses in Kayseri, one of which was full of hyperberi, the other two being full of drachmas.[3]

The description of Anatolia by the Dominican friar Simon de Saint-Quentin, based on his visit around 1246, impresses us with the Seljuk sultan's wealth and power. Anatolia's natural resources of mines and extensive pastureland for animals, whose products could be exported as far as distant northern Europe, earned the sultan the riches to support a large army. Simon's use of the term 'Turkey' (*Turquie regnum*), one of its earliest attestations, is suggestive of Seljuk rule's profound influence in the transformation of Anatolia from a largely Christian – above all Greek and Armenian – part of the Byzantine empire into a land with a substantial Muslim and Turkish component following the Byzantines' abandonment of much of Anatolia in the wake of their defeat at Manzikert in 1071 by the Great Seljuk ruler Alp Arslan.

Yet if from the west Seljuk Anatolia seemed a land of riches and power – despite its formal incoporation into the Mongol empire shortly before Simon's visit in the wake of the Battle of Kösedağ in 1243 – this view is not reflected in our Muslim sources. Anatolia features rarely in histories and geographies produced in Iraq, Syria or Egypt, the heartlands of the medieval Islamic world. When it does, it little resembles the prosperous, all-powerful kingdom of our friar. Take the account of the Moroccan Ibn Saʿīd, also written in the mid thirteenth century, perhaps a decade or so after Simon's visit. Although Ibn Saʿīd does briefly mention the existence of silver and iron mines, he is more impressed by the huge numbers of nomadic Turkmen – 200,000 households near Denizli, 30,000 near Ankara and 100,000 near Kastamonu. In contrast to the hundred major cities Simon claims for the Seljuk realm, Ibn Saʿīd – rather more credibly – notes only 24. He remarks on the existence of a Turkmen carpet-making industry, but the only other major product he finds worthy of mentioning is the abundant fruit that Anatolia produced. He states there were 400,000 agricultural estates (*ḍīʿa*), of which

36,000 were ruined. In Konya, the Seljuk capital, the houses were of mud except for those of the ruler and the elite, which had marble panels. There is no mention of the sultan's income.[4] So where Simon found wealth, splendour and power, Ibn Saʿīd found nomads, destroyed agricultural land and fruit. The differences between them doubtless come down to a matter of expectations. Where for Simon the Seljuk lands were the exotic east, the route through which prized luxuries came to Europe, from the point of view of the Middle East and the broader Islamic world, Anatolia was the wild west, a barely Islamised frontier land that produced few scholars or literary men.[5] It was a place where one might seek one's fortune, to be sure, as plenty of refugees and immigrants from the Iranian and Arab lands did, but culturally, geographically and historically, it was a different world.

This acute sense of difference from the broader Muslim world is also reflected in our sources, or the lack of them. In contrast to the profusion of historical writing in the central Islamic lands under the Seljuks' contemporaries, the Seljuk sultanate of Anatolia found very few chroniclers. Unlike the situation in most of the rest of the Islamic world of the time (or at least its developed centres), no biographical dictionaries record the lives and teaching of the Anatolian *ʿulamāʾ*, no works extol the virtues (*faḍāʾil*) of Konya or any other Anatolian city. The panegyric poets who so lavishly praise the Ayyubids, Mamluks and Great Seljuks of Iran are largely silent on the rulers of Anatolia. Muslim Anatolian rulers do not even leave much in the way of epigraphic or numismatic evidence until the second half of the twelfth century. Thus even the customary sources for Islamic history are largely absent for Anatolia.

The uniqueness of Anatolia therefore demands that the historian employ different methods from those commonly used to study other areas of the Muslim world. With the comparative paucity of literary sources, or at least chronicles, material evidence from archaeology and architecture as well as epigraphy and numismatics becomes a vital tool for interpreting the Anatolian past rather than the optional extra it is often seen as elsewhere. The linguistic diversity of the the written primary sources that do exist – Arabic, Armenian, Greek, Persian and Syriac are key, while Georgian, Latin and Turkish are also useful – presents a hurdle few individuals could hope to surmount.

Cooperation between scholars from different disciplines is thus essential, yet to date little has been done in this respect.[6]

This volume, which arises from a conference held in Istanbul in 2009, brings together scholars from various backgrounds ranging from Armenian studies to Islamic archaeology. We focus above all on the late twelfth to late thirteenth centuries, a period of tumultuous change in Anatolia that witnessed the rise of the Seljuk state to its brief apogee in the reign of 'Alā' al-Dīn Kayqubād I (1219–37) followed by the humiliation of Mongol domination from the mid century onwards. This era saw the development of a sophisticated culture that drew on Iranian, Byzantine, Ayyubid and common Levantine elements, while the Seljuk court became the political, artistic and cultural centre of Anatolia. At the same time, the wider society, both Christian and Muslim, was affected by developments in religion and culture. The rise of Sufi groups – sometimes through court patronage, perhaps sometimes through a broader appeal of their own – may have played a part in spreading Islam to a broader audience. More certainly, *ṭarīqat*-based Sufism influenced the institution of *futuwwa*, a type of religiously inspired guild and social organisation that came to dominate Anatolian urban life by the end of the thirteenth century. The religiously and ethnically diverse society in which the Seljuks lived was reflected in the life of the court and the ruling dynasty itself, while the Perso-Islamic culture and religion that the court publicly supported resonated far beyond the elite Muslim circles of Konya and the few other major Muslim cities of Anatolia.

We explore how court and society interacted and shaped one other, aiming to move beyond the more purely political history that has dominated to date. We have also tried to represent the political, as well as ethnic and religious, diversity of Anatolia. The Seljuks were the pre-eminent Muslim dynasty in the thirteenth century, but they were not the only one, and other, sometimes rival, sometimes allied dynasties such as the Mengüjekids in the north-east also played a role in Anatolian history – albeit one that is often overlooked. To enable the reader to appreciate the contribution of this volume, we shall firstly outline the state of the art of the historiography to date, before sketching what the Seljuk court was and how it operated. We

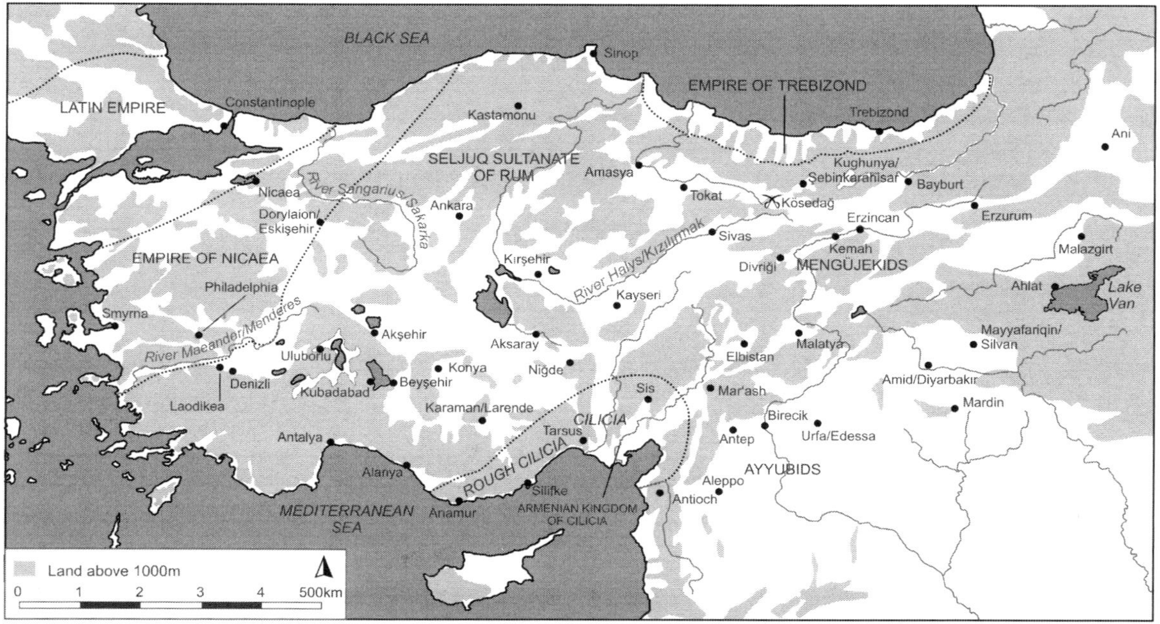

Figure 1.1 Map of Anatolia in the time of 'Alā' al-Dīn Kayqubād I (1219–37).

will then conclude this introduction by surveying the chapters in this book.

The Seljuk Sultanate of Rūm: Sources and Approaches

It is essential to distinguish between the Great Seljuk sultanate, based in Iran, Iraq and Central Asia (c.1040–1194) and the Seljuk sultanate of Rūm, as Anatolia was generally known to the Muslims (c.1081–1308). The Anatolian branch of the family had little to do with their cousins, with whom relations were tense owing to disputes over legitimate leadership. Alp Arslan, the Great Seljuk sultan who in 1071 won the Battle of Manzikert against the Byzantines, the event which is conventionally seen as marking the establishment of Turkish rule in Anatolia, does not seem to have intended to conquer the region. For a good 40 years before the battle Asia Minor had been penetrated by migratory Turkish groups in search of pastureland, with whom the Byzantines had proved wholly incapable of dealing. Neither Alp Arslan nor his successor Malikshāh played any role in the establishment of the sultanate of Rūm, and Malikshāh's efforts to exert his authority in the west came to naught in the long run.[7]

The two Seljuk states were very different in many ways, even if the one in Anatolia continued to draw on the prestige of their shared dynastic name long after the collapse of the Great Seljuks. Yet there is a widepread tendency to assume a certain identity between them, or at least that their institutions and culture were insufficiently different to be worth commenting on. In part this assumption of parallels is perhaps a natural reaction to the extreme paucity of sources for Seljuk Anatolia. As early as the thirteenth century, one Muslim historian was lamenting the absence of relevant historical information. Ibn Bībī, whose elaborate Persian chronicle *al-Awāmir al-ʿalāʾīya fī ʾl-umūr al-ʿalāʾīya*, completed in 1282, is our principal source for the history of the Seljuk sultanate, declared that he was obliged to start his work with Ghiyāth al-Dīn Kaykhusraw I (r. 1192–6, 1205–11) owing to the lack of information about earlier periods (see the comments by Pancaroğlu on pp. 25–6 below).[8] Our other main Islamic sources are also in Persian, and written after the demise of the Seljuk dynasty:

the *Musāmarat al-akhbār* of Āqsarā'ī, which is detailed only for the period of Mongol domination, and an anonymous chronicle written probably by several hands in Konya in the early to mid fourteenth century. We may also mention the work of Aḥmad of Niğde, writing in 1333, called *al-Walad al-shafīq*, which preserves an abridged version of a history of the Seljuk dynasty by the same author.[9] However, *al-Walad al-shafīq* is more valuable for the snippets of information about the author's home town of Niğde that it occasionally provides than for any new details of dynastic history. Apart from these we are largely reliant on occasional references in Arabic chronicles produced in Iraq and Syria, such as Ibn al-Athīr's *al-Kāmil fī 'l-ta'rīkh* (1222) or the anonymous *Ta'rīkh al-manṣūrī*.

Given the relative paucity of Muslim sources, Christian ones assume a greater importance. Without them, we would know virtually nothing about the Seljuk sultanate and its Muslim contemporaries in twelfth-century Anatolia. They also provide a useful supplement to our Persian and Arabic sources for later periods. Yet they suffer from a certain distance: the Seljuks may have had a Greek chancery,[10] but all the Greek chronicles surviving were composed in Byzantium or the capitals of its successor states, such as Panaretos' chronicle of Trebizond. Armenian and Syriac chronicles were composed within the Seljuk realm but are also removed from court life, and the chroniclers are usually more preoccupied with, say, Armenian church politics than with the deeds of their Seljuk overlords. In her chapter in this volume, Rachel Goshgarian notes the striking lack of Armenian references to the Mengüjekid rulers of Erzincan, despite the wealth of Armenian texts produced in and around that city.

Yet it is these Muslim and Christian chronicles that have supplied the basic thread of the narrative of Seljuk history. Their acute limitations perhaps explain why the study of Seljuk history seems in some respects to have stagnated for the last 40 years. Without any new 'evidence' in the form of previously unknown chronicles it may have seemed difficult to move beyond the two works which dominate the the field, despite their somewhat problematic assumptions. The first of these was *Pre-Ottoman Turkey*, published in 1968 by the prominent French medievalist Claude Cahen. In large part based on work carried out by Cahen in the 1940s, it provides an overview of the Seljuks and their contemporaries which has remained standard in the west to date (although the revised French edition of 1988, which provides references, is to be preferred).[11] Shortly afterwards, in 1971, Osman Turan produced *Selçuklular Zamanında Türkiye: Siyasi Tarih Alp Arslan'dan Osman Gazi'ye, 1071–1318* ('Turkey in Seljuk Times: Political History from Alp Arslan to Osman Gazi, 1071–1318'), which offers a detailed chronological survey for a Turkish-speaking audience. In addition to the narrative source base in Persian, Arabic and Latin, Cahen and Turan also occasionally drew on numismatic and epigraphic evidence. Turan's history supercedes Cahen's pioneering work in detail and depth. Both works, however, are limited by a certain assumption that is evident in their titles: that the history of Anatolia is identical with the history of Turkey. Despite the use of the term 'Turquie' by Simon de Saint-Quentin and other Latin authors of the Middle Ages, there is no equivalent in any of our Islamic sources: the Seljuk sultanate, Anatolia, Greeks and Byzantines are all described by the term Rūm (meaning Rome), and the Anatolian Seljuk ruler was known as the Sultan of Rūm. Although the territories that comprised Rūm were never exactly defined, it certainly was not identical with the borders of modern Turkey. Throughout the existence of the Sultanate of Rūm (the dates of which are conventionally given as 1081 to 1308, although the reality is more complicated), large parts of western, north-eastern and southern Anatolia remained in the hands of Christian rulers – firstly Byzantium, then its successor states in Nicaea and Trebizond (from 1204) and the Armenian kingdom of Cilicia (from the late twelfth century). Much of what is now eastern Turkey never or only very fleetingly formed part of the Seljuks' domains, with the south-east retaining closer links to Syria and Iraq and the north-east largely comprising part of the medieval Caucasian and Iranian worlds.

Thus 'Turkey' is a rather anachronistic concept to apply to medieval Muslim Anatolia. Nor are the continuities between the Seljuks and Ottomans clear, as was claimed by what has been dubbed 'the Ottoman dynastic myth' of the fifteenth century.[12] The Ottoman principality arose on the far western periphery of Anatolia, in a frontier land over which the Seljuk sultans had probably rarely exerted much authority, and almost certainly none by the time of the rise of Osman Ghazi around 1300. The Ottoman empire was a major European power before it was an Asian one, and key Seljuk territories such as south-central Anatolia were not definitively annexed to the Ottoman state for a good century and a half after the demise of the Seljuks: Konya itself, for instance, was only taken by Mehmed the Conqueror in 1468. Furthermore, the Seljuk domination of most of Anatolia was a relatively short-lived phenomenon of the first half of the thirteenth century. Up until the 1220s, the Seljuks shared Anatolia with various other Turkish, Muslim dynasties as well as Christian ones. In the north-east, Erzincan, Koloneia (Şebinkarahisar) and Divriği were subject to the Mengüjekids and, until the late twelfth century, north-central Anatolia was dominated by the Danishmendids. Erzurum, a Saltuqid possession in the twelfth century, was briefly ruled by a rival Seljuk at odds with his relatives in Konya in the early thirteenth century. In the second half of the thirteenth century the introduction of Mongol rule gradually weakened the Seljuk polity, and underaged sultans were dominated by amirs who consolidated their political power as clients of the Mongol rulers. By the final decades of the thirteenth century the Seljuk sultanate was no more than a historical relic, and its abolition in the early fourteenth century goes unnoticed by most sources: indeed, even the date of its demise is a matter of debate.[13] Space precludes a lengthy discussion of all these complex and little-understood dynamics, but it is salutary to remember that Muslim Anatolia does not automatically equal Seljuk Rūm, and that the latter itself was far from being a monolithic, centralised state.

Many publications on the Seljuks have appeared in Turkey since Turan's and Cahen's *magnum opuses*. The quality of many of these is distinctly poor, and they have rarely succeeded in adding to (or subtracting from) the works of Turan and Cahen. The assumption of the identity of Seljuk Anatolia with Anatolian Turkey and the presumption that the Seljuks were the direct predecessors of the Ottomans remain largely unchallenged. This paradigm unproblematically places the Seljuks as another link in the chain of great Turkish states in between the pre-Islamic Turkish polities of Inner Asia and culminating with the Ottoman empire and modern Turkish Republic, and has remained more or less intact ever since it was first articulated in 1922 by Ziya Gökalp in his *Türk Devletinin Tekâmülü*. Undoubtedly, this is another reason for the assumption of the identity of the Great Seljuk and Anatolin Seljuk cultures.

Partly as a result of a sparse and difficult source base, combined with ideological considerations, the religious and intellectual history of medieval Anatolia has been approached as a *tabula rasa*, with scholarship dominated by modern nationalist concerns, primarily through the great imaginative powers of the pioneering scholar, Mehmed Fuad Köprülü (1890–1966). Köprülü's Seljuk Anatolia – the homeland of the Turks – was populated with migrating nomadic Turkmen, the religious faith of whom remained essentially shamanistic, barely disguised by a thin veneer of Islamic faith and practice.[14] Köprülü privileged the Turkmen as the main agent of change responsible for transforming the Anatolian landscape into a predominantly Turkish, heterodox and syncretistic Muslim one, under the guidance of antinomian dervishes and spiritual leaders from Khurasan, who, in essence, were no more than superficially Islamicised shamans. Influenced by Durkheim's approach to the study of religion through primitive origins, Köprülü sought for traces of old ethnic traditions under new Islamic forms – ethnic traces that were distinctive of an essential and timeless 'national character' of the Turks and that had their origins in Central Asia. Köprülü aimed to recover the Turkish cultural heritage long dominated by Persian-, and later by European-influenced works.

Köprülü's model, the initial framework of which was put into place in 1918, continues to inform how and what aspects of religious and cultural history are studied today. With no serious theoretical challenge to Köprülü's paradigm, other aspects of medieval Anatolian cultural and religious history remain unexplored. There is no detailed synthetic historical study of the intellectual and religious landscape of thirteenth-century Anatolia. We have no history of the *'ulamā'*, nor of intellectual trends. While there are many studies dealing with the life and works of religious luminaries such as Mawlānā

Jalāl al-Dīn al-Rūmī and Ṣadr al-Dīn al-Qūnawī, these figures have been viewed largely in isolation, detached from the political landscape and bereft of the greater socio-religious context shaping their careers and thought.

Studies of Sufism predominate in modern scholarship on medieval Anatolian Muslim religious and intellectual life, reflecting Köprülü's influence. These works tend to approach Sufism according to the dichotomy of conformist urban Sufis vs. non-conformist rural Sufis. To pick a typical example of this approach, the 'non-Sunni' Sufi order of the Qalandarīya (or Kalander), Ahmet Yaşar Ocak argues, broadly appealed to the Turkmen communities of the thirteenth century because they were only superficially Islamised, and their practices better accommodated local pre-Islamic beliefs and traditions.[15] For, as Ocak points out, Sufism probably meant little more for them 'than a form of social life, rather than being a means of attaining any mystic goals'.[16] Indeed, according to the predominant paradigms of the field, popular religion has been rendered static, unchanging and undynamic, set in a framework informed by a strict dichotomy between high and low Islam.

Although there have been a few works rejecting the Köprülü paradigm, their impact remains relatively limited. In his *God's Unruly Friends*, Ahmet T. Karamustafa criticises the two-tiered model of religion of a high (normative) and low (antinomian) Islam for failing to generate explanatory analysis or to account for a historical dimension for popular religion. Karamustafa contends that originally extraneous beliefs and practices to Islam were neither 'survival' nor 'traces', but rather 'the building blocks of a new Islamic synthesis'.[17] Devin DeWeese likewise objects to the notion that Central Asian nomadic Turks were merely superficially Islamic, and that their 'conversion' was in name only. DeWeese argues that Islamisation was both transformative and at the same time characteristically attuned to pre-Islamic traditions.[18] Although we have a few voices such as Karamustafa and DeWeese pleading for new ways of regarding the problem of deviant dervishes or the Islam of nomads, their work focuses neither on the Seljuk period (in the case of Karamustafa), nor on Anatolia (DeWeese).

If research on the political, religious and intellectual history of Seljuk Anatolia has atrophied, much greater progress has been made in recent years with regard to the material culture of medieval Anatolia, often suggesting conclusions of broader significance. Recent studies on the landscape and architectural history of the region have added valuable fresh perspectives on Seljuk Anatolian culture and society. For instance, in his study of the Anatolian Seljuk tradition of suburban palace-garden complexes, Scott Redford compares the Seljuk suburban palace, garden and hunting practices and traditions with those of their neighbours to the east and west.[19] Proposing that these garden and hunting preserves formed 'a communality of chivalric practice', Redford argues that the Seljuk traditions may be conceived of as a 'shared chivalric garden culture in the Mediterranean and Islamic world of the Middle Ages'.[20] Redford's examination of garden culture offers a unique view of elite culture which transcended religious, linguistic or regional geographical boundaries. Such interdisciplinary approaches will further enrich the field of Seljuk studies.

The Anatolian Seljuk Court and Society

This volume addresses how dynastic power and authority based at the court interacted with broader social, political and religious communities throughout the realm. The reasons for the emphasis on the court are twofold: firstly, because as in most premodern Islamic (and non-Islamic) polities the court was the focus of political, artistic and cultural life; and secondly, because notwithstanding that fact, it has received very little attention in the medieval Anatolian context – and indeed, has been surprisingly neglected in studies of Middle Eastern and Islamic history to date.[21] It would be instructive to say a few words about the internal dynamics and make-up of the Anatolian Seljuk court, but the dearth of critical studies on the subject is paralleled by the absence of even a single modern Turkish word conveying the broad meaning of 'court' as a social and cultural world. The closest word in modern Turkish to court is *saray*, which strictly means palace; indeed, the Seljuk court in modern Turkish historiography has been conceptualised as a palace complex and its institutions rendered most commonly as the *saray teşkilatı*, 'the apparatus of the palace'.[22]

If one turns to contemporary record, one does not find a single comprehensive term for court, but rather a variety of related words. Ibn Bībī commonly uses *bārgāh* and *dargāh* to refer to the 'inner' and 'outer' courts of what could be considered an imperial complex. Thus, the European court, with its inner chamber and outer hall distinction, is clearly paralleled in the inner and outer courts of the Seljuk royal complex, which may be also compared to the inner and outer court in the Ottoman context (*enderūn* and *birūn*), and the inner and outer court in the imperial Chinese context.[23] Palace complexes were generally divided into secluded inner areas and zones of wider presence. It is these two spheres which come into interaction to form the court.[24] The court structure of *bārgāh and dargāh* appears applicable to urban palace complexes located within the citadel of the main Seljuk centres of Konya, Kayseri and Alanya (Alā'iyya).[25]

The inner court, or *bārgāh*, was the space relegated to the sultan's household centred at the palace, including his harem and entourage of extended family members, servants, favorites (*khawāṣṣ*), military retainers (*sarwārān-i bārgāh*), young nobles in attendance (*mulāzim*) and household staff of *ghulām*s.[26] This was a restricted space consisting of various chambers with different functions centring around the *saray*, or palace, the living quarters and personal space of the sultan. Thus the sultan would receive private audiences at the *dīwān-i bārgāh*.[27] He likewise would attend the *ṣuffa-yi bār* or *bārgāh* to dispense justice, presumably receiving petitions and making judgements.[28]

Access to the inner palace complex, or *bārgāh* was limited; Ibn Bībī impresses upon us how important the security of the *bārgāh* was for the sultan sometimes. Early on his reign, 'Alā' al-Dīn Kayqubād I, fearful for his life from the potentially hostile and powerful commanders that he inherited from his deceased brother and enemy, took measures to increase the security of the *bārgāh*. The sultan ordered that any amir seeking an audience with him at the *bārgāh* would enter alone and accompanied by one of his *ghulām*s. In order to impress the seriousness of these measures, he had the commander of the imperial curtains (*amīr-i pardadārān-i khāṣṣa*) clubbed 50 times in front of the *dargāh* for having admitted commanders into the *bārgāh* in the company of large groups of heavily armed retainers (*khawāshi-yi umarā'*).[29]

The outer court of the palace complex, the *dargāh*, constituted the space of public interaction between the sultan and his entourage and the rest of the ruling elite, military commandership and state dignitaries.[30] One may see the *dargāh* as equivalent in some ways to the *birūn* of the Ottoman court; it could hence be translated as 'porte'.[31] The *umarā'-yi dargāh* were the amirs restricted to the outer court. The commanders of the outer court were commonly manumitted *ghulām* granted provincial military commands and governorships. Unlike the denizens of the *bārgāh*, the ruling elite restricted to the *dargāh* maintained separate households located outside of the *dargāh*. Scott Redford identifies the residences of these commanders in Konya as lying a little to the north of the citadel, in view of the Alaeddin Köşkü, the imperial palace astride the citadel wall.[32] The outer court of the *dargāh* likewise consisted of different buildings for different functions. The *dawlatkhāna* was also the site of official enthronements and other such public-oriented activies. The *dawlatkhāna* likewise contained a section for the *bazmkhāna*, where drinking *majlis*, or symposia, were held.[33] The *dargāh* was thus the site of imperial pageantry demonstrating hierarchy and order, and the conspicuous display of the Seljuk porte's magnificence (*shukūh-i dargāh-i sulṭānī*).[34] Ibn Bībī refers to the Seljuk court collectively in metaphoric terms as the *dargāh-i jahān-panāh-i pādishāh,* 'the porte of the *padishah* under whom the world finds refuge'.[35]

The *dīwān*, or governing council, likewise was held presumably in the vicinity of the *dargāh*, although Ibn Bībī sheds little light on its exact location. Ibn Bībī, however, does make a distinction between the members of the *dīwān* and the *dargāh* (*mu'tabarān-i dīwān u dargāh*).[36] Although more research is necessary for identifying more accurately the make-up of the Anatolian Seljuk *dīwān* as well as its functions, it seems that its membership consisted of the top echelons of the ruling elite drawn from both the *bārgāh* and the *dargāh*, including the vizier, the *parwāna* (in charge of the royal chancery, also known as the *ṭughrā'ī*),[37] the *nā'ib al-salṭanat* (in charge of overall administration of the realm),[38] the *ustādhār* (or *ustādh al-dār*, the steward of the *bārgāh* and personal treasurer of the sultan).[39]

Members of both the *bargāh* and *dargāh* regularly interacted when court was in session, when various members of the military or political elite of the realm were summoned before the sultan. For instance, the newly enthroned 'Alā' al-Dīn Kayqubād I 'held court' with his military commanders as he toured the city of Konya, and announced the order for his commanders to refortify the city walls. Indeed, Ibn Bībī tells us specifically that it was from the *bārgāh* or inner court that the sultan departed as he mounted his steed to tour the city with the commanders of the outer and inner courts (*bā umarā'-yi dargāh wa sarwarān-i bārgāh*).[40] The *ghulām* corps constituted the most important network connecting the inner and outer courts. Although manumitted and promoted to a provincial commandership, and thus having 'graduated' into the realm of the outer court, commanders of palace *ghulām* origins would retain their palace *laqab* as a social marker of and sign of prestige, a clear indication of one's palace connections and intimacy with the sultan. That we see many top provincial commanders bearing the title *chashnīgīr*, or royal food taster – yet no longer functioning as such – is the most salient example of the use of such titles: Shams al-Dīn Altun-aba *chashnīgīr*, Mubāriz al-Dīn Chavlı *chashnīgīr*, Sayf al-Dīn Türkeri *chashnīgīr*, and Sirāj al-Dīn Sarija *chashnīgīr*. In fact, moving to the outer court not only signalled a new status for a *ghulām*, it also indicated new power bases with the creation of personal retinues – and hence, the development of autonomous spheres of power. It was this source of independent military power which increased the military potential of the Seljuk polity as an efficient means for extending Seljuk power throughout the realm in the absence of the sultan's physical presence. Yet at the same time this autonomy posed a potential threat to the sultan, especially if bonds of loyalty were questionable as in the case of young and newly enthroned 'Alā' al-Dīn Kayqubād *vis-à-vis* his elder brother's powerful and hostile amirs. Thus, an important dynamic of Seljuk political culture may be found in the struggle to maintain a balance between powerful provincial amirs and powerful administrators who often had a 'foot' in both the inner and outer spheres of the court, and those closest to the sultan forming his immediate household and entourage.

Like other medieval polities, Seljuk politics was based on social networks rather than institutional bodies. Furthermore, Seljuk elites, as elsewhere in the linguistically and ethnically diverse medieval Mediterranean world, constituted a social system which shared common values, status symbols and ruling patterns found among the elite throughout the region. Malcolm Vale has written of early medieval northern Europe that '[t]here was little, if any, sense of ethnic or national exclusiveness in this milieu. Court culture was open to external forces: it was essentially permeable and absorptive of a wide range of influences.'[41] The same was certainly true of the Seljuk case, as the chapters in this volume demonstrate, suggesting the necessity for finding alternatives to the nationalist paradigms that have dominated the study of Anatolia.

The Present Volume

The 2009 Istanbul conference which inspired this volume aimed to develop a more sophisticated approach to the study of medieval Muslim Anatolia, as far as possible on its own terms rather than with the benefit of hindsight as a prelude to the Ottoman or Turkish states. For that reason, this volume avoids the description of the Anatolian Seljuk dynasty as 'the Seljuks of Turkey' (*Türkiye Selçukluları*), so common in contemporary Turkish scholarship. The conference brought together scholars seeking new approaches to understanding the history of the Seljuks and their contemporaries. As the title of the volume indicates, our aim was to move beyond the confines of political history to understand the underlying dynamics of the Seljuk state and its contemporaries, as it sought to establish its legitimacy among both its Muslim and Christian subjects on this remote frontier of Islamdom.

As the chapters published here illustrate, there is, in fact, no dearth of new, untapped sources on Muslim Anatolia. The classic sources for Islamic history such as chronicles are indeed limited, but both literary and material sources can offer new insights. Particularly promising is the study of epigraphy, which forms the basis for the chapters by two of our contributors (Pancaroğlu and Redford). Although Christian sources have long been recognised as important for political history, the insights provided by Greek and Armenian sources into the functioning of society and even the Seljuk court itself has been undervalued to date (see the contributions by Korobeinikov, Shukurov and Goshgarian). Yet there is also much to be learned from the published sources, above all in Persian. After all, the complete text of our main Persian chronicle for the period, Ibn Bībī, remains available only in facsimile. Conclusions drawn on the basis of the edited abridged version or translations derived from it are often tendentious, and a complete edition of this major but extremely difficult source remains a desideratum. The chronicles we have also contain valuable material that is sometimes pushed aside in the search for 'facts': the chapters by Yıldız (Chapter Four) and Yıldız and Şahin (Chapter Seven) illustrate how the published chronicles of Rāwandī and Ibn Bībī still have much potential to improve our understanding of the Seljuk court. The tendency in scholarship to prioritise pure political history has meant that more literary sources have often been neglected. The letters of Jalāl al-Dīn Rūmī, for instance, and the poems of his son Sulṭān Walad shed much light on relations between Sufis and the Seljuk court, as Peacock discusses (Chapter Eight), but have not previously been exploited for historical purposes. As Gary Leiser points out in his concluding chapter, a rich range of sources exists beyond those exploited by the contributors to this volume.

The chapters are divided into the three sections, the first of which deals with dynastic identity and the Great Seljuk heritage. Oya Pancaroğlu examines dynastic self-identification and self-proclamation at a time of flux in Anatolia and beyond with her exploration of the building activities of Sayf al-Dīn Shāhanshāh (r. c.1171–96) of the Divriği branch of the Mengüjekid dynasty, which focuses on this local ruler's epigraphic expressions of claims of wide rulership. This underlines that Seljuk hegemony in Anatolia was not to be taken for granted, and in moments of weakness rival dynasties were ready to assert themselves – a point which appears again later in the volume in Scott Redford's investigation of the Erzurum branch of the Seljuk dynasty. The means by which the Seljuks themselves sought to assert their right to rule are investigated by the next two chapters. Dimitri Korobeinikov argues that the Anatolian dynasty rooted its right to rule in the Great Seljuk heritage and did not, as sometimes thought, see itself as heir to Byzantium – unlike, significantly, the Ottomans. Sara Nur Yıldız, meanwhile, shows how this emphasis on the Great Seljuk heritage was promoted after the collapse of the dynasty in Iran.

The second section deals with the royal household. Rustam Shukurov investigates the innermost part of the sultans' court, the harem, using a rich range of Christian and Muslim sources to illuminate the functioning of this most obscure institution. Arguing that the Christian women of the royal household profoundly influenced the identity of the Seljuk sultans, his conclusions are suggestive for our understanding of medieval Anatolian society more generally. Scott Redford addresses the question of royal women from another angle, combining epigraphic and literary evidence to reconstruct the life of 'Iṣmat al-Dunyā wa 'l-Dīn, a wife of 'Alā' al-Dīn Kayqubād I who was 'written out' of Ibn Bībī's history.

The third section examines the role of Sufism at court and in society. Sara Nur Yıldız and Haşim Şahin's chapter, 'In the proximity of sultans: Majd al-Din Isḥāq, Ibn 'Arabī and the Seljuk court', explores the contacts between these two major figures in the religious history of early thirteenth-century Anatolia and the courts of Ghiyāth al-Dīn Kaykhusraw I and 'Izz al-Dīn Kaykā'ūs I. Andrew Peacock, meanwhile, examines the links in the later thirteenth century between Jalāl al-Dīn Rūmī and his son Sulṭān Walad on the one hand and the elite on the other. Both these studies argue for much closer and more complex links between Sufi circles and the court than has hitherto been appreciated. Rachel Goshgarian, meanwhile, takes us back to north-eastern Anatolia where we began, with a study of the role of *futuwwa* among the Christians of Erzincan. Her work underlines the close links and mutual influences between Muslim and Christian communities in Anatolia.

The volume concludes with a chapter by Gary Leiser that points to further avenues for research, both in terms of themes and sources. The select bibliography is intended merely to highlight some of the major studies to which our contributors have referred and to act as a very preliminary guide to further reading. Indeed, this volume is far from being the final word on Seljuk Anatolia. Research on this difficult but extremely rich and rewarding area of study has scarcely begun, and these chapters are published rather in the hope that by illustrating the diversity of sources and approaches and their vast potential for transforming how we think about medieval Muslim Anatolia, they will in some small way encourage future work that may address some of the lacunae we have outlined above. Of course, there will always be large gaps in our knowledge: many parts of twelfth-century history, in particular, are always likely to remain obscure. Yet by adjusting our questions to the evidence rather than vice versa, there is still much we can learn about the Seljuks and their contemporaries.

Notes

1. We are very grateful to Peter Maxwell-Stuart for the translation of this passage.
2. There is a misprint in the Latin text. For *alumnis* read *aluminis*.
3. Simon de Saint-Quentin, *Histoire des Tartares*, ed. Jean Richard (Paris: Librairie Orientaliste Paul Geuthner, 1965), XXXI.142, XXXII.143 (pp. 66, 68–70).
4. Ibn Saʿīd, *Kitāb al-jughrāfīya*, ed. Ismāʿīl al-ʿArabī (Beirut: al-Maktab al-Tijārī, 1970), pp. 184–7, 195.
5. On Anatolia as the 'wild west', see Charles Melville, 'Anatolia under the Mongols' in Kate Fleet (ed.), *The Cambridge History of Turkey*, i: *Byzantium to Turkey, 1071–1453* (Cambridge: Cambridge University Press, 2009), p. 52.
6. The only other collection of essays dealing with Seljuk Anatolia in a western language is Gary Leiser (ed.), *Les Seljoukides d'Anatolie* (*Mésogeios* 25–6 [2005]).
7. See A.C.S. Peacock, *Early Seljuq History: A New Interpretation* (London: Routledge, 2010).
8. Ibn Bībī, *al-Awāmir al-ʿalāʾīya fīʾl-umūr al-ʿalāʾīya*, facsimile edition prepared by Adnan Sadık Erzi as İbn-i Bībī, *El-Evāmirüʾl-ʿAlāʾiyye fīʾl-Umūri l-ʿAlāʾiyye* (Ankara: Türk Tarih Kurumu, 1956), p. 11.

9. For more on these narrative sources, see Charles Melville, 'The early Persian historiography of Anatolia' in Judith Pfeiffer, Sholeh A. Quinn, and Ernest Tucker (eds), *History and Historiography of Post-Mongol Asia and the Middle East: Studies in Honor of John E. Woods* (Wiesbaden: Harrassowitz, 2006), pp. 135–66 and A. C. S. Peacock, 'Aḥmad of Niğde's *Al-Walad al-Shafīq* and the Seljuk past', *Anatolian Studies* 54 (2004), pp. 95–107.
10. See Dimitri Korobeinikov, '"The King of the East and the West": the Seljuk Dynastic Concept and Titles in the Muslim and Christian sources' in this volume, pp. 76–7.
11. Claude Cahen, *Pre-Ottoman Turkey: A general survey of the material and spiritual culture and history c. 1071–1330* (London: Sidgwick and Jackson, 1968); idem, *La Turquie pré-ottomane* (Istanbul: Institut Français d'Études Anatoliennes, 1988); a second English version was made from the French, but omitting most of the notes which make the latter so valuable: idem, *The Formation of Turkey: The Seljukid Sultanate of Rum: Eleventh to Fourteenth Century*, trans. and ed. P.M. Holt (London: Longman, 2001).
12. Colin Imber, 'The Ottoman dynastic myth', *Turcica* 19 (1987), pp. 7–27.
13. See A.C.S. Peacock, 'Seljuq legitimacy in Islamic history' in Christian Lange and Songül Mecit (eds), *The Seljuqs: History, Politics and Culture* (Edinburgh: Edinburgh University Press, 2011), pp. 79–95.
14. For a sample of his scholarship in English, see Mehmet Fuad Köprülü, *Islam in Anatolia after the Turkish Invasion*, trans. Gary Leiser (Salt Lake City: University of Utah Press, 1993).
15. Ahmet Yaşar Ocak, 'Social, cultural and intellectual life, 1071–1453', in Kate Fleet (ed.), *The Cambridge History of Turkey*, i: *Byzantium to Turkey, 1071–1453* (Cambridge: Cambridge University Press, 2009), p. 392.
16. Ibid., p. 392.
17. Ahmet T. Karamustafa, *God's Unruly Friends: Dervish Groups in the Islamic Later Middle Period, 1200–1550* (Salt Lake City: University of Utah Press, 1994), p. 11.

18. Devin DeWeese, *Islamization and Native Religion in the Golden Horde. Baba Tükles and Conversion to Islam in Historical and Epic Tradition* (University Park, Penn.: The Pennsylvania State University Press, 1994), p. 7ff.
19. Scott Redford, *Landscape and the State in Medieval Anatolia: Seljuk Gardens and Pavilions of Alanya, Turkey* (Oxford: Archeopress, 2000), p. 2.
20. Ibid., p. 108.
21. A recent exception is the important volume edited by Albrecht Fuess and Jan Peter Hartung, *Court Cultures in the Muslim World: Seventh to nineteenth centuries* (London: Routledge, 2011).
22. First used by İ.H. Uzunçarşılı, *Osmanlı Devleti Teşkilatına Medhal* (Ankara: Türk Tarih Kurumu, 1941; 4th edition, 1988), pp. 78–86, the term *saray teşkilatı* is likewise employed by Erdoğan Merçil in his *Selçuklular'da Saray ve Saray Teşkilatı* (Istanbul: Bilge Kültür Sanatı, 2011).
23. For more on the distinction of inner and outer courts, see Jeroen Duindam, 'Royal courts in dynastic states and empires', in Jeroen Duindam, Tülay Artan and Metin Kunt (eds), *Royal Courts in Dynastic States and Empires: A Global Perspective* (Leiden: Brill, 2011), p. 1; İ. Metin Kunt, 'Turks in the Ottoman imperial palace', in Duindam, Artan and Kunt (eds), *Royal Courts*, p. 293; Hans Bielenstein, *The Bureaucracy of Han Times* (Cambridge: Cambridge University Press, 1980), pp. 154–5; Andrew Eisenberg, 'Retired emperorship in medieval China: the Northern Wei', *T'oung Pao* Second Series, 77 (1991), nos. 1–3, pp. 51–2; Denis Twitchett and Paul Jakov Smith (eds), *The Cambridge History of China*, v/i: *The Sung Dynasty and Its Precursors, 907–1279* (Cambridge: Cambridge University Press, 2009), pp. 26–7, 31, 639, 720–1, 726–7.
24. Rita Coast Gomes, *The Making of a Court Society: Kings and Nobles in Late Medieval Portugal* (Cambridge: Cambridge University Press, 2003), pp. 3, 18.
25. Scott Redford, 'Thirteenth-century Rūm Seljuq palaces and palace imagery', *Ars Orientalis* 23 (1994), p. 200.

26. Ibn Bībī also uses *khāwāshī u ḥasham* as a general phrase for the sultan's men (Ibn Bībī, *al-Awāmir al-ʿalāʾīya*, p. 624).
27. Ibid., p. 218.
28. Ibid., p. 228.
29. Ibid., p. 267.
30. Ibid., p. 540.
31. Suzan Yalman thus renders *dargāh* as 'porte' as in *umarāʾ-yi dargāh*, 'commanders of the porte' ('Building the Sultanate of Rūm: Memory, Urbanism and Mysticism in the Architectural Patronage of 'Ala al-Din Kayqubad, r. 1220–1237' [PhD Dissertation, Harvard University, 2011], p. 166).
32. Scott Redford, *Landscape and the State in Medieval Anatolia: Seljuk Gardens and Pavilions of Alanya, Turkey* (Oxford: Archeopress, 2000), p. 59.
33. Ibn Bībī, *al-Awāmir al-ʿalāʾīya*, p. 267.
34. Ibid., p. 540.
35. Ibid., p. 707.
36. Ibid., p. 623.
37. Uzunçarşılı, *Medhal*, pp. 95, 97. The *parwāna* was in charge of the issuance of *farmān*s related to the business of the imperial council and treasury, as well as the the granting of *iqṭāʿ*s and other imperial gifts.
38. Sadi Kucur, 'Nāib-i saltanat', *Türkiye Diyanet Vakfı İslam Ansiklopedisi*, xxxii (2006), pp. 313–4.
39. Uzunçarşılı, *Medhal*, p. 80; Sadi S. Kucur, 'Vekīl-i Hāsslık ve Selçuklu Saraylarında Üstādü'd-dārlık', *Türk Kültürü İncelemeleri Dergisi* 14 (2006), p. 7; P.M. Holt, 'The mamluk institution', in Youssef M. Choueiri (ed.), *A Companion to the History of the Middle East* (Malden, Mass. and Oxford: Blackwell Publishing, 2005), p. 163.
40. Ibn Bībī, *al-Awāmir al-ʿalāʾīya*, p. 253.
41. Malcolm Vale, *The Princely Court. Medieval Courts and Culture in North-West Europe, 1270–1380* (Oxford: Oxford University Press, 2001), p. 2.

PART ONE

DYNASTIC IDENTITY AND THE GREAT SELJUK INHERITANCE

CHAPTER TWO

THE HOUSE OF MENGÜJEK IN DİVRİĞİ: CONSTRUCTIONS OF DYNASTIC IDENTITY IN THE LATE TWELFTH CENTURY[1]

Oya Pancaroğlu

In his introduction to the history of the Seljuks, Ibn Bībī gives a curious explanation for effectively omitting the dynasty's first century from his account.

> [This work starts] from the beginning of the crown princehood of the fortunate (i.e. late) martyr sultan Ghiyāth al-Dīn Kaykhusraw, the father of the great sultan 'Alā' al-Dīn Kayqubād — may God shelter both of them in His forgiveness — for the reason that the particulars of the rule of sultan Sulaymān b. Qutlumush and the circumstances of the events [concerning] the great amirs such as amir Mengüjek, amir Artuq and amir Danishmend were not certain. The books of the historians of that realm had excessive difficulties and consulting them was not easy; the oral reports of distant times

> did not warrant confidence because of the inconsistency of the accounts and repose of mind did not result from those words; [thus] comprehension [of them] escaped [one].[2]

The explanation is seemingly convincing: Ibn Bībī claims to have had at his disposal both written sources and oral reports concerning the late eleventh and twelfth centuries, which he cast aside on account of their alleged difficulty, unreliability and inconsistency. Reading between the lines, however, one wonders whether the actual problem was not so much the shortcomings of these sources as his suspicion that the period in question – with its ever-shifting balance of power among numerous players and its manifold ups and downs for the Seljuks – might detract from his mission to present a cohesive account of the Seljuk dynasty through the twelfth and into the thirteenth century.

Nevertheless, it is hard to disagree with Ibn Bībī that Anatolia's twelfth century presents special challenges of historical reconstruction, compounded by the presumable loss of at least some of those unnamed written sources that he rejected. The story of the twelfth-century Turkmen dynasties in Anatolia – Seljuk, Danishmendid, Mengüjekid and Saltuqid – is told, for the greater part, by outsiders who weaved in and out of the political lives of these dynasties as needed by their narratives.[3] The modern task of reconstruction has necessarily relied upon these patchy accounts in order to establish a basic outline of the political relations among the Anatolian Turkmen dynasties and their neighbours such as the Byzantines, Georgians, Armenians, Great Seljuks, Zangids and Ayyubids. That there is more to their stories than what has so far been gleaned from textual reconstruction alone is the motivation for this chapter, which approaches the Divriği branch of the Mengüjekid dynasty in the last two decades of the twelfth century through the architectural works built by Sayf al-Dīn Shāhanshāh (r. c.1171–96).

The Family of Mengüjek

What makes Divriği particularly significant as a case study for exploring the question of dynastic identity in the late twelfth century is the fact that no surviving medieval historical text explicitly mentions this branch of the Mengüjekids, whose existence is known solely from numismatic and architectural–epigraphic evidence. The town, marked by a citadel in the upper Euphrates catchment area, is remarkably rich in inscriptions that provide an invaluable conduit to the history of the Mengüjekid dynasty, while the buildings themselves attest its notable position in the network of artistic resources of medieval Anatolia. In fact, little is known about even the general history of the Mengüjekids whose main branch, based in Erzincan, is only intermittently mentioned by the medieval historians.

As in the case of the other early Turkmen dynasties of Anatolia, the current state of knowledge about the origins of the Mengüjekids amounts to little more than speculation.[4] The eponym Mengüjek (or Mangūjak, Mangūjuk) is thought to belong to a military commander once in the service of the Great Seljuks who was active in the upper Euphrates region in the decades following the Battle of Manzikert. Some time in the middle of the twelfth century, after the death of Isḥāq (Mengüjek's son) around 1140, the Mengüjekid family entered into a power-sharing arrangement with bases in Erzincan, Kemah and Divriği. Şebinkarahisar (Koloneia/Kūghuniya) was probably added around the turn of the thirteenth century. It is generally assumed that the rulers in these towns led their own branch of the dynasty in the pattern of family-based power-sharing schemes seen in most early and medieval Turkic dynasties. Of these rulers, Fakhr al-Dīn Bahrāmshāh, who ruled from Erzincan for over 60 years between some time in the early 1160s until his death in 1225, is by far the most renowned. He was featured at length by Ibn Bībī and briefly by Rāwandī, with both authors agreeing on his exemplary rulership in terms of justice, generosity and courage. Furthermore, thanks to his patronage of the poet Niẓāmī's didactic *mathnawī*, the *Makhzan al-asrār* ('Treasury of Secrets', 1160s or 1170s), Bahrāmshāh's name was also immortalised in the Persian literary realm. The striking longevity of Bahrāmshāh's reign must have been due at least in part to the careful course of diplomacy which he followed, especially with regard to the Seljuks whenever the latter's stars were on the rise. Bahrāmshāh was probably also a noteworthy patron of architecture, but no evidence of this has survived in the extremely earthquake-prone city of Erzincan located on the North Anatolian Fault.[5]

While Bahrāmshāh held sway in Erzincan and evidently appointed his sons to rule in Kemah and Şebinkarahisar, Divriği was ruled from around 1171 by his first cousin, Sayf al-Dīn Shāhanshāh, who died in 1196 leaving behind the earliest surviving Mengüjekid architecture, which forms the subject of this chapter. These latter decades of the twelfth century witnessed a number of critical events in the political landscape of Anatolia and the neighbouring regions, which undoubtedly impacted Mengüjekid rule in its various centres. Closest to home, the Seljuks under sultan Qılıch Arslan II (r. 1155–92) consolidated their power over much of central Anatolia with their victory at the Battle of Myriokephalon in 1176, thus crushing Byzantine hopes for regaining territorial control. In 1178 the Seljuks likewise eliminated their main Turkmen rivals, the Danishmendids. In the face of this ascendancy, both Bahrāmshāh and Shāhanshāh appear to have aligned themselves in a favourably subordinate position to Qılıch Arslan II and to have pledged some form of allegiance to the Seljuk ruler, whether through marriage arrangements with the Seljuk family as in the case of Bahrāmshāh, or through copper coinage acknowledging the superiority of Seljuk power as in the case of Shāhanshāh. Farther afield the 1170s were marked by the collapse of the Fatimid caliphate and empire – once the ideological and political challenge to the Sunni powers of the medieval Islamic world – and the unification of much of Syria under the Zangids (especially Nūr al-Dīn) whose torch passed in 1174 to the Ayyubids under Saladin. The counter-Crusade mission of these two dynasties, which saw its first major milestone in the capture of Edessa by ʿImād al-Dīn Zangī in 1144, reached its climax with the capture of Jerusalem by Saladin in 1187. The ideological repercussions of these events in greater Syria and Egypt were felt far and wide, not least in Anatolia where such shifts in regional power entailed a necessary attunement to the wider political landscape.

Shāhanshāh's coinage, limited to three known types in copper, succinctly records the pulsation of Seljuk power in late twelfth-century

Anatolia as perceived in Divriği.[6] The earliest type is dated 567 (1171–2) and is inscribed with the name and title of Qılıch Arslan II on the obverse and the name of Shāhanshāh on the reverse. This coin dates approximately from the period when Shāhanshāh took power in Divriği (the precise year is not known) at a time when Seljuk fortunes were on the rise, presumably necessitating this numismatic expression of subordination to Qılıch Arslan II. A second coin type of Shāhanshāh, however, omits the name of the Seljuk sultan; though undated, it is probable that this type corresponds to the period immediately before or after the death of Qılıch Arslan II in 1192 when the latter's numerous sons – assigned various appanages around the country since around 1188 – competed and clashed with each other in a bid to ascend the Seljuk throne. The Seljuk interregnum in Anatolia lasted until 1196 when Rukn al-Dīn Sulaymānshāh finally gained the upper hand and seized the throne in Konya from his brother, Ghiyāth al-Dīn Kaykhusraw I and sent him into exile. The third and last type among Shāhanshāh's coins dates from this same year and includes the title and name of Rukn al-Dīn Sulaymānshāh on the obverse, revealing Shāhanshāh's prudent recognition of renewed Seljuk supremacy after several years of political confusion.

The turmoil of the 1190s was further compounded by the politically and militarily destructive central Anatolian passage of the Third Crusade in 1190. Further east, the same decade also saw the definitive dissolution of the Great Seljuk empire in western Iran in 1194, intensifying the scramble for power among the successor states of *atabeg*s, notably those in Azerbaijan. Thus, when Shāhanshāh died in 1196 – probably within a month of issuing his last coin type – a new order was dawning in both Anatolia and the surrounding regions with the surge of Seljuk and Ayyubid power. The survival of the Mengüjekid dynasty well into the thirteenth century, when Seljuk and Ayyubid rivalry manifested itself in territorial expansionism, must be credited to the political astuteness of both Bahrāmshāh and Shāhanshāh, who safeguarded their dynastic identity throughout the turmoil of the late twelfth century. The jewel in Divriği's architectural crown, the mosque and hospital complex, built jointly in

1228–9 by Shāhanshāh's grandson, Aḥmadshāh, and Bahrāmshāh's daughter, the princess Tūrān Malik, is arguably the most remarkable testimony to artistic creativity in medieval Anatolia, affirming Divriği as a significant nexus in a complex web of cultural resources.[7] Whereas Erzincan and its political dependencies of Kemah and Şebinkarahisar were ultimately annexed by the Seljuks in 1226–8, Divriği apparently remained in Mengüjekid hands until sometime after 1252 when Shāhanshāh's great-grandson, Malik Ṣāliḥ, erected the last known Mengüjekid inscription on the Divriği citadel, which shows no sign of political subjugation.[8] The monumentality of this lion-flanked inscription mounted on the most imposing tower of the citadel (the Arslanburç) reveals a most remarkable sense of local entitlement retained by the rulers of Divriği even as they entered the choppy waters of the second half of the thirteenth century. How Mengüjekid claims to power continued to be broadcast in Divriği beyond the expansionist agenda of 'Alā' al-Dīn Kayqubād in the 1220s and 1230s and the Mongol invasion in the nearby Battle of Kösedağ in 1243 is quite puzzling. Proclaiming Malik Ṣāliḥ as the 'crown of the family of Mengüjek' (*tāj-i āl-i Mangūjak*), the roots of the dynastic pride expressed in the Arslanburç inscription can be traced to the last decades of the twelfth century when Sayf al-Dīn Shāhanshāh ruled in Divriği.

Building for Divriği's 'King of Kings': The Architecture of Sayf al-Dīn Shāhanshāh

Two buildings – a mosque and a tomb – from the patronage of Shāhanshāh in Divriği reflect the intersection of political ambition with architectural projects at the end of the twelfth century, providing a focal point for investigating aspects of dynastic self-identification and self-proclamation at a time of flux in Anatolia and beyond. The earlier of these two monuments is the Kale Camii ('Citadel Mosque'), one of the earliest dated mosques in Anatolia preserved nearly intact, perched on the pinnacle of Divriği's lofty citadel.[9] A well-known early example of the so-called 'basilica' type mosque, the

Kale Camii constitutes the earliest sign of Mengüjekid presence in Divriği in the form of a standing building (figs. 2.1 and 2.2). Its inscriptions are concentrated on its portal and on a surviving fragment of its wooden *minbar* (now preserved in the Sivas Museum). There are two inscriptions on the mosque portal; the first, in two lines, is situated at the top above the arch and the second, a single line, just above the door. Both inscriptions were written in a type of foliated Kufic script which, in the second case especially, presents some difficulties in reading.[10]

Upper inscription:
(1) amara bi-'imārat (sic) *hādh{ā} al-masjid al-mubārak al-amīr al-isfahsālār al-ajall Sayf al-Dunyā wa 'l-Dīn (2) Abū 'l-Muẓaffar Shāhanshāh bin Sulaymān bin a{m}īr Isḥaq [sic] ḥusām amīr al-mu'minīn fī sanat sitta wa saba'īn*(?) *wa khamsmi'a*

(1) The building of this blessed mosque was ordered by the great amir commander Sayf al-Dunyā wa 'l-Dīn (2) Abū 'l-Muẓaffar Shāhanshāh son of Sulaymān son of the amir Isḥaq [*sic*], the

Figure 2.1 Kale Camii, Divriği; general view.

Figure 2.2 Kale Camii, Divriği; portal.

sword of the Commander of the Faithful, in the year five hundred and seventy(?)-six (=1180–1).

Lower inscription:
al-'āmil ustādh Ḥasan(?) bin Pīrūz(?) al-Marāghī(?)

The builder [is] the master Ḥasan(?) son of Pīrūz(?) al-Marāghī(?).

The designation of the building as a masjid rather than a *jāmi'* suggests that it was envisioned as the royal prayer hall of the citadel – probably sited in proximity to the palace, of which no standing remains survive – rather than as the main congregational Friday mosque for the entire Muslim populace of the town. This is also borne out by its location at the highest point of the citadel at some distance from the gates that led out to the lower town, which must have had a Friday mosque of some sort already prior to the construction of the mosque–hospital complex in 1228–9. It is, of course, impossible to estimate the sizes of the Muslim and Christian (primarily Armenian) communities of *extra-muros* Divriği in the late twelfth century, although some sense of the demographic situation of the nearby villages at least may be gleaned retrospectively from the information preserved in the Ottoman tax registers of 1519 and 1530 wherein some villages indicated as being Armenian are listed among the endowments of the thirteenth and later centuries.[11] The upper portal inscription further reveals that Shāhanshāh, presumably in keeping with his predecessors, had assumed the title of *al-amīr al-isfahsālār*[12] and presented himself as a supporter of the caliph. The absence from this inscription of Qılıch Arslan II's name – which one may have expected to find in the common formula *fī ayyām* ... ('during the days of ...') – may be taken as evidence of the more private context of this mosque, in contrast to the public circulation of Shāhanshāh's coinage bearing the Seljuk sultan's name.

According to the lower portal inscription, Shāhanshāh availed himself of the services of a master architect who – if the name is correctly read – seems to have hailed from Maragha in Azerbaijan. The prominence of this master's signature placed just above the door must indicate the prestige associated with the builder's name and/or the tradition he represented. The portal, constructed in stone like the rest of the building but also with a limited application of brick and glazed tiles, conforms to the style of brick architecture which extended across the greater Iranian world at this time and is notably similar to, for example, the portal design of the contemporary Mosque of Maghak-i 'Aṭṭār in Bukhara dated 1178–9.[13] The floriated Kufic style of the inscriptions, though showing some affinity to examples from regions further south (for example, Diyarbakır), also has counterparts in both brick and stone in the Caucasus from the end of the eleventh century onwards.[14] The arcaded interior of the mosque features robust columns known especially from early and later medieval Armenian and Georgian stone architecture in eastern Anatolia and Transcaucasia. It is probable that stonemasons of local or regional extraction were employed for the construction, so that the work of the builder named at the entrance may well have been limited mainly to the design of the portal (and perhaps also to the general supervision of the construction). The encounter of styles and techniques seen on the portal is replayed in the interior, especially in the mihrab where a carved niche loosely approximating a *muqarnas* hood created from a single block of stone could be explained as the product of a tentative phase in the introduction of this Islamic architectonic ornamental form (which probably first developed in plaster or brick in Iraq) to Anatolian stone architecture.[15] From the surviving fragment of the *minbar*, the following partial reading of its inscription[16] written in a somewhat inept *naskh* script can be established:

> *(1) … al-Islām wa 'l-muslimīn qātil al-kafara … (2) … al-mutamarridīn za'īm juyūsh al-Muslimīn … (3) … kahf {al-ḍu'afā'?} wa 'l-masākīn iftikhār āl Mangū{jak} … (4) … pahlawān al-Rūm {wa 'l-Shām?} wa 'l-Arman {sipah-bād?} … (5) Shāhanshāh b. Sulaymān ḥusām amīr al-mu'{minīn} …*
>
> (1) … of Islam and Muslims, the slayer of the infidels … (2) … of the rebellious, the leader of the armies of the Muslims … (3) … refuge of [the weak?] and the indigent, the pride of the family of Mengü[jek] … (4) … hero of Rūm [and Shām?] and Arman, [commander?] (5) Shāhanshāh son of Sulaymān, the sword of the commander of the fai[thful] …

Extending the titulature of the upper portal inscription, the *minbar* inscription endowed Shāhanshāh with further epithets encapsulating both militant and charitable qualities within a named dynastic identity (*āl Mangūjak*) and a named geographic framework (Rūm, [Shām, i.e., Syria?] and Arman, i.e., Armenia).[17] Despite the elaborateness of its content, the execution of the *minbar* inscription is characterised by problems not dissimilar to the inscription of the portal, suggesting in both cases either an artisanal problem in the transference of the text in question from paper to stone or wood or a case of moderate ineptness affecting Divriği's overall epigraphic production at this time. In either case, the Kale Camii represents a probable gathering of artistic skill from various sources which can be read from the conspicuousness of some of its seams.

The near synthesis of styles in the Kale Camii appears to have paved the way for Shāhanshāh's second surviving monument in Divriği, his mausoleum known as Sitte Melik.[18] Built as an octagonal tomb tower with a portal and a pyramidal dome, Sitte Melik's form complies with the general trend of Muslim funerary architecture but, unlike a great many medieval Anatolian tombs, it does not have a crypt (figs. 2.3–2.6).[19] Situated at the south-western foot of the citadel, Sitte Melik is built in fine ashlar masonry, its portal incorporating a proper *muqarnas* niche in four tiers, skilfully adapted to stone. This niche is contained within a rectangular frame outlined by an articulated high-relief moulding and decorated with a matrix of low-relief interlocking octagons. In addition to this elaborate portal design, two elongated niches – one triangular, the other rounded in section – were placed on the sides flanking the entrance, evoking similar niches found on the exterior apse walls of medieval Georgian

Figure 2.3 Sitte Melik Tomb, Divriği; general view.

Figure 2.4 Sitte Melik Tomb, Divriği; portal.

and Armenian churches. Below the pyramidal dome of the tomb is a striking cornice composition consisting of a band of low-relief interlacing geometric ornament surmounted by a fine *muqarnas* register and topped by an inscriptional frieze.

Sitte Melik's frieze inscription is possibly the most remarkable to survive from any medieval Anatolian tomb. Written in an elongated (or *thuluth*-like) *naskh* style on a plain ground with some filler ornamentation, this inscription runs around the eight sides of the building.[20] Though not entirely devoid of orthographic errors these

Figure 2.5 Sitte Melik Tomb, Divriği; side niche.

Figure 2.6 Sitte Melik Tomb, Divriği; section of frieze inscription.

are relatively minor and allow a nearly complete reading, with lacunae limited to the beginning and the end of the text corresponding to the damaged segment of cornice on its entrance façade and two contiguous façades [numbered (1), (7) and (8)] to the right of the entrance.

(1) … wa 'l-muslimīn tāj al-anām (2) ẓahr al-imām 'imād al-ayyām (?) *'alā' al-dawla najm al-milla bahā' al-umma shams al-ma'ālī kahf al-ghuzāt al-muwaḥḥidūn ḥāmī thughūr al-mu'minīn (3) qātil al-kafara wa 'l-mushrikīn qāmi' {al-ilḥād}*[21] *wa 'l-mutamarridīn qāhir al-zanādiqa wa 'l-mutabaddi'īn 'umdat al-khilāfa 'izz al-mulūk wa 'l-salāṭīn (4) maljā' al-ḍu'afā' wa 'l-masākīn abū 'l-aytām wa 'l-maẓlūmīn al-mutanaṣṣif min al-ẓālimīn pahlawān al-Rūm wa 'l-Shām wa 'l-A(5)rman alp qutlugh ulugh humāyūn jabūghā tughrultakīn mafkhar āl Mangūjak Abū 'l-Muẓaffar Shāhanshāh bin (6) Sulaymān bin Isḥāq bin al-marḥūm al-sa'īd al-shahīd al-ghāzī al-amīr Mangūjak ẓahīr amīr al-mu'minīn (7) {khallada Allāhu ?} dawlatahu wa ḍā'afa {iqtidārahu ?} wa adāma fī* [four illegible words] *aḥad min shuhūr sanat {ithnayn wa ?} tis'{īn wa-khamsmi'a} (8) …*

(1) … and of Muslims, crown of the people, (2) helper of the imam, support of the reign (?), greatness of the state, star of the religion, brilliance of the community, sun of virtues, cave of the monotheist ghazis, protector of the border regions of the faithful, (3) slayer of the infidels and the polytheists, suppressor of heresy and rebels, vanquisher of heretics and innovators, support of the caliphate, the glory of kings and sultans, (4) refuge of the weak and the indigent, father of orphans and the oppressed, enforcer of justice against the oppressors, the *hero* of Rūm, Shām, and A(5)rman (Armenia), *the brave and blessed exalted sovereign, the lord falcon-prince,*[22] the pride of the family of Mangūjak, Abū 'l-Muẓaffar Shāhanshāh son of (6) Sulaymān son of Isḥāq son of the late fortunate martyr warrior amir Mengüjek, the support of the Commander of the Faithful (7) [may God perpetuate ?] his fortune, strengthen [his power ?],

and continue in [...] one of the months of the year [five hundred and] nine[ty-two?] (8) ...

On the portal façade of the tomb are two more inscriptions in *naskh*, placed one below the other, just above the top of the *muqarnas* arch. While the upper one identifying the tomb's occupant has an intricate background scroll, the lower one was written on plain ground, neither one exhibiting a particularly noteworthy mastery over the script. It is generally assumed that the lower one was added at the time of Shāhanshāh's death, so that its date of 592 (1196–7) (which may or may not have repeated the partly legible date in the frieze inscription) is taken as the *terminus ante quem* of the building.

Upper inscription:
hādhā (sic) *turbat* (sic) *sharīf al-amīr sipāsalār* (sic) *Sayf al-Dīn Shāhanshāh bin Sulaymān al-mawt bāb kullu dakhalahu.*
This is the noble tomb of the amir commander Sayf al-Dīn Shāhanshāh son of Sulaymān. Death is a gate which all [must] enter.

Lower inscription:
bi-tārīkh sanat ithnā wa tis'īn wa khams mi'a
On the date of year five hundred and ninety-two (=1196–7).

Like the Kale Camii, Sitte Melik was also signed but the name of its builder, inscribed on a block of stone on the side to the right of the entrance façade, was never completely deciphered mainly due to the worn surface of the inscription. Although this signature is now entirely missing (probably replaced by a plain block of stone in the course of restoration), a comparison of its photograph from 1967[23] with a signature on the portal of Alay Han, an undated Seljuk caravanserai near Aksaray,[24] confirms that both buildings were in fact the work of the same architect from the city of Ahlat (figs. 2.7–2.8). Both signatures start with the word *'amal-i* ('work of') and a name which may be tentatively read as *Tūtbeg*, followed by the patronymic

Figure 2.7 Sitte Melik Tomb, Divriği; signature block (reproduced from Sakaoğlu, *Türk Anadolu'da Mengücekoğulları*, p. 394).

Figure 2.8 Alay Han, Aksaray; signature block (photograph: Suzan Yalman).

Figure 2.9 Alay Han, Aksaray; portal (photograph: Suzan Yalman).

bin Bahrām. In the Alay Han signature, the same name and patronymic are clearly followed by the *nisba* (relational name) *al-Khilāṭī* ('from Ahlat') which on the Sitte Melik remained illegible except for the first two letters (*alif-lām* = *al-*).[25] The Alay Han signature ends with an additional word which is most likely *al-najjār* ('woodworker'). The personal name Tutbeg, though apparently not previously encountered, fits in with better-known medieval Turkic names such as Tutush or Iltutmish, which are derived from the root verb *tut*, meaning to seize, grasp or hold.[26]

Alay Han is generally assumed to have been built in the last years of the reign of sultan Qılıch Arslan II which, if correct, means that it is earlier than Sitte Melik.[27] Though built on a larger scale, the portal with its *muqarnas* niche and other decorative elements closely resembles that of Sitte Melik (fig. 2.9). The architect of both, Tutbeg b. Bahrām, was probably an itinerant master builder (and woodworker?) who made his services available to at least two of Anatolia's twelfth-century dynasties and brought Ahlat's tradition of fine stone craftsmanship to regions with an apparent demand for such novel elements as *muqarnas*, the expertise for which could not be sourced

Figure 2.10 Sultan Melik Tomb, Kemah; general view.

locally. The employment of the same architect by the Seljuks and the Mengüjekids underlines the critical role played by the mobility of artists, combined with the competitive aspect of patronage in the 1180s and 1190s.

The novelty of the style displayed by Sitte Melik is also apparent when it is compared to the two other extant examples of Mengüjekid tomb architecture from the 1190s. One of these, popularly known as Sultan Melik, is located in the cemetery just on the outskirts of Kemah and is attributed, based on circumstantial evidence, to the patronage of Bahrāmshāh's son Saljūqshāh and dated to the 1190s (fig. 2.10).[28] It was fashioned entirely in the Iranian tradition of brick architecture with an overt structural connection to such Azerbaijani tombs as Mu'mina Khātūn in Nakhchivan dated 1186–7 and Gunbad-i Kabūd in Maragha dated 1196–7. Sultan Melik, however, is a more modest rendition, employing embedded glazed bowls on its portal instead of glazed bricks and tiles, which were perhaps not as readily available in Kemah at this time as they were in Azerbaijan. The other tomb, which is known as Kamereddin, is located in Divriği and carries an inscription identifying a high-ranking court official as *al-amīr al-ḥājib al-ajall al-kabīr Qamar al-Dīn bin al-Ḥājj wa* (*sic*) *al-Ḥaramayn Rūzbih* ('the exalted and grand amir chamberlain Qamar al-Dīn son of Ruzbih the pilgrim to the holy shrines').[29] A second inscription giving the date of 20 Sha'bān 592 (19 July 1196) indicates that Kamereddin was built around the same year as Sitte Melik. Provided with a polylobed arch to accentuate its entrance and a series of embedded glazed bowls (recalling Sultan Melik in Kemah) to highlight the cornice of its otherwise plain exterior, Kamereddin has no apparent resemblance to Sitte Melik (fig. 2.11).[30] Nevertheless, the

Figure 2.11 Kamereddin Tomb, Divriği; general view.

two tombs were built in the same high-quality stone masonry, which, along with the coincidence of their dates, strongly suggests that they are the work of the same architect or workshop. The stylistic discrepancy between the two monuments may reflect the protocol of the local power structure through the visual rhetoric of architecture. The ongoing modulation of architectural style in Divriği can thus be seen through a comparison between the four Mengüjekid buildings of the late twelfth century. Whereas Sultan Melik in Kemah represents a faithful emulation of Iranian–Azerbaijani architectural style, the Kale Camii suggests that already by the 1180s Shāhanshāh's patronage favoured a more dynamic and divergent search for the visual expression of its dynastic identity. The outcome of this search is epitomised by Sitte Melik and the distinct artistic work of Tutbeg from Ahlat, which, judging by the stylistic detachment conveyed by the contemporary Kamereddin, was most likely seen as the prerogative of the ruler.

The Realms of Royal Rhetoric

Shāhanshāh's visual rhetoric was complemented by the message of the inscriptions of the Kale Camii and Sitte Melik, affording a broad view of the realm of royal self-identification on which his image was projected. The Sitte Melik frieze inscription, which subsumes and extends the message of the Kale Camii's portal and *minbar* inscriptions, necessitates a closer look at the language and imagery deployed in order to chart this rhetorical realm and to locate Shāhanshāh's self-proclaimed place in it. At first glance, the Sitte Melik frieze inscription appears as a long list of epithets and titles with a multiplicity of references followed by invocations and dates. Upon closer inspection, however, the inscription's register of epithets discloses itself as a structured composition of themes which culminate in the name of Shāhanshāh and his dynastic lineage. Although the individual and combined elements of the inscription are not novel as such, understanding the nature of the selection brings a nuanced insight into Shāhanshāh's self-perceived place in his socio-political world.[31]

The beginning of the frieze inscription has not survived but it must have started with some variation of the following phrase: 'This tomb was ordered by …'. This phrase was most likely followed by Shāhanshāh's main title, *al-amīr al-isfahsālār*, and probably a series of single-word epithets before his *laqab* (honorific name), Sayf al-Dunyā wa 'l-Dīn. In most examples of twelfth-century titulature the *laqab* is followed by a series of compound epithets, and this is where Sitte Melik's inscription in its surviving form begins by first depicting Shāhanshāh as a virtuous ruler who is an asset to both his subjects and his religion (*tāj al-anām ẓahr al-imām 'imād al-ayyām 'alā' al-dawla najm al-milla bahā' al-umma shams al-ma'ālī*). From here, the compound epithets shift in tone with an ideologically charged set which is based on militant exclusion and condemnation of the 'other'. This set begins by referencing both sides of an undefined border zone (*thughūr*) – on one side, the Muslim faithful in general, and, on the other side, the so-called infidels, polytheists, heretics, rebels and innovators (*kahf al-ghuzāt al-muwaḥḥidūn ḥāmī thughūr al-mu'minīn qātil al-kafara wa 'l-mushrikīn qāmi' {al-ilḥād} wa 'l-mutamarridīn qāhir al-zanādiqa wa 'l-mutabaddi'īn*). From this expression of censure and exclusion the text turns affirmative once again with a set of epithets that place Shāhanshāh within the intersecting orbits of the caliphate and the sultanate, thus conferring on him the aura of legitimacy with which he fulfils the role not only of the just and benevolent ruler but also of the redeemer of a humanity in need of his protection (*'umdat al-khilāfa 'izz al-mulūk wa 'l-salāṭīn maljā' al-ḍu'afā' wa 'l-masākīn abū 'l-aytām wa 'l-maẓlūmīn al-mutanaṣṣif min al-ẓālimīn*). Up to this point, the language of the text is entirely in Arabic and its discourse is wholly Islamic. The following set of epithets, starting with *pahlawān*, introduce Persian and Turkic terms of heroism in conjunction with the geographical coordinates of Shāhanshāh's sovereignty – Rūm, Shām, and Arman[32] – thereby conjoining the mythic with the current to arrive at the grand finale where Abū 'l-Muẓaffar Shāhanshāh is exalted as the current progeny of the house of the legendary Mengüjek (*pahlawān al-Rūm wa 'l-Shām wa 'l-Arman alp qutlugh ulugh humāyūn jabūghā tughrultakīn mafkhar āl Mangūjak Abū 'l-Muẓaffar Shāhanshāh bin Sulaymān bin Isḥāq bin al-marḥūm al-sa'īd al-shahīd al-ghāzī al-amīr Mangūjak ẓahīr amīr al-mu'minīn*). The invocations at the end carry all of these claims to the divine plane as a pious final disclaimer characteristic of much of medieval Islamic foundation inscriptions.

The frieze inscription was thus constructed as a text incorporating a definite structural and thematic rhythm, with points and counterpoints of affirmation and condemnation accentuating a scale of concepts relating to sovereignty and building up to a crescendo in the dynastic figure of Shāhanshāh. While this may be perceived as simply one elaborate composition of epithets and titles used by many rulers of the day (including Shāhanshāh himself already, in the *minbar* of the Kale Camii), three aspects of the textual composition – the geopolitical delineation of Rūm, Shām and Arman; the use of Turkic and Persian titles; and the extended discourse on heresy – are particularly noteworthy in terms of the observations they elicit about the construction of Shāhanshāh's image, which in turn complemented the construction of his tomb.

In both the Sitte Melik and the Kale Camii (*minbar*) inscriptions, the geographic arena of Shāhanshāh's dominion comprises Rūm, Shām and Arman. Like many medieval Islamic regional designations inserted into such texts, these were conceived not so much as discrete territories with defined boundaries on the ground but more as contiguous terrains in a state of flux, potentially subject to conquest and open to confluence under the aegis of a legitimate(d) sovereign. The confluence of geographies in the titles of rulers recalls the Abbasid caliph al-Qā'im's bestowal of the title *malik al-mashriq wa 'l-maghrib* ('king of the east and the west') upon the Great Seljuk ruler Tughrul in 1058.[33] Later Great Seljuk sultans such as Malikshāh also used binary ethno-geographic designations in inscriptions such as *mawlā al-'arab wa 'l-'ajam* ('master of Arabs and non-Arabs').[34] Such epithets also resonated with the Anatolian Turkmen dynasties whose first and foremost claim of geographic sovereignty was naturally Rūm. The term Rūm in this context indicated at once the lands conquered from the Byzantines (Romans) in the post-Manzikert era and the more notional 'Roman space' of the Byzantine/Roman empire.[35] Although Rūm could stand alone in an epithet claiming territorial sovereignty, it was often joined to one or more further geographic designations. A most common geographic combination involved the pairing of Rūm and Arman. The epithet *pahlawān al-Rūm wa 'l-Arman*, for example, was employed by Qılıch Arslan II in an inscription on the *minbar* of the Ulu Cami in Aksaray (c.1155) while he was still the crown prince.[36] This pairing was, on the one hand, a matter-of-fact territorial delineation reflecting demographic and historical realities, and, on the other hand, a conceptual augmentation of claims of sovereignty on the binary east–west pattern of *al-mashriq wa 'l-maghrib* or *al-'arab wa 'l-'ajam*.[37] Thus, when the poet Niẓāmī extolled his Mengüjekid patron Bahrāmshāh in the introduction to the *Makhzan al-asrār*, he deployed the paired terms *malik-i Arman* and *shāh-i Rūm* as well as *Rūm-sitānanda* ('conqueror of Rūm') and *Abkhāz-gīr* ('captor of Abkhaz/Georgia').[38] In the first pair, Niẓāmī denoted the confluence of two cultural and historico-political territories under the sovereignty of one ruler, while in the second pair he engaged the ideals of conquest and expansion as a necessary attribute of rulership.[39]

For the Mengüjekid rulers located in the upper Euphrates region, the pairing of Rūm and Arman accurately reflected the historical legacy of their territory, once part of the Roman–Byzantine frontier province of Armenia. It also reflected the current demographic reality as, according to the early thirteenth-century geographer Yāqūt, Erzincan had a majority Armenian population and a similar situation was probably the case in Divriği.[40] However, the Sitte Melik inscription includes a third geography, Shām (Syria), which does not coincide with the reality of Shāhanshāh's sphere of authority confined as it was to the western reaches of the upper Euphrates basin. This region was at a considerable distance from even the most generous definition of greater Syria, which was under successive Great Seljuk, Burid, Zangid and Ayyubid control during the twelfth century. Shāhanshāh's claim over Shām may therefore seem as nothing more than sheer inflation with not even a partial basis in reality. Yet, seen from the vantage point of Rūm, Shām (or at least its northern reaches) was contested territory and the source of tension and periodic conflict especially between the Seljuks of Anatolia and their succession of neighbours to the east, starting with the Great Seljuks at the turn of the twelfth century and continuing intermittently with their successors the Zangids and the Ayyubids.[41] Although we have no information on Shāhanshāh's military activities, it is probable that he was a participant in or a political supporter of Qılıch Arslan II's confrontations with Syrian powers (especially Nūr al-Dīn b. Zangī and Saladin) and thereby saw it fit to include Shām in his epithet. Indeed, Shāhanshāh's absorption of Shām into his geopolitical epithet may have been similar to Niẓāmī's appellation of Bahrāmshāh as *Abkhāz-gīr*. Mengüjekid rhetorical claims over Georgia and Syria were thus most likely predicated upon military participation or even just military aspiration rather than any actual territorial gain or military success. The same could be said about Qılıch Arslan II when he employed the seemingly improbable quadripartite geopolitical epithet of *sulṭān bilād al-Rūm wa 'l-Arman wa 'l-Afranj wa 'l-Shām* in an inscription on the *minbar* of the royal Seljuk mosque in Konya (Alaeddin Camii) dated AH 550 (1155–6), the year of his accession.[42] In this case, the mention of Afranj ('Franks') was probably justified by the successful Seljuk attack against the German forces of the Second Crusade at the second Battle of Dorylaeum in 1147 under the leadership of Qılıch Arslan II's father, Mas'ūd I.[43] The 'lands of the Franks' could refer to the remaining Frankish presence in greater Syria after the elimination of the County of Edessa in 1144 by 'Imād al-Dīn Zangī. Qılıch Arslan II's listing of Afranj alongside Shām was a double-edged rhetorical sword, which engaged not only the long-standing Anatolian Seljuk rivalry with Syria but also the common Muslim cause against the Franks in Syria.

For Shāhanshāh in the latter decades of the twelfth century, the net effect of listing Rūm, Shām and Arman together was to convey the idea of an expansive realm with a potential for further expansion in a composite framework which served to magnify the rhetoric of rulership on the geopolitical arena of his time. A second composite framework in the Sitte Melik inscription emerges from the embedding of Persian and Turkic titles (*pahlawān al-Rūm wa 'l-Shām wa 'l-Arman alp qutlugh ulugh humāyūn jabūghā tughrultakīn*) into the otherwise Arabic language of the text, thereby extending the horizons of Shāhanshāh's political image to include the Turco-Iranian space of the Islamic world. This multi-lingual rhetoric is encountered in the titulature of other Turkic rulers of the twelfth century, not only in Anatolia but also in Syria and Azerbaijan. Limited use of Turkic titles such as *qutlugh atabeg* can be attested already in the inscriptions of the Burids in Damascus from the beginning of the twelfth century.[44] The practice appears to have gained momentum under another *atabeg*, ʿImād al-Dīn Zangī, whose inscription on the walls of Baalbek employs the titles *alp ghāzī īnānch qutlugh tughrultakīn atābeg*.[45] Qılıch Arslan II also made use of Turkic titles (*alp īnānch qutlugh bilge*) on the Aksaray *minbar* when he was still the crown prince, but omitted them altogether from the Konya *minbar* when he assumed the supreme title sultan after his accession to the throne.[46] In the 1160s, the Artuqids and Ahmadilis also employed such Turkic titles although they are noticeably absent from the titulature of Nūr al-Dīn b. Zangī.[47]

The use of Turkic titles could be perceived as a reflection of the relevance of ethnicity in the projection of political identity, and of a cultural continuity between pre-Islamic (or para-Islamic) Turkic identity and medieval Turco-Islamic states. It is probable that such terms resonated with Turkmen rulers and subjects who, even as they adopted the tenets of Islamic rulership and strove to cement their legitimate place within the Islamic world, maintained both concepts of sovereignty and narratives of heroism from their Turkic heritage. The endurance of heroic narratives is made especially evident in the cycle of stories, incorporating multiple layers of orally transmitted epic and mythic tales, which were eventually written down under the name of Dede Korkut in eastern Anatolia in the late medieval period.[48] However, even as these Turkic terms undoubtedly held meaning for the Turkic-speaking populations and rulers from ʿImād al-Dīn Zangī to Shāhanshāh, it is probable that they were not perceived to operate in semantic isolation as an entirely discrete set of concepts derived from a wholly separate realm of rhetoric or culture. This observation is suggested by the inclusion of the Persian royal term *humāyūn* in Shāhanshāh's sequence of Turkic titles or the Arabic term *ghāzī* in Zangī's. The primary appeal of the Turkic terms must have derived less from their indication of specific ethno-cultural identity and more from the access they provided into the world of royal epics and myths of a synthesised Turco-Iranian past as embedded into the Islamic present. In other words, the force of these titles turned on the power exerted by ancient Turkic and Iranian narratives of heroism and royalty on the identity of twelfth-century rulers in need of political legitimacy and prestige, and ever ready for chances to demonstrate their capacity for battle and conquest for the Islamic world. This is all the more evident in the Sitte Melik inscription from the introduction of these Turkic titles immediately following the geopolitical referencing of Rūm, Shām and Arman governed by the Persian epic title of *pahlawān* (hero). In the case of Zangī, the Turkic titles are preceded by an even more epic combination of Persian title and geopolitical element: *shahriyār al-Shām wa 'l-'Irāqayn, pahlawān-i jahān, khusraw-i Irān* ('sovereign of Shām and the two Iraqs, hero of the world, Chosroes of Iran').[49]

Far more ostentatious than Shāhanshāh's claims in this category, Zangī's Persian titles – *shahriyār*, *pahlawān* and *khusraw* – epitomise the key concepts of sovereignty, heroism and justice[50] respectively, for which the Iranian tradition provided the main framework in the eastern Islamic world of the Great Seljuks and their successors. It is from the same framework that Shāhanshāh's primary title of *al-amīr al-isfahsālār* was derived. This combined Arabic–Persian title, first encountered with Great Seljuk amirs in Iran and Syria in the early twelfth century, became fairly widespread later in the same century, being adopted by (or conferred by the caliph upon) regional rulers emerging from the dissolution of the Great Seljuks, in particular those in the frontier regions or involved in the confrontation with the Crusaders.[51] Thus, the term *isfahsālār*, an Arabicised version of the Middle Persian military title *spah-salar* (or *spah-badh*), appears to have retained its Sasanian connotation of high-ranking military commanders assigned to the governance and defence of border regions. As such, it is a title distilled out of the Iranian cultural horizon of the Great Seljuk successor states, not necessarily with a precise lexical understanding of its Middle Persian usage (though the coincidence is remarkable) but probably with a sense of its signification of the ancient Persian royal-military protocol.

The compound title *al-amīr al-isfahsālār* mainly functioned in tandem with ensuing Turkic and/or Persian titles, so that the assumption of a grander title such as sultan could entail the discontinuation of any and all non-Arabic titles from a ruler's titular sequence. This is exemplified in the case of both Nūr al-Dīn b. Zangī and Qılıch Arslan II, whose respective rise in power in the middle decades of the twelfth century resulted in the apparent discarding of their previously held Turkic and/or Persian titles and the assumption of exclusively Arabic titles and epithets amounting to a thoroughly Islamic/universal rhetoric of rulership.[52] The recourse to Turkic and Persian titles thus seems to have gone hand in hand with lower strata of rulership, in which the pressures exerted by expansionist neighbours combined with the aspirations of the ruler in question gave meaning to the evocation of legendary Turco-Iranian notions of heroism and regalism. Judging by his epigraphic record, Shāhanshāh retained the title *al-amīr al-isfahsālār* throughout his career while buttressing his status and legitimacy in this lower-tier rulership by maximising on a range of concepts, including composite geopolitical claims and Turco-Iranian titles.

Integral to the composite geographic and linguistic framework of Shāhanshāh's political identity as expressed in the Sitte Melik inscription is the notion of a border zone where not only conceptual confluencing and amalgamation could be effected but also opposition, exclusion, and differentiation. This is first signalled in the explicit and twofold declaration of Shāhanshāh as *kahf al-ghuzāt al-muwaḥḥidūn ḥāmī thughūr al-mu'minīn* ('cave of the monotheist ghazis [and] protector of the borders of the faithful') which engages the idea of the protection of true belief from the threat posed by the world lying beyond the borders of true belief.[53] An expanded rhetoric on heresy and unbelief follows immediately, using a series of epithets which amount to an intense invective against infidels, polytheists, heretics and rebels (*qātil al-kafara wa 'l-mushrikīn qāmi' [al-ilḥād] wa 'l-mutamarridīn qāhir al-zanādiqa wa 'l-mutabaddi'īn*). Similar epithets were first introduced in the earlier decades of the twelfth century in the inscriptions of ʿImād al-Dīn Zangī and continued by his son Nūr al-Dīn b. Zangī.[54] Zangid epigraphic condemnation of unbelievers and heretics was choreographed in the immediate context of counter-Crusade military activity and ideology (*jihād*). Similar epithets were used in inscriptions of the Artuqids, who also had a history of military activity against the Franks in the twelfth century.[55] That the Franks figured prominently in the ideological concerns of the second half of the twelfth century is likewise evident from Qılıch Arslan II's Aksaray *minbar* inscription with its mention of the Afranj as discussed earlier. Nevertheless, because the intended target of such invectives is not identified their 'reach' could also extend further, at least theoretically, to the non-Sunni Muslim adversaries *du jour*, most notably the Fatimid caliphate – then on its last legs in Egypt – and perhaps even various strands of Ismaʿili agents active elsewhere, including Syria. This becomes especially relevant in the case of Nūr al-Dīn whose agent Saladin brought down the Fatimid state in 1172. Indeed, such invectives could be easily deployed to lend ideological justification to the persecution of inconveniently influential individuals – as happened in the ominous execution of the mystic–philosopher Shihāb al-Dīn Yaḥyā al-Suhrawardī on the order of Saladin in 1191, on trumped-up charges of heresy which appear to have been rather a cover-up for political motives.[56]

In the case of Shāhanshāh tucked away in Divriği, condemnation of heresy and associated deviances from a presumed norm indicate Mengüjekid participation in a common Sunni ideological front which took shape in the latter decades of the twelfth century. This seemingly unifying ideological front soared high above the political landscape, with its realities of irreversible fragmentation, expansion and contraction. Though unlikely to have been affected directly either by Crusader passage through Anatolia or Frankish presence in greater Syria, the Mengüjekid polity in Divriği led by the figure of Shāhanshāh had much to gain from the up-to-date enhancement of its geopolitical image. As in the demarcation of Rūm, Shām and Arman, the maintenance of Mengüjekid dynastic identity depended on conceptually reaching well beyond the limits and politics of local authority, an exercise which was undertaken by both Bahrāmshāh and Shāhanshāh. The titular discourse on heresy should likewise be seen more as extended and elevated political rhetoric, modelled after celebrated rulers of the twelfth century such as 'Imād al-Dīn and Nūr al-Dīn, than as the focused expression of a strict dogmatic position on any particular non-Muslim or non-Sunni opponent.[57]

The World of Tutbeg b. Bahrām al-Khilāṭī

The expression of Shāhanshāh's public image as declared in the Sitte Melik frieze inscription must have been composed in Divriği by a secretary–scribe in tune with both his patron's aspirations and the wider world of twelfth-century diplomatic and chancery texts in which royal titulature evolved. As the carefully composed text was transferred directly from penned document to the stonemason's chisel, it retained permanent marks of the secretary's handwriting in the form of certain ligatures between the letters (fig.2.6). Besides these fingerprint-like signs, there remain no further traces of this anonymous secretary whose experience in the world of bureaucracy must have been no less than the architect's experience in his craft. The self-confidence of the frieze inscription thus finds its counterpart in the architectural work of Tutbeg b. Bahrām, who evidently possessed the necessary visual vocabulary and design skills to match his patron's geopolitical aspirations by composing discrete visual elements – *muqarnas* portal, epigraphic frieze, elongated exterior niches – into a monument which in itself could be read as a conceptual confluence masterfully translated into stone. In other words, the Sitte Melik can be perceived as an embodiment of Shāhanshāh's public image, giving tangible and visible form to his claims on Rūm, Shām and Arman as well as his amalgamations of Islamic, Iranian and Turkic horizons of sovereignty. The favourable conjunctions in the figure of the sovereign as depicted in the inscription and in the architecture of his tomb coalesced to represent Shāhanshāh as a fixed pivot in a political realm composed of multiple and movable rhetorical parts.

Given the absence of information about the specific circumstances which led to and governed Tutbeg's employment in the Sitte Melik project in Divriği, it is not possible to go beyond speculation on the question of intention on the part of the architect or patron. Yet the combination of Tutbeg's apparent artistic background in Ahlat and Shāhanshāh's rhetorical amplification of his political persona suggest that Divriği was not simply the unwitting recipient of the work of random itinerant builders who happened to be passing by. From 1100 until 1207, Ahlat was the centre of a principality first established by Sökmen (Sukmān) al-Quṭbī, a former Turkic slave amir in the service of the Great Seljuks, and ruling the regions surrounding Lake Van.[58] The dynastic name, Shāh-i Arman, derives from the primarily Armenian ethnic make-up and political history of the region ruled by this Turkmen family. Sources extol the commercial prosperity and cultural reputation of twelfth-century Ahlat, especially during the long reign of Nāṣir al-Dīn Sökmen II (r. 1128–85) who was married to Shāhbānū, the daughter of the Saltuqid ruler of Erzurum, 'Izz al-Dīn Saltuq II. Shāhbānū is said to have personally initiated in 1164 a major building campaign of roads and stone bridges (replacing earlier wooden ones) leading into the city and large commercial inns, as well as rebuilding the citadel which had been left in ruins. For the latter, she employed an engineer named Qaraqush who gained renown for completing the mammoth task in just a few months. Such intensive building activity in a short time would have required significant numbers of builders and stonemasons, whose high-quality work can be deduced from the account of the Khwārazmshāh Jalāl al-Dīn's brutal eight-month winter siege of the city in 1229–30 which required massive effort and machinery to breach and destroy the same citadel.[59] For his part, Sökmen II was apparently responsible for the establishment of a town known in the medieval sources as Sukmānābād said to be west of Khuy, on the caravan road going east from Ahlat to Tabriz. No trace of Ahlat's medieval architecture prior to the late thirteenth century survives, an unfortunate loss which is undoubtedly due to the destruction brought on by the invading Khwārazmshāh and the Mongols as well as two devastating earthquakes (1246 and 1276) which destroyed most of the city.[60] Nevertheless, building activity associated with Sökmen II and Shāhbānū in the sources leaves little doubt about a wealth of new architecture in the twelfth century, sustained by commercial prosperity and artistic resources.

When Sökmen II died in 1185, he left no heir to follow him, which triggered a period of political instability for the Shāh-i Arman as a series of slave amirs ruled in succession until 1207 when Ahlat was taken by the Ayyubids. It may be supposed that the demise of the dynastic line in 1185 created conditions which were not favourable for the employment of large numbers of skilled builders, some of whom probably began to seek employment elsewhere. Tutbeg's employment at the Alay Han and the Sitte Melik in the 1190s could thus be linked to the changing circumstances in his home town. It is also tempting to link the demise of the dynastic line with the sudden emergence of Ahlat's celebrated funerary stelae, the earliest examples of which in fact date to the 1180s and 1190s.[61] Both the travels of Tutbeg and the remarkable craftsmanship and design elements displayed on the stelae suggest that craftsmen had to adapt themselves to the changing circumstances at the end of the twelfth century. Their success in this respect is evident from the continuing association of Ahlat with the highest-quality stonework. The funerary stelae especially furnish important clues about the merits of these craftsmen in terms of design and artistic execution, which they continued to showcase by carrying contemporary Islamic geometric motifs onto a new type of grave marker echoing the form of the Armenian commemorative stele known as *khatchkar*. Given the resourcefulness of its craftsmen, who have left behind numerous signatures, it is highly probable that Ahlat was also the main artistic centre where such Islamic forms as *muqarnas* – first developed in brick or stucco and wood in Iran and Iraq – were translated into stone and thence introduced into the Islamic architecture of Anatolia and the Armenian architecture of Transcaucasia, eastern Anatolia and Upper Mesopotamia where they flourished throughout the thirteenth century.[62] The difference between the *muqarnas* niches of the Kale Camii and Sitte Melik in Divriği is fairly compelling evidence for presuming Ahlat to be the source of stone *muqarnas* production in Anatolia. By virtue of its location at a regional and cultural junction and its vibrant commercial and professional life, twelfth-century

Ahlat afforded its artists the opportunity to encounter and process a variety of visual forms (notably those coming from the Armenian and Islamic traditions) which were then transmitted to regions such as central Anatolia where their novelty would have rendered them particularly prestigious.[63]

Through his two known works – Alay Han and Sitte Melik – Tutbeg emerges as a pioneer architect in late twelfth-century Anatolia, responsible for the earliest extant examples of the fine *muqarnas* stone portals which would become a hallmark of public buildings from the early thirteenth century onwards. As an itinerant artist, Tutbeg was perhaps accompanied by a small team of stonemasons proficient in geometric patterns and *muqarnas* construction. It is equally probable that Tutbeg's primary role was that of a master designer who planned and directed the stone construction and decoration. If the last word following Tutbeg's signature in the Alay Han inscription is indeed *al-najjār* (woodworker) it would confirm his expertise in designing and creating in more than one medium.[64] This kind of cross-medium proficiency in medieval Anatolia is also indicated in the signature on Qılıch Arslan II's Aksaray *minbar* of c.1155, wherein Nushtegin (Nūshtakīn) al-Jamālī is represented as the 'architect of the mosque and the *minbar*' (*mi'mār al-masjid wa 'l-minbar*).[65] Here the word *mi'mār* signified responsibility for the design of both the mosque and its wooden *minbar* (and perhaps other furnishings as well). Nushtegin also bore the title *khwāja* ('master') and the epithets *ṣalāḥ al-dawla* ('rectitude of the state') and *zayn al-ḥājj* ('ornament of pilgrimage'), all of which indicate a learned and well-travelled individual of rank. A similar background can be assumed for the maker of Qılıch Arslan II's Konya *minbar*, who signed his name as *ustādh Mangūmbartī al-ḥājjī al-Akhlāṭī*.[66] This master craftsmen who hailed from Ahlat clearly excelled in the area of geometric patterning and it is probable that he worked as a designer on more than one medium. The presence of master designers in Ahlat is also known from the record of the funerary stelae, on which occupational titles such as *muzayyin* ('designer') can be encountered, and in several master–student relationships detected from the end of the thirteenth century into the fourteenth century when Ahlat's architecture can once again be documented from extant buildings.[67] It is this aspect of Ahlat's artistic activity which ensured it a continuous brilliance between the twelfth and fifteenth centuries. Despite vicious political and military upheavals in the early thirteenth century, two of the most distinct buildings in Anatolia at this time – the Tomb of Mama Hatun in Tercan[68] and the mosque–hospital complex of Divriği – were both signed by masters from Ahlat.

As Tutbeg b. Bahrām made his way around Anatolia in the 1190s, he must have benefited from a dynamic network of master craftsmen and architects among whom his Ahlat pedigree probably served him particularly well in securing commissions. For his Mengüjekid patron, the image-conscious Shāhanshāh, Tutbeg offered the winning combination of high-quality stonemasonry with a distinctly novel design which was just beginning to make its stamp on the built environment of Anatolia. At a time when the fortunes of the less powerful, such as the Mengüjekids and the Shāh-i Arman, ultimately depended on their ability to navigate the tidal waves caused by the tremors emanating from the more powerful, such as the Seljuks and the Ayyubids, this fortunate conjunction of patron and architect in the safe haven of Divriği ensured the creation of a monument which not only commemorates the figure of Shāhanshāh but also embodies the workings of a dynastic image well-attuned to the world outside of Divriği. Embedded into the story of Shāhanshāh's patronage of Kale Camii and Sitte Melik are the terms of artistic and political engagement which defined the circuits of connectivity in medieval Anatolia.

Notes

1. The idea for this chapter was conceived during a research trip to Divriği in September 2009. I would like to acknowledge the kind assistance and hospitality extended to me there by Dr Erdal Eser (Cumhuriyet University, Sivas), director of the Divriği citadel excavation project, and his team of students.
2. Ibn Bībī, *al-Awāmir al-'alā'īya fī 'l-umūr al-'alā'īya*, facsimile edition prepared by Adnan Sadık Erzi as İbn-i Bībī, *El-Evāmirü'l-*

'Alā'iyye fī 'l-Umūri'l-'Alā'iyye (Ankara: Türk Tarih Kurumu, 1956), p. 11. See also printed partial edition of Ibn Bībī's unabridged text by Necati Lugal and Adnan Sadık Erzi: İbn-i Bībī, *El-Evāmirü'l-'alā'iyye fī 'l-umūri'l-'alā'iyye. I. Cild (II. Kılıç Arslan'ın Vefâtından I. 'Ala'ü'd-Dīn Keyḳubâd'ın Cülûsuna Kadar)*, (Ankara: Ankara Üniversitesi İlahiyat Fakültesi Yayınları, 1957), p. 41.

3. In addition to the relevant entries in the *Encyclopaedia of Islam* (2nd edition); the *Türkiye Diyanet Vakfı İslam Ansiklopedisi*; and two chapters in Claude Cahen, *La Turquie pré-ottomane* (Istanbul: Institut Français d'Études Anatoliennes, 1988), pp. 33–54; the two main secondary sources covering these dynasties (with the exception of the Danishmendids) are Osman Turan, *Doğu Anadolu Türk Devletleri Tarihi* (1973; reprint, Istanbul: Ötüken, 2001) and Faruk Sümer, *Selçuklular Devrinde Doğu Anadolu'da Türk Beylikleri* (Ankara: Türk Tarih Kurumu, 1990). For a brief overview of the primary sources in Arabic, Persian, Armenian, Georgian and Syriac, which provide the bulk of the admittedly scanty information from which the history of these dynasties is assembled, see Turan, *Doğu Anadolu Türk Devletleri Tarihi*, pp. 12–4. For the Mengüjekids, two further secondary sources are Max van Berchem and Halil Edhem, *Matériaux pour un Corpus Inscriptionum Arabicorum, Troisième partie, Asie Mineure, Tome premier, Siwas, Diwrigi* (Cairo: Institut Français d'Archéologie Orientale, 1917) and Necdet Sakaoğlu, *Türk Anadolu'da Mengücekoğulları* (Istanbul: Yapı Kredi Yayınları, 2005).
4. The following account of the Mengüjekids is based on a cautious assessment of the sources given above in note 3, in combination with the evidence provided for cultural history by the surviving architecture. See also Oya Pancaroğlu, 'The Mosque-Hospital complex in Divriği: a history of relations and transitions', *Anadolu ve Çevresinde Ortaçağ* 3 (2009), pp. 169–98.
5. T.A. Sinclair, *Eastern Turkey: An Architectural and Archaeological Survey* (London: Pindar Press, 1987–90, 4 vols), ii, pp. 426–30.
6. Sakaoğlu, *Türk Anadolu'da Mengücekoğulları*, pp. 136–41.

7. Doğan Kuban, *Divriği Mucizesi: Selçuklu Çağında İslam Bezeme Sanatı Üzerine Bir Deneme* (Istanbul: Yapı Kredi Yayınları, 1997); Sakaoğlu, *Türk Anadolu'da Mengücekoğulları*, pp. 239–385; Pancaroğlu, 'The Mosque-Hospital complex in Divriği'.
8. Berchem and Edhem, *Siwas, Diwrigi*, pp. 89–90; Sakaoğlu, *Türk Anadolu'da Mengücekoğulları*, p. 205. On the citadel of Divriği, see also Sinclair, *Eastern Turkey*, ii, pp. 400–2.
9. Berchem and Edhem, *Siwas, Diwrigi*, pp. 56–62; Sakaoğlu, *Türk Anadolu'da Mengücekoğulları*, pp. 217–26; Ali Boran, *Anadolu'daki İç Kale Cami ve Mescidleri* (Ankara: Türk Tarih Kurumu, 2001), pp. 60–5.
10. These are discussed at length in Berchem and Edhem, *Siwas, Diwrigi*, pp. 56–62.
11. Ersin Gülsoy and Mehmet Taştemir, *1530 Tarihli Malatya, Behisni, Gerger, Kâhta, Hısn-ı Mansur, Divriği ve Darende Kazâları Vakıf ve Mülk Defteri* (Ankara: Türk Tarih Kurumu, 2007), pp. xlix-lvii, 212–71; Ersin Gülsoy, 'XVI. asrın ilk yarısında Divriği Kazası vakıfları', *İlmî Araştırmalar 1* (1995), pp. 107–30; Zeki Arıkan, 'Divriği Kazası'nın ilk sayımı', *Osmanlı Araştırmaları* 11 (1991), pp. 49–71.
12. This title will be discussed in detail in the next section.
13. Michael Meinecke, *Fayencedekorationen seldschukischer Sakralbauten in Kleinasien* (Tübingen: Wasmuth, 1976), i, p. 15, n. 40. Triangular glazed tiles once highlighted the spandrels of the portal arch. The few remaining examples, visible until recently, appear not to have survived the regrettable restoration of the building undertaken by the Directorate General of Endowments in 2007–8.
14. For Diyarbakır, see Max van Berchem and Josef Strzygowski, *Amida* (Heidelberg: Carl Winter, 1910). For the Caucasus, see N. Khanikoff, 'Les inscriptions musulmanes du Caucase', *Journal Asiatique 20* (August 1862), pp. 57–155.
15. For the Kale Camii mihrab, see Ömür Bakırer, *Onüç ve Ondördüncü Yüzyıllarda Anadolu Mihrabları* (Ankara: Türk Tarih Kurumu, 1976), pp. 71, 128–9. For the development of *muqarnas*, see Yasser Tabbaa, *The Transformation of Islamic Art during the Sunni*

Revival (Seattle: University of Washington Press, 2001), pp. 103–24, 150–5.

16. Sakaoğlu, *Türk Anadolu'da Mengücekoğulları*, pp. 229–30. The reading here is a slightly amended version of the one offered by Sakaoğlu. The problems in the reading are due not only to orthographic mistakes but also to the fact that this fragment was salvaged from the original *minbar* which ended up as firewood when the Ottoman mosque (Cedidpaşa) to which it had been moved was converted into a temporary prison in 1949 (ibid., p. 227).
17. These geographic designations and the other terms used here are discussed in the next section.
18. Berchem and Edhem, *Siwas, Diwrigi*, pp. 63–9; Sakaoğlu, *Türk Anadolu'da Mengücekoğulları*, pp. 389–97; Hakkı Önkal, *Anadolu Selçuklu Türbeleri* (Ankara: Atatürk Kültür, Dil ve Tarih Yüksek Kurumu, 1996), pp. 37–42. The name of the tomb, which incorporates the female title *sitte* (from the Arabic *sayyida* for lady), is a popular appellation for which no secure explanation exists, although the possibility that it transferred to the tomb as a result of associated royal female patronage or endowment is most likely. Indeed, an entry in the 1530 tax register lists an endowment dated to 593 (1196–7) for the 'Türbe-i Sitti Melike Hatun', which, judging by its date, must almost certainly be related to the Sitte Melik Tomb (Gülsoy and Taştemir, *Vakıf ve Mülk Defteri*, p. 245). It may be that Shāhanshāh's wife (or daughter) had made these endowments for her husband's (or father's) tomb a year after its construction (or his death) in 592 and that she was buried in the same tomb at a later date (though no inscribed cenotaphs are to be found in the tomb to ascertain this), which caused her name to be perpetuated in association with the tomb. The important role of female members of the Mengüjekid family in architectural patronage and endowments is apparent from the evidence preserved in the tax registers, which also reveal the active existence of Mengüjekid identity in the sixteenth century (Pancaroğlu, 'The Mosque-Hospital complex in Divriği,' pp. 171 note 9, 173 note 13).

19. In fact, none of the other medieval (Mengüjekid to Mamluk) tombs in Divriği were built with crypts. This observation might suggest that funerary practices here did not involve the embalming of the deceased, a procedure which is associated with the presence of accessible tomb crypts elsewhere in Anatolia. In a survey of 136 medieval Anatolian tombs, it was found that at least 67 were definitely furnished with crypts: Ülkü Bates, 'The Anatolian Mausoleum of the Twelfth, Thirteenth and Fourteenth centuries' (PhD Dissertation, University of Michigan, 1970), pp. 405–8.
20. On the *thuluth*-like *naskh* script in the Seljuk realms and its connections to scribal practices of the chancery, see Scott Redford and Gary Leiser, *Victory Inscribed. The Seljuk* Fetiḥnāme *on the Citadel Walls of Antalya, Turkey/Taşa Yazılan Zafer. Antalya İçkale Surlarındaki Selçuklu Fetihnamesi* (Antalya: Suna-İnan Kıraç Akdeniz Medeniyetleri Araştırma Enstitüsü, 2008), pp. 113–21.
21. This word is mistakenly written as *ilāh ilḥād.*
22. The Persian and Turkic terms have been italicised in the translation to distinguish them from the rest of the Arabic text. The significance of these terms (and the preceding geographic designations) are discussed in the next section. Translations of the Turkic terms have been checked against definitions and usages offered in Gerard Clauson, *An Etymological Dictionary of Pre-Thirteenth-Century Turkish* (Oxford: Clarendon Press, 1972) and Gerhard Doerfer, *Türkische und mongolische Elemente im Neupersischen* (Wiesbaden: Franz Steiner Verlag, 1963–75). Nevertheless, the line between title and personal name is somewhat blurred and the distinction is difficult to make without further evidence. Thus, it may be that the final term in this sequence, *tughrultakīn*, is not a title (as the translation 'falcon-prince' here would suggest) but rather Shāhanshāh's Turkic personal name. As such, it would combine with the preceding term, *jabūghā* (a variant of *yabghū*), possibly to indicate Shāhanshāh's secondary rank within the Mengüjekid family hierarchy. An ancient title, *yabghū/jabūghā* (loosely translated here as 'lord') was typically applied

in Turkic societies to a member of the ruling family who occupied a position second or third in rank to the great *kāghān/khān*. This inscription is one of the last known instances of its usage, at least in the western Turkic world. For some examples of the earlier usage and variants of this term, see (in addition to Clauson and Doerfer) Berchem and Edhem, *Siwas, Diwrigi*, pp. 67–8; *Ḥudūd al-ʿālam, 'The Regions of the World'. A Persian Geography 372 A.H. – 982 A.D.*, trans. Vladimir Minorsky (Cambridge: E.J.W. Gibb Memorial, 1970, 2nd edition), pp. 288–9; and *The Sea of Precious Virtues (Baḥr al-Favāʾid)*, trans. Julie Scott Meisami (Salt Lake City: University of Utah Press, 1991), p. 331 note 11. For a discussion of *tughrultakīn* as personal name vs. title, see Max van Berchem, 'Monuments et inscriptions de l'ātabek Lu'lu' de Mossoul', in Carl Bezold (ed.), *Orientalische Studien. Theodor Nöldeke zum siebzigsten Geburtstag* (Gieszen: Alfred Töpelmann, 1906), i, pp. 200–1 notes 6–7.

23. Sakaoğlu mentions that the Sitte Melik underwent initial restoration in the 1950s when the conical dome was reconstructed, apparently causing some damage to the upper courses of the masonry but not, it seems, to the signature block which was photographed in 1967 (*Türk Anadolu'da Mengücekoğulları*, p. 391); for the photograph of the signature block, see ibid., p. 394. This block most probably disappeared in the course of the recent restoration undertaken by the Directorate General of Endowments in 2007–8.
24. This signature was first noticed by İbrahim Hakkı Konyalı (*Âbideleri ve Kitabeleri ile Niğde, Aksaray Tarihi* [Istanbul: Fatih Yayınevi, 1974], i, pp. 1100–6), but his attempt to read it was hampered by the high placement of the inscription. He offered a tentative reading which has been reproduced wholesale in the most recent publication on Alay Han, which seems to have overlooked Konyalı's caveat. This publication, ironically, provides a good-quality photograph of the signature, from which it is possible to decipher most of the actual inscription; Bekir Deniz, 'Alay Han', in Hakkı Acun (ed.), *Anadolu Selçuklu Dönemi Kervansarayları* (Ankara: Kültür ve Turizm Bakanlığı Yayınları, 2007), pp. 51–75

(photograph on p. 66). For references to earlier publications which noted the stylistic and technical similarity between Sitte Melik and Alay Han portals, see ibid., p. 57 note 16.

25. Both Berchem and Edhem (*Siwas, Diwrigi*, p. 69) and Sakaoğlu (*Türk Anadolu'da Mengücekoğulları*, p. 394) read the letter following the initial *alif-lām* as *mīm* which led Sakaoğlu to propose that the *nisba* might be al-Marāghī. What they took to be a *mīm*, however, is the little loop in the connection between the *lām* and the *khā'* in the beginning of *al-Khilāṭī*.
26. Clauson, *Etymological Dictionary*, p. 451.
27. Konyalı mentions that the caravanserai's older name, Pervane, might link it to Ẓāhir al-Dīn Ili, a Danishmendid prince who entered the service of Qılıch Arslan II after the fall of his dynasty and occupied the court office of the *parwāna*; *Aksaray Tarihi*, p. 1106.
28. Although the tomb is popularly identified as that of Mengüjek Ghāzī (modern Turkish, Mengücek Gazi), the founder of the dynasty, this is quite improbable. An associated structure next to it – possibly a *zāwīya* from the same period – has a very similar portal but this is too damaged make any specific observations. For a summary of the issues of identification and dating surrounding these two buildings along with references, see Pancaroğlu, 'The Mosque-Hospital complex in Divriği', pp. 178–9.
29. Berchem and Edhem, *Siwas, Diwrigi*, pp. 62–3; Önkal, *Anadolu Selçuklu Türbeleri*, pp. 42–6; Sakaoğlu, *Türk Anadolu'da Mengücekoğulları*, pp. 398–402.
30. On polylobed arches in twelfth-century Zangid Syria (including Harran), see Tabbaa, *The Transformation of Islamic Art*, pp. 140–4.
31. Studies on medieval Islamic titulature and honorifics are few and far between. The following discussion has benefited from these works focused on the late twelfth and early thirteenth centuries: Berchem, 'Monuments et inscriptions de l'ātabek Lu'lu' de Mossoul'; Nikita Elisséeff, 'La titulature de Nūr ad-Dīn d'après ses inscriptions', *Bulletin d'Études Orientales 14* (1952–4), pp. 155–96; Rustam Shukurov, 'Turkoman and Byzantine self-identity. Some reflections on the logic of title-making in twelfth- and

thirteenth-century Anatolia', in Antony Eastmond (ed.), *Eastern Approaches to Byzantium* (Aldershot: Ashgate, 2001), pp. 259–76; Clifford Edmund Bosworth, 'Laḳab', *EI*², v, pp. 618–31.

32. These geographic designations may be translated, respectively, as Anatolia, Syria and Armenia. However, these translations are not used in this chapter so as to retain the fluid medieval sense of the regions in question and to avoid modern connotations burdened by notions of borderlines and national identities.
33. Bosworth, 'Laḳab,' p. 622.
34. See, for example, Malikshāh's Diyarbakır Great Mosque inscription; Berchem and Strzygowski, *Amida*, p. 53.
35. Shukurov, 'Turkoman and Byzantine self-identity', pp. 264–70.
36. Zeki Oral, 'Anadolu'da san'at değeri olan ahşap minberler, kitabeleri ve tarihçeleri', *Vakıflar Dergisi* 5 (1962), p. 26.
37. The east–west coupling in geographic epithets was also taken up by the Danishmendids, on whose bilingual coinage this binary concept was translated into Greek as Rhomania and Anatoli; Shukurov, 'Turkoman and Byzantine self-identity', pp. 264–72.
38. Niẓāmī Ganjawī, *Kulliyāt-i khamsa-yi ḥakīm Niẓāmī Ganjawī*, ed. S. Nuʻmānī (1374; 3rd printing, Tehran: Ahmadi, 1995), i, pp. 21–2.
39. The term *Abkhāz-gīr* should be seen in the context of the Muslim campaigns against Georgia, starting in 1161 and 1163, in which a number of Turkmen dynasties of eastern Anatolia and Azerbaijan as well as the Great Seljuks participated; A.C.S. Peacock, 'Georgia and the Anatolian Turks in the 12th and 13th Centuries', *Anatolian Studies* 56 (2006), pp. 127–46. Bahrāmshāh's participation in the 1203 campaign to Georgia headed by Rukn al-Dīn Sulaymānshāh was praised by Rāwandī on account of the ruler's readiness for self-sacrifice; Rāwandī, *Rāḥat al-ṣudūr wa āyāt al-surūr*, ed. Muḥammad Iqbāl (Leiden and London: Brill and Luzac & Co, 1921), p. 217.
40. Yāqūt al-Ḥamawī, *Muʻjam al-buldān* (Beirut: Dar Ṣādir, 1977), i, p. 150.

41. Turan, *Selçuklular Zamanında Türkiye: Siyasi Tarih Alp Arslan'dan Osman Gazi'ye (1071–1318)* (Istanbul: Turan Neşriyatı Yurdu, 1971), pp. 73–6, 142–7, 200–5, 211–13; Cahen, *La Turquie pré-ottomane*, pp. 33–48.
42. Oral, 'Anadolu'da san'at değeri olan ahşap minberler', p. 29.
43. Turan, *Selçuklular Zamanında Türkiye*, pp. 182–6.
44. See, for example, the inscription of the *atabeg* Tughtakīn (who succeeded the Great Seljuks in Damascus and established the Burid dynasty) on the Great Mosque of Damascus dated 503 (1109–10); Étienne Combe et al., *Répertoire chronologique d'épigraphie arabe* (Cairo: Institut Français d'Archéologie Orientale, 1931–91, 18 vols), viii, no. 2933.
45. Combe et al., *Répertoire chronologique d'épigraphie arabe*, viii, no. 3111. Although undated, this inscription must have been placed after Zangī's capture of Baalbek from the Burids in 1139. A second inscription in the name of 'Imād al-Dīn Zangī in Aleppo dated 1142 has an even longer Turkic sequence: *alp ghāzī u(lu)gh arslān īnānch qutlugh tughrultakīn atābeg*; ibid., viii, no. 3112.
46. Oral, 'Anadolu'da san'at değeri olan ahşap minberler', pp. 26, 29.
47. For the Ahmadilis' use of Turkic titles (*alp qutlugh jabūghā ulugh atābeg*), see *The Sea of Precious Virtues*, pp. vii-viii. For an early Artuqid example in Mayyāfariqīn/Silvan (*alp īnānch qutlugh beg*), see Combe et al., *Répertoire chronologique d'épigraphie arabe*, ix, no. 3272. Nūr al-Dīn's titulature is discussed in Elisséeff, 'La titulature de Nūr ad-Dīn'.
48. *The Book of Dede Korkut*, trans. Geoffrey Lewis (Harmondsworth: Penguin, 1974).
49. Combe et al., *Répertoire chronologique d'épigraphie arabe*, viii, no. 3112. Much of the titulature of the rulers in Anatolia, Syria and Iraq through the twelfth and into the thirteenth century would have been composed in the chancery (*dīwān al-inshā'*), which frequently employed secretaries and scribes of Persianate background who effected a suitable fusion of established Iranian practices and Turkic traditions (such as the integration of the *ṭughrā*) within

an Islamic framework; Cahen, *La Turquie pré-ottomane*, pp. 184–8; Osman Turan, *Türkiye Selçukluları Hakkında Resmî Vesikalar* (Ankara: Türk Tarih Kurumu, 1958), pp. 22–7. The weight of the Iranian tradition on the Turkmen rulers of twelfth-century Anatolia is most palpable in the choice of Persian royal names given especially to the Seljuk and Mengüjekid princes of the generation of Shāhanshāh. Up until the middle of the twelfth century, the princes in these two dynasties had received either Turkic or Arabic (notably Old Testament) names. Names compounded with *-shāh* made their contemporaneous debut with the generation of Shāhanshāh and Bahrāmshāh in the Mengüjekid dynasty, and with the sons of Qılıch Arslan II in the Seljuk dynasty.

50. Elisséeff, 'La titulature de Nūr ad-Dīn', pp. 177–8.
51. Clifford Edmund Bosworth, 'Ispahsālār, Sipahsālār', *EI*², iv, pp. 204–9; Elisséeff, 'La titulature de Nūr ad-Dīn', pp. 167–9.
52. Persian titles only appear in Nūr al-Dīn's earliest known inscription dated 1148; Elisséeff, 'La titulature de Nūr ad-Dīn', p. 178. In the case of Qılıch Arslan II, the shift is apparent in the Aksaray and Konya *minbar* inscriptions dated within about a year of each other and separated by the accession of Qılıch Arslan to the sultanate; Oral, 'Anadolu'da san'at değeri olan ahşap minberler', pp. 26, 29.
53. This conceptual coupling of border zones and caves also had a counterpart in the articulation of medieval Anatolia's sacred topography; Oya Pancaroğlu, 'Caves, borderlands and configurations of sacred topography in medieval Anatolia', in Gary Leiser (ed.), *Les Seldjoukides d'Anatolie* (*Mésogeios* 25–26 [2005]), pp. 249–82.
54. Elisséeff, 'La titulature de Nūr ad-Dīn', pp. 187–91.
55. Ibid. For Muslim–Crusader encounters in the twelfth century, see Carole Hillenbrand, *The Crusades: Islamic Perspectives* (New York: Routledge, 2000).
56. Hossein Ziai, 'The source and nature of authority: a study of Suhrawardī's illuminationist political doctrine', in Charles Butterworth (ed.), *The Political Aspects of Islamic Philosophy* (Cambridge, Mass.: Harvard University Press, 1992), pp. 304–44.

Suhrawardī was branded by his persecuters as *zindīq*, *mulḥid* and *kāfir* – all terms with correspondences in the titulature of the twelfth and thirteenth centuries, including that of Shāhanshāh in the Sitte Melik inscription. See Daniella Talmon-Heller, *Islamic Piety in Medieval Syria* (Leiden: Brill, 2007), pp. 233–4.

57. It may be pointed out that in the ninth century, Divriği (Tephrike) was the main site at which Paulicians, a dualist sect persecuted by the Byzantines as heretics but supported by the Arabs, were brutally defeated by Byzantine forces and apparently dispersed. The close connection between Divriği and the history of the so-called Paulician heresy is, however, unlikely to have informed the rhetoric of Sitte Melik's frieze inscription, which appeared some 300 years later.
58. Turan, *Doğu Anadolu Türk Devletleri Tarihi*, pp. 101–48; Sümer, *Doğu Anadolu'da Türk Beylikleri*, pp. 52–6, 67–84; Carole Hillenbrand, 'Shāh-i Arman', *EI*^{2}, ix, p. 193.
59. Turan, *Doğu Anadolu Türk Devletleri Tarihi*, p. 136.
60. Sümer, *Doğu Anadolu'da Türk Beylikleri*, p. 57.
61. Beyhan Karamağaralı, *Ahlat Mezartaşları* (Ankara: Selçuklu Tarih ve Medeniyeti Ensitüsü, 1972).
62. For the early development of Syrian stone *muqarnas* in Aleppo, see Tabbaa, *The Transformation of Islamic Art*, pp. 150–5.
63. Pancaroğlu, 'The Mosque-Hospital complex in Divriği', pp. 185–9.
64. For professional connections between carpentry and architecture, especially in relation to geometric designs, see Gülru Necipoğlu, *The Topkapı Scroll: Geometry and Ornament in Islamic Architecture* (Santa Monica: Getty Center, 1995), pp. 150–2.
65. Oral, 'Anadolu'da san'at değeri olan ahşap minberler', p. 26.
66. Ibid., p. 30.
67. Pancaroğlu, 'The Mosque-Hospital complex in Divriği', p. 187.
68. Önkal, *Anadolu Selçuklu Türbeleri*, pp. 437–43.

CHAPTER THREE

'THE KING OF THE EAST AND THE WEST': THE SELJUK DYNASTIC CONCEPT AND TITLES IN THE MUSLIM AND CHRISTIAN SOURCES[1]

Dimitri Korobeinikov

Muslim states in Anatolia are often thought to have depicted themselves as successors to Byzantium. The Ottoman sultans, at least from the sixteenth century, described themselves as the rulers of 'Rūm', showing their aspirations to be viewed as inheritors of 'Rome' or the 'Rhomaioi', the Byzantines. Süleyman the Magnificent (1520–66), for instance, styled himself '*qaysar-i Rūm*', 'the emperor (lit. Caesar) of the Romans' in an inscription dated 1538 at Bender.[2] One can also find the title 'the throne of justice, the rule of the Caesar' in the list of titles employed by sixteenth-century Ottoman sultans in official correspondence.[3] So successful was this appropriation of 'Roman' identity that the word *Rūmī* (or variants thereof) became the common way to refer to Ottoman subjects in the wider world, even among Christian enemies like Portugal.[4] Yet, although the Seljuk polity in Anatolia is commonly known as the 'Sultanate of Rūm', there has been little discussion to date as to which Byzantine influences played a role in determining the state's formal political identity. In this chapter, I investigate the titles used by the Anatolian Seljuks and compare them with those of the Great Seljuks, suggesting that it was to the latter, rather than Byzantium, that the Seljuk rulers of Rūm looked as a source of legitimacy.

Both the Byzantine and Great Seljuk empires aspired to universal rule. The Byzantine emperor was the heir of the *imperium romanum* that embraced, as the Byzantines believed, the whole of the civilised world. In 1294, the famous Byzantine statesman, Theodore Metochites, referred to the land beyond Byzantine borders as the 'blind marsh, or Scythian cold, or waterless sands, full of wild beasts', filled with 'the lawless, undisciplined, never adequate or sound in mind crowd of people',[5] thus suggesting that the land and society within the Byzantine borders represented the opposite. Metochites' words were by no means a 'voice of one crying in the wilderness' as his opinion was supported by many Byzantine writers, most notably by Emperor John VI Kantakouzenos (1347–54), who described the empire of the Romans as 'the source of all piety and the teacher of law and sanctification' in a letter to Symeon the Proud (1341–53), the Grand Duke of Moscow, dated September 1347.[6] Indeed, the Byzantine emperor, anointed at his coronation as *basileus* and *autocrat* of the Romans, i.e. of all Christians, was believed to have been 'the lord and master of the *oikoumene*', the natural king whose laws and ordinances were accepted throughout the world.[7] By the mid fourteenth century this notion was recognised by the Mamluk sultans, who then addressed the emperors not only as the heads of Orthodox Christendom but also as masters of non-Christian people, in particular the Turks.[8] Likewise, one of the main titles of the Great Seljuk sultans was *malik al-mashriq wa 'l-maghrib*, 'king of the East and the West', and thus, by implication, the whole world.

Universal Rulership in the Seljuk Tradition

The title *malik al-mashriq wa 'l-maghrib* was granted to the first sultan, Tughrul (r. 1040–63), by the Caliph al-Qā'im bi-Amr Allāh (r. 1031–75) on Saturday 25 Dhū 'l-Qa'da 449/24 January 1058. The Islamic sources recount at length the audience at which Tughrul was granted this title. They underline that Tughrul saw himself very much as heir to Iranian traditions of rulership, which shared with Byzantium aspirations to universality.[9] The caliph bestowed on Tughrul seven robes of honour, each of which had a black hem, or collar (*zīq*). This was followed by a turban of gold brocade perfumed with musk (*'imāma miskayya mudhhaba*), a jewel-encrusted crown, necklace and a gilded sword. The outfit, especially the crown, was so heavy that the mighty Turk was unable to make his final bow down to the ground. The caliph also bestowed on him banners and another sword, and concluded the ceremony by proclaiming Tughrul 'the King of the East and the West'.[10]

All items bestowed as part of the ceremony had a special meaning. The splendid heavy crown was worthy of a Sasanian *shāhanshāh* and appropriately called *al-tāj al-khusrawī*, literally 'the crown of Chosroes', Khusraw or Chosroes being the name of the two most famous Sasanian *shāhanshāh*s, Khusraw I Anūshirwān (531–79) and Khusraw II Parvēz (590–628). The crown had two components, the turban and the crown per se, which symbolised the power of the sultan over two 'nations': the Arabs and the non-Arabs (*al-'ajam*), the latter usually meaning the Persians. This was a ceremonial representation of the title 'Lord of the Arabs and the Persians' (*mawlā al-'arab wa 'l-'ajam*) in the inscriptions,[11] hence Tughrul's royal epithet *al-mutawwaj al-mu'ammam* (literally, 'the crowned and turbaned one'), which suggested his royal prerogatives to govern the Muslim community. Likewise, the seven robes of honour symbolised the seven 'climes' into which ancient Iranian geographers divided the earth, pointing to Tughrul's aspirations to be ruler of the world. Finally, the two swords were given as tokens of the sultan's role as master of 'two empires' (*dawlatayn*), and symbolic of Tughrul's proclamation as 'the King of the East and the West'.[12]

The title *malik al-mashriq wa 'l-maghrib* thus embodied these claims to universal sovereignty. The extant inscriptions of Tughrul and Alp Arslan are scanty,[13] but it is clear that Tughrul used the title in his charters and official correspondence;[14] Alp Arslan likewise struck it on his coinage in 457 (13 December 1064 to 2 December 1065).[15] Although Malikshāh does not seem to have used this particular title, his titulature nevertheless expressed his aspirations to universal rule in the Iranian tradition (see the extant inscription from Nishapur in eastern Iran quoted below, p. 73). However, in later times, *malik al-mashriq wa 'l-maghrib*, even if sparsely used, was never abandoned. Its Persian form, *pādishāh-i sharq u gharb*, 'the King of the East and the West', was used by Sultan Sanjar (r. 1118–57).[16]

The Seljuks and Anatolia

Despite their conquests in the region in the eleventh century, the Great Seljuks never styled themselves as rulers of Rūm, although it was common practice to include in their titles the different territories over which they ruled. For instance, the *Jadwal mashāhīr ayyām al-dawla al-qāhira* 'List of the famous people of the days of the victorious state' (the expression 'the victorious state' being an epithet of the Great Seljuk empire) gives the names of the countries which various sultans possessed or claimed, yet Rūm never appears among them. According to our list, Tughrul was considered to be lord of Iraq, Azerbaijan, Mazandaran, Quhistan and Georgia (Abkhaz), while his brother Chaghrı was in charge of Khurasan, Khwarazm and Kirman. Alp Arslan ruled over Khurasan, Iraq, Azerbaijan, Syria, Khwarazm and Georgia; his son Malikshāh, during whose reign the Great Seljuk state reached its zenith, was master of Iraq, Fars, Syria, Azerbaijan, Khwarazm, Khurasan, Georgia and Transoxiana. While Rūm is mentioned as a territory raided (*ghazā*) by Alp Arslan and Malikshāh, it is not included in the list of their territories (*mamālik*).[17]

Unlike the state of the Great Seljuks, the Sultanate of Rūm was centred in the formerly Byzantine provinces in Asia Minor and was largely surrounded by Byzantine lands. We should recall the circumstances of its establishment. Sulaymān b. Qutlumush, the founder of the sultanate, 'was reported to have come from the Turkmen of [the confederation of] *al-nāwakīya* who dwelt in Syria'.[18] The name *al-nāwakīya* derived from the Persian word *nāwak* 'a small arrow', usually used for shooting birds.[19] This name may have originated as a designation of the Turkic confederations that formed the left wing of the Seljuk army: according to legend, the tribes of the right wing, whose symbol was the broken bow, were called 'the people of the broken [bow]' (*būz ūq/boz ok*); whilst the tribes of the left wing, whose symbol was three arrows, were 'the people of the three [arrows]' (*üç ūq/ok*).[20]

Some of the *nāwakīya* Turkmen had entered Asia Minor in 1070 even before Sulaymān's rise; their leader was Arīsghī, Chrysoskoulos of the Byzantine sources.[21] The emperor Romanos IV Diogenes, and then his successor, Michael VII Doukas, settled them in western Anatolia, but most of the *al-nāwakīya* Turkmen made for Syria. It was from Syria that Sulaymān came to Anatolia in 1075, ousted by the supporters of the Great Seljuk Sultan Malikshāh.[22] Sulaymān's chance came in October 1077, when Nikephoros Botaniates started his rebellion against Michael VII. Arīsghī/Chrysoskoulos and his *nāwakīya* Turks supported Botaniates in Phrygia, as did Sulaymān, in command of another group of *nāwakīya* near Cotyaeum/Kütahya, at the beginning of 1078, recognising the new emperor as his suzerain.[23] Only three years later, by June 1081, Sulaymān had felt himself strong enough to shake off the weak Byzantine suzerainty.[24] Thus the Seljuk sultanate of Rūm, which was not recognised by Malikshāh until 1084 (and only as a subordinate state),[25] for the first six to ten years of its existence was a Byzantine 'client' state.

Upon their independence, the Seljuk sultans in Rūm had to tackle two problems: firstly, to gain the respect of other Muslim states; and secondly, and most importantly, to win the support of other Turks in the peninsula as well as their numerous Christian subordinates. They achieved this by advancing the notion of loyalty to the Seljuk dynasty. In doing so, they distinguished themselves from the other Turkic dynasties in Anatolia. They did not advance a claim to the Byzantine inheritance, as the Danishmendid

Turkish rulers of north-central Anatolia had done by accepting the title of ὁ μέγας μελήκις πάσης Ῥωμανίας καὶ Ἀνατολῆς, 'the great maliks of all the Romania and the East'.[26] For the Danishmendid lands could have been considered the 'East' only from the Byzantine point of view; from the Muslim perspective, these territories were the 'West'. When the sultans of Rūm seized the Danishmendids' territories, they were nevertheless still called the *shāhanshāh-i maghrib*, 'the kings of the West', in diplomatic correspondence based on Great Seljuk usage.[27]

Unfortunately we have no reliable evidence for Anatolian Seljuk royal titles until the mid twelfth century. The claim of the Byzantine sources and the Syriac chronicler Michael the Syrian that Sulaymān b. Qutlumush used the title of sultan is not supported by any Muslim evidence and may reflect outsiders' perceptions rather than the reality.[28] The first evidence for the full title of the sultan of Rūm refers to Qılıch Arslan II (r. 1156–92) in c.551/1156:

> the great sultan, the august *shāhanshāh*, chief of the sultans of the Arabs and the Persians, master of the nations, glory of the world and religion, pillar of Islam and the Muslims, glory of kings and sultans, defender of the law, destroyer of the infidels and the polytheists, helper of the fighters for faith, guardian of the countries of Allah, protector of the servants of Allah, sultan of the lands of Rum, Armenia, the Franks, and Syria, Abū 'l-Fatḥ Qılıch Arslan b. Mas'ūd b. Qılıch Arslan, helper of the Commander of the Faithful.[29]

This represents an extended version of some of the titles used by the Great Seljuk Sultan Malikshāh, as illustrated by inscription attributed to the latter at Nishapur:

> ... the great sultan, the august *shāhanshāh*, lord of the Arabs and the Persians, sultan of the land of Allah, ruler of the countries of Allah, pillar of Islam and the Muslims, strengthener of the world and religion, Abū 'l-Fatḥ Malikshāh b. Muḥammad b. Da'ūd, the right hand of the Commander of the Faithful ...[30]

These titles sought to emphasise the power of the Great Seljuks over the Muslim *orbis terrarum*. There was, however, a difference: since Qılıch Arslan II lacked both the rank and the prestige of the Great Seljuk sultans, he did not describe his realm in the terms of a borderless universal power (like the state of the Great Seljuks), but rather as a lower-ranking state confined to the region of 'Rum, Armenia, [the lands] of the Franks, and Syria'. Despite the reference to Rūm, the sultan did not style himself as successor of the Byzantine emperors over the former Byzantine lands. This is confirmed by the letter which Qılıch Arslan II sent to Michael the Syrian, the Jacobite *catholicos*, some time in 1185, and of which a Syriac copy was incorporated into Michael's famous chronicle. The relevant part of the sultan's titles reads: *sultan d-Qapaduqya w-Surya w-Armanya* ('the sultan of Cappadocia, Syria and Armenia').[31] Whereas Qılıch Arslan's inscription described him as lord of Rūm, Armenia and Syria, Michael the Syrian refused to accord the sultan the designation 'sultan of Rūm', substituting Cappadocia for Rūm. This suggests that Michael saw the only legitimate ruler of the Byzantine lands of 'Rūm' as 'the emperor and autocrat of the Romans, faithful in Christ God' (ἐν Χριστῷ Θεῷ πιστὸς βασιλεὺς καὶ αὐτοκράτωρ Ῥωμαίων) who still resided in Constantinople.

Universal Aspirations in Anatolian Seljuk Titulature

After the division of the sultanate between the sons of Qılıch Arslan II and the consequent dynastic struggle, which ended in 1205 with the return of the sultan Ghiyāth al-Dīn Kaykhusraw I (1192–6, 1205–11) to the throne, a period of consolidation began. With the collapse of the remnants of the Great Seljuk sultanate in Iran in 1194, and more particularly after the conquests of Antalya and Sinop, sultanic titulature in Anatolia began to change. Sultan 'Izz al-Dīn Kaykā'ūs I (1211–19) rejected the very idea of the geographical limits of his empire and described himself on the walls of both cities as universal ruler *par excellence*, without any mention of Rum or any other province; the only geographic notion that suggested any location was expressed in the title 'the Sultan of the Two Seas' (namely the Mediterranean and the Black Sea), obviously in relation to the recent re-conquest of Antalya in 1216 and Sinop in 1214. But other 'universal' titles borrowed, or indeed, derived from those of the Great Seljuks, were carefully preserved: the sultan was 'the shadow of the Lord over the East and West' (*ẓill Allāh fī 'l-khāfiqayn*), 'chief of the sultans of the Arabs and the Persians' (*sayyid salāṭīn al-'arab wa 'l-'ajam*) and, finally, 'king of the kings of the world' (*malik mulūk al-'ālam*)[32]. Moreover, it was only after the victory over the Grand Komnenos, Alexios I (who, though master of Trebizond, claimed to have been the true Byzantine emperor), and the conquest of Sinop that the sultan felt strong enough to write about himself (in August 1215) as if he were a Great Seljuk:

> The victorious sultan, *king of the East and the West*, chief of the sultans of the world, *lord of the Arabs and the Persians*, glory of the world and Islam, *succour to Islam and the Muslims*, sultan of the sea and land, Abū 'l-Fatḥ Kaykā'ūs b. Kaykhusraw, proof of the Commander of the Faithful.[33]

Claims to universal rule were also stressed by the Anatolian Seljuks in their diplomatic correspondence. The letters addressed by the last Khwārazmshāh Jalāl al-Dīn (r. 1220–31) to 'Alā' al-Dīn Kayqubād I (r. 1219–37),[34] and the letter sent by Sultan Rukn al-Dīn Qılıch Arslan IV to his brother 'Izz al-Dīn Kaykā'ūs II in 1256,[35] have one thing in common. By omitting almost any geographical limits they underlined the universal power of the sultan: he was 'the great sultan, the victorious, the fighter for faith (*mujāhid*), the Marabout (*murābiṭ*), succour to Islam and the Muslims, destroyer of the infidels and the polytheists'.[36] Yet these universal aspirations might on occasion be tempered. Neither the Khwārazmshāh nor Rukn al-Dīn Qılıch Arslan IV named their addressees 'kings of the East and the West', but rather only 'kings of the West' (*shahriyār-i* or *shāhanshāh-i maghrib*).[37] In Rukn al-Dīn Qılıch Arslan IV's letter to 'Izz al-Dīn Kaykā'ūs II, the latter is addressed as 'the glory of the sultans, the pride of the Seljuk dynasty, Chosroes of Greece (*khusraw-i Yūnān*), King of the West, proof of the Commander of the Faithful',[38] though earlier, in 1254, another brother of Kaykā'ūs II, 'Alā' al-Dīn Kayqubād II, had called him (according to Āqsarā'ī), 'the sultan of sultans of the East and the West'.[39] Yet the titles in Āqsarā'ī are so flattering that a degree of authorial exaggeration may have been at play.

Likewise, when communicating with their Christian subjects, the sultans of Rūm did not stress the fact that they ruled the former Byzantine lands; they did not present themselves as heirs of the Byzantine emperors in Asia Minor. Despite the evident Byzantine features in Anatolian Seljuk chancery practice, such as the Greek chancery of the sultans and the use of the 'sworn chrysobulls' in the correspondence,[40] as far as titles were concerned the sultans preferred to stress that they were the victorious descendants of Seljuk, members of the noble dynasty destined to rule the world. Let me list the examples. The first one is the colophon of Basil of Melitene in 1226:

> The present {Gospel-}book, {written} in perfect and carefully lined miniature minuscule calligraphy, of the four Gospels of the great God's messengers and evangelists Matthew, Mark, Luke and John was completed by the hand of me, the protonotary Basil of Melitene (βασιλείου πρῶτονοταρίου μελιτηνιώτου), son of the priest Orestes {...}[41], at the time when my holy sovereign the most high great sultan Kayqubād, son of Ghiyāth al-Dīn Kaykhusraw was lord of Rhomania, Armenia, Syria and all the territories and provinces of the Turks on the sea and the land. {The Gospel-book} was completed in Great Caesarea (Kayseri) ...[42]

Basil's Greek colophon is full of appalling mistakes, yet his two Armenian colophons were written in elegant and grammatically correct language. Basil, however, was so proud of his status that in one of his colophons in Armenian he again mentioned that he was a protonotary (*dprapet*);[43] both statements, in Greek and in Armenian, suggest that he was protonotary (the chief scribe) of the Armenian chancery of the sultan. He thus had access to chancery documents.[44] Little wonder that his colophon is reminiscent of the sultan's titles in the Greek letters which Hugh I of Cyprus (1205–18) exchanged with Sultan 'Izz al-Dīn Kaykā'ūs I in 1214–18, and of the preamble to the treaty concluded between 'Alā' al-Dīn Kayqubād I and the Venetian *podestà* Jacopo Tiepolo in Constantinople in 1220.

The fourth letter of Hugh I addressed the sultan as τῷ ὑψηλοτάτῳ, κραταιοτάτῳ, εὐτυχεστάτῳ, μεγαλογενεῖ, μεγάλῳ σουλτάνῳ, τροπαιούχῳ καὶ νικιτῇ πάσης τῆς ὑπὸ τῶν Τούρκων χώρας, γῆς τε καὶ θαλάσσης, τῷ Ἀζατήν ('to the most high, most powerful, most fortunate, [the one] of noble descent, the great sultan 'Izz al-Dīn, the victorious (literally 'the one to whom trophies are dedicated'), the conqueror of all the provinces of the Turks on land and sea').[45] A slightly different form is given in the first letter dated January 1214; the text reads: τῷ ὑψηλοτάτῳ, κραταιῷ καὶ εὐτυχεῖ, μεγαλογενεῖ, μεγάλῳ σουλτάνῳ, τροπαιούχῳ καὶ νικιτῇ πάσης τῆς κατὰ τῶν Τούρκων χώρας, γῆς τε καὶ θαλάσσης ('to the most high, powerful, fortunate, [the one] of noble descent, the great sultan, the victorious, the conqueror of the all the provinces of the Turks on land and sea').[46] Likewise, the Latin copy of the treaty in 1220 named the sultan as *altitenentis, felicis, magni generis, magni Soldani Turkie, domini Alatini Caicopadi* ('the high, fortunate, [the one] of noble (literally, 'great') descent, the great Sultan of Turkey lord 'Alā' al-Dīn Kayqubād').[47]

What did these sources (three in Greek and one in Latin) have in common? They emphasise the following two notions: that the sultan belonged to an illustrious family (hence the honorifics *megalogenos* and *magni generis*, the counterpart of the 'pride of the dynasty of Seljuk'), and that he was the victorious master of many territories on the sea and the land (the counterpart of the Arab title 'sultan of the sea and the land'). From this point of view the translation of 'Rūm' as 'Turkey' in the treaty and the letters of Hugh I was not offensive to 'Alā' al-Dīn Kayqubād I: he had other, more substantial, sources by which to legitimise his power.

Islamic sources also tend to stress the legitimacy of the Anatolian Seljuks by referring to their illustrious lineage. An allusion to such a link is found in Ibn Bībī's report of the meeting in 1203 in Constantinople between the exiled sultan Ghiyāth al-Dīn Kaykhusraw I and the emperor Alexios III Angelos (1195–1203).

According to Ibn Bībī, the sultan addressed his Byzantine host in the following terms:

> Your Majesty knows that I am the son of Qılıch Arslan and am from the family of Malikshāh and Alp Arslan. The two wings of [the army] of my ancestors and paternal uncles (*a'mām*)[48] conquered with their sword the worldly kingdoms of yours (*mamālik-i jahān-i turā*) from the east to the west, as is recognised by all the people. They put a yoke of submission on the necks of those haughty; and your ancestors always sent tribute and revenue (*kharāj* and *bāj*)[49] to their treasury and you [continued] to do the same to mine.[50]

We even read in Ibn Bībī that in the autumn of 1196 the city-dwellers of Laodicea, called Combusta, or Cecaumenē (literally, 'the burnt one'), refused free passage to the sultan Kaykhusraw I when he fled from Konya facing the advance of his brother Rukn al-Dīn Sulaymānshāh. Kaykhusraw I intended to go to Constantinople, where he expected to meet the emperor Alexios III, his ally. Despite the fact that the Laodiceans prevented (for a while) the alliance between Kaykhusraw I and Alexios III against Rukn al-Dīn Sulaymānshāh, the latter, when in Konya,

> said that ... anyone who committed rudeness and arrogance towards the Seljuks and was fond of fraternising with the infidels, should receive proper retribution; he [then] ordered the town of Laodicea be punished again by fire, and since that time they call [it] 'burnt Lādhīq' (*Lādhīq-i sūkhta*).[51]

The expression 'the Seljuks' here refers to the members of the Seljuk dynasty; and the statement '[those] fond of fraternising with the infidels' means the Muslim population of Laodicea, which united with its Greek neighbours against the unpopular sultan Kaykhusraw I, whom Sulaymānshāh had forced to flee from Konya.[52] Nevertheless, the principle of loyalty to the dynasty, rather than to a particular sultan, was more important in the eyes of Sulaymānshāh.

Although the reliability of this rather later literary evidence is somewhat questionable, we are on surer ground with Ghiyāth al-Dīn Kaykhusraw I's son, 'Alā' al-Dīn Kayqubād I. Epigraphic evidence shows that by 1226 he was using a new title, 'the crown (*tāj*) of the dynasty of Seljuk'.[53] The emphasis on dynastic loyalty may be related to the fact that by the early thirteenth century, the sultans of Konya were by no means the sole dynasty to claim rule over Rūm. Titles asserting sovereignty over 'Rūm' are also attested among the Erzurum branch of the Seljuk dynasty, the Saltuqid dynasty in the same area, the Artuqids of Diyarbakır and perhaps the Mengüjekids of Erzincan too.[54] In this context, it may have seemed attractive to members of the dynasty in Konya to emphasise their lineage as a way of differentiating themselves from their rivals.

Sultans of Rūm?

The name 'Sultanate of Rūm' itself was based on the idiom *sulṭān al-Rūm* and its variants, which Muslim chroniclers outside the borders of the sultanate (and modern scholars after them) applied to the sultans in Konya: *al-sulṭān min al-Rūm* ('the sultan from Rūm'), *ṣāhib al-Rūm* ('master of Rūm') or even *malik al-Rūm* ('the king of Rūm'), though the latter was traditionally associated with the titles of the Byzantine emperors. One of the chief historians dealing with the Seljuks of Anatolia in the second part of the thirteenth and the beginning of the fourteenth century, Āqsarā'ī (d. between 1323 and 1327) also makes it clear that the land under the rule of the sultans in Konya was called Rūm, and he employs various designations such as *mulk-i Rūm* ('the kingdom of Rūm'),[55] *mamālik-i Rūm* ('the kingdoms of Rūm'),[56] *dīyār-i Rūm* ('the countries of Rūm'),[57] *bilād-i Rūm* ('the lands of Rūm'),[58] *wilāyat-i Rūm* ('the province of Rūm')[59] and even *salṭanat-i Rūm* ('the Sultanate of Rūm').[60] All these names served as descriptions of the Seljuk realm in Anatolia, but we cannot say that Āqsarā'ī suggested that any of these expressions were the official name of the Seljuk state. The most likely candidate, the *salṭanat-i Rūm*, was mentioned almost exclusively in relation to the *yarlıgh*s (decrees) of the Ilkhans, who entrusted various Seljuk officials, including the sultans themselves, with authority over the sultanate.[61] Likewise, in Āqsarā'ī's text power over Rūm is expressed as *imārat-i Rūm* ('authority over Rūm' or 'command over Rūm')[62] or *ḥukūmat-i Rūm* ('governorship over Rūm'),[63] suggesting something rather less than absolute sovereignty.

Āqsarā'ī wrote shortly after the disappearance of the sultanate of Rūm, it having been a Ilkhanid client state for 50 years by that time. His references to the *salṭānat-i Rūm*, are, with only one exception,[64] derived from Ilkhanid, not Seljuk, documents. The reader must therefore conclude that the expression '*salṭanat-i Rūm*' was certainly in use in the Ilkhanid chancery, but the issue of how the Seljuks of Rūm finally settled on their own formal designation remains unresolved. The text of Āqsarā'ī demonstrates that the official Seljuk state ideology was far more complex and could not have been entirely reduced to the expression 'the sultanate of Rūm', with an emphasis on its geographical location. Āqsarā'ī himself took special care to explain to his future readers that

> at this time[65] when the dynasty of the house of Seljuk (*dawlat-i āl-i Saljūq*) in the kingdom of Iraq (*dar mulk-i 'Irāq*) came to an end and that kingdom fell into disorder, and the sultanate of Sultan Tughrul expired, the kingdom of Rūm (*mamlakat-i Rūm*) was in [the] possession of the Sultan 'Alā' al-Dīn Qılıch Arslan[66] b. Mas'ūd b. Qılıch Arslan b. Sulaymānshāh, as [will be] mentioned if God the Highest is willing.[67]

Āqsarā'ī thus places the Seljuks of Rūm in the wider context of the history of the Great Seljuk state. Similar attempts to link the Anatolian Seljuks to the Great Seljuks were made by his contemporary, Aḥmad of Niğde, in his unpublished *al-Walad al-shafīq*. Aḥmad goes to the extent of excising Qutlumush from the genealogy of the Seljuks of Rūm in order to present an unbroken transfer of power from the Great Seljuks to Qılıch Arslan II.[68]

Throughout his text, Āqsarā'ī confines himself to the title '*sulṭān*' to which he customarily added the name of one or other Seljuk sovereign in Rūm. Only on one occasion does Āqsarā'ī use the more precise expression *sulṭān-i Rūm* (in its plural form),[69] but this was evidently an allusion to the already-mentioned 'sultans of Iran from the dynasty of Seljuk' (*salāṭīn-i 'ajam az āl-i Saljūq*).[70] The chief criteria which helped Āqsarā'ī to distinguish the Seljuk masters of Rūm from other Muslim rulers was the fact that the former belonged to the famous Seljuk dynasty and had the prestigious title of sultan.[71] They possessed Rūm, the core of their realm, but from the point of view of their sovereign rights their possessions could not have been ultimately reduced to the lands in Asia Minor.

Thus, in constructing their empire, the Seljuks, 'the kings of the East and the West', did not adhere to the Byzantine notion of 'Rome', 'Rūm', as a symbol of their state. In this, they differed from the later Ottomans. From the Seljuk perspective, the name 'sultanate of Rūm' could hardly have been justified any more than was the attribution to the eastern Roman empire of the title 'the empire of the Greeks' or, even less aptly, 'Byzantium'. On those occasions where the territorial designation Rūm does occur in texts derived from Anatolian Seljuk official practice, it is not – unlike the references to noble lineage – the defining feature of their titulature. It was not a statement of a desire to be recognised as successors to Byzantium, but merely a geographical reference to the territories where their state was based, along with Armenia and Syria. To some extent, the sultans of Rūm resorted to the Great Seljuks' notions of universal rule to legitimise their state, but this appears to have been done only occasionally. Perhaps the realities of Anatolia's position as a distant outpost of the Muslim world made such universal claims seem unrealistic for all but the most ambitious and victorious of sultans. Above all, it was the prestige of the sultans' own lineage, their glorious Seljuk descent, on which they based their right to rule. It is thus no surprise that rebels against the Seljuk sultans, and indeed later against the Ottomans, based their own claims to legitimacy on possession of a Seljuk lineage.[72]

Notes

1. I wish to express my thanks to Dr M.E. Martin, who read the chapter and offered various suggestions concerning language and

style, and to Dr A.C.S. Peacock who offered important additions and sent me his chapter 'Seljuq legitimacy in Islamic history' prior to its publication (see infra, note 72). All mistakes are, however, my own.

2. Z. Abrahamovicz, 'Osmanskii sultan kak vostochnorimskii imperator (*qayser-i Rūm*)', in I.V. Zaitsev and S.F. Oreshkova (eds), *Turcica et Ottomanica. Sbornik statei v chest' 70-letiia M.S. Meyera* (Moscow: Vostochnaia literatura, 2006), pp. 103–5.
3. Feridun Bey Ahmed, *Münşeat-i Selatin* (Istanbul, 1274/1857), i, p. 4; on the titles in Feridun Bey's work, see H. İnalcik, 'Power relationships between Russia, the Crimea and the Ottoman Empire as reflected in titulature', in Ch. Lemercier-Quelquejay, G. Veinstein and S.E. Wimbush (eds), *Passé turco-tatar, présent soviétique: études offertes à Alexandre Bennigsen (=Turco-Tatar Past, Soviet Present: studies presented to Alexandre Bennigsen)* (Paris: Éditions Peeters, Éditions de l'École des hautes études en sciences sociales, 1986), pp. 192–9.
4. On the Ottoman usage of Rūm and Rūmī, see Cemal Kafadar, 'A Rome of one's own: cultural geography and identity in the lands of Rum', *Muqarnas* 24 (2007), pp. 10–8; Salih Özbaran, *Bir Osmanlı Kimliği: 14.-17. Yuyıllarda Rûm/Rûmi Aidiyet ve İmgeleri* (Istanbul: Kitap Yayınevi, 2004).
5. Theodore Metochites, Βασιλικὸς δεύτερος (Second Imperial oration), MS Cod. Vindobon. Philol. Gr. 95, fol. 154r; idem, Οἱ Δύο Βασιλικοὶ Λόγοι, ed. I. Polemis (Athens: Ekdoseis Kanakē, 2007), p. 376, ll. 9–10.
6. D. Obolensky, *The Byzantine Commonwealth: Eastern Europe, 500–1453* (London: Weidenfeld and Nicolson, 1971), pp. 265–6. For the Greek original, see H. Hunger, O. Kresten and J. Koder (eds), *Das Register des Patriarchats von Konstantinopel* (Vienna: Verlag des Österreichischen Akademie der Wissenschaften, 1981–2001, 3 vols), ii: *Edition und Übersetzung der Urkunden aus den Jahren 1337–1350*, N 168, p. 478, ll. 1–8.
7. Obolensky, *The Byzantine Commonwealth*, p. 264.
8. D.A. Korobeinikov, 'Diplomatic correspondence between Byzantium and the Mamlūk sultanate in the fourteenth century', *al-Masāq* 16 (2004), pp. 60–1.

9. On the relationship between Iranian and Byzantine traditions of rulership, see M.P. Canepa, *The Two Eyes of the Earth: Art and Ritual of Kingship between Rome and Sasanian Iran* (Berkeley, Calif.: University of California Press, 2009).
10. Sibṭ b. al-Jawzī, *Mir'āt al-zamān fī tārīkh al-a'yān*, selections edited by Ali Sevim as Sibt İbnü'l-Cevzî, *Mir'âtü'z-zeman fî Tarihi'l-âyân, Selçuklularla ilgili bölümler* (Ankara: Dil ve Tarih Coğrafyası Fakültesi, 1968), pp. 24–6 – reprinted with additions in A. Sevim, 'Mir'âtü'z-Zaman Fî Tarihi'l-Âyan (Kayıp Uyûnü't-Tevârîh'ten Naklen Selçuklularla İlgili Bölümler) Sıbt İbnü'l Cevzî', *Belgeler* 14, no. 18 (1989–92), pp. 47–9; Ṣadr al-Dīn 'Alī al-Ḥusaynī, *Akhbār al-dawlat al-saljūqiyya,* ed. Muhammad Iqbāl (Beirut: Dār al-Āfāq al-Jadīda, 1984), p. 18; 'Abd al-Raḥmān b. 'Alī Ibn al-Jawzī, *al-Muntaẓam fī ta'rīkh al-mulūk wa 'l-umam* (Hyderabad, Deccan: Dā'irat al-Ma'ārif al-'Uthmāniyya, 1940–2, 10 vols), viii, p. 182; idem, *al-Muntaẓam fī ta'rīkh al-mulūk wa 'l-umam* (Beirut: Dār al-Kutub al-'Ilmīya, 1992, 18 vols), xvi, pp. 19–20; Bundārī, *Zubdat al-nuṣra wa nukhbat al-'uṣra*, in M.T. Houtsma (ed.), *Histoire des Seldjoucides de l'Irâq par al-Bondârî, d'après Imâd ad-dîn al-Kâtib al-Isfahânî* (Leiden: E.J. Brill, 1889; Recueil de textes relatifs à l'histoire des Seldjoucides 2), pp. 13–5; 'Izz al-Dīn Ibn al-Athīr, *al-Kāmil fī 'l-tārīkh* (Beirut: Dār Ṣādir, 1965–7, 13 vols), ix, pp. 633–4; *The Annals of the Saljuq Turks. Selections from al-Kāmil fī 'l-Tārīkh of 'Izz al-Dīn Ibn al-Athīr*, trans. D.S. Richards (London: RoutledgeCurzon, 2002), pp. 114–5; Bar Hebraeus, *The Chronography of Gregory Abu'l-Faraj*, trans. Ernest A. Wallis Budge (London: Oxford University Press, 1932, 2 vols), i, pp. 211–2; ii: MS Bodleian Library, Hunt 52, fol. 74r, col. ii – 74v, col. i; the shortened Arabic version of the *Chronography* of Bar Hebraeus is silent about Tughrul's coronation, and mentions only his *khuṭba*: Ghrīghūrīyūs Abū 'l-Faraj b. al-'Ibrī, *Tārīkh mukhtaṣar al-duwal*, ed. A. Ṣāliḥānī (Beirut: Maṭba'at al-Kāthūlīkiyya lil-Ābā' al-Yasū'īyyin, 1890), p. 321; Mīrkhwānd, *Tārīkh-i rawḍat al-ṣafā*, ed. N. Sabūkhī (Tehran: Pīrūz, 1338–9), iv, pp. 261–3; C.E. Bosworth, 'The political and dynastic history of the Iranian World (A.D. 1000–1217)', in J.A. Boyle (ed.), *The Cambridge History of Iran*, v: *The Saljuq*

and Mongol Periods (Cambridge: Cambridge University Press, 1968–91), pp. 46–7.

11. Sheila Blair, *The Monumental Inscriptions from Early Islamic Iran and Transoxiana* (Leiden: Brill, 1992), pp. 170–1, n. 64.
12. Bundārī, *Zubdat al-nuṣra*, p. 14; R.A. Guseinov, 'Sultan i Khalif (iz istorii siuzereniteta i vassaliteta na Blizhnem Vostoke XI-XII vv.)', *Palestinskii Sbornik* 19 (82) (1969), pp. 130–1; idem, 'Le sultan et le calife (de l'histoire de suzeraineté et de vassalité en Asie occidentale aux XIe et XIIe siècles)', *Bedi Kartlisa* 28 (1971), pp. 199–207.
13. There are no surviving inscriptions of Tughrul; as to Alp Arslan, only one inscription on a silver plate (of questionable authenticity) is listed in Étienne Combe et al. (eds), *Répertoire chronologique d'épigraphie arabe* (Cairo: Institut français d'archéologie orientale, 1931–91, 18 vols), vii, pp. 164–5, no. 2661, in which the sultan is styled as 'His most sublime Majesty, the great sultan Alp Arslān'.
14. Sibṭ b. al-Jawzī, *Mir'āt al-zamān*, p. 87 (*Belgeler* 14, no. 18, p. 106); Ibn al-Jawzī, *al-Muntaẓam*, viii, p. 223; Bosworth, 'The Political and Dynastic History', p. 48.
15. Dominique Sourdel, 'Un trésor de dinars ġaznawides et salǧuqides découvert en Afganistan', *Bulletin d'Études Orientales* 18 (1963–4), p. 215.
16. *İstanbul'un fethinden önce yazılmış tarihî takvimler*, ed. Osman Turan (Ankara: Türk Tarih Kurumu, 1954), pp. 94–5; Rustam Shukurov, 'Turkoman and Byzantine self-identity. Some reflections on the logic of the title-making in twelfth- and thirteenth-century Anatolia', in Antony Eastmond (ed.), *Eastern Approaches to Byzantium* (Aldershot: Ashgate, 2001), p. 271 and n. 50.
17. *İstanbul'un fethinden önce yazılmış tarihî takvimler*, pp. 3, 84–91.
18. Sibṭ b. al-Jawzī, *Mir'āt al-zamān*, p. 243 (*Belgeler* 14, no. 18, p. 256).
19. D.A. Korobeinikov, 'Raiders and neighbours: the Turks (1040–1304)', in Jonathan Shepard (ed.), *The Cambridge History of the Byzantine Empire, c. 500–1492* (Cambridge: Cambridge University Press, 2008), p. 706.

20. Cf. Rashīd al-Dīn, *Oghūz-nāme*, MS Topkapı Sarayı, Bağdat Köşkü 282, fol. 596b; idem, *Oghūz-nāme*, trans. R.M. Shukiurova (Baku: Elm, 1987), pp. 61–2; idem, *Die Geschichte der Oğuzen des Rašīd ad-Dīn*, ed. K. Jahn (Vienna: Böhlau, 1969), p. 43; idem, *Jāmi' al-tawārīkh*, MS Bodleian Library, Elliott 377, fol. 341v; Abū 'l-Ghāzī, the Khan of Khīvā, *Şecere-i Terākime (Rodoslovnaia Turkmen)*, ed. A.N. Kononov (Moscow and Leningrad: Izdatel'stvo Akademii Nauk SSSR, 1958), p. 28, ll. 456–65 (Chaghatay text); p. 49 (Russian translation).
21. Sibṭ b. al-Jawzī, *Mir'āt al-zamān*, pp. 144, 146–7 (*Belgeler* 14, no. 18, pp. 166, 168); Nicephorus Bryennius, *Histoire*, ed. P. Gautier (Brussels: Byzantion, 1975), pp. 100–3.
22. Sibṭ b. al-Jawzī, *Mir'āt al-zamān*, pp. 174–5 (*Belgeler* 14, no. 18, p. 194); *Anadolu Selçukluları Devleti Tarihi* III: *Histoire des Seljoukides d'Asie Mineure par un anonyme*, fasc. and Turkish trans. Feridun Nâfiz Uzluk (Ankara: Örnek Matbaası, 1952; Anadolu Selçukluları Gününde Mevlevi Bitikleri 5), pp. 35–6, edited by Nādira Jalālī as *Tārīkh-i āl-i Saljūq dar Ānāṭūlī* (Tehran: Mīrāth-i Maktūb, 1999), pp. 78–9.
23. Michael Attaleiates, *Historia*, ed. and trans. I. Pérez Martín (Madrid: Consejo Superior de Investigaciones Científicas, 2002), pp. 191–9; Bryennius, *Histoire*, pp. 238–41.
24. Michel le Syrien, *Chronique*, ed. and trans. J.B. Chabot (Paris: Ernest Leroux, 1899–1910), iii, p. 172 (French translation), iv, pp. 579–80 (Syriac text); *The Edessa-Aleppo Syriac Codex of Michael the Great*, ed. Gregorios Yuhanna Ibrahim, text summary by S. Brock (Piscataway, N.J.: Gorgias Press, 2009; Texts and Translations of the Chronicle of Michael the Great, ed. G. Kiraz, vol. i), fol. 290r-v [pp. 582–3]. Bryennius names Sulaymān sultan in 1080–81, during the reign of Nikephoros Botaneiates: Bryennius, *Histoire*, p. 303, l. 26. Anna Comnena calls the residence of Sulaymān 'the Sultan's [possession]' (σουλτανίκιον, obviously from Turkish *sultanıñ*, -ιον being the Greek ending for foreign words) in 1081 and suggests that he had assumed the title of sultan by 1084: Anna Comnena, *Alexias,* eds. D.R. Reinsch

and A. Kambylis (Berlin: Walter de Gruyter, 2001), Book III: xi, pp. 114–5, ll. 38–49, Book VI: ix, pp. 186–7, l. 65–84.

25. Ibn al-Athīr, *al-Kāmil*, x, p. 139; *The Annals of the Saljuq Turks*, p. 218.
26. Shukurov, 'Turkoman and Byzantine self-identity', p. 264.
27. O. Turan, *Türkiye Selçukluları hakkında resmî vesikalar* (Ankara: Türk Tarih Kurumu, 1958), p. ۹۸.
28. See above, note 24.
29. Combe et al., *Répertoire chronologique d'épigraphie arabe*, ix, pp. 11–12, no. 3218; Carole Hillenbrand, *Turkish Myth and Muslim Symbol: The Battle of Manzikert* (Edinburgh: Edinburgh University Press, 2007), p. 161.
30. Blair, *The Monumental Inscriptions from Early Islamic Iran and Transoxiana*, n. 64, p. 170. Cf. similar inscriptions: Combe et al., *Répertoire chronologique d'épigraphie arabe*, vii, pp. 214–5, 245–6, 251, 253–4, 264, nos. 2734, 2773, 2780, 2783, 2792; viii, pp. 82, 99–103, 117–9, 122–3, nos. 2934, 2960, 2961, 2973, 2974, 2978.
31. Michel le Syrien, *Chronique*, iii, p. 394 (French translation); iv, p. 728 (Syriac text); *The Edessa-Aleppo Syriac Codex of Michael the Great*, fol. 364v [p. 731].
32. Scott Redford and Gary Leiser, *Victory Inscribed: The Seljuk* Fetiḥnāme *on the Citadel Walls of Antalya, Turkey/Taşa Yazılan Zafer. Antalya İçkale Surlarındaki Selçuklu Fetihnamesi* (Antalya: Suna-İnan Kıraç Akdeniz Medeniyetleri Araştırma Enstitüsü, 2008), pp. 30–4, 108–12.
33. Combe et al., *Répertoire chronologique d'épigraphie arabe*, x, p. 114, no. 3761; M. Şakir Ülkütaşır, 'Sinop'ta Selçukiler zamanına ait tarihî eserler', *Türk Tarih, Arkeologya ve Etnografya Dergisi* 5 (1949), p. 122. The traditional Great Seljuk titles are given in italics. Cf. R.M. Shukurov, '«Novyi Mantzikert» imperatora Feodora I Laskarisa', in G.G. Litavrin (ed.), *Vizantiia mezhdu Zapadom i Vostokom. Opyt istoricheskoi kharakteristiki* (St Petersburg: Aletheia, 1999), pp. 409–27.
34. Turan, *Türkiye Selçukluları hakkında resmî vesikalar*, pp. ۹۴-۱۰۱.
35. Ibid., pp. ۸۴-۸۹.

36. Ibid., pp. ۸۴, ۹۴, ۹۷-۹۸.
37. Ibid., pp. ۸۴, ۹۸.
38. Ibid., p. ۸۴.
39. Āqsarā'ī, *Musāmarat al-akhbār*, edited by Osman Turan as Kerîmüddin Mahmud Aksarayi (Aksaraylı), *Müsameret ül-ahbâr: Moğollar zamanında Türkiye Selçukluları Tarihi* (Ankara: Türk Tarih Kurumu, 1944), p. 38.
40. On Seljuk diplomatic practice, see M.E. Martin, 'The Venetian-Seljuk Treaty of 1220', *English Historical Review* 95 (1980), pp. 321–3; Speros Vryonis, *The Decline of Medieval Hellenism in Asia Minor and the Process of Islamization, from the Eleventh through the Fifteenth century* (Berkeley, Calif.: University of California Press, 1971), p. 470.
41. Three or four letters were erased.
42. MS Bibl.Genn. 1.5, fol. 166r-v; J. Bick, *Die Schreiber der Wiener griechischen Handschriften* (Vienna: Museion; Verlag E. Strache, 1920), pp. 67–8, no. 60; E. Coche de la Ferté et al. (eds), *Collection Hélène Stathatos:* ii; *Les objets byzantins et post-byzantins* (Strasbourg: P. Amandry, 1953–71), ii, plate XIV, 110, 3–4; A.S. Mat'evosyan, *Hayeren jeṙagreri hishatakaranner, xiii dar (Colophons of Armenian Manuscripts, xiii century)* (Erevan: Armenian Academy of Sciences, 1988), N 107 (g), p. 145.
43. Mat'evosyan, *Hishatakaranner*, N 107 (a), p. 145.
44. Dimtri Korobeinikov, 'A Greek Orthodox Armenian in the Seljukid service: the colophon of Basil of Melitina', in Rustam Shukurov (ed.), *Mare et litora: Essays presented to S. Karpov for his* 60th *birthday* (Moscow: Indrik, 2009), pp. 709–24.
45. Alexander Beihammer (ed.), *Griechische Briefe und Urkunden aus dem Zypern der Kreuzfahrerzeit. Die Formularsammlung eines königlichen Sekretärs im Vaticanus Palatinus Graecus* 367 (Nicosia: Zyprisches Forschungszentrum, 2007), N 32, pp. 183–4. The letter was sent between 1216 and 1218.
46. Ibid., N 19, p. 170.
47. G.L.F. Tafel and G.M. Thomas, *Urkunden zur älteren Handels- und Staatgeschichte der Republik Venedig, mit besonderer Beziehung auf Byzanz und die Levante {Fontes rerum Austriacarum, Abt. II:*

Diplomata et Acta, vols. xii-xiv] (Vienna: Aus der Kaiserlich-Königlichen Hof- und Staatsdruckerei, 1856–7), ii, p. 221.

48. Alp Arslan (1063–73) and Malikshāh (1073–92) were not direct ancestors of the sultan Ghiyāth al-Dīn Kaykhusraw I. Alp Arslan was the cousin of Sulaymān b. Qutlumush, the founder of the dynasty of the Seljuks of Rūm.
49. The *kharāj* was a land tax, whilst the *bāj* was a tribute, sometimes the sums collected from the customs levy. In this particular case the expression *kharāj* and *bāj* meant the money and gifts that the Byzantine emperors sent to the Seljuk sultans. The Byzantines regarded these as a reward for the 'service' that the sultans gave to the emperors, while the Seljuks considered the *kharāj* and *bāj* a tribute.
50. Ibn Bībī, *al-Awāmir al-'alā'īya fī 'l-umūr al-'alā'īya*, facsimile edition prepared by Adnan Sadık Erzi as İbn-i Bībī, *El-Evāmirü'l-'Alā'iyye fī'l-Umūri'l-'Alā'iyye* (Ankara: Türk Tarih Kurumu, 1956), p. 53. Cf. the abridged version: *Histoire des Seldjoucides d'Asie Mineure, d'après l'abrégé du Seldjouknāmeh d'Ibn-Bībī: texte persan,* ed. M.Th. Houtsma (Leiden: E.J. Brill, 1902; Recueil de textes relatifs à l'histoire des Seldjoucides 4), p. 15 and H. Duda, *Die Seltschukengeschichte des Ibn Bibi* (Copenhagen: Munksgaard, 1959), p. 28.
51. Ibn Bībī, *al-Awāmir al-'alā'īya*, p. 39.
52. Ibid., pp. 36–9.
53. Combe et al., *Répertoire chronologique d'épigraphie arabe*, x, pp. 240–1, no. 3957.
54. Shukurov, 'Turkoman and Byzantine self-identity', p. 269.
55. Āqsarā'ī, *Musāmarat al-akhbār*, pp. 61, 137, 208, 271.
56. Ibid., pp. 43, 140, 153, 190, 209, 210, 278, 279, 313.
57. Ibid., pp. 93, 201, 217, 257.
58. Ibid., p. 125.
59. Ibid., pp. 148, 154, 213.
60. Ibid., pp. 61, 242, 270, 278, 294. On these expressions, or simply *salṭanat*, see idem, pp. 279, 287, 294, 295, 301.
61. For example, the first mention of the *salṭanat-i Rūm* in Āqsarā'ī (p. 61), is obviously a citation of the *yarlıgh* issued by Hülegü

in 1258, in which he sanctioned the division of the sultanate between 'Izz al-Dīn Kaykā'ūs II and Rukn al-Dīn Qılıch Arslan IV. Likewise, the second mention (p. 242) of the *salṭanat-i Rūm* refers to the appointments made by the Ilkhan in AH 698 (9 October 1298 to 28 September 1299) during the revolt of the Mongol commander Sülemish in Asia Minor (on the date, see idem, pp. 239, 245); cf. similar cases of the usage of the *salṭanat-i Rūm*: idem, pp. 278, 294. Only in one place does Āqsarā'ī (p. 270) mention a certain Sa'd Köse, a chancery clerk, who was responsible for 'some ancient records of the [state] *dīwān* of the Sultanate of Rūm (*salṭanat-i Rūm*)' in AH 698 (1299). This is the *only* statement in Āqsarā'ī that could suggest the expression '*salṭanat-i Rūm*' was employed by the Seljuk chancery as an official name of the sultanate. The term '*salṭanat-i Rūm*' might have been written as the official title in the book of the state records of the *dīwān* of Rūm. However, this is only a suggestion.

62. Āqsarā'ī, *Musāmarat al-akhbār*, pp. 148, 285, 312.
63. Ibid., pp. 156, 158, 190, 302, 312.
64. See supra, note 61.
65. Āqsarā'ī is referring to the end of the reign of Tughrul (III) (1176–94), the last of the Seljuk dynasty in Iran and Iraq.
66. Qılıch Arslan II of Rūm (1156–92).
67. Āqsarā'ī, *Musāmarat al-akhbār*, p. 26.
68. A.C.S. Peacock, 'Aḥmad of Niğde's *al-Walad al-Shafīq* and the Seljuk past', *Anatolian Studies* 54 (2004), p. 102.
69. Āqsarā'ī, *Musāmarat al-akhbār*, p. 27.
70. Ibid., p. 21.
71. Indeed, that the caliph recognised the title 'Sultan' for the Seljuks was a remarkable achievement of the Grand Seljuk rulers (and then of other puppet Seljuk dynasties). For example, the Khwārazmshāh Jalāl al-Dīn, though himself styled as sultan, did not manage to obtain permission from the caliph to be named as such in the correspondence with Baghdad. The caliph only agreed to name him as *shāhanshāh*, but not as sultan. Shihāb al-Dīn Muḥammad al-Nasawī, *Sīrat al-sultān Jalāl al-Dīn Mankburnı (Zhizneopisanie sultana Jalal ad-Dina Mankburny)*,

ed. Z.M. Buniatov (Moscow: Vostochnaia literatura, 1996), pp. 215–6 (Arabic text), pp. 230–1 (Russian translation).

72. A.C.S. Peacock, 'Seljuq legitimacy in Islamic history', in Christian Lange and Songül Mecit (eds), *The Seljuqs: History, Politics and Culture* (Edinburgh: Edinburgh University Press, 2011), pp. 79–95.

CHAPTER FOUR

A *NADĪM* FOR THE SULTAN: RĀWANDĪ AND THE ANATOLIAN SELJUKS[1]

Sara Nur Yıldız

'As long as the world turns, may Khusraw be just! / the sovereign of men and creatures alike, may Khusraw be just.'[2] Thus opens the *qaṣīda* which brings Muḥammad b. 'Alī Rāwandī's *Rāḥat al-ṣudūr wa-āyāt al-surūr* to a conclusion. The short *qaṣīda* of 30 couplets with the *radīf* (repeating final rhyme) '*Khusraw bā dād bād*' ('may Khusraw be just!') not only associates its addressee, Sultan Ghiyāth al-Dīn Kaykhusraw I (r. 1192–6, 1205–11), with the quintessential just ruler, the Sasanian king Khusraw Anūshīrwān (r. 531–79) through a play on names, but also exhorts him, as 'the imperial one', to be just – the running theme of the poem – and to live up to the image of world conqueror and generous patron:

> The commander of the world and propitious potentate [that is] Ghiyāth al-Dīn,
> May the realm-conquering blessed *khusraw* [the emperor] be just!

Sarwar-i gītī Ghiyāth al-Dīn wa dawlat-shahriyār
Mulk-gīr u kāmrān Khusraw bā dād bād

He takes tribute from enemies, and bestows crowns
on friends;
May the *khusraw* [the emperor] be just on earth for eternity!
Bāj-gīr az dushmanān wa tāj-bakhsh-i dūstān
dar jahān tā jāwidān Khusraw bā dād bād

The *qaṣīda* urges the sultan, as the 'conqueror of ten lands' (*dah kishwar-gushāy*), ruler of the seven climes and the lord of the auspicious conjunction (*ṣāḥib-qirān*), to dispense justice and be 'clement upon his flock'.[3] The poet likewise portrays Kaykhusraw as a universal monarch reigning over the world: 'the sovereign of Rūm and Rus, of the Turk and the Chinese, Egypt and Syria [ruling] as far as the borders of India'. The poem intimates that, with the demise of the Great Seljuk dynastic house based in western Iran and Mesopotamia ('Irāq-i 'ajam), their traditional claim to the sultanate now reverted to their kin, the Seljuks of Rūm; the sovereign is thus reminded that that he is the inheritor of the Seljuk dynastic legacy: '[Now that] the nest of the sultanate has become barren *(shud 'aqīm īn āshyān-i salṭanat),* Khusraw shall become its auspicious offspring.' Hoping that the sultan be '[generous and bountiful as] the ocean and quarry', and act as 'bestower of riches to his eulogists arriving from surrounding lands', the poet's desire for patronage emerges in the final couplets. The sultan is thus requested to 'disperse gold upon the head of the traveller who has arrived as panegyrist after a journey of two months', 'redeem all of the indignities and injustices suffered by this poor one at the hands of base people', and 'greet, lodge and provide for this poor one, and dispense silver upon him'.[4]

Articulating the desire for Ghiyāth al-Dīn Kaykhusraw I's protection and patronage, this *qaṣīda* reveals much about Rāwandī's aspirations as a poet, and the function of compilation, the *Rāḥat al-ṣudūr*, which it concludes. K. A. Luther was the first to propose that, through a display of his literary and rhetorical skills in this work, Rāwandī hoped to obtain a post at the Seljuk court.[5] I take Luther's argument further by claiming that Rāwandī compiled the *Rāḥat al-ṣudūr* with the particular goal of gaining employment as *nadīm* ('boon companion') at the Seljuk court.[6] The *Rāḥat al-ṣudūr* was thus his showcase of skills, talents and practical knowledge qualifying him for the post of court boon companion. Rāwandī highlights his past intimate association with the Great Seljuk court in Hamadan as a selling point for such a post at the Anatolian Seljuk court; indeed, Rāwandī hoped to convince Kaykhusraw I of his familiarity with Great Seljuk court culture and thus demonstrate his competency in transferring this cultural capital, together with its accompanying dynastic charisma and legacy, to the Seljuk Anatolian court in the capacity as *nadīm*.[7]

This chapter reviews the post of the *nadīm* in Anatolia in conjunction with the *Rāḥat al-ṣudūr* and its Anatolian Seljuk political and cultural context, including the reception of Rāwandī at the Seljuk court. These topics have been largely overlooked as a result of the predominant scholarly interest in the historical section of Rāwandī's compilation, despite its characterisation as derivative and deficient, lacking in literary merit and marred by extensive verse, heavy rhetoric and 'curious' extraneous material.[8] Indeed, there is very little original material in Rāwandī's *Rāḥat al-ṣudūr*. The historical section was copied verbatim from Ẓahīr al-Dīn Nīshāpūrī's *Saljūqnāma*, about which much has been said.[9] Likewise, material in the introduction was taken, sometimes word for word, from Muntajab al-Dīn Badī' al-Juwaynī's *'Atabat al-kataba*, a collection of documents from the reign of the Great Seljuk sultan Sanjar (1117–57).[10] In an effort to rescue the *Rāḥat al-ṣudūr* from its detractors,[11] Julie Meisami has shown us how the work should be understood as a 'hybrid' text, the historical section of which had primarily a morally edifying function.[12] Meisami's analysis of the work, however, remains limited to the historical section. In a detailed study, Dagmar Riedel likewise stresses the didactic aspects of Rāwandī's work yet, unlike Meisami, considers the work holistically. Describing the three interlinking parts of the compilation as a 'coherent text from different sources', Riedel points out that it was designed as a kind of textbook which served as 'a personalized curriculum of Great Seljuq politics and courtly etiquette'.[13] Framed as it is according to the sections of a Persian panegyric *qaṣīda*, Riedel points out that the tripartite structure of the *Rāḥat al-ṣudūr* focuses on justice, institutional history and courtly etiquette.[14] Yet despite her careful textual analysis, which illuminates many aspects of the *Rāḥat al-ṣudūr*, Riedel does not connect the author's aspirations at the Anatolian Seljuk court specifically with the boon companionship. Indeed, her characterisation of Rāwandī as 'an obscure calligrapher and theologian' overlooks his vocation as aspiring *nadīm*.[15] It is this gap that I consider in this chapter – the relationship of Rāwandī's text with courtly *adab* literature and the position of the *munādama*, or boon companionship, at the Anatolian Seljuk court.

Rāwandī and the Rāḥat al-ṣudūr

Originally from the small town of Rāwand in the outskirts of Kashan, Abū Bakr Najm al-Dīn Muḥammad al-Rāwandī was born into a family of scholars famed for their calligraphic skills.[16] Rāwandī took up residence in Hamadan at the court of the Seljuk sultan Tughrul III during the years 1181–9, serving as apprentice to his uncle, a renowned court calligrapher. Following the death of Tughrul III in 1194 and the subsequent collapse of Great Seljuk power in 'Irāq-i 'ajam,[17] Rāwandī took up service as tutor to the sons of a family of local notables, the 'Arabshāh. Although trained for imperial court employment, Rāwandī discovered that his career prospects in western Iran remained limited to tutoring the sons of a local Shi'ite household of means. Rāwandī's hopes for a career at court were thus dashed as the sultanate disintegrated into petty warring principalities throughout the 1190s and early 1200s, and Persian Iraq was plundered by the former sultan's *ghulām*s and commanders, the army of the Khwarazmians and the caliphal army under the control of the vizier Mu'ayyid al-Dīn.[18] It was under these straitened circumstances and outbreak of political turmoil that the *Rāḥat al-ṣudūr* took its final shape, and its author sought the patronage of the Seljuks of Rūm – the formerly hostile cousins of the Great Seljuks and previously obscure branch of the dynastic family.

Although it seems he originally intended the work for Tughrul III,[19] Rāwandī readjusted his text for submission to Kaykhusaw I with added material on the Rūm Seljuk sultan's background, conquests and military exploits against Christian lands, completing the final version of the *Rāḥat al-ṣudūr* in 1210.[20]

Rāwandī tells us that he learned of Kaykhusraw I's military activities from an Anatolian merchant visiting Hamadan, Jamāl al-Dīn Abū Bakr al-Rūmī, who, acting as an agent and propagandist of the sultan, spread the news of Kaykhusraw's conquest of Antalya (1207), his struggle against the 'infidel' Armenians and other deeds (*manāqib*). The merchant also relayed the sultan's injunction to those in 'Irāq-i 'ajam to muster armies and march against the lands of the infidels (perhaps rather than squabble among themselves). This propaganda gained the distant sultan adherents and supporters from among the 'Iraqi amirs, notables and ruling elite.[21] Like many other members of the political elite, through contact with the merchant-agent Jamāl al-Dīn Abū Bakr al-Rūmī, Rāwandī placed hopes in Kaykhusraw I as a possible saviour of his homeland torn apart by political tumult and military strife.[22]

The *Rāḥat al-ṣudūr* is divided into three sections: an extensive introduction, a history of the Great Seljuks and an overview of *adab* as the *nadīm*'s requisite repertoire of courtly etiquette, skills and talents. The introduction begins with a fourteen-couplet *mathnawī* with eulogies to the prophets ending with Muḥammad, the Prophet's companions, the *ahl-i bayt* and various other religious figures. Rāwandī then launches into a discourse on the notion of justice as meted out by God, the caliphs and Iranian kings, followed by two long *qaṣīda*s, one by the compiler praising his dedicatee, Kaykhusraw I, and one composed by the famous poet Jamāl al-Dīn al-Iṣfahānī on the vicissitudes of fate.[23] The text then turns to the life and circumstances of the author, beginning with how the Great Seljuk sultan Tughrul III received instruction in calligraphy from Rāwandī's uncle. This section is interspersed with *qaṣīda*s praising the author's uncle and associates, as well as the intellectual elite of Hamadan, emphasising their fame as mentors of the Seljuk sultans. The author provides the details of his own education and explains how he came to compile his work. The introduction concludes with a description of the work's content, the *fihrist*, a discursus on why a sultan should strive to leave behind a good name by doing good deeds, and an exhortation that the sultan should endear himself to his subjects.

The second section, the history of the Great Seljuks of Iran and Iraq up to the invasion of the Khwārazmshāh, comprises the bulk of the work. Based verbatim on Nīshāpūrī's *Saljūqnāma*, this section contains extensive selections of verse inserted into the narrative for illustrative or edifying purposes. *Qaṣīda*s by the author in the praise of the work's dedicatee, Kaykhusraw I, are inserted in between the reigns of sultans, and Arabic and Persian poetic selections, including verses from Firdawsī's *Shāhnāma* as well as Sanā'ī, are also interspersed throughout the text.[24] Poetic selections provide moral and edifying commentary, as well as serve to heighten the reader's emotional response to tragic events. Thus, with verse by the renowned Seljuk poet Mu'izzī, Nishapur, after its destruction by the Ghuzz in 1153, is compared to the desolate remains of a familiar encampment turned into ruins haunted only by birds and wild beasts.[25] The poetic selections from the repertoire of Niẓāmī, Anwarī, 'Imādī, Jamāl al-Dīn al-Iṣfahānī, and Mujīr al-Dīn Baylaqānī appear to have been drawn by Rāwandī from the illustrated anthology of contemporary poems compiled for Tughrul III by his uncle for entertainment at the sultan's *majlis* (assemblies).[26] The historical section ends with the panegyric composed by Rāwandī for Kaykhusraw I, whom he exhorts to deliver his homeland from Khwarazmian oppression.

The third section of Rāwandī's work focuses on the courtly accomplishments (*ādāb*) of the *nadīm*,[27] in six sections (*faṣl*), ranging from a discussion on the benefits of playing chess and its different forms (*faṣl-i dar dhikr-i ādāb-i nadama* [?] *wa sharḥ-i bākhtan-i shaṭranj wa nard*, pp. 404–15); on the proper way to prepare and drink wine (*faṣl fī 'l-sharāb*, pp. 416–27); on horse-racing and archery (*faṣl dar musābaqat wa tīr-andākht*, pp. 428–31); on hunting (*faṣl dar shikār kardan*, pp. 431–3); on the author's expertise in calligraphy (*faṣl fī ma'rifat uṣūl al-khaṭṭ min al-dā'īra wa 'l-niqā*, pp. 437–47);[28] and, finally, on divination through the numerical values of letters, referred to as the 'conqueror' and the 'conquered' (*faṣl fī 'l-ghālib wa 'l-maghlūb*, pp. 447–56). This method 'of calculating the results of contests between rivals' was a form of divination specifically used for military decisions; it was supposedly of ancient origins going back to Alexander the Great, who learned it from his tutor, Aristotle.[29]

The third part of Rāwandī's work, the section on the arts of the *nadīm*, has received little attention from scholars. Indeed, if one is looking for new information on the practice of these activities one will be disappointed, for this section is as derivative as the other two.[30] This section, however, provides important clues to the author's intent: by concluding his work with this summary excursion through the arts of a *nadīm*, as well as highlighting his special skills in calligraphy, Rāwandī appears to have been alerting his reader to his qualifications for this court position. By stressing his intimate knowledge of and his extensive experience at the Seljuk court in Hamadan under sultan Tughrul III, Rāwandī demonstrates his special qualifications as a *nadīm par excellence*, capable of assisting the Anatolian Seljuk sultan in fulfilling his role as the supreme power in the Turco-Iranian world and inheritor of the entire Seljuk legacy. As an intimate of the sultan, Rāwandī would thus convey the political memory (through his historical narrative), the literary culture (with the verse of Great Seljuk poets) and court practice (with the instruction of *adab*) of the defunct Iranian Seljuks to the Anatolian Seljuk court.

Adab, *Ethics and the* Nadīm

What exactly was the post of *nadīm* to which Rāwandī aspired? Despite the many medieval works on *adab* written by *nadīms*,[31] there is little modern scholarship focusing on the role of the *nadīm* in medieval Islamic polities, and none at all with reference to Anatolia.[32] Although research to date has largely concentrated on the Abbasid *nadīm*, one can draw on this literature for the Seljuk case since court practice of the Great Seljuks was modelled largely on that of the Abbasids (via Ghaznavid and Samanid models).[33] As for the Anatolian context of the Seljuks, however, we have little to go by. Although Ibn Bībī, our main source for the thirteenth-century Anatolian Seljuk dynasty and author of a work deeply entrenched in court politics, makes mention of this courtly occupation (as will be discussed further below), he provides little specific information to illuminate the Anatolian Seljuk context.

The prestigious and influential post of the boon companion, as *nadīm* is usually translated, developed in the early Abbasid period around the same time as the vizierate, yet in a sphere separate from the administrative offices. The duty of the boon companion required first and foremost 'befriending' the caliph according to a set of rigorous requirements and protocol.[34] The boon companion was to observe proper deportment, and to cultivate the virtues of forbearance, humility, brevity in speech and discretion.[35] The *nadīm* was on duty during the caliph's 'private' time, or as Chejne expresses it 'in his time of solitude, hunting parties, chess games, and drinking and literary sessions'. He was likewise indispensible to the *majlis*, the intellectual or literary assemblies held by the caliph.[36]

Famous poets often served as boon companion to the caliphs and tutor to their sons, as in the case of the celebrated Abū Nuwās (d. c.815). They were often historian–littérateurs and chess experts such as Abū Bakr Muḥammad al-Ṣūlī (d. 947), whose work, *Akhbār al-'Abbās*, contains valuable information on the institution in reference to literary and drinking sessions.[37] Ibn Iskandar, the eleventh-century author of the *Qābūsnāma*, outlines the skills that the *nadīm* should possess: he should be trained in the epistolary arts in Arabic and Persian so that he may act as personal secretary for the ruler; he should have considerable expertise in poetry, having committed poems to memory both in Arabic and Persian; he should also be able to distinguish good verse from bad; he should know the Qur'an by heart and be able to comment upon it; he should likewise be well versed in the hadith, jurisprudence and the application of the law; he should have some knowledge of medicine and astrology; he should be a talented raconteur and knowledgeable about the lives of monarchs and their character; and finally, he should be able to play a musical instrument, and be skilful in backgammon and chess.[38] It is for this reason that the *Rāḥat al-ṣudūr* covers this wealth of different topics:

Rāwandī aims in his book to show his mastery of all the appropriate skills for a *nadīm*.

A further important characteristic of the *nadīm* was connected with *adab*, in the sense of 'correct behaviour' as much as 'literature', as is demonstrated by the career of Miskawayh (c.936–1030), who stands out as the exemplary Abbasid boon companion *adīb*.[39] It was during his long and illustrious career of service to the Shi'ite Buyids, a period of flourishing Islamic learning, that Miskawayh brought an intellectual depth to *adab* literature never before witnessed, nor ever to be matched. Critical of the shallowness of the court culture of his time, Miskawayh developed a system known as 'virtue ethics', which permeated much of later *adab* works. As intellectual advisor and companion to the ruler, the *nadīm* was to be well versed in ethics and moral philosophy, and have a good command of the sacred and secular sciences, including divinity, mathematics, alchemy and cooking.[40] To this body of knowledge, one must add history writing, for history facilitated the acquisition of virtues by providing concrete examples of ethical theory with the exposition of the unfolding of the divine plan as manifested by events.[41] Miskawayh thus composed a world history as a model of prudent management of the realm according to the concept of *tadbīr*, or 'sound government'.[42] In the Islamic world this body of general practical knowledge came to be defined as *adab*: the 'manners, culture, the root and substance of *ta'dīb*, education, discipline, culture'.[43]

Miskawayh's ethical framework exerted much influence over subsequent *adab* literature, and in particular over the conceptualisation of the boon-companion. In his *Siyar al-mulūk* ('The Conduct of Kings'), the eleventh-century Seljuk vizier Niẓām al-Mulk points out that, '[a] boon-companion is the reflexion of his ruler. If he is affable, liberal, patient, gracious, the ruler is likely to be so.'[44] The early fourteenth-century author, Ibn al-Ṭiqṭaqā, likewise equates the character of the ruler with that of his *nadīm*.[45] Drawing on the same tradition, Rāwandī elaborates on the ethical qualities of the *nadīm*:

> Boon companionship (*munādamat*) and attending majlis (*mujālasat*) with the *pādishāh* is a grave business (*amrī-yi 'aẓīm-*

> *ast*) and a weighty or dangerous occupation (*kārī-yi khaṭīr-ast*). The boon companion is the manifestation of the intelligence and the proof of the excellence of the *pādishāh*: men take on the qualities of those with whom they spend time.[46]

Thus the *nadīm* was much more than the drinking companion and source of entertainment for the sultan.[47] The *nadīm*'s access to the sultan, as well as his influence on him, made him a participant in court politics, albeit as a member of the imperial entourage rather than of the administrative *dīwān*. It may be illustrative to repeat Matthew Innes's observation that 'the exercise of power was rooted in the everyday, in the give and take of face-to-face relationships of cooperation, patronage, and mutual backscratching, ... and thus, bound up in patterns of movement and meeting'.[48] In other words, social relationships formed the main basis of medieval political power, with informal and fluid ties of personal loyalty, rather than formal structured institutions, lying behind the political and social dynamics of the period. Thus, as Matthew Innes argues, medieval rulers and elites lacked a stable institutional basis for the exercise of power, and thus dominated 'socially rather than administratively'.[49] Indeed, similar to that of other medieval polities, Seljuk political culture – in both Anatolia and Iran – was based on personal rule. Thus, if one views the sultan's drinking parties with the elites of his court and realm as a political practice which was part and parcel of personal rule, then the *nadīm* must likewise been seen as more than an entertainer and drinking partner of the sultan, but also as a political actor.

The Nadīm *at the Seljuk Court of Rūm and the Reception of Rāwandī's* Rāḥat al-ṣudūr

Our major source for the position of the *nadīm* in Seljuk Anatolia is Ibn Bībī. He refers to the *nadīm* in a somewhat stereotypical way, always using the plural form *nudamā'* paired with *ḥurafā'* (intimates), and, in one instance, with *julasā'* (companions).[50] Mention is made of the *nudamā'* in descriptions of enthronement ceremonies during which the recital of panegyric poetry took place,[51] or in references to the *majlis-i bazmī* (wine symposiums) which followed celebratory feasts.[52] Only once does Ibn Bībī mention the name of a *nadīm*: a certain Nūr al-Dīn pasar-i Shash Ṭalā-yī Akhlāṭī, who appears in the company of the sultan 'Alā' al-Dīn Kayqubād I (r. 1219–37).[53] Thus, although Ibn Bībī does not tell us much about the *nadīm*, it is clear it was very much part of Anatolian Seljuk court life.

It is Ibn Bībī's description of the activities and moral probity of Alā' al-Dīn Kayqubād, however, that strikes a chord with Rāwandī's text with regard to the *nadīm*'s role in reinforcing the moral probity of the ruler. Rather than looking to the *nadīm* as the reinforcer of the sacred role of the ruler as dispenser of justice and upholder of ethical behaviour, as we see in Rāwandī, Ibn Bībī portrays the sultan, in this case, Kayqubād I, as fulfilling all ethical requirements of his position as monarch. Ibn Bībī thus presents us with a description of the sultan's activities, both in the official capacity as ruler as well as during his leisure time, which reinforce the notion that justice was the central preoccupation of the monarch, around which all other royal activities gravitated. Thus, in a chapter describing 'the sultan's virtues, love of justice and other attractive features',[54] Ibn Bībī provides a rather detailed description of Kayqubād's daily routine. After the morning prayers (done in accordance to Shafi'i rites, although the Hanafi prescriptions prevailed in all other matters), the sultan would go to the court of justice where petitioners were received. There the sultan carried on the daily business of 'dispensing justice'.[55] So inordinately just was Kayqubād, Ibn Bībī tells us, that the smallest creature such as an ant would not be denied his due. After dispensing justice all day, when night fell the sultan would preside over the magnificent imperial *majlis*.[56] To the accompaniment of music and wine, the exploits of kings (*tawārīkh-i mulūk*) would be recited; indeed, the sultan in particular relished the discussion of praiseworthy *pādishāh*s of old, such as Maḥmūd of Ghazna, whom he held as exemplary models. Sometimes the sultan would recite his own verse. Everyone was expected to conform to a standard of decency at the risk of banishment. As Ibn Bībī explains, 'if one of his intimates or nadims (*ḥurafā' wa nudamā*) transgressed their rank or duty (*birūn-i martaba wa waẓīfa*) with inappropriate speech or behaviour, he would scold them and distance them from the court, and never allow them entrance to the *majlis* again'.[57] Ibn Bībī likewise informs us that Kayqubād was well versed in Persian edifying and ethical works such as Ghazzālī's *Kīmiyā-yi sa'ādat* and Niẓām al-Mulk's *Siyāsatnāma*. He ends this section with a brief overview of the sultan's abilities in other occupations. Kayqubād was thoroughly trained in various crafts of the artisan, and in particular knew the value of precious stones; he played chess and backgammon well, and was an avid polo (*gūyī*) player and hunter.[58]

In contrast, Kayquabād's son and successor Ghiyāth al-Dīn Kaykhusraw II (r. 1237–46) lacked his father's exemplary character and seemed to have little interest in state affairs or ruling his realm with justice. Immediately after the Seljuk defeat at Kösedağ (1243), the landmark battle ushering in the period of Mongol dominance in Anatolia, the elderly Seljuk commander Mubāriz al-Dīn Chavlı chided Kaykhusraw II for bringing disaster on the sultanate. Indeed, the Seljuk hostilities with the Mongols could possibly have been avoided if the sultan had followed a different policy. The young and inexperienced sultan's biggest offence, according to Chavlı, was receiving the wrong counsel. In general, the sultan was guilty of associating with the wrong types – base associates, vulgar boon companions and ignorant intimates (*julasā'-yi arādhīl wa nudamā'-yi asāfil wa ḥurafā'-yi jāhil*).[59] Kaykhusraw II was a wayward sultan in need of rehabilitation.

It has been assumed that Rāwandī never actually travelled to the Seljuk court in Konya, but instead sent his work.[60] The final *qaṣīda*, however, makes specific reference to the poet's arrival at the court with the line 'the traveller who has arrived as panegyrist after a journey of two months'.[61] Rāwandī, for reasons which remain unknown, did not however succeed in entrenching himself at the Seljuk court in Konya. His hopes to gain a position as *nadīm* to Kaykhusraw I may have been dashed when the sultan died in battle against the Byzantines in 1211, the year Rāwandī may possibly have arrived at court. Thus, while we do not know of Rāwandī's subsequent fate – whether he remained in Konya, left for another court or died – we do know that the only extant version of the *Rāḥat al-ṣudūr* was copied in mid April 1238 (the beginning of Ramadan 635), by al-Ḥāfiẓ Ḥājjī Ilyās b. 'Abdallāh, as he is named in the manuscript, a member of the *'ulamā'* as his title al-Ḥāfiẓ (memoriser of the Qur'an) indicates.[62] His son, Abū Sa'īd b. Ilyās al-Ḥāfiẓ *muḥtasib al-'asākir*,[63] appears among the ranks of the Seljuk political elite as a religious official, as can be seen in a reference to him among the witnesses of the Seljuk statesman Jalāl al-Dīn Qaratay's *waqfīya* dating from 651/1253–4.[64] The production of this copy of the *Rāḥat al-ṣudūr* – the single copy to have survived into modern times – coincides with troubled times for the Seljuk sultanate. Shortly after the young Seljuk sultan Kaykhusraw II took the throne in 1237, he remained for approximately a year under the tyrannical hold and dangerous influence of the Seljuk official, Sa'd al-Dīn Köpek. Indeed, Köpek's reign of terror and purging of important generals and statesmen had dire consequences for the Seljuk elite and the stability of the empire on the eve of the Mongol invasions.[65] The situation reminds one of Niẓām al-Mulk's caveat against employing as boon companions those who hold administrative posts; intimates of the sultan should not have additional sources of power or administrative responsibilities, otherwise the manipulation of the sultan through their intimate influence had the potential to upset the balance of power distributed among the members of the court and *dīwān*.[66] The case of Köpek provides a striking example of this dangerous situation. After having isolated Kaykhusraw II from the influence of all other officials and amirs, Köpek seized complete control of the reins of government through his grip over the sultan and proceeded to destroy the empire's ruling elite, until he was murdered some time in the summer of 1238.

How may we interpret the copying of this text during this period of crisis for the Seljuk sultanate? Was it a response to Köpek's regime and manipulation of the sultan and the state apparatus? Did Rāwandī's concluding *qaṣīda* with its exhortation to rule justly (*Khusraw bā dād bād*), originally directed to Kaykhusraw I, have special resonance in 1238? It is possible. Rāwandī's ethically oriented compilation would have been appropriate material for the rehabilitation of the young sultan's ways, especially after the damaging effects of his contact with Köpek. It thus may have been copied by al-Ḥāfiẓ

Ḥājjī Ilyās b. 'Abdallāh as a way to to urge Kaykhusraw II to return to the path of just rule.

Conclusion

The title of Rāwandī's work, *Rāḥāt al-ṣudūr wa-āyāt al-surūr* has been translated in various ways. Jan Rypka renders it as 'Recreation of the Breast and Symbol of Joy',[67] Meisami as 'Ease for Breasts and Marvel of Happiness'[68] and Riedel as 'Comfort of Hearts and Wonder of Delights'.[69] I propose the alternative translation of 'Comfort at the Bosoms (of Leaders) and Delight in the Auspicious Signs'. My translation takes into account the author's intentions in compiling this work, rendering *rāḥat al-ṣudūr* as 'comfort of one's breast', that is, inner peace, in reference to the ease or comfort of living (*rāḥat*) in relation to the power of those at the helm of government (*ṣudūr*, the plural of *ṣadr*, ministers or chiefs). The second part of the title, *āyāt al-surūr* ('signs of joy'), may be interpreted as intimating the bright future of the greater Seljuk world with the auspicious rise to power of Kaykhusraw I. This hybrid work, to use Meisami's term, with its mixture of history, poetry and didactic discussions of justice, as well as its overview of the arts of *adab* at which a *nadīm* should be proficient, was compiled with the symbiotic relationship of the *nadīm* and sultan in mind.

It was likewise the symbiotic relationship of power between courtiers such as the *nadīm* and the sultan that was expressed through *qaṣīdas* such as Rāwandī's *Khusraw bā dād bād*. Just as the *nadīm* was a core member of the *majlis*, or court assembly, the recital of the *qaṣīda* was his ritualistic literary counterpart, reflecting the ideal qualities of rulership. Considered 'the courtly poem par excellence',[70] the *qaṣīda* recited in praise of caliphs, sultans and notables took a central role in the ceremonial ritual of court life in the medieval Islamic world.[71] The fiction of imperial glory based on divine will and dependent upon the exercise of justice was the 'glue' between the sultan and his court officials, whose livelihoods were dependent upon the imperial personage of the ruler. When the ideological fiction of the power and glory of the sultanate was subverted, such as we see under the brief regime of Köpek, the court, if not the entire sultanate, was endangered. This was particuarly important in the case of political structures which lacked a hereditary caste of nobility, but rather were manned by a meritorious aristocracy supporting a hereditary sultan. When a sovereign, such as Kaykhusraw II, was born into a role which may not suit his personal tendencies, it was up to the men of his court to help him fulfil that role. Courtiers such as the *nadīm* thus strove to cast the sultan in the role of 'warrior', decision-maker and power-balancer through their representations of the royal personage, a strategy of subterfuge necessary to justify the continuance of a hereditary dynasty.

The recitation of panegyric *qaṣīda*s is likened by Stefan Sperl to a public ritual of the renewal of faith in the state, which at the same time reminded the sovereign of the duties of his high office. Following their ritualistic recitation at the court assembly, their authors were awarded with *khil'a*, or robes of honour, and large sums of money, as convention dictated.[72] As Sperl points out, 'the sumptuous award of the court poet is part of the ceremony: it is a public demonstration of generosity and symbolizes the life-giving function of the King'.[73] The aspiring *nadīm* Rāwandī, with his compilation of the *Raḥāt al-ṣudūr*, took on the role of agent of cultural continuity through the transfer of literary and other cultural forms. Rāwandī's particular project was the renewal of the Great Seljuk political and cultural legacy in the lands of Rūm under the rising Anatolian Seljuks.

Notes

1. I dedicate this chapter to the memory of K. Allin Luther, whose course on Perso-Islamic civilisation at the University of Michigan inspired me to study the medieval Turco-Iranian world.
2. Muḥammad b. 'Alī Rāwandī, *Raḥāt al-ṣudūr wa-āyāt al-surūr*, ed. Muhammad Iqbal (Leiden and London: E. J. Brill and Luzac and Co., 1921), p. 465. This edition is based on the unique manuscript, Paris, Bibliotheque Nationale, MS Suppl. Persan 1314. A Turkish translation has been rendered by Ahmed Ateş, *Râhat-üs-sudûr ve Âyet-üs-sürûr (Gönüllerin Rahatı ve Sevinç Alâmeti*

(Ankara: Türk Tarih Kurumu, 1960, 2 vols), cited hereafter as Rāwandī, trans. Ateş.

3. *Ṣāḥib-qirān*, a term with pre-Islamic Iranian origins, means world 'conqueror and universal sovereign' (Cornell Fleischer, 'Royal authority, dynastic cyclism, and "Ibn Khaldunism" in sixteenth-century Ottoman letters', *Journal of Asian and African Studies* 18, no. 304 [1983], p. 206); the term is known for its implications of important planetary conjunctions: Naindeep Sigh Chann, 'Lord of the auspicious conjunction: origins of the *Ṣāḥib-Qirān*', *Iran and the Caucasus 13* (2009), pp. 93–4.
4. Rāwandī, *Rāḥat al-ṣudūr*, p. 465.
5. K. Allin Luther, 'Islamic rhetoric and the Persian historians, 1100–1300 A.D.', in James A. Bellamy (ed.), *Studies in Near Eastern Culture and History in Memory of Ernest T. Abdel-Massih* (Ann Arbor, Mich.: Center for Near Eastern and North African Studies, 1990), pp. 90–8.
6. For the first in-depth study of the work as a literary composition, see Dagmar A. Riedel's dissertation, 'Searching for the Islamic Episteme: The Status of Historical Information in Medieval Middle-Eastern Anthological Writing' (PhD Dissertation, Indiana University, 2004).
7. For more on the dissolution of the Great Seljuks, see Julie Scott Meisami, 'The collapse of the Great Saljuqs', in Chase F. Robinson (ed.), *Texts, Documents and Artefacts: Islamic Studies in Honour of D. S. Richards* (Leiden: Brill, 2003), pp. 265–300.
8. For a critique of earlier modern reception of Rāwandī, see Julie Scott Meisami, 'Rāvandī's *Rāḥat al-ṣudūr*: history or hybrid?', *Edebiyat* 5, no. 2 (1994), pp. 183–5; eadem, *Persian Historiography to the end of the twelfth century* (Edinburgh: Edinburgh University Press, 1999), p. 237; Hillenbrand, 'Rāvandī, the Seljuk court at Konya, and the Persianisation of Anatolian Cities', *Mésogeios* 25–36 (2005), p. 162. Hillenbrand comments that the work ends with 'a rather curious section of miscellaneous items'.
9. For more on Ẓahīr al-Dīn Nīshāpūrī's *Saljūq-nāma*, upon which Rāwandī based his historical section, see A.H. Morton, *The Saljūqnāma of Ẓahīr al-Dīn Nīshāpūrī. A critical text making use of the*

unique manuscript in the Library of the Royal Asiatic Society (London: E. J. W. Gibb Memorial Trust, 2004).

10. G. M. Curpalidis, 'Selçuklu Devletinin Tarihiyle İlgili Fars Kaynaklarının Tekstolojik Tahlili ("Atebet El-Ketebe" Adlı XII. Yüzyılın. Belge Derlemesi Ve Muhammed Er-Râvendî'nin "Rahat Es-sudûr ve Âyet Es-surûr" Eserinin Kıyaslandırılması Temelinde)', in *Uluslararası Osmanlı Öncesi Türk Kültürü Kongresi Bildirileri* (Ankara: Atatürk Kültür Merkezi, 1997), p. 121. For more on al-Juwaynī's *'Atabat al-kataba*, see A.K.S. Lambton, 'The administration of Sanjar's empire as illustrated in the *'Atabat al-kataba'*, *Bulletin of the School of Oriental and African Studies* 20, no. 1 (1957), pp. 367–88.
11. Meisami, *Persian Historiography*, pp. 237–9; eadem, 'The historian and the poet: Rāvandī, Nizami and the rhetoric of history', in Kamran Talatof, Jerome W. Clinton and K. Allin Luther (eds), *The poetry of Nizami Ganjavi: knowledge, love, and rhetoric* (New York: Palgrave, 2000), pp. 97–128; eadem, 'Rāvandī's *Rāḥat al-ṣudūr*,' pp. 183–215.
12. Meisami, 'Rāvandī's *Rāḥat al-ṣudūr*,' pp. 183–4; eadem 'The historian and the poet', 97 ff.
13. Riedel, 'Searching for the Islamic Episteme', pp. iii, 4, 18.
14. Ibid., pp. 224, 259–60.
15. Ibid., p. iii.
16. Rāwandī, *Rāḥat al-ṣudūr*, p. iv.
17. The Seljuks of Iraq constituted a large appanage under the loose overlordship of the Great Seljuk Sultan Sanjar (d. 1155), and considered themselves to be his heirs and continuators: K. Allin Luther, 'The end of Saljuk dominion in Khurasan', in Louis L. Orlin (ed.), *Michigan Oriental Studies in honor of George C. Cameron* (Ann Arbor, Mich.: Department of Near Eastern Studies, University of Michigan, 1976), p. 219.
18. Kenneth Allin Luther, 'Ravandi's report on the administrative changes of Muhammad Jahan Pahlavan', in C.E. Bosworth (ed.), *Iran and Islam: In Memory of the Late Vladimir Minorsky* (Edinburgh: Edinburgh University Press, 1971), p. 400.
19. Julie Scott Meisami, 'The collapse of the Great Saljuqs', p. 265.

20. Reidel, 'Searching for the Islamic Episteme', pp. xv-xxii, 178, 184
21. Rāwandī, *Rāḥat al-ṣudūr*, p. 462: *'wa dar ḥidmat-i umarā'-yi 'Irāq wa ṣudūr u buzurgān sharḥ-i sīrat wa 'adl farmūdan va lashgar ārāstan wa kāfir kāstan wa maṣṣāf {maṣāf} dādan wa bilād-i kufr gushādan mī-dād wa umarā'-yi 'Irāq-rā dūstdār-i khudāwand-i 'ālam karda-ast …'*
22. Ibid.
23. For more on Jamāl al-Dīn al-Iṣfahānī, see Michael Glünz, *Die Panegyrische Qaṣīda bei Kamāl al-Dīn Ismā'il aus Isfahan: eine Studie zur persischen Lobdichtung um den Beginn des 7./13. Jahrhunderts* (Stuttgart: Steinter, 1993) pp. 8–9.
24. Ateş points out that a total of 2799 verse couplets are found in the work, 511 of which are by the author himself in praise of Kaykhusraw I (Rāwandī, trans. Ateş, i, p. xx).
25. For more on the poet Mu'izzī, see G.E. Tetley, *The Ghaznavid and Seljuq Turks. Poetry as a Source for Iranian History* (London and New York: Routledge, 2009).
26. Rāwandī, *Rāḥat al-ṣudūr*, pp. xv–xxii; 57: *'wa khudāvand-i 'ālam majlis bi-dān mī-ārāst'*.
27. Ibid., p. 404.
28. Ibid., pp. xxvii–xxviii; 64.
29. Ibid., p. xxviii.
30. Iqbal writes: 'The contents of the sundry sections at the end of the book are to my mind not so important as might appear at first sight. Of these the two sections on shooting (with arrows) and horse-racing (pp. 428–434) can be dismissed as entirely uninteresting, for they only discuss the lawfulness or otherwise of these practices under various conditions, from a religious point of view …' 'The section on chess contains nothing that is extraordinary or instructive … more or less a repetition of what has been so often told by earlier and later writers on chess in Arabic as well as in Persian …' (Rāwandī, *Rāḥat al-ṣudūr*, pp. xxvi–xxvii).
31. See Anwar G. Chejne, 'The boon-companion in early 'Abbāsid times', *Journal of the American Oriental Society* 85, no. 3 (1965), p. 328.

32. This stagnant state of affairs has begun to change in recent years with the important study by Samer M. Ali, *Arabic Literary Salons in the Islamic Middle Ages: Poetry, Public Performance, and the Presentation of the Past* (Notre Dame: University of Notre Dame Press, 2010).
33. For examples of the institution of the *nadīm* under the Great Seljuks, see Tetley, *The Ghaznavid and Seljuk Turks*, p. 13 and passim, for a survey of Great Seljuk panegyric literature.
34. Chejne, 'The boon-companion', pp. 327–30.
35. Ibid., p. 330.
36. Ibid., p. 335.
37. Ibid. Also see Stefan Leder, 'al-Ṣūlī', EI^2, ix, pp. 846–8. Reminiscent of Rāwandī, Ṣūlī produced a recension of the *dīwān* of Abū Nūwas and a work on chess. For a study of Ṣūlī at the Abbasid court, see Letizia Osti, 'The wisdom of youth: legitimising the Caliph al-Muqtadir', *Al-Masāq* 19, no. 1 (2007), pp. 17–27. Osti tells us, 'In the *Kitāb al-awrāq*, his major historical work, Ṣūlī mixed accounts of political and military events with anecdotes of life at court and events in his own life'. Al-Ṣūlī expanded and embellished his historical narrative with a prodigious use of verse (Osti, 'The wisdom of youth', pp. 19–20).
38. Chejne, 'The boon-companion', p. 332.
39. Lenn E. Goodman, *Islamic Humanism* (Oxford: Oxford University Press, 2003), pp. 102–3.
40. Ibid., p. 108.
41. Meisami, *Persian Historiography*, p. 81.
42. Goodman, *Islamic Humanism*, pp. 199–200.
43. Ibid., p. 107.
44. Quoted in Chejne, 'The boon-companion', p. 331.
45. Ibid, pp. 331, 331 n. 38.
46. Rāwandī, *Rāḥat al-ṣudūr*, p. 405: *Nadīm bayān-i 'aql wa burhān-i faḍl-i pādishāh bāshad.*
47. J. Sadan, 'Nadīm', EI^2, vi, pp. 849–52.
48. Matthew Innes, *State and Society in the Early Middle Ages: The Middle Rhine Valley, 400–1000* (Cambridge: Cambridge University Press, 2000), pp. 139–40.

49. Ibid., p. 261.
50. Ibn Bībī, *al-Awāmir al-ʿalāʾīya fī ʾl-umūr al-ʿalāʾīya*, facsimile edition prepared by Adnan Sadık Erzi as İbn-i Bībī, *El-Evāmirü'l-ʿAlāʾiyye fī'l-Umūri'l-ʿAlāʾiyye* (Ankara: Türk Tarih Kurumu, 1956), pp. 218, 228, 237, 273, 504, 526.
51. Ibid., p. 217.
52. Ibid., pp. 218, 237, 504.
53. Ibid., p. 273.
54. Ibid., p. 222.
55. Ibid., pp. 227–8.
56. Ibid., p. 228.
57. Ibid.
58. Ibid.
59. Ibid., p. 526.
60. Based on this assumption Riedel theorises: 'Since Rāwandī himself did not travel to Anatolia to plead in person for the patronage of Kay Khusraw, he designed the *Rāḥat* as his representative. The miscellany is a written record of Great Seljuq politics, organized in accordance with oral practices that were indispensible to a Rūm Seljuq identity. The *Rāḥat* therefore illustrates how writing can be employed to adhere to oral practices, even though they were changed by being represented in writing' (Reidel, 'Searching for the Islamic Episteme', p. 262).
61. Rāwandī, *Rāḥat al-ṣudūr*, p. 465.
62. Meisami, *Persian Historiography*, p. 439. Riedel's careful description of the manuscript informs us that copyists's *nisba* of al-Qunawī appears to be a later addition (Riedel, 'Searching for the Islamic Episteme', p. 79).
63. I cannot identify with any exactitude the specific post of *muḥtasib al-ʿasākir*. For more on the *muḥtasib* in the Great Seljuk context, see Christian Lange, *Justice, Punishment and the Medieval Muslim Imagination* (Cambridge: Cambridge University Press, 2008) and Richard Wittmann, 'The *muḥtasib* in Seljuq times: insights from four chancery manuals', *Harvard Middle Eastern and Islamic Review* 7 (2006), pp. 108–128. In addition to his duties as overseer of commercial transactions, the *muḥtasib* exercised punitive

authority in various ways (Lange, *Justice, Punishment and the Medieval Muslim Imagination*, p. 55). See also Ronald P. Buckley, 'The muhtasib', *Arabica 39* (1992), pp. 59–117; Wilhelm Floor, 'The office of muhtasib in Iran', *Iranian Studies* 18, no. 1 (1985), pp. 53–74.

64. M. Ferid Uğur and M. Mes'ud Koman, *Selçuk Büyüklerinden Celâlüddin Karatay İle Kardeşlerinin Hayat ve Eserleri* (Konya: Yeni Kitap Basımevi, 1940), p. 82; Osman Turan, 'Selçuk Vakfiyeleri III. Celâleddin Karatay, Vakıfları ve Vakfiyeleri', *Belleten* 12, no. 45 (1948), p. 144.
65. See Sara Nur Yıldız, 'The rise and fall of a tyrant in Seljuk Anatolia: Sa'd al-Din Köpek's reign of terror, 1237–1238', in Robert Hillenbrand, A.C.S. Peacock and Firuza Abdullaeva (eds), *Ferdowsi, the Mongols and Iranian History: Art, Literature and Culture from Early Islam to Qajar Persia* (London: I.B. Tauris, forthcoming).
66. Chejne, 'The boon-companion', p. 331.
67. Jan Rypka, *History of Iranian Literature* (Dordrecht, Holland: D. Reidel Publishing Company, 1968), p. 242.
68. Meisami, *Persian Historiography*, p. 237.
69. Riedel, 'Searching for the Islamic Episteme', p. iii.
70. Julie Meisami, 'Poetic microcosms: The Persian qasida to the end of the twelfth century', in Stefan Sperl and C. Shackle (eds), *Qasida Poetry in Islamic Asia and Africa* (Leiden: Brill, 1996), p. 139.
71. Stefan Sperl, 'Islamic kingship and Arabic panegyric poetry in the early 9th century', *Journal of Arabic Literature 8* (1977), p. 20.
72. Ibid., p. 20.
73. Ibid., p. 34.

PART TWO

THE ROYAL HOUSEHOLD

CHAPTER FIVE

HAREM CHRISTIANITY: THE BYZANTINE IDENTITY OF SELJUK PRINCES

Rustam Shukurov

Relations between the Byzantines and the Anatolian Turks in the twelfth and the thirteenth centuries have been the subject of extensive scholarly investigation, covering rivalry and alliances in politics, economic exchange and cultural influences. Muslim Anatolia was the usual destination for Byzantine political fugitives, often Byzantine aristocrats who had fallen out of favour with the authorities. Conversely, Seljuk sultans and princes frequently fled from their political enemies to Constantinople. This supports the impression that the Byzantine and Muslim Anatolian spaces represented a sort of continuum wherein the cultural boundaries between the Christian Byzantine and Seljuk Muslim elements were blurred and permeable, such as has been postulated, for instance, by Michel Balivet and the late Keith Hopwood.[1] The persistence of these blurred boundaries appears to be confirmed both by contemporary Byzantine and Muslim sources. In the present chapter, I attempt to reconstruct the nature of the fuzziness and permeability of borders between the

Byzantine and Seljuk cultural spaces. The study focuses on Seljuk identity, and especially on those models of identity that prevailed among the Seljuk ruling house, the Seljuk nobility and, possibly, even more among the middle and lower classes of the Muslim population. My hypothesis, which is to be discussed below, is that the identity of Anatolian Muslims, and especially the Muslim elite, was extremely complex and included Byzantine (Greek and Christian) elements. In other words, under certain conditions a member of the Seljuk elite could act as a Byzantine, and even deem himself to be Greek and Christian. This hypothesis has grown out of my reflections on the role of Greek women in Anatolian Muslim social life. I therefore begin my study with the question of the Greek wives and concubines in the Seljuk harem.

The Greek Lineage of the Seljuks

Let us start with the genealogy of the Seljuks in order to identify which sultans had Greek wives and concubines or Greek mothers. The surviving information is rather scant and only covers the end of the twelfth to the mid-thirteenth century.

1. ʿIzz al-Dīn Qılıch Arslan II (1156–92), the son of the sultan Masʿūd I and, probably, a Christian mother, the granddaughter of the Grand Prince Sviatoslav II (r. 1073–6)[2]
   ∞ N/a., *wife or concubine, Greek* (mother of Ghiyāth al-Dīn Kaykhusraw I)
2. Ghiyāth al-Dīn Kaykhusraw I (1192–6, 1205–11)
   ∞ N/a., *wife, Greek, daughter of Manuel Maurozomos*
3. ʿAlāʾ al-Dīn Kayqubād I (1219–37)
   ∞ Māhparī Khātūn (Khwānd Khātūn), *wife, Greek* (mother of Ghiyāth al-Dīn Kaykhusraw II)
4. Ghiyāth al-Dīn Kaykhusraw II (1237–46)
   ∞ Bardūliya/Προδουλία, *wife, Greek* (mother of ʿIzz al-Dīn Kaykāʾūs II)

5. Ghiyāth al-Dīn Kaykhusraw II
   ∞ N/a., *Greek slave concubine* (mother of Rukn al-Dīn Qılıch Arslan IV)[3]
6. 'Izz al-Dīn Kaykā'ūs II (1245–61)
   ∞ N/a., *wife, Greek* (?)

Number 1: One of the wives or concubines of 'Izz al-Dīn Qılıch Arslan II was Greek. She gave birth to Ghiyāth al-Dīn Kaykhusraw I. The Greek origin of Kaykhusraw's mother is attested by Niketas Choniates.[4] 'Izz al-Dīn Qılıch Arslan II, when dividing his territories among his nine sons, a brother and a nephew, gave Kaykhusraw I Sozopolis (Uluborlu), on the borders of the Byzantine territory, perhaps, as Claude Cahen suggested, because he was the son of a Greek mother. The Greek identity of Kaykhusraw I probably facilitated his contacts with the Byzantines.[5]

Number 2: One of the wives of Ghiyāth al-Dīn Kaykhusraw I was a noble Greek from Byzantium. During his exile in Byzantium, Kaykhusraw I married the daughter of Manuel Mavrozomes. It is unknown, however, if this Byzantine wife bore him any children.[6]

Number 3: One of the wives of 'Alā' al-Dīn Kayqubād I and the mother of Ghiyāth al-Dīn Kaykhusraw II was Greek. Her name was Māhparī Khātūn and very likely she was the daughter of Kīr Fārid (that is, *Kyr* Bardas), the Greek ruler of Kalonoros (Alanya) who handed over the city to the Seljuks in 1221.[7] Around the same year, he married off his daughter to 'Alā' al-Dīn Kayqubād I. The Greek identity of Māhparī Khātūn is attested by 'Azīz Astarābādī, who referred to her as *rūmīya li-aṣl* ('Roman/Byzantine/Greek by origin').[8]

Number 4: The first wife who gave birth to 'Izz al-Dīn Kaykā'ūs II was called by Ibn Bībī *Bardūliya/Pardūliya*, which as I have suggested elsewhere can be read as the Greek personal name Προδουλία (Prodoulia). The Greek identity of Prodoulia is referred to both by Christian and Muslim authors. Bar Hebraeus in the Arabic version of his chronicle says that she was Rūmī/Roman, adding that she was a daughter of a priest (*rūmīya ibnat qissīs*).[9] Her descent from the family of a Greek priest is confirmed by Simon de Saint-Quentin ('hunc genuerat ipse de filia cujusdam sacerdotis Greci').[10] Pachymeres characterises her as 'an extremely good Christian' (χριστιανῇ ἐς τὰ μάλιστα οὔσῃ).[11] Nikephoros Gregoras indirectly confirms her Christian identity, saying that the sultan 'Izz al-Dīn Kaykā'ūs II was 'an offspring of Christian forbears' – χριστιανων τε ὑπῆρχε γονέων υἱός – seemingly implying by γονέων not so much 'parents' but rather generally 'forbears', that is his mother, his paternal grandmother, and possibly his great-grandmother who also were Greek.[12] Indirect references to her Christian and Greek identity are also found in the accounts of Muslim historians of the time: Ibn Bībī, Āqsarā'ī and Baybars al-Manṣūrī all refer to the Christian and Rūmī affiliation of Prodoulia's brothers Kīr Khāya and Kīr Kadīd (← Gk. Kattidios).[13] The life of Prodoulia was full of vicissitudes, which I have recently discussed in detail elsewhere; it is sufficient to mention here that she ended her life in Byzantium, perhaps in Berrhoia, after 1264.[14]

Number 5: The woman who gave birth to the future sultan Rukn al-Dīn Qılıch Arslan IV, and whose name we do not know, was a Greek slave. However, the question of her ethnic origin is debatable. Claude Cahen argues that in fact she was a Turk, and bases upon this assumption a far-reaching hypothesis about the nature of internal strife in the Seljuk sultanate in the 1250s: due to his Greek blood 'Izz al-Dīn symbolised the anti-Mongol party, while Rukn al-Dīn, an offspring of a Turkish mother, became a symbol of the pro-Mongol orientation of a section of the Seljuk elite. Of course, Cahen was too experienced a scholar to formulate such statements explicitly; however, this sort of logic is quite recognisable in his studies.[15]

Cahen bases his assumption upon two pieces of evidence. The first is William of Rubruck's statement that the two sons of the sultan Ghiyāth al-Dīn Kaykhusraw II were born of Christian women while the third one (that is, Rukn al-Dīn) was born of a Turkish woman.[16] The second piece of evidence comes from Ibn Bībī who maintains that Rukn al-Dīn's mother was 'from among the Rūmī slaves' (*az jārīya-yi rūmīya*), where 'Rūmī' presumably was understood by Cahen as 'Anatolian Turk'.

On the other hand, Bar Hebraeus writes that the mother of Ghiyāth al-Dīn's second son Rukn al-Dīn 'also was a Greek woman' (*wa-ummuhu ayḍan rūmīya*) like 'Izz al-Dīn's mother.[17] Consequently, Ibn Bībī's expression *jārīya-yi rūmīya* should be only understood as 'Greek bondwoman' in contrast to the case of Prodoulia, who was a free Greek. The authority of these two best informed and most reliable historians would seem to invalidate Rubruck's statement. Moreover, Simon de Saint-Quentin, who was better informed and more accurate than Rubruck, wrote that Rukn al-Dīn's mother was a daughter of a resident of Konya ('*filia, ut dicitur, cujusdam burgensis Yconii seu pretorii*');[18] Saint-Quentin's evidence does not exclude the possibility of her being Greek. To sum up, Cahen's belief, based upon Rubruck's evidence, seems to be wrong, and it would appear to be the case that Rukn al-Dīn's mother was in fact a Greek slave and concubine of the sultan.[19]

Ghiyāth al-Dīn Kaykhusraw II likewise had as wife a Georgian princess by the name of Tamar, but popularly known as Gurjī Khātūn (i.e. 'the Georgian Lady'). She was the mother of his youngest son 'Alā' al-Dīn Kayqubād II. Tamar was his most beloved wife and bore the honorary title *Malikat al-malikāt*, i.e. 'the Queen of Queens'.[20] Seemingly Ghiyāth al-Dīn Kaykhusraw II, the son of a Greek mother, had a special passion for Christian women.

Number 6: The origin of 'Izz al-Dīn Kaykā'ūs II's wife remains obscure. Byzantine sources mention that during his exile in Constantinople 'Izz al-Dīn Kaykā'ūs II was accompanied by his wife, but there is no mention of her religious or ethnic affiliation.[21] Kirakos of Gandzak reports that 'Izz al-Dīn became 'a son-in-law' of John III Doukas Vatatzes (1222–54) in the year 1249.[22] Cahen assumes that Kirakos' information might well have been true.[23] The early Ottoman tradition relates that 'Izz al-Dīn's wife was Greek and her name was Anna.[24] Neither Kirakos nor Ottoman tradition, however, are fully reliable. If 'Izz al-Dīn's wife was Greek of Byzantine imperial descent, it should have been mentioned by other Byzantine or eastern authors of the time.[25] Since this evidence has no confirmation in other, more reliable sources, the supposed marriage of 'Izz al-Dīn to a daughter from the house of Doukas-Vatatzes seems doubtful. However, taking into account the evidence of Kirakos and the Ottoman tradition, we cannot exclude the possibility that 'Izz al-Dīn's wife was of Greek origin. It is not improbable that her Greek ancestry was refracted in different ways in the prism of Kirakos and the Ottoman tradition.

The Seljuk Harem

Let us place this genealogical information into a broader anthropological context. Naturally, the aforementioned Greek women lived in the royal harem. Ibn Bībī occasionally refers to the harem directly (*mukhaddarāt-i ḥaram*, *ḥaram*, *ḥaram-i humāyūn*),[26] or indirectly with descriptive expressions such as 'the children and womenfolk' (*khawātīn u atfāl*, *atfāl u 'iyāl wa 'awrāt*) and 'the children and women, the mother and the sons' (*atfāl u 'iyāl wa wālida u walad*).[27] In a few instances he even refers to the harem as a source of expensive jewellery which could be extracted to meet urgent state needs: for instance, Mu'izz al-Dīn Qayṣarshāh removed from his harem an expensive headband (*kalla-band*) valued at 50,000 dinars, while 'Alā' al-Dīn Kayqubād took from his harem an exquisite shawl (*dastārcha-yi sarī*) worth 12,000 dinars.[28] Other than this, however, we have little information about the harem in Seljuk sources. We know disappointingly little about its structure, governance and role in the political life of the sultanate. This is mostly due to the fact that sources normally avoid describing private family life; we do not even know the names of the majority of women who are referred to in medieval Muslim historical narratives.

Nonetheless, we may derive some additional retrospective information about the Seljuk harem from the better-documented Ottoman harem in Leslie Peirce's pioneering study, *The Imperial Harem*,[29] which has shaped how Ottomanists have come to view the harem's role in sexual and dynastic politics.[30] Although the study makes no comparisons with the Seljuk harem and its Byzantine equivalent, the nobles' *gynaeceum* (γυναικών, γυναικωνιτικός),[31] both may have had influence on Ottoman practice, as some common features suggest. Apparently, like its Ottoman equivalent, the Seljuk harem was a complicated institution consisting of both female and male members of the sultan's family, which also had its own associates and attendants (*khadam-i ḥaram*). From Ibn Bībī we know that the sultan's mother, sisters, wives and concubines could be present in the royal harem at the same time.[32] The Seljuk harem was thus a household comprising several generations of women in addition to male infants and daughters. The harem also included eunuchs and female servants who performed administrative and household functions. Like the Ottomans, the Seljuks, at least in the thirteenth century, seem to have followed a 'one mother–one son' policy. This meant that a wife or concubine who had given birth to a male child was excluded subsequently from being a sexual partner of the sultan, passing into the group of post-sexual females. Again, as in the Ottoman harem, in Seljuk times it is likely that these post-sexual females, including the sultan's mother and sultan's consorts, had the highest status in the hierarchy of the harem.[33] Just as the sultans in early Ottoman times preferred Christian women, so too does this seem to be true of the Seljuks, as the genealogical table discussed above suggests.[34] Greek women were clearly dominant in the Seljuk harem. Very likely several generations of Greek women normally lived at the same time in the harem: the oldest generation of the sultan's mother and probably even his grandmother, the sultan's wives and slave concubines. In summary, sources directly refer to the Christian affiliation of at least three Greek women: these were first, the anonymous mother of Ghiyāth al-Dīn Kaykhusraw I; second, Māhparī Khātūn, Ghiyāth al-Dīn Kaykhusraw II's mother; and third, Prodoulia, the mother of 'Izz al-Dīn Kaykhusraw II. We can add to these the Georgian wife of Ghiyāth al-Dīn Kaykhusraw II: Tamar, or Gurjī Khātūn.

Contemporary sources likewise indicate that royal women were allowed to practise Christianity freely. In 1243, the Latin emperor Baldwin II (1237–61) in his letter to the French Queen Blanche of Castile mentions his recent negotiations with the Seljuk sultan Ghiyāth al-Dīn Kaykhusraw II who had requested the hand of a princess from Baldwin's family. According to Baldwin II, Kaykhusraw II promised that the Latin princess would enjoy complete freedom in religion, would have a chapel in the palace and be accompanied by priests. The sultan points out that this was common practice at the Seljuk court, as his own Greek mother (i.e. Māhparī Khātūn) observed Christian rites ('lege Christiana Graeca') during the lifetime of his father.[35] The Latin princess would have been the fourth Christian wife of the sultan, but the planned union never took place.

Ghiyāth al-Dīn Kaykhusraw II likewise promised the Georgian queen Rusudan that her daughter Tamar would be allowed to keep her Christian religion on their marriage in 1238. The Georgian princess was accompanied by senior Christian ecclesiastics and attendants. [36] Adopting Islam later in her life did not prevent Tamar from acting as patron of a church in Beliserama, Cappadocia, in the 1280s, long after the death of the sultan, thus maintaining her links with his subjects in the Christian community.[37]

We do not know much about the Christian servants of Greek wives. A certain Fakhr al-Dīn Sīwāstūs was a slave of Māhparī (*ghulām-i wālida-yi sulṭān Ghiyāth al-Dīn*) who, judging by his second name, was Greek (< σεβαστός).[38] In 1240s he played a prominent role as a supporter of Rukn al-Dīn Qılıch Arslan IV.[39] One more example: one of the associates of Gurjī Khātūn in the 1280s was a certain Basileios Giagoupes, who was depicted together with Gurjī Khātūn on a fresco in the Church of St George in Beliserama, Cappadocia.[40] It is perhaps appropriate to adduce a Golden Horde parallel, although Golden Horde practices concerning women differed considerably from the Anatolian ones. The Byzantine wife of Khān Özbeg (1313–41), who was known in the Golden Horde under the name Bayalūn (بيلون), was most likely Maria, the illegitimate daughter of the emperor Andronikos II. In the early 1300s she was married to Tuqtay (1291–1312); after the latter's death she became the wife of his nephew Özbeg Khan.[41] Ibn Baṭṭūta gives a detailed description of her retinue, in which a prominent place was occupied by the Greeks: Greek female slaves along with Turkish and Nubian (i.e. African?) ones, in total a hundred (*mi'at jārīya rūmīyāt wa turkīyāt wa nūbīyāt*) and Greek pages (*al-rūmīyīn al-fityān*), Greek chamberlains (*al-ḥujjāb min rijāl al-Rūm*), 200 Greek soldiers of the escort, headed by a certain Michael Lūlū the Greek, as well as her Greek steward Sārūja (ساروجة الرومى).[42] Thus a Greek woman in the harem could have had many of her compatriots among her attendants, both women and men of different statuses ranging from slave to administrator.

Judging by these cases, one can suggest that the presence of a church or a chapel, icons, priests and Christian attendants would have been normal practice in the Seljuk harem. In other words, the harem possessed the sort of Christian religious and cultural infrastructure which made the functioning and continuation of a Christian inner life possible. V. Mecit Tekinalp has recently argued that the vanished church Eflatun Mescit in the Konya Citadel (St Amphilochios) and the church in the Seljuk palace of Alanya were probably kept by the sultans for the use of their Christian spouses as well as other Christian associates and servants of the Seljuk court. Tekinalp shows that the church in Alanya was repaired, or even built, at the time when 'Alā' al-Dīn Kayqubād I was constructing his palace. The interior of the church of Alanya has no signs of a *miḥrāb*, showing that it was never converted into a mosque. With regard to the Eflatun Mescit in Konya,[43] Tekinalp argues convincingly that the Eflatun church was converted into a mosque at a much later date, somewhere between 1466 and 1476.[44] In addition, I suggest that that the castle churches in İspir and Bayburt, which being Trapezuntine in type may be dated no earlier than the thirteenth century, were likewise built to accommodate the local Muslim rulers' predominantly Christian harem.[45] It is possible that the situation at the early Ottoman imperial harem until the second half of the fourteenth century was similar. Indeed, the first Ottoman rulers, from Osman (c.1299–1320) to Bayezid I (1389–1404) had Christian wives and concubines, while one of them, Theodora, daughter of John VI Kantakouzenos, even encouraged the local Christian converts to Islam to return to their former faith, thus manifesting her Christian identity.[46]

These royal women's continued adherence to the Christian faith, and the presence of priests and Christian attendants in their entourage, was not unique to Anatolia and neighbouring lands. For instance, when Maria, the illegitimate daughter of Michael VIII Palaiologos became the wife of Abaqa Khan in 1265, she kept her Christian religion at the Mongol court. She arrived at court in the company of

Theodosios Prinkips, the abbot of the Pantocrator monastery, who as the bride's escort, was entrusted with her personal wealth and a portable church in the form of a tent made of expensive textiles. Upon the death of Abaqa in 1282, she returned to Byzantium and became a nun, taking the name Melane.[47] Numerous princesses of the Grand Komnenoi of Trebizond married neighbouring Muslim amirs and sultans and very likely continued to confess Christianity. The most detailed account of the life of a Trapezuntine princess in a Muslim environment is that concerning Theodora Komnene (of the Grand Komnenoi), the wife of the Aqquyunlu sultan Uzun Ḥasan. According to Italian travellers in Persia, Theodora kept her Christian religion and had a chapel at the court with Orthodox priests and Greek maidens from the noble Trapezuntine families.[48] As we can see, the preservation of Christian identity by Greek brides in non-Christian environments was normal practice in the vast region comprising Anatolia and Western Iran.[49]

The Evidence of Byzantine Canon Law

Here I wish to make a brief digression in order to place the problem of mixed Muslim and Christian marriages in Seljuk Anatolia in a broader historical context. In the days of the Patriarch of Constantinople Loukas Chrysoberges, between 1157 and 1170, some 'Hagarenes' (that is, Anatolian Turks) appeared in the Holy Synod and, when they were required to be baptised, said that Orthodox priests in their homeland had already administered this rite to them. The synod's investigation revealed that it was the custom in Anatolia for all the Muslim infants to accept baptism because their parents deemed that otherwise their children would be possessed by demons and stink like dogs (κατὰ κύνας ὄζειν; see also further below). The synod decreed that the baptism of the Hagerenes in this case was a medicine or charm rather than a spiritual purifier. Therefore, their baptism was not accepted as valid. Moreover, some of these Hagarenes claimed that they had Orthodox mothers (μητέρας … ἔχειν ὀρθοδόξους) who had had them baptised by Orthodox priests. By 'Orthodox mothers', Anatolian Greek women who had married local Muslims are clearly meant. Nonetheless, the synod decided that these half-Greek 'Hagarenes' should be baptised anew because the Church had no solid evidence substantiated by witnesses that the baptism had actually taken place and that the correct procedure had been followed.[50]

The issue of the baptised Hagarenes remained current throughout the twelfth to fourteenth centuries, and was discussed again by two famous Orthodox canonists: by Theodore Balsamon at the end of the twelfth century, and by Matthew Blastares in the fourteenth century. If Balsamon simply repeats the decisions of the Patriarch Loukas Chrysoberges,[51] Blastares adds some new details concerning the baptism of the Hagarenes. He maintains that many of Hagarenes did not circumcise their children before the Christian priests baptised them.[52] Thus Muslim infants were baptised first, and only then were they circumcised.

Western authors give additional details about mixed marriages and the children born into such unions. The Latin historians of the Crusades noted in Anatolia a specific group of the Turkopouli (that is, 'the children of the Turks') who were born of a Greek mother and a Turkish father.[53] For the beginning of the fourteenth century, the Catalan soldier and chronicler Ramon Muntaner reports that the Turks of western Anatolia married girls from noble Greek families. It is especially interesting that the male children of these mixed marriages 'became Turks and were circumcised', while for female children the choice of religion was free. The same difference between the religious affiliation of boys and girls was reported by Ludolf von Suchen in the middle of the fourteenth century. Von Suchen maintains that when the Turks married Christian women, the boys of the mixed marriages followed the Muslim religion of their fathers while the girls maintained the Christian faith of their mothers.[54] However, as we have seen in Byzantine canonical texts, boys also could be baptised by their mothers.

These reports confirm that, firstly, mixed marriages between Muslims and Greek women were common throughout the centuries, and, secondly, that the children of both Muslim and mixed marriages were baptised according to Orthodox Greek rites. The popularity of mixed marriages in Muslim lands has been very clearly demonstrated by a passage from the Byzantine historian of the fifteenth century, Doukas, who, with considerable arrogance, made the following observance about the Ottoman Turks:

> The people of this shameless and savage nation, moreover, do the following: if they seize a Greek woman or an Italian woman or a woman of another nation or a captive or a deserter, they embrace her as an Aphrodite or Semele, but a woman of their own nation or of their own tongue they loathe as though she were a bear or a hyena.[55]

The predominance of Greek women at the Seljuk harem thus seems to have been merely a royal variation of a common practice in Muslim Anatolia. Greek women were valued as the most prestigious marriage partners among all strata of Muslim society. It was Greek women who guided their Muslim husbands and masters into the refined Byzantine way of life and the world of Byzantine luxury, introducing among other things new cuisines and ways of structuring the household. Although the information on Seljuk marriage policy in the eleventh to twelfth century is scarce, it seems highly probably that the Seljuk harem was modelled along similar lines as other strata of Muslim Anatolian society, with a preference of marriage to Greek women who in turn acted as mediators to the old world of the 'empire of the Romans'.

The Christian Faith

Greek blood flowed in the veins of the Seljuk sultans whose mothers and grandmothers were Greek women, often of noble descent. These blood ties of the sultans with Greeks are extremely important for an understanding of the cultural environment at the Seljuk court. One cannot underestimate the impact of several generations of Greek women at the harem. Their presence inevitably affected the cultural experience of the Seljuk princes and princesses, including even those who were born to Muslim wives and concubines but who lived in the harem along with its Greek members. Such influence was unavoidable since Christian women continued to confess Christianity, praying in the harem churches and surrounded by Christian attendants, servants and priests. In other words, Christian ladies had all the necessary prerequisites to replicate Christian culture – though mostly only within the confines of their small harem world, the intimate world of women and children. Significantly, Christianity and Byzantine culture (language and customs) existed in the harem not as a relic of the former life of these women, but as a living system which contributed to shaping the future.

Given that male infants were raised by their mothers in the harem until the age of ten or eleven,[56] we may suggest that in the harem future sultans became familiar with Byzantine culture and customs as well as basic concepts of the Christian faith and rites. In one case, we know for certain that infant Seljuk princes were baptised in Konya. I refer to the scandal concerning the Christian identity of the sultan ʻIzz al-Dīn Kaykāʼūs II and his male children (who can be identified as Ghiyāth al-Dīn Masʻūd, Rukn al-Dīn Gayūmarth and Constantine Melikes, or Malik Constantine and Sabbas as the latter two were known in Byzantium).[57] According to the testimony of the Pisidian metropolitan Makarios, ʻIzz al-Dīn Kaykāʼūs II and his sons were baptised long before the escape of the sultan and his family to Constantinople in 1261.[58] Indeed, it seems that the sultan's sons had been baptised upon birth. During the stay of the sultan ʻIzz al-Dīn and his family in Constantinople, the Patriarch of Constantinople, Arsenios, relying upon Makarios' testimony, treated them as good Christians, allowing them to attend religious services.[59] After ʻIzz al-Dīn Kaykāʼūs II's escape from Byzantium to the Golden Horde, the Christian affiliation of the sultan was called into question and the patriarch Arsenios was accused of canonically inadmissible conduct with the infidels. When Kaykāʼūs II learned of the trial against the patriarch, he contacted Constantinople from the Crimea, and, somewhat surprisingly, claimed that he was a true Christian and had the necessary evidence to prove it.[60]

It is worth noting in connection with this interesting case that if the royal infants had been baptised in the proper way (as the metropolitan Makarios insisted), they must have borne Christian baptismal names along with their Muslim ones. Unfortunately we do not know the Christian names of 'Izz al-Dīn Kaykā'ūs II or of his sons, Ghiyāth al-Dīn Mas'ūd II and Rukn al-Dīn Gayūmarth. However, thanks to Byzantine sources, we know that another son of 'Izz al-Dīn was probably baptised as Constantine – a rather lofty imperial-sounding name – although we have no information about his official Muslim name.[61]

Besides 'Izz al-Dīn Kay-Kā'ūs II and his sons, 'Izz al-Dīn's grandfather, Ghiyāth al-Dīn Kaykhusraw I, was Christian. Ghiyāth al-Dīn Kaykhusraw I, having been expelled from the sultanate by his brother Rukn al-Dīn Sulaymān II (r. 1196–1204), lived in Constantinople, apart from a brief interval, from 1197 to 1203. He is said to have been baptised there and adopted by the emperor, Alexios III Angelos (1195–1203), meaning that the emperor became the sultan's godfather. As Ruth Macrides suggests, it is not impossible that he was even adopted by the emperor.[62] Kaykhusraw I was on friendly terms with Theodore Laskaris, the future founder of the Nicaean empire. He addressed Laskaris' wife Anna as 'sister'. In fact, Anna was the daughter of Alexios III Angelos, and, naturally, the sultan as the spiritual son of her father (or adoptive son) considered Anna as his sister.[63] A distorted echo of these relationships can be found in the Seljuk tradition according to which the mother of Kaykhusraw I was 'the sister of the wife of *Kālūyān-takfūr*' (*az khwāhar-i zan-i Kālūyān-takfūr*). Undoubtedly, by *Kālūyān-takfūr* Alexios III is meant.[64] This assertion is not true, formally speaking, but it does accurately reflect the family relationships between the sultan and the emperor. It is plausible that he was baptised by his mother, because Niketas Choniates qualifies him as a 'Christian on his mother's side' (μητρόθεν Χριστιανόν).[65] In any case, Ghiyāth al-Dīn Kaykhusraw I was rebaptised (or baptised?) in Constantinople by the emperor Alexios III, as I have already mentioned.

Some additional information about the baptisms of the princes of the Anatolian ruling houses can be found in later sources. For instance, the baptism of the Muslim noble infants is mentioned by Bertrandon de la Broquière who visited Muslim Anatolia in 1432. He relates that Ramazan (Ramaḍān), a Turkmen chieftain of south-east

Anatolia, was baptised by his Greek mother in order to purify him from an unpleasant smell.[66] When Bertrandon de la Broquière visited Konya, he heard a similar story about the son of Ibrāhīm Beg of Karaman, whose Greek mother likewise had him baptised according to the Greek rite to rid him of a bad odour.[67] Such customs also were reported by later authors of the sixteenth and seventeenth centuries (such as Busbecq and Casalius).[68] Anatolian Christians believed that baptism of children purified them from a 'bad smell' similar to that of the 'smell of dog,' as Byzantine canons explain (see above). This, according to F.W. Hasluck, was a way for local Christians (presumably Greeks and Armenians) to explain the strict Muslim rules of ritual purity such as ablution before prayer.[69]

Given the popularity of baptism among Anatolian Muslims, we can only speculate which other Seljuk sultans and princes may have been baptised by their mothers. I would not be surprised if a majority of the Seljuk rulers, and especially those who had Christian mothers, experienced baptism. This Christian affiliation of the sultans is confirmed by Seljuk policy toward local Christians. According to a late thirteenth-century Greek author, Christian Greeks were still numerous in Muslim Anatolia and freely performed their rites.[70] The Orthodox, Armenian and Monophysite churches functioned in the sultanate without obstacle or hindrance. Judging by the documents of the Constantinople patriarchate, church authorities in Constantinople continued to administer the Anatolian Orthodox bishoprics and to resolve disputes among the Orthodox community. The personal attitude and behaviour of the sultans towards the local Christians was likewise quite favourable, as is witnessed by 'Izz al-Dīn Kaykā'ūs II's warm relations with abbot Mar Dionysios, whose monastery of Bar Sawma near Malatya the sultan visited in 1259.[71] There are multiple similar examples. Seljuk policy towards the Christian churches in Anatolia deserves futher study.

The Greek Language

Another important consequence of the harem experience of the Seljuk princes was linguistic. The role of the Greek language in the life of the Muslim states of Anatolia, including the Seljuk sultanate, has not been properly investigated. Information about the Greek language at the Seljuk court, and about the level of its knowledge by the elite, is very scanty; however, we have some evidence indicating that Greek was far from alien to them. As Cahen has noted, Seljuk royal refugees usually fled to Byzantium and rarely to the Muslim countries of the region.[72] Indeed, starting at the end of the eleventh century, the usual destination of a refugee Seljuk sovereign or nobleman was Byzantium. Thus we may pose the question as to which language these noble refugees used to communicate with the Byzantine Greeks. Neither Byzantine nor Seljuk sources, in their extensive accounts of the life of the refugee sultans in Constantinople, mention the use of interpreters between the emperor and the sultan. This is probably because the refugee sultans spoke Greek. In two instances, Ibn Bībī implies that the sultan Ghiyāth al-Dīn Kaykhusraw I spoke Greek. The first case is the visit of the *ḥājib* Zakariyā (who probably was Greek ← Ζαχαρίας) to the court of Manuel Mavrozomes in 1204 or 1205. When Zakariyā appeared before Mavrozomes and the sultan, the latter recognised him and, offering apologies to Mavrozomes, 'immediately switched to Persian' (lest Mavrozomes should understand him) and told his servants to take care of Zakariyā.[73] Which language did the sultan speak with Mavrozomes before switching to Persian? Obviously, it must have been Greek. Thus we may derive some important conclusions from this story. Firstly, at that time the Persian language, along with its official and cultural status in the Seljuk society, was used as the primary language of communication between the sultan and his servants. Secondly, the sultan communicated with his Greek hosts in Greek, using Persian only to ensure that they did not understand what he said to his servants.

The second case deals with the battle by Antioch-on-the-Maeander between the forces of Ghiyāth al-Dīn Kaykhusraw I and Theodore Laskaris in 1211. When the two rulers met on the battlefield, Kaykhusraw I attracted the attention of the emperor by exclaiming: !كوندوس (*ay kūndūs!*). Ibn Bībī translated كوندوس as 'bald, hairless' (يعنى اى كل 'that is "hey, bald"').[74] However, it seems that Ibn Bībī misunderstood the word *kūndūs* (كوندوس) which, in fact, was an equivalent of the Greek κονδός (variants: κόνδος, κοντός): 'short, short man.'[75] The definition κονδός, 'short', fits well in the context of the narrative: Kaykhusraw I was a very tall and large man while Theodore, in fact, was short.[76] The sultan thus addressed the emperor in a somewhat pejorative and humiliating way as he challenged his enemy to battle. Here the Persian historian made the sultan speak Greek.

References to the knowledge of Greek by the children of mixed marriages can be found in contemporary sources. Thus, Anna Comnena, the Byzantine princess and writer of the first half of the twelfth century, asserts more than once that such children spoke Greek and, being bilingual, sometimes acted like translators; she calls them μιξοβάρβαροι ἑλληνίζοντες, that is 'Greek-speaking half-barbarians'.[77] The Turks of Aydın spoke Greek during the negotiations with John Kantakouzenos in 1331;[78] in all probability, the men negotiating with the Greeks were the offspring of mixed Turkish and Greek marriages. Finally, as an anonymous Italian traveller at the beginning of the fifteenth century reports, the two daughters of Theodora Komnene by Uzun Ḥasan were bilingual, speaking both the local language (Persian and Turkic?) and Pontic Greek like their mother.[79] This evidence implies that the children of the mixed marriages were as a rule bilingual.

I am inclined to suggest that the majority of the members of the Seljuk ruling house spoke Greek to some extent, especially those whose mothers were Greek. If so, the flight of the Seljuk sultans to Constantinople was understandable: there they found themselves in a comfortable cultural environment which was familiar to them from their childhood experience in the harem. In Constantinople the Seljuk refugees found themselves in their childhood world, dominated by the Christian faith and the Greek language and customs.

The sources provide scant information about the role of the spoken Greek language in the sultan's court as well as among the nobility and intellectual elite of the sultanate. Yet we have valuable evidence that the Greek language was known by the Seljuk nobles. Ibn Bībī reports that the above-mentioned *ḥājib* Zakariyā/Zacharias was fluent in the five languages of Anatolia,[80] which probably were Greek,

Persian, Turkish, Armenian and Arabic. As a Persian author, Ibn Bībī is unusual in his inclusion of Greek words in his text, words which may have entered the Anatolian Persian language of the time. In his coverage of the war between the Seljuks and the Empire of Trebizond in 1214, Ibn Bībī informs us that the draft copy of the peace treaty between ʿIzz al-Dīn I and the Grand Komnenos Alexios I was compiled by the sultan's *nūṭārān* (نوطاران sing. نوطار ← νοτάριος), that is the Greek secretaries of the chancery.[81] The official use of the Greek language by the Seljuk chancery is well known. A Greek epistle from 1216 of ʿIzz al-Dīn Kaykāʾūs I to the Cypriot king Hugh I Lusignan (1205–18) is an authentic product of the Greek secretaries.[82] The Greek production of the Muslim Anatolian chanceries also can be seen in the Greek epigraphy in early Turkmen coinage and Seljuk official inscriptions in Greek on buildings, such as that of 1215 on the tower of Sinop Citadel.[83] This is just one example of how the Greek language was used in symbolic statements of Muslim political power.

Furthermore, Ibn Bībī uses the Greek term *fāsiliyūs* (فاسليوس ← βασιλεύς) for the Byzantine emperor[84] and twice the Greek *qadirghahā* (قدرغها, sing. قدرغه ← κάτεργον) for a battleship.[85] Moreover, the fifteenth-century Turkish translation of Ibn Bībī by Yazıcızade ʿAlī contains a long Greek expression rendered into Arabic script: ايستم بستم متى خر ستو متى بنايا (*īstim bistim matā khiristū matā banāyā*), which in Greek script is: εἰς τὴν πίστιν, μὰ τὸ Χριστὸ, μὰ τὴ Παναγιά! ('[I swear] by [my] faith, by Christ, by the Virgin!').[86] This is the oath the emperor Alexios III Angelos made to Kaykhusraw I before the well-known duel between the sultan and a Frankish knight in Constantinople some time in 1203. I am inclined to support Dmitri Korobeinikov's suggestion that this Greek exclamation most likely was taken by Yazıcızade ʿAlī from a copy of Ibn Bībī's work which has not survived to the present day.[87]

Among Anatolian intellectuals, Ibn Bībī was not unique in his interest in Greek vocabulary. Jalāl al-Dīn Rūmī and his son Sulṭān Walad, who both married Greek women, wrote quite extensive verses of colloquial Greek in the Arabic script which have been deciphered by Burguière and Mantran.[88] Versifying in Greek was thus not a bizarre caprice of two men of genius but, when placed in its context, rather indicates the interest of the Muslim elite in the Greek language and the latter's prevalence in Seljuk Anatolia.

Conclusion: Anatolian Seljuk Sultans and Dual Identity

I have outlined in this study several issues requiring further in-depth elaboration on the basis of available sources from both the eastern and western cultural spaces. My study does not claim to resolve all the questions raised, but rather seeks to point out possible new perspectives for future research. These questions include the systematic study of the history of the Seljuk harem and the place of women in Seljuk society, the role of the Greek ethnic element and the Greek language in Muslim Anatolia, and the functioning of Orthodox Christianity in the Anatolian Muslim lands. Nevertheless, some preliminary conclusions may be drawn. Christianity and the Greek language were indispensable parts of the cultural and religious environment of Muslim Anatolia. Moreover, Christianity and the Greek language were not exterior to local Muslim culture but rather formed some of its constituent elements. This profound Hellenisation was a characteristic feature of Seljuk Anatolian culture, which makes it unlike other Muslim societies of the Near East.

I suggest that at least three Anatolian Seljuk sultans – Ghiyāth al-Dīn Kaykhusraw I, his grandson ʿIzz al-Dīn Kaykāʾūs II and the latter's son Masʿūd II – had dual Christian and Muslim identity, an identity which was further complicated by dual Turkic/Persian and Greek ethnic identity. It is very much possible that ʿAlā al-Dīn Kayqubād I and ʿIzz al-Din Kaykāʾūs I, who spent much time with their father Ghiyāth al-Dīn Kaykhusraw I in Byzantium, had the same type of dual identity. Furthermore, it seems likely that Ghiyāth al-Dīn Kaykhusraw II, the son of ʿAlā al-Dīn Kayqubād I and a Greek wife, and himself another sultan who expressed great interest in Greek women, bore a dual confessional and ethnic identity. The same may be said of Kaykhusraw II's son Rukn al-Dīn Qılıch Arslan

IV, as well as 'Alā' al-Dīn Kayqubād II whose identity included Turkish/Persian Muslim and Christian Georgian elements.

Claude Cahen repeatedly emphasised the religious tolerance of the Anatolian Seljuks, exceptional for the Muslim world.[89] I would prefer to interpret the place of Christianity and the Greek language in the Seljuk identity in a different way. I will adduce one more parallel to the Seljuk situation. A symptomatic description of a similar phenomenon belongs to the continuator of Bar Hebraeus. He describes the character of Baidu, the Mongol Khan of Iran who ruled for few months only in 1295. Baidu was close to the Byzantine princess Maria, the wife of Abaqa, and due to her he was favourably disposed towards Christians and even referred to himself as Christian. However, at some point he adopted Islam. The continuator of Bar Hebraeus describes the identity of Baidu thus: 'To the Christians he used to say, "I am a Christian", and he hung a cross on his neck. To the Muslims he showed that he was a Muslim, but he was never able to learn the ablutions and the fasts.'[90] The Syriac author gives an excellent example of a specific kind of identity, which I would call *dual identity*.

Dual identity supposes that one of the two identities is in active mode while the other is in deferred mode. When in a Christian environment, such persons would identify themselves as Christian, deferring their Muslim identity. They would, however, embrace their Muslim identity when in a Muslim space, in turn deferring their Christian self for the time being. Such a paradigm has little to do with religious and cultural tolerance in the proper sense because tolerance means an ability to tolerate others, while the sultans bore both religions and both cultures in their selves. Of course, such a paradigm is completely different from religious or cultural syncretism, which means the combining of the elements of differing worlds. Differing beliefs, languages and modes of life seemingly were present unmixed in the mentality of such persons. Depending on the circumstances, one of the two parts of their dual self was activated while the other receded into deferred status.

Notes

1. See, for instance, Michel Balivet, *Romanie byzantine et pays de Rûm turc: Histoire d'un espace d'imbrication gréco-turque* (Istanbul: Isis, 1994); Keith Hopwood, 'Nomads or bandits? The pastoralist/sedentarist interface in Anatolia', in A. Bryer and M. Ursinus (eds), 'Manzikert to Lepanto. The Byzantine World and the Turks 1071–1571', *Byzantinische Forschungen* 16 (1991), pp. 179–94; Keith Hopwood, 'Peoples, territories, and states: The formation of the Begliks of Pre-Ottoman Turkey', in C.E. Farah (ed.), *Decision Making and Change in the Ottoman Empire* (Kirksville, Mo.: Truman State University Press, 1993), pp. 129–38.
2. Arnoldi, Chronica Slavorum, ed. G.H. Pertz (Hannoverae: Impensis bibliopolii Hahniani, 1868), p. 24: 'Quedam nobilis matrona de terra Theutonicorum nupsit regi Ruthenorum, qui genuit ex ea filiam, cuius filia devenit in terram nostram, de qua ego descendi.'
3. Abū 'l-Faraj, *Ta'rīkh mukhtaṣar al-duwal* (Beirut: Al-Hazmiyya, 1994), p. 447.
4. Nicetas Choniates, *Historia*, ed. J.A. van Dieten (Berlin and New York: De Gruyter, 1975), i, p. 521, l. 89.
5. Claude Cahen, 'Kaykhusraw', *EI*^{2}, iv, p. 816; Claude Cahen, *La Turquie pré-ottomane* (Istanbul: Institut Français des Etudes Anatoliennes, 1988), p. 60.
6. Ibn Bībī, *al-Awāmir al-'alā'īya fī 'l-umūr al-'alā'īya*, facsimile edition prepared by Adnan Sadık Erzi as İbn-i Bībī, *El-Evāmirü'l-Alā'iyye fi'l-umūri'l-Alā'iyye* (Ankara: Türk Tarih Kurumu, 1956), p. 305; H.W. Duda, *Die Seltschukengeschichte des Ibn Bibi* (Copenhagen: Munksgaard, 1959), pp. 330–1 note 83; Osman Turan, *Selçuklular Zamanında Türkiye: Siyasi Tarih Alp Arslan'dan Osman Gazi'ye (1071–1318)* (Istanbul: Turan Neşriyat Yurdu, 1971), p. 282; Osman Turan, 'Les souverains seldjoukides et leurs sujets non-musulmans', *Studia Islamica* 1 (1953), p. 80; K. Varzos, Ἡ γενεαλογία τῶν Κομνηνῶν (Thessaloníki: Κέντρον Βυζαντινών Ερευνών, 1984), i, p. 475.

7. Cahen, *La Turquie pré-ottomane*, pp. 74, 170 (on the Greek origin of Kīr Fārid); Turan, *Selçuklular*, pp. 336–7, 403–4; V.M. Tekinalp, 'Palace churches of the Anatolian Seljuks: tolerance or necessity?', *Byzantine and Modern Greek Studies* 33, no. 2 (2009), p. 161; Ibn Bībī, *al-Awāmir al-'alā'īya*, p. 247; *Histoire des Seldjoucides d'Asie Mineure d'après l'abrégé du Seldjouknameh d'Ibn-Bibi*, ed. M.Th. Houtsma (Leiden: E.J. Brill, 1902; Recueil de textes relatifs à l'histoire des Seldjoucides 4), p. 102. Vincent de Beauvais referred to her (very likely mistakenly) as a concubine, see *A History of the Crusades,* ed. K.M. Setton, ii: R. Wolff and H. Hazard (eds), *The Later Crusades. 1189–1311* (Madison, Wis., Milwaukee, Wis. and London: The University of Wisconsin Press, 1969), p. 692 note 12.
8. 'Azīz b. Ardashīr Astarābādī, *Bazm u razm*, ed. M.F. Köprülü-zade (Istanbul: Evkaf Matbaası, 1928), p. 45. In 1243, during the war with the Mongols, Māhparī Khātūn, along with Kaykhusraw II's wife and daughter, took asylum in the kingdom of Cilician Armenia. The sultan sent his mother and his wife to Kayseri, and after the battle at Kösedağ and the Mongol advance to Kayseri the women fled to Sis (Kozan) in Cilician Armenia, probably making for Aleppo. However, when the news about the Seljuk defeat at Kösedağ reached Cilician Armenia, the Armenians detained the women and handed them over to the Mongols. According to Kirakos of Gandzak and Smbat the Constable, King Het'um I was ordered by the Mongol commander Baiju to send the sultan's mother, wife and daughter; the king did this against his will out of fear of the Mongols. Baiju was extremely happy at seizing the sultan's harem and richly rewarded the Armenian embassy (Ibn Bībī, *al-Awāmir al-'alā'īya*, pp. 528, 536). Ibn Bībī only mentions the sultan's mother and daughter (p. 536):
والده و کریمه سلطان را باز داشتند و نگذاشتند که ببلاد اسلام گذرند آخر الامر بمغل سپردند
Translation: '[the Armenians] detained the sultan's mother and daughter and prevented them from passing to the Muslim lands, and finally handed them over to the Mongols.' On the presence

of the sultan's wife among the captured women, see Kirakos Gandzaketsi, *Istoriia Armenii*, trans. L.A. Khanlarian (Moscow: Nauka, 1976) p. 178. Smbat Sparapet refers to the sultan's mother and sister: A. Galstian, *Armianskie istochniki o mongolakh: izvlecheniya iz rukopiesi XIII-XIV vv.* (Moscow: Nauka, 1962), p. 47. See also Cahen, *La Turquie pré-ottomane*, p. 230. It seems that by 1254 Māhparī Khātūn had already come back to Anatolia from Mongol captivity (she is mentioned in connection with the embassy of 'Alā' al-Dīn Kayqubād II in 1254), see Ibn Bībī, *al-Awāmir al-'alā'īya*, pp. 607–8; Ibn Bībī, *Histoire des Seljoucides*, ed. Houtsma, p. 277; Duda, *Seltschukengeschichte*, p. 264. Cf. Wolff and Hazard (eds), *The Later Crusades, 1189–1311*, p. 692. On Māhparī, and especially her building activity, see Antony Eastmond, 'Gender and patronage between Christianity and Islam in the thirteenth century', in Ayla Ödekan, Engin Akyürek and Nevra Necipoğlu (eds), *First International Sevgi Gönül Byzantine Studies Symposium* (Istanbul: Vehbi Koç Vakfı, 2010), pp. 78–88.

9. Abū 'l-Faraj, *Mukhtaṣar*, p. 447.
10. Simon de Saint-Quentin, *Histoire des Tartares*, ed. J. Richard (Paris: Paul Geuthner, 1965), XXXII. 26, p. 82.
11. Georges Pachymérès, *Relations Historiques*, ed. A. Failler (Paris: Belles Lettres, 1984–2000, 5 vols) II.24, vol. i, p. 183, l. 23. Cf. Nicephori Gregorae, *Byzantina historia*, ed. L. Schopen and I. Bekker (Bonn: Impensis B. Weberi, 1829–55, 3 vols), IV.4, vol. i, p. 94, ll. 13–4, who refers to the Christian ancestry of the sultan 'Izz al-Dīn Kaykhusraw II implying the Christian and Byzantine identity of his mother Προδουλία.
12. Gregoras, *Byzantina historia*, IV.4, vol. i, p. 94, ll. 13–4.
13. Ibn Bībī, *al-Awāmir al-'alā'īya*, pp. 609, 638; Āqsarā'ī, *Musāmarat al-akhbār* edited by Osman Turan as Kerimüddin Mahmud oğlu Aksaraylı, *Müsameret ul-ahbar. Moğollar zamanında Turkiye selçuklular tarihi* (Ankara: Türk Tarih Kurumu, 1944), pp. 40, 82; Baybars al-Manṣūrī al-Dawādār, *Zubdat al-fikra fi ta'rīkh al-hijra. History of the Early Mamluk Period*, ed. D.S Richards (Beirut and Berlin: Das Arabische Buch, 1998), p. 73.

14. For further details, see my Russian-language article: R.M. Shukurov, 'Semeistvo 'Izz al-Dina Kai-Kavusa II v Vizantii', *Vizantiiskii Vremennik* 67 (2008), pp. 90–6.
15. Cahen, *La Turquie pré-ottomane*, pp. 230, 239ff; Claude Cahen, 'Kaykā'ūs', *EI*², iv, pp. 813–4.
16. M. Komroff (ed.), *Contemporaries of Marco Polo, consisting of the travel records to the eastern parts of the world of William of Rubruck (1253–1255); the journey of John of Pian de Carpini (1245–1247); the journal of Friar Odoric (1318–1330) & the oriental travels of Rabbi Benjamin of Tudela (1160–1173)* (New York: Liveright Publishing Corp., 1928), p. 208.
17. Abū 'l-Faraj, *Mukhtaṣar*, p. 447.
18. Simon de Saint-Quentin, *Histoire*, XXXII. 26, p. 82. Here Saint-Quentin speaks of «Azadinus», that is, 'Izz al-Dīn. However here, as well as through the entire Chapter 26 and onwards, he confuses the names of the two brothers 'Izz al-Dīn and Rukn al-Dīn (Raconadius), ascribing the deeds of one to the other, and in particular ascribing to Rukn al-Dīn primogeniture and an origin from the daughter of a Greek priest.
19. Osman Turan is of the same opinion, i.e. that Rukn al-Dīn's mother was a Greek slave: Turan, *Selçuklular Zamanında Türkiye*, p. 458. It is worth noting that in the Persian language of the time, expressions such as *jārīya-yi rūmī* and *kanīz-i rūmī* were an idiom referring to a woman with white skin and blonde hair, while *rūmī* generally referred to something or someone very white. In contrast, the expression *kanīz-i zangī* meant 'black bondwomen from Africa' while *zangī* denoted the colour black in general. Note by way of illustration the following *bayt* in 'Azīz Astarabādī's *Bazm u razm*:
    یا رومی روم باش یا زنگی زنگ
    ون بوقلمون مباش رنگ اندر رنگ
20. Aflākī, *Manāqib al-'ārifīn*, ed. Tahsin Yazıcı as Şams al-Dīn Aḥmad al-Aflākī al-'Ārifī, *Manāḳib al-'Ārifīn* (Ankara: Türk Tarih Kurumu, 1959–61), i, p. 92 (referred to as the sultan's wife), p. 263 (referred to as 'the Queen of Queens').

21. Pachymérès, *Rélations historiques*, II.24 (vol. i, p. 183, l. 24), III.25 (vol. i, 1, pp. 303, ll. 16–17, 313, l. 14); Gregoras, *Byzantina historia*, IV, 6, vol. i, p. 101. Two of the three passages of Pachymeres refer to several wives in the sultan's harem, but it seems that in fact 'Izz al-Dīn arrived in Constantinople with only one spouse. Cf. Ibn Bībī's references to the family of the sultan: Ibn Bībī, *al-Awāmir al-'alā'īya*, pp. 623, 625, 637 (*L'histoire des Seldjoucides*, ed. Houtsma, vol. iv, pp. 287, 289). For more details, see Shukurov, 'Semeistvo 'Izz al-Dina', pp. 106, 107.
22. Kirakos Ganzaketsi, *Istoriia Armenii* (Moscow: Nauka, 1976), p. 196. In fact Kirakos made some mistakes, which can, however, be easily corrected on the basis of the general logic of his account. He argues that 'the brother of the Sultan Ghiyāth al-Dīn' became 'the son-in-law of Laskaris', implying under the former 'Izz al-Dīn II and John Vatatzes III under the latter.
23. Cahen, *La Turquie pré-ottomane*, p. 239. Zhavornkov too believes that 'Izz al-Dīn was a son-in-law of John III: P.I. Zhavoronkov, 'Nikeiskaia imperiia i Vostok', *Vizantiiskii Vremennik* 39 (1978), pp. 94–5.
24. J. von Hammer, *Histoire de l'empire ottoman depuis son origine jusqu'a nos jours*, trans. J.-J. Hellert (Paris: Henri Dupuy, 1835), i, pp. 46–7 (with reference to the Ottoman historian Lütfi). The same is repeated by N. Bees, *Die Inschriftenaufzeichnung des Codex Sinaiticus Graecus, 508 (976) und die Maria Spiläotissa Klosterkirche bei Sille (Lykaonien), mit Exkursen zur Geschichte der Seldschuken-Türken* (Berlin: Verlag der 'Byzantinisch-Neugrieschischen Jahrbücher', 1922), pp. 46–7.
25. It seems that John III Doukas Vatatzes had no daughter. Polemis, in his prosopographical study of the Doukas family, does not discuss such a marriage: D.I. Polemis, *The Doukai: A Contribution to Byzantine Prosopography* (London: The Athlone Press, 1968), pp. 107–9, no. 72.
26. Ibn Bībī, *al-Awāmir al-'alā'īya*, pp. 42, 247 ('Alā' al-Dīn's wedding to Kīr Fārid's daughter), p. 299 ('Alā' al-Dīn's wedding to an Ayyūbid princes), p. 363 ('Alā' al-Dīn's wedding to

a Mengüjekid princess) and some general references on pp. 172, 177, 623.

27. Ibid., pp. 448, 476, 618, 625, 637.
28. Ibid., pp. 42, 116.
29. Leslie Peirce, *The Imperial Harem: Women and Sovereignty in the Ottoman Empire* (New York: Oxford University Press, 1993). See also a recent study providing some parallel material to Anatolian practices: Delia Cortese and Simonetta Calderini, *Women and the Fatimids in the World of Islam* (Edinburgh: Edinburgh University Press, 2006). On the Abbasid harem, see N.M. El-Cheikh, 'The qahramâna in the Abbasid court: position and functions', *Studia Islamica* 97 (2003), pp. 41–55. For general information about Near Eastern women, including life in a harem, see Lois Beck and Guity Nashat (eds), *Women in Iran from the rise of Islam to 1800* (Champaign, Ill.: The University of Illinois Press, 2003), especially the chapters by J.S. Meisami and Maria Szuppe.
30. See, for instance, Colin Imber, *The Ottoman Empire, 1330–1650* (New York: Palgrave Macmillan, 2002), p. 87ff.
31. On women's seclusion and women's quarters in Byzantine noble houses, see Lynda Garland, 'The life and ideology of Byzantine women', *Byzantion* 58 (1988), pp. 371–2, 379–81; on the wearing of veils by Byzantine noble women, see Ph. Koukoules, 'Βυζαντινὰ καὶ οὐχὶ τουρκικὰ ἔθιμα', *Byzantinische Zeitschrift* 30 (1929–30), pp. 182–3. Interestingly, Pachymeres calls the sultan's harem γυναικωνῖτις (*Rélations historiques*, i, p. 185, l. 16).
32. Ibn Bībī, *al-Awāmir al-'alā'īya*, p. 637 (mother and wives), p. 116 (the sultan's sister).
33. Peirce, *The Imperial Harem*, pp. 23, 40ff.
34. Ibid., pp. 29–37.
35. In addition, the sultan promised that churches would be built in every city, which would be ready to pay for their maintenance, and the sultan would also ensure the recognition of the supremacy of the Patriarch of Constantinople and the Roman Church by local Greek, Armenian and other bishops. See the text of the letter in: A. Du Chesne and F. Du Chesne, *Historiæ Francorum scriptores*

coaetanei, ab ipsius gentis origine (Paris: Cramoisy, 1649), v, pp. 424–6; other editions of the letter, see B. Hendrickx, 'Régestes des empereurs latins de Constantinople (1204–1261/1272)', Βυζαντινά 14 (1988), p. 143, no. 221; commentaries in Du Cange, *Histoire de l'empire de Constantinople sous les empereurs français*, ed. J.A. Buchon (Paris: Firmin Didot, 1826), pp. 289–91; and, especially, Eastmond, 'Gender and patronage', p. 84.

36. Bar Hebraeus, *The Chronography of Gregory Abu'l-Faraj*, trans. and ed. Ernest A.W. Budge (London: Oxford University Press, 1932, 2 vols), i, p. 403–4; M. Brosset, *Histoire de la Géorgie depuis l'antiquité jusqu'au XIXe siècle* (St Petersburg: Imprimerie de l'Académie impériale des sciences, 1849–56, 2 vols), i, pp. 501–2. For a detailed account of her life, see Speros Vryonis, 'Another note on the inscription of the Church of St. George of Beliserama', *Byzantina* 9 (1977), pp. 11–22. Vryonis suggests, not without reason, that her close association with Rūmī could have been misinterpreted by Bar Hebraeus as conversion to Islam (p. 19).
37. Vryonis, 'Another note on the inscription', pp. 11–8 and now R.M. Shukurov, 'Iagupy: tiurskaya familiia na vizantiiskoi sluzhbe', in G.G. Litavrin (ed.), *Vizantiiskie Ocherki* (St Petersburg: Ataleia, 2006) pp. 210–7.
38. B.A. Gordlevskii, *Gosudarstvo Sel'dzhukidov Maloi Azii* (Moscow and Leningrad: Izdatel'stvo Akademii Nauk SSSR, 1941), p. 160; Cahen, *La Turquie pré-ottomane*, p. 170; Ibn Bībī, *al-Awāmir al-'alā'īya*, p. 584; Duda, *Seltschukengeschichte*, p. 253.
39. His high-sounding sobriquet Sīwāstūs could hardly have implied his extraction from a noble lineage. In Byzantium at that time the family name Σεβαστός (Sebastos) often belonged to common people (*paroikoi*, manuscript copyists, priests), see *Prosopographisches Lexikon der Palaiologenzeit* (Vienna: Verlag der Österreichischen Akademie der Wissenschaften, 1976–96, 12 vols), nos. 25087–96. If this sobriquet derived from the Byzantine title σεβαστός (for instance, from the title of some of Sīwāstūs' forefathers), it indicated a lower official of the Byzantine state;

for more details, see A.P. Kazhdan, 'Sebastos', in A. Kazhdan and A.M. Talbot (eds), *Oxford Dictionary of Byzantium* (Oxford: Oxford University Press, 1991, 3 vols), iii, p. 1863; R. Guilland, *Recherches sur les institutions byzantines* (Berlin: Akademie Verlag, Amsterdam: A.M. Hakkert, 1967, 2 vols), ii, p. 25; Pseudo-Kodinos, *Traité des offices*, ed. and trans. J. Verpeaux (Paris: CNRS Editions, 1966), p. 139 (see also Index); L. Stiernon, 'Notes de prosopographie et de titulature byzantines. Sébaste et gambros', *Revue des études byzantines* 23 (1965), pp. 222–43; L. Stiernon, 'Note de titulature et de prosopographie byzantines. Théodora Comnène et Andronic Lapardas, sébastes', *Revue des études byzantines* 24 (1966), pp. 89–96.

40. Marcel Restle, *Byzantine Wall Painting in Asia Minor* (Greenwich, Conn.: New York Graphic Society 1967), i, pp. 66, 176–7, III, pl. LX; Natalia Teteriatnikov, *The Liturgical Planning of Byzantine Churches in Cappadocia* (Rome: Pontificio Istituto Orientale, 1966), pp. 136, 224; Shukurov, 'Iagupy'.

41. Pachymérès, *Rélations historiques*, iii, p. 295 (the wedding of Tuqtay and Maria); *Prosopographisches Lexikon der Palaiologenzeit*, no. 92632. Judging by Ibn Duqmāq, Ibn Khaldūn and al-'Aynī, Bayalūn had had at least two husbands before getting married to Özbeg Khan: V. G. Tizengauzen [Tiesenhausen], *Sbornik materialov otnosiaschikhsya k istorii Zolotoi Ordy,* i: *Izvlecheniya iz arabskikh sochinenii* (St Petersburg: Imperatorskaya Akademiya Nauk, 1884), pp. 316, 384, 486. It appears from a letter of Gregory Akindynos that she was still alive by the beginning of 1341: *Letters of Gregory Akindynos*, Greek text and English trans. A.C. Hero (Washington, D.C.: Dumbarton Oaks Research Library and Collection, 1983), pp. 56–57, no. 12. Cf. with a common belief that Bayalūn was a daughter of Andronikos III, which does not fit the chronology of the latter's lifetime: Stephen Runciman, 'The ladies of the Mongols', in *Εις μνήμην Κ. Αμάντου* (Athens: Τυπογραφείον Μυρτίδη, 1960), pp. 47–8; *Letters of Gregory Akindynos*, pp. 331–2 (commentaries by Hero on the aforementioned letter of Akindynos with further bibliographical references).

42. *Voyages d'Ibn Batoutah*, Arabic text and French trans. C. Defrémery and B.R. Sanguinetti (Paris: L'imprimerie impériale, 1853–8, 4 vols), ii, pp. 394, 413–14, 417. Ibn Baṭṭūta describes travelling to Constantinople in the suite of Bayalūn Khātūn; however, it is unlikely that he undertook that journey himself: his story has too many chronological and geographical inconsistencies.
43. For the most thorough study of the Eflatun Mescidi to date, see Semavi Eyice, 'Konya'nın Alaeddin Tepesinde Selçuklu Öncesine Ait Bir Eser: Eflâtûn Mescit', *Sanat Tarihi Yıllığı* 4 (1970–1), pp. 269–302.
44. Tekinalp, 'Palace churches', pp. 150–60.
45. Further details, see R. Shukurov, 'Tserkvi v tsitadeliakh Ispira i Bayburta: relikt garemnogo khristianstva?', in M.V. Bibikov (ed.) *Vizantiiskie ocherki* (St Petersburg: Aleteia, 2011), pp. 228–42. Anthony Bryer suggests that both churches were built by the local Muslim vassals of the Grand Komnenoi (and most likely by Mughīth al-Dīn Tughrulshāh, the Seljuk ruler of Erzerum in 1201/1203–25) as a token of their political allegience to the Greek emperors of Trebizond. However, I believe that political allegiance by itself can hardly explain why the churches were built right inside citadels, beside the mosques and dwelling places of Muslim rulers. See Bryer's discussion and description of the churches: Anthony Bryer and David Winfield, *The Byzantine Monuments and Topography of the Pontos* (Washington, D.C.: Dumbarton Oaks Research Library and Collection, 1985, 2 vols), i, pp. 354–5, fig. 121, pls. 287a-288c for the İspir church and pl. 290a, b for the Bayburt church. On the church in the castle of Bayburt and its ground plan, see also Selina Balance, 'The Byzantine churches of Trebizond', *Anatolian Studies* 10 (1960), p. 167 and fig. 20. Detailed description of the citadel church in İspir: David Winfield and June Wainwright, 'Some Byzantine churches from the Pontus', *Anatolian Studies* 12 (1962), pp. 150–3 and fig. 10, pl. XXV b and c. See also more recently T.A. Sinclair, *Eastern Turkey: An Architectural and Archaeological Survey* (London: The Pindar Press, 1987–90, 4 vols), ii, pp. 255, 265–6, 283. Cf. Tekinalp, 'Palace churches', p. 150 note 3, which refers to Bryer and

Winfield's *Byzantine Monuments* without qualifying the Bayburt and İspir churches as harem ones.

46. Anthony Bryer, 'Greek historians on the Turks: the case of the first Byzantine-Ottoman marriage', in R. Davis and J. Wallace-Hadrill (eds) *The writing of history in the Middle Ages. Essays presented to R.W. Southern* (Oxford: Oxford University Press, 1981), pp. 471–93; Peirce, *The Imperial Harem*, p. 42.
47. Pachymérès, *Rélations historiques*, III.3, p. 235; *Prosopographisches Lexikon der Palaiologenzeit*, no. 21395; Runciman, 'The ladies of the Mongols', pp. 48–53.
48. Anthony Bryer, 'Greeks and Turkmens: the Pontic exception', *Dumbarton Oaks Papers,* 29 (1975), Appendix II note 146; M. Kuršanskis, 'Autour de la dernière princesse de Trébizonde: Théodora, fille de Jean IV et épouse d'Uzun Hasan', *Archeion Pontou* 34 (1977–8), pp. 77–8; *Travels to Tana and Persia by Barbaro and Contarini. A Narrative of Italian Travels in Persia, in the Fifteenth and Sixteenth Centuries*, ed. Lord Stanley of Alderley (London: The Hakluyt Society, 1873), p. 178.
49. During the rule of the ardent Muslim Özbeg Khan, the khan's wives probably did not keep their original Christian faith. Judging by Ibn Baṭṭūta's account, Bayalūn lived the Muslim way of life when among the Golden Horde, but once in Byzantine territory she ceased to perform Muslim rites and began openly to consume pork and wine (*Voyages d'Ibn Batoutah*, ii, p. 419). However, it is unclear whether Bayalūn practised Christianity or Islam during the lifetime of her first husband Tuqtay. On Bayalūn, see also Devin DeWeese, *Islamization and Native Religion in the Golden Horde: Baba Tükles and Conversion to Islam in Historical and Epic Tradition* (University Park, Penn.: Pennsylvania State University Press, 1994), pp. 119–23, 150–2, however DeWeese skips the question of the Greek identity of one of the wives of Özbeg Khan. On Christians in the Fatimid harem, see Cortese and Calderini, *Women and the Fatimids*, p. 78.
50. J. P. Migne (ed), *Patrologiae cursus completus. Series Graeca* (Paris: Lutetiae Parisiorum, 1864), cxix, col. 785; V. Grumel, V.

Laurent and J. Darrouzès (eds), *Les regestes des actes du patriarcat de Constantinople* (Paris: Institut français d'études byzantines, 1932–79, 2 vols), i, fasc. II-III: *Les regestes de 715 à 1206*, no. 1088; Charles Brand, 'The Turkish element in Byzantium, 11th-12th centuries', *Dumbarton Oaks Papers* 43 (1989) pp. 16–17. See also Oikonomidès' comments: N. Oikonomidès, 'La brebis égarée et retrouvée: l'apostat et son retour', in Dieter Simon (ed.), *Religiöse Devianz: Untersuchungen zu sozialen, rechtlichen und theologischen Reaktionen auf religiöse Abweichung im westlichen und östlichen Mittelalter* (Frankfurt am Main: Klostermann, Vittorio, 1990), p. 155. Those Latins who had adopted Orthodox Christianity had to be anointed only but not to be baptised anew. See for instance, A.I. Almazov, *Neizdannye kanonicheskie otvety Konstaninopol'skogo patriarkha Luki Khrizoverga i mitropolita Rodosskogo Nila* (Odessa: Ekonomicheskaia tipografiia, 1903), p. 61 (the response of the metroplitan Neilos dating to 1350–60).

51. K. Rhalles and M. Potles, *Σύνταγμα τῶν θείων καὶ ἱερῶν κανόνων* (Athens: Εκ της Τυπογραφίας Γ. Χαρτοφύλακος, 1852–9, 6 vols), ii, pp. 497–8.
52. Rhalles and Potles, *Σύνταγμα*, vi, p. 120: ἔθος γοῦν ἐστι τῶν Ἀγαρηνῶν τοῖς πλείστοις, μὴ πρότερον τὰ σφέτερα περιτέμνειν βρέφη, πρὶν ἂν οἱ ὑποτελεῖς ὄντες αὐτοῖς τῶν Χριστιανῶν ἱερεῖς, καὶ ἄκοντες ἀναγκασθῶσι ταῦτα βαπτίσαι… . .
53. Speros Vryonis, 'Byzantine and Turkish societies and their sources of manpower', in idem, *Studies on Byzantium, Seljuks, and Ottomans: Reprinted Studies* (Malibu. Calif.: Undena Publications, 1981) no. III, p. 133.
54. Ramon Muntaner, *Les Almogavres: L'expédition des Catalans en Orient*, ed. and trans. J.-M. Barberà (Toulouse: Anacharsis, 2002), p. 44; Ludolphus de Sudheim, *De itinere Terre Sancte*, ed. G.A. Neumann, in *Archives de l'Orient latin* 2 (1884), p. 375. For further details on intermarriages in Anatolia and the Balkans for the Ottoman period, see Vryonis, 'Manpower', pp. 143–4.
55. Ducae, *Historia Turco-Byzantina (1341–1462)*, ed. V. Grecu (Bucharest: Editio Academiae Reipublicae Popularis Romanicae,

1958) IX.1, p. 59, ll. 14–8: καὶ ταῦτα τὸ ἀναιδὲς καὶ ἀπάνθρωπον ἔθνος, εἰ Ἑλληνίδα ἢ Ἰταλὴν ἢ ἄλλην τινὰ ἑτερογενῆ προσλάβηται ἢ αἰχμάλωτον ἢ αὐτόμολον, ὡς Ἀφροδίτην τινὰ ἢ Σεμέλην ἀσπάζονται, τὴν ὁμογενῆ δὲ καὶ αὐτόγλωτον ὡς ἄρκτον ἢ ὕαινα βδελύττοντες. English translation: H.J. Magoulias, *Decline and Fall of Byzantium to the Ottoman Turks by Doukas* (Detroit, Mich.: Wayne State University Press, 1975), p. 93.

56. In particular, this was the custom in the Ottoman harem in the fifteenth century: Peirce, *The Imperial Harem*, p. 47.
57. Shukurov, 'Semeistvo,' pp. 107–13.
58. Pachymérès, *Relations Historiques*, ii, pp. 339, ll. 9–12, 349, ll. 10–12. On the metropolitan Makarios, see also *Prosopographisches Lexikon der Palaiologenzeit*, no. 16271.
59. Pachymérès, *Relations Historiques,* ii, pp. 337, 339. On Makarios' testimony, the patriarch Arsenios wrote: Τουτέστιν ὥρισα κοινωνῆσαι τοῦς τοῦ σουλτάνου παῖδας τῆς Ἐκκλησίας με ἐξώθησέ καὶ ταῦτα τοῦ πανιερωτάτου μητροπολίτου Πισσιδίας ἐγγράφως ὁμολογήσαντος ὡς ἐκεῖνος καὶ ἐβάπτισε τούτους καὶ ἐκοινώνησε (Arsenios, 'Testamentum', in Migne (ed), *Patrologiae cursus completus*, cxl, col. 956).
60. Pachymérès, *Relations Historiques*, ii, p. 347, ll. 9–15. On the Christian affiliation of the sultan, see also Gregoras, *Byzantina historia*, IV.4, vol. i, p. 94.
61. On the Byzantine career of Malik Constantine, see V. Laurent, 'Une famille turque au service de Byzance. Les Mélikès', *Byzantinische Zeitschrift* 49 (1956), pp. 349–68.
62. Acropolites, *Georgii Acropolitae Opera*, ed. A. Heisenberg and P. Wirth (Stuttgart: In aedibus B.G. Teubneri, 1978), i, p. 14.14; George Akropolites, *The History*, introduction, translation and commentary by Ruth Macrides (Oxford: Oxford University Press, 2007), p. 124, and Macrides' comments: p. 128 note 20 and also Ruth Macrides, 'The Byzantine godfather', *Byzantine and Modern Greek Studies* 11 (1987), p. 151; Georgii Akropolit, *Istoriia*, trans. P.I. Zhavoronkov (St Petersburg: Aleteia, 2003) pp. 53, 174–5 (notes 154–5 of Zhavoronkov's commentary).

63. Acropolites, *Opera*, i, p. 14, l. 23; Polemis, *The Doukai. A Contribution to Byzantine Prosopography*, p. 131 (no. 101: Euphrosyne); D.A. Korobeinikov, 'A sultan in Constantinople: the feasts of Ghiyāth al-Dīn Kay-Khusraw I', in Leslie Brubaker and Kallirroe Linardou (eds), *Eat, Drink, and be Merry (Luke 12:19): Food and Wine in Byzantium. In Honour of Professor A.A.M. Bryer* (London: Ashgate, 2007), pp. 96–102.
64. *Tārīkh-i āl-i Saljūq dar Anāṭūlī*, ed. Nādira Jalālī (Tehran: Mīrāth-i Maktūb, 1999), p. 84.
65. Nicetas Choniates, *Historia*, p. 521, l. 89.
66. Bertrandon de la Broquière, *Le voyage d'Outremer*, ed. Ch. Schefer (Paris: Ernest Leroux, 1892), p. 90: 'Ramedang ... avoit esté filz d'une femme crestienne laquelle l'avoit fait baptisier à la loy gregiesque pour luy enlever le flair et le senteur qu'ont ceulx qui ne sont point baptisiez. Il n'estoit ne bon crestien ne bon sarazin.'
67. Ibid., p. 115: 'Il avoit esté baptisié en la loy greguesque pour oster le flair, aussy duquel la mere avoit esté crestienne, comme on me dist.'
68. For more details, see F.W. Hasluck, *Christianity and Islam under the Sultans* (Oxford: Oxford University Press, 1929), i, pp. 32–4.
69. Ibid., i, pp. 32–3.
70. This follows from the *vita* of Niketas Junior compiled by Theodore Mouzalon before 1294: Εἰ γὰρ καὶ δουλεύει Πέρσαις χρόνον ἤδη μακρὸν τῇ βαρβαρικῇ καὶ ἀθέῳ τούτων δυναστείᾳ ὑποπεσοῦσα, ἀλλ' οὖν ἔτι περισῴζει οὐ βραχύ τι μέρος χριστιανῶν, παρ' οἷς ἐκεῖ καὶ τὴν ἐκκλησίαν, ψαλλόντων τε καὶ ἀνομολογούντων τὸν κύριον ..., and further on: Ἦ γὰρ οὐκ ἴστε ὡς χριστιανοὶ μὲν ἡμεῖς, πολλοὶ δὲ χριστιανῶν τὴν Περσικὴν χώραν οἰκοῦντες τὰ χριστιανῶν σὺν παρρησίᾳ λατρεύομεν; etc. (Theodorus Muzalon, 'Oratio ad sanctum martyrem Nicetam iuniorem', in F. Halkin, *Hagiographica inedita decem* [*Corpus Christianorum. Series Graeca* 21] (Turnhout and Leuven: Brepols and Leuven University Press, 1989), p. 130, ll. 48–52, p. 134, ll. 215–7). See also V. Laurent, 'Note additionnelle.

L'inscription de l'église Saint-Georges de Bélisérama', *Revue des études byzantines* 26 (1968), p. 369.

71. Bar Hebraeus, *The Chronography*, p. 435.
72. Cahen, *La Turquie pré-ottomane*, p. 171.
73. Ibn Bībī, *al-Awāmir al-'alā'īya*, p. 79:

سلطان در زمان اورا بشناخت و تفحص احوال را بحکم تفرسی که در آن حالت نمود اهمال فرمود واز ملک
مفرزوم در باب اوعذری که موافق مزاج وقت بود خواست و بیکی از خواص بزبان پارسی فرمود که اورا جائی باز
دارد تا چون طلب [فرماید] زود حاضرآید چون سرای از اغیار خالی شد حالی سلطان زکریا را طلب فرمود

Cf. İbn-i Bībī, *El-Evāmirü'l-Alā'iyye fi'l-Umūri'l-Alā'iyye. I Cild (II Kılıç Arslan'ın Vefâtından I 'Ala'ü'd-Dīn Keyḳubâd'ın Cülûsuna Kadar)*, ed. Necati Lugal and Adnan Sadık Erzi (Ankara: Ankara Üniversitesi İlahiyat Fakültesi Yayınları, 1957), p. 115, ll. 12–14. Not all the readings of Lugal and Erzi are satisfactory here.

74. Ibn Bībī, *al-Awāmir al-'alā'īya*, pp. 109–10; ibid., ed. Lugal and Erzi, p. 156, l. 18.
75. *Lexikon zur byzantinischen Gräzität besonders des 9.-12. Jahrhunderts*, ed. Erich Trapp et al. (Vienna: Verlag der Österreichischen Akademie der Wiessenschaften, 1994-) p. 857.
76. For a physical description of Kaykhusraw I, see Gregoras, *Byzantina historia*, i, p. 20, ll. 15–17, German translation by J.L. van Dieten as Nikephoros Gregoras, *Rhomäische Geschichte* (Stuttgart: Anton Hiersemann, 1973), i, p. 73; and also Acropolites, *Opera*, p. 16, ll. 26–7. For a physical description of Theodoros Laskaris, see Acropolites, *Opera*, p. 31, ll. 22ff., and the English translation: George Akropolites, *The History*, p. 157.
77. See for instance: Anna Comnène, *Alexiade*, ed. B. Leib (Paris: Les Belles lettres, 1967), VII, 8, 3, l. 13 (ῥωμαΐζοντες); XV, 5, 2, l. 18 (μιξοβάρβαροι ἑλληνίζοντες).
78. *Ioannis Cantacuzeni eximperatoris Historiarum libri iv*, ed. L. Schopen (Bonn: Impensis Ed. Weberi, 1828–32, 3 vols), i, p. 471, l.25: οἱ βάρβαροι πρότερον Ἑλληνιστὶ πρὸς Ῥωμαίους εἶπον... . See also Speros Vryonis, *The Decline of Medieval Hellenism in Asia Minor and the Process of Islamization from the Eleventh through the Fifteenth Century* (Berkley: University of California Press, 1971), pp. 461–2.

79. *Travels to Tana and Persia by Barbaro and Contarini*, p. 183; Anthony Bryer, 'Ludovico da Bologna and the Georgian and Anatolian Embassy of 1460–1461', *Bedi Kartlisa* 19–20 (1965), p. 197 note 7; S.P. Karpov, 'Kul'tura Trapezundzskoi Imperii', in *Kul'tura Vizantii* (Moscow: Nauka, 1991), iii, p. 118.
80. Ibn Bībī, *al-Awāmir al-'alā'īya*, p. 77; ibid., ed. Lugal and Erzi, p. 112, ll. 7–12.
81. İbn-i Bibi, *el-Evāmirü'l-'alā'īya*, ed. Lugal and Erzi, p. 215; Duda, *Seltschukengeschichte*, p. 67 note b. On Greek secretaries in the Seljuk chancery, see also Vryonis, *The Decline of Medieval Hellenism*, pp. 233, 470; and Cahen, *La Turquie pré-ottomane*, p. 187.
82. S. Lampros, ''Η 'Ελληνική ὡς ἐπίσημος γλῶσσα τῶν Σουλτάνων', *Νέος Ἑλληνομνήμων* 5 (1908) pp. 51–2; M. Delilbaşi, 'Greek as a diplomatic language in the Turkish chancery', in N.G. Moschonas (ed.), Η επικοινωνία στο Βυζάντιο: πρακτικά του Β Διεθνούς Συμποσίου, 4–6 Οκτωβρίου 1990 (Athens: Κέντρο Βυζαντινών Ερευνών, 1993), pp. 147–8.
83. A. Heisenberg, 'Neue Quellen zur Geschichte des lateinischen Kaisertums und der Kirchenunion', *Sitzungsberichte Bayerischen Akademie der Wissenschaften, philosophisch-philologische und historische Klasse* 3 (1923), p. 71.
84. See, for instance Ibn Bībī, *al-Awāmir al-'alā'īya*, pp. 637ff., 735ff.; ibid., ed. Lugal and Erzi, pp. 74ff.
85. Ibn Bībī, *al-Awāmir al-'alā'īya*, pp. 637, 729.
86. Yazıcızâde 'Alī, *Histoire des Seldjoucides d'Asie Mineure d'après l'abrégé du Seldjoucnameh d'Ibn-Bibi*, ed. M. Th. Houtsma (Leiden: E.J. Brill, 1897), p. 40, ll. 18–19. The Greek of the expression is colloquial, and close to Modern Greek. The most plausible accentuation of Παναγιά (which is closer to the relevant Arabic word) is a colloquial variant of the standard Παναγία. Probably, the initial 'π' in πίστιν and Παναγιά was pronounced as 'b' and the final 'ν' in τὴν and πίστιν sounded rather like 'm' due to the assimilation; these phonetic features were probably reflected in the Arabic transcription. My thanks are due

to Michael Gratsianskiy, Peter Mackridge, David Holton, and Marjiolijne and Caroline Janssen for their stimulating discussion of the phrase.

87. Korobeinikov, 'A Sultan in Constantinople', p. 100. Korobeinikov, however, repeats Houtsma's old reading of the Greek expression εἰς τὴν πίστιν μετὰ Χριστοῦ μετὰ Παναγίας, where μετά is hardly relevant and makes no sense. Cf. Yazıcızâde 'Alī, *Histoire*, p. 40 note a; P.I. Melioranskii, 'Sel'dzhukname kak istochnik dlya istorii Vizantii XII-XIII vv', *Vizantiiskii Vremennik* 1 (1894), p. 618 note 2.
88. One of the wives of Jalāl al-Dīn Rūmī was Kirā Khātūn (his other wife, Gawhar Khātūn, was from Samarqand), while the wife of Sulṭān Walad was known as Kirākā Khātūn (or Faṭīma); both women, judging by their names, undoubtedly were Greek (Aflākī, *Manāqib al-'Ārifīn*, Index of names, p. 1203; Vryonis, 'Another note on the inscription', p. 16). On the Greek verses, see R. Burguière and R. Mantran, 'Quelques vers grecs du XIIIe siècle en caractères arabes', *Byzantion* 22 (1952), pp. 63–80; C.D. Mertzios, 'Quelques vers grecs du XIIIe siècle en caractères arabes', *Byzantinische Zeitschrift* 51 (1958), pp. 15–6. In general on Greek linguistic influence upon later Anatolian Turkish, see bibliographical references in Vryonis, *The Decline of Medieval Hellenism*, p. 462 note 65.
89. Cahen, *La Turquie pré-ottomane*, pp. 163–5.
90. Bar Hebraeus, *The Chronography*, pp. 504–5.

CHAPTER SIX

PAPER, STONE, SCISSORS: 'ALĀ' AL-DĪN KAYQUBĀD, 'IṢMAT AL-DUNYĀ WA 'L-DĪN, AND THE WRITING OF SELJUK HISTORY[1]

Scott Redford

This chapter addresses three main issues relating to writing a history of the Seljuks. The first is the accordance, or lack thereof, between two different historical sources: chronicles and inscriptions (the 'paper' and 'stone' in the title). The second concerns sultans' wives and their place in the Seljuk social order, and the third is legitimacy. These weighty issues cluster around 'Iṣmat al-Dunyā wa 'l-Dīn, the cousin and wife of the Seljuk sultan 'Alā' al-Dīn Kayqubād I (r. 1219–37). Despite being a prominent member of the ruling family in her own right she figures not at all in the main chronicle of Seljuk Anatolia, Ibn Bībī's *al-Awāmir al-'alā'īya fī 'l-umūr al-'alā'īya*. Instead, we glean information about her from other historians' accounts of 'Alā' al-Dīn Kayqubād's taking of Erzurum, where she lived, and their marriage. Even in these accounts, she remains nameless, and is not mentioned in chronicles again. She only gains a name thanks to two surviving building inscriptions. Why did Ibn Bībī excise (hence the 'scissors' in the title) her from history in his account of this dynasty?

Here, I examine evidence for 'Iṣmat al-Dunya wa 'l-Dīn's life in reverse chronological order, starting with inscriptions in south-central and southern Anatolia made during her years as a wife of 'Alā' al-Dīn Kayqubād and, after his death, as an ally of his son and successor, Ghiyāth al-Dīn Kaykhusraw II (r. 1237–46). Subsequently, I review her brief appearance in Erzurum in 1230 as a princess, a sister, a cousin and a spoil of war, as presented in the narrative sources.

Part 1: Uluborlu

In an article appearing in 1912, Halil Edhem published an inscription dating to Rajab 629/May 1232 from the mosque now known as the Alaeddin Camii in Uluborlu, a town in the lake district of south-central Turkey. Many decades later, Osman Turan noted the historical importance of this inscription. In a footnote of his 1971 book, *Selçuklular Zamanında Türkiye,* he remarked that 'Iṣmat al-Dunya wa 'l-Dīn, the woman recorded in this inscription as the patron of this mosque, unlike other wives of 'Alā' al-Dīn Kayqubād, is not mentioned at all in Ibn Bībī's history. From this inscription, and this inscription alone, we learn that she was the daughter of 'Alā' al-Dīn Kayqubād's uncle, Mughīth al-Dīn Tughrulshāh, who ruled Erzurum between the Seljuk conquest of the city from the Saltuqids in 1202 and his death in 1225. Among the many sons of Qılıch Arslan II, only Mughīth al-Dīn Tughrulshāh had continued to rule even after his brother Ghiyāth al-Dīn Kaykhusraw I (r. 1192–6 and 1205–11) regained the throne in Konya and reunited the Seljuk domains, which had been divided by their father among his sons sometime in the 1180s. As mentioned above, 'Iṣmat al-Dunyā wa 'l-Dīn makes no appearance in Ibn Bībī's chronicle, which does

Figure 6.1 Inscription of 'Iṣmat al-Dunyā wa'l-Dīn, Uluborlu. Photograph courtesy of the Uluborlu Museum.

mention the sultan's other known wives, Māhparī (Khwand Khātūn) and al-Malika al-'Ādilīya.[2]

The Uluborlu inscription records 'Iṣmat al-Dunyā wa 'l-Dīn as a queen – *malika* –indubitably a wife of 'Alā' al-Dīn Kayqubād, whose name begins the inscription, and in whose territories the mosque in question was built. In an article published four years after Turan's book, J.M. Rogers remarked on an unusual feature of this inscription, the fact that it makes clear that 'Iṣmat al-Dunyā wa 'l-Dīn built this mosque with her own money, but did not speculate on the reason for this.[3]

Unfortunately this inscription, along with the mosque where it was located, burned in 1910. A portion of it survives in the Uluborlu Museum (Figure 6.1). From the surviving lower right-hand corner, we can observe that when complete it was as large as a normal sultanic building inscription of the time. The height of the lines is approximately 12 centimetres – making the original five-line inscription (and these are long lines) over 60 centimetres high. The following reproduces the Arabic of Edhem's published text, with the addition of line breaks recorded by another author. The parentheses mark those parts of the inscription that remain.[4]

1 بنى هذا المسجد المبارك فى ايام دولة السلطان
2 (الاعظم) شاهنشاه المعظم ظل الله فى العالم
3 (علأ الدنيا و الدين ا)بو الفتح كيقباذ بن كيخسرو و من مال الملكة
4 (العالمة العادلة عصمة الدنيا و الد)ين صفوة الاسلام و المسلمين بنت
5 (الملك الشهيد طغرلشاه بن ق)لج ارسلان دام اقبا(لها فى رجب) سنة (تسع) و عشرين و ستماية

Translated, it runs as follows:

> This blessed masjid was built in the days of the reign of the greatest sultan, the great Shāhanshāh, God's shadow on earth, 'Alā' al-Dunyā wa 'l-Dīn, Father of Victory, Kayqubād, son of Kaykhusraw, and with the wealth of the learned and just queen, 'Iṣmat al-Dunyā wa 'l Dīn, Quintessence of Islam and of Muslims, daughter of the martyred king Tughrulshāh, son of Qılıch Arslan, may [God] extend her success, in Rajab of the year 629 (May 1232).

In addition to its size and length, this inscription is unusual, and therefore notable, for many reasons, all of them relating to its patron. Indeed, *min māl* ('with the wealth of') is a rare formulation, appearing in only one other Seljuk inscription that I know of, also featuring a female patron (about which, more later). This phrase emphasises the independence of the queen's wealth from that of the sultan. While other sub-sultanic patrons used their own wealth to erect buildings in Seljuk Anatolia, they, too, as here, used the formula *fī ayyām* ('in the days of'), but the fact that their names appeared at all must have been deemed sufficient indication of their patronage.

As well as demonstrating this queen's own financial contribution, the Uluborlu Mosque inscription endows 'Iṣmat al-Dunyā wa 'l-Dīn with three unusual things: firstly, a title; secondly, a three-generation genealogy back to Qılıch Arslan II, the grandfather she shared with her husband; and thirdly, a benediction: something this inscription does not grant the sultan himself. The inscription also calls her learned and just, *'ālima* and *'ādila*, attributes which combine with her title to give her an unassailable Islamic index of purity, knowledge and justice. These last titles also link her to her father, whose inscriptions on the citadel of Bayburt in north-east Anatolia also use them; they are not titles used, however, by the sultans of the Konya branch of the family. Moreover, her genealogy extends to three generations, his to only two. This has the effect, of course, of emphasising her sultanic bloodline rather than their common ancestor, Qılıch Arslan II, who does not appear in his genealogy. Once again, she may have learned this trick from her father, whose Bayburt inscriptions also trot out longer genealogies than those found in the inscriptions of the Konya branch of the family. Actually, we would know that she was a woman of sultanic lineage even without the genealogy listed here, because 'Iṣmat al-Dunya wa 'l-Dīn, following Anatolian Seljuk practice, is more of a title than a name: the name 'Iṣmat is one only given to women of the ruling house. Other sultanic wives *not* originating from ruling houses, like Māhparī, assume the name/title of Ṣafwat al-Dunyā wa 'l-Dīn.[5] In this sense, there is at least one *other* name hiding behind this name/title. The very fact of her insistence on it, and it alone, may be seen as another index of display of her high status.

The style of writing of the inscription as well as its size makes it the equal of many, if not most, sultanic inscriptions of the time. While the inscription suffers from the usual generous size and spacing of the first line and crowding on the last, it is in general better planned and executed than most of its contemporaries. (The only unusual practice that is remarkable in the surviving part is the unusual form of the letter *hā'* in the word *shahīd*: it is as if that letter started out life as an *'ayn*, with the calligrapher realising too late that there was no room for the formula *al-sa'īd al-shahīd*.) In other words, this inscription was formulated and executed by a person or persons conversant with the practice of the dynasty. This is no surprise, given the nuanced elevation of the queen relative to the ruling sultan in the inscription and her financial independence. She must have had a scribe in her retinue who had mastered the rules of chancery practice because, in my opinion, this is not an inscriptional text that could have been written by someone in the sultan's central administration and sent out to Uluborlu. Based on Seljuk inscriptional evidence from Sinop, I have argued elsewhere that scribes attached to the retinues of sultanic and non-sultanic patrons wrote foundation inscriptions like this, albeit based on common formulas.[6]

To summarise: the Uluborlu Alaeddin Mosque inscription emphasises 'Iṣmat al-Dunyā wa 'l-Dīn's importance as a member of the Seljuk ruling dynasty in her own right, her relationship to her father's 'dynasty' in Erzurum, her independence from the sultan, her own noble qualities and her personal fortune. What 'Alā' al-Dīn Kayqubād would have thought of this had he seen the inscription remains speculative: it is such a declaration of autonomy that it strongly suggests that she was banished here within two short years of their marriage, and that he did not venture to Uluborlu to see it, or her.

In the great division of Seljuk lands by Sultan Qılıch Arslan II, Uluborlu had been granted to 'Alā' al-Dīn's father Ghiyāth al-Dīn Kaykhusraw I, and from there must have passed to his children, first 'Izz al-Dīn Kaykā'ūs I, and then to 'Alā' al-Dīn himself as sultanic property. It is possible that 'Iṣmat al-Dunyā wa 'l-Dīn's epigraphic presence here denotes her being granted this town, its territories and its revenues by 'Alā' al-Dīn. This supposition is based not only on the inscription discussed above, but also on two inscriptions which point to a concentration of her architectural patronage in this region, a practice that has been recognised for other architectural patrons of the Seljuk dynasty like her fellow wife Māhparī Khātūn.

A recent article on two other Seljuk foundation inscriptions – one a fragmentary inscription from the now-ruined caravanserai at Derebucak in the mountains south of Beyşehir and the other the foundation inscription of the Kırkgöz Han, a caravanserai on the road between Antalya and Burdur – points to 'Iṣmat al-Dunyā wa 'l-Dīn as the patron of both. Granted neither of these buildings is *very* near Uluborlu, but they lie on routes that connect it to the coast from the west and the east. She is not known from building inscriptions anywhere else in Anatolia. Uluborlu must also have gained in importance after 'Alā' al-Dīn's founding of the palace of Kubadabad (Qubādābād) on the shores of Lake Beyşehir to its east; this palace continued to be used by his son and successor.[7]

What remains of the Derebucak caravanserai inscription is identical in content to the beginning of the Kırkgöz one, the common text suggesting a common patron. We can therefore presume that the fragmentary Derebucak inscription also bore her name because the Kırkgöz Han inscription does. The similarity of these texts in turn implies a scribe working for the patron herself – a practice which, I propose, extended back in time to the Uluborlu Mosque inscription. The Kırkgöz Han inscription, which had until recently only been partially read, dates to the reign of Sultan Ghiyāth al-Dīn Kaykhusraw II between 1237 and 1246. Even though the Kırkgöz Han is not finely decorated, its immense size and kiosk mosque have led many to assume that it was a sultanic foundation. Now we know that it was not a king-sized but a queen-sized caravanserai, built by this queen! The Kırkgöz Han inscription allies 'Iṣmat al-Dunyā wa 'l-Dīn intimately with Sultan Ghiyāth al-Din Kaykhusraw II: in it, after his names and titles, she is called 'the exalted lady, queen of the climes of the world, pearl of the crown of nations' (*al-sitt al-'ālīya malikat aqālīm al-'ālam 'Iṣmat al-Dunyā wa 'l-Dīn durrat tāj al-duwal*) and given a benediction four times longer than that of the sultan himself.

A large inscription of Sultan Ghiyāth al-Dīn Kaykhusraw II in Uluborlu itself attests to his building activities there. It refers to 'the completion of this blessed construction' (*ikmāl hādhihi 'l-'imārat al-mubāraka*), so it could even derive from the same mosque, or more likely the nearby fortifications, although it is at present in secondary reuse in a fountain building nearby. Most striking is its date: the year after he acceded to power. This too serves to underline an alliance between the two, which seems to be supported by Ibn Bībī. In detailing the imbroglio surrounding Ghiyāth al-Dīn Kaykhusraw II's accession to the throne, Ibn Bībī describes the arrest of the mother of the heir apparent (the former Ayyubid princess al-Malika al-'Ādilīya) as well as his half-brothers, her sons, in Kayseri. The queen was taken to Ankara where she was strangled, while the brothers were imprisoned in Uluborlu. Kaykhusraw II ordered his son's *atabeg* (tutor), Mubāriz al-Dīn Armaghānshāh, to murder the incarcerated princes. Armaghānshāh, however, did not have the stomach to murder a Seljuk prince's brothers. Instead the amir killed two *ghulām*s, or household slaves, and passed them off as the sultan's younger brothers in order to placate him.[8]

Although the evidence is circumstantial, in this case history derived from both the inscriptional record and that of chronicles coincides in associating 'Iṣmat al-Dunyā wa 'l-Dīn with the new sultan from the beginning until near the end of his reign. As we will see in the next section, their acquaintanceship could easily have dated to much earlier years, when, as a boy, Ghiyāth al-Dīn Kaykhusraw resided in Erzincan, where he served as *malik* (prince), and 'Iṣmat al-Dunyā wa 'l-Dīn lived in nearby Erzurum. Given Ibn Bībī's exaltation of the accomplishments of 'Alā al-Dīn Kayqubād I, it might be that 'Iṣmat al-Dunyā wa 'l-Dīn's complicity in Ghiyāth al-Dīn Kaykhusraw's power grab led Ibn Bībī to excise her from history in his chronicle.[9]

Part 2: Erzurum

Placed in the context of intra-Seljuk rivalry, these inscriptions naturally cause us to turn our gaze from this region of south-central Anatolia to north-east Anatolia, to Erzurum, where 'Iṣmat al-Dunyā wa 'l-Dīn must have grown up in her father's and brother's court, and, to a lesser degree, to Erzincan, where Ibn Bībī tells us Ghiyāth al-Dīn Kaykhusraw II spent part of his boyhood under the tutelage of Mubāriz al-Dīn Ertokush, who was appointed his *atabeg*. As mentioned earlier, Ibn Bībī tells us that Erzurum had been granted as an appanage to 'Iṣmat al-Dunyā wa 'l-Dīn's father, Mughīth al-Dīn Tughrulshāh, by Rukn al-Dīn Sulaymānshāh in 1202, when it was taken over from the Saltuqids. After Tughrulshāh's death in 1225, his son Rukn al-Dīn Jahānshāh continued family rule in Erzurum, constituting a local Seljuk dynasty that lasted almost 30 years.

Both father and son are given the title of *malik*, roughly equivalent to prince, in Ibn Bībī's history, meaning that they were subject to the sultanate based in Konya. Both use this title on most of their inscriptions. Be this as it may, the inscriptional and numismatic records point to an assertion of sovereignty separate from the main Seljuk sultanate. An inscription of the father from the mosque at Ispir refers to him not as *malik* but as sultan. He minted silver currency (called dinars on the coins themselves), which, while they do not use the title 'sultan', do record that they were minted in Erzurum and give the name of the ruling caliph in Baghdad, al-Nāṣir li-Dīn Allāh (Figures 6.2 and 6.3). Although there is no caliphally granted title on these coins, this, too, constitutes an expression of independence, since a *malik* usually only issues coins (copper and silver) of a recognisably different type: not aniconic, as these are, but bearing the image of a horse and rider. Finally, even though the Bayburt Citadel inscriptions are ambivalent in that some of them name Mughith al-Din as *malik* and some as sultan, in ways both direct and indirect their sum total points towards independence. Two of those that name him *malik* nevertheless give him a caliphally-granted title, *nāṣir amīr al-mu'minīn*, call him *kamāl āl saljūq* (Consummation of the House of Seljuk) and give him a genealogy that extends four generations back to Rukn al-Dīn Sulaymān b. Qutlumush (d. 1086), the longest genealogy I know from the Seljuk inscriptional record. Other inscriptions, including two situated in a prominent location and carefully carved, name him *al-sulṭān al-a'ẓam, shāhanshāh al-mu'aẓẓam* and *al-sulṭān al-mu'aẓẓam, shāhanshāh al-a'ẓam*, Seljuk sultanic titles if there ever were ones. Minting silver coinage of a non-princely type, using caliphally granted titles, and calling yourself sultan constitute expressions of independence: emphasising your Seljuk pedigree constitutes a challenge to your cousins in Konya.[10]

Another indication of the separate track they followed comes from the geographer Yāqūt who, in the entry on Erzurum in his *Mu'jam al-buldān*, praises the ruler of Erzurum, presumably Mughīth al-Dīn

Figure 6.2 and 6.3 Dinar of Mughīth al-Dīn Tughrulshāh.
Photographs courtesy of Şennur Şentürk, Curator, Yapı Kredi Numismatic Collection, Istanbul. Accession number 8337.

Figure 6.2:

Obverse:

1) *Al-Imām*
2) *La ilaha illa Allāh*
3) *Waḥdahu la sharīka lahu*
4) *Al-Nāṣir li-Dīn Allāh*
5) *Amīr al-mu'minīn*

Marginal:

ḍuriba hadhā al-dīnār bi-Arzurūm

Tughrulshāh, as a just and enlightened ruler, calling him the sultan of an independent state:

> Arzan al-Rūm [Erzurum] is another city in Armenia (*bilād Arminīya*). Its people are Armenians. And it is at present larger and greater than the first [the town of Arzan, now ruined, east of Silvan]. It has an independent (*mustaqill*) sultan who resides there. Its territory and regions are extensive and full of resources (*khayrāt*). And the beneficence (*iḥsān*) of its ruler to his subjects is evident in his justice towards them, except that

Figure 6.3:
Reverse:

1) *Muḥammad rasūl Allāh*
2) *Mughīth al-Dunyā wa 'l-Dīn*
3) *Abū'l-Fatḥ Ṭughrul Shāh*
4) *Bin Qilij Arslān*

Marginal:
{sanat} thamān wa sitta mi'ā

sinfulness (*fisq*) and the drinking of wine and the perpetration of forbidden things there is widespread ...[11]

Traditionally, the Seljuk rulers in Erzurum have been treated as a sideshow, and placed in a teleological historical narrative relating to the size, strength and growth of the Seljuk state, an expansion leading to direct conflict in the subsequent decade with the Mongols. This small state has mainly attracted the attention of historians due to an event unusual in Islamic history: the apostasy of one of 'Iṣmat al-Dunyā wa 'l-Dīn's brothers, who converted to Christianity in order to marry the Georgian queen Rusudan. The daughter of this marriage, Tamar/Gurjī Khātūn, was betrothed to Ghiyāth al-Dīn Kaykhusraw II, who, as we have stated, was ruling as *malik* in nearby Erzincan.[12]

While coins and inscriptions give us indications of independence, Ibn al-Athīr reports that Rukn al-Dīn Jahānshāh's open rupture with his cousin and alliance with the Khwārazmshāhs, rather than Khwarazmian activity alone, was the impetus for the Ayyubid–Seljuk attack against the combined armies of Khwarazm and Erzurum, which ended in the Seljuk–Ayyubid victory at the Battle of Yassı Çimen in 1230. This was followed immediately by either an attack on Erzurum, leading to its surrender to 'Alā' al-Dīn, or by a simple surrender of the city. Most historical sources relating to the aftermath of this battle report that 'Alā' al-Dīn Kayqubād imprisoned and killed Rukn al-Dīn Jahānshāh – all, in fact, save Ibn Bībī, who reports that during feasting by the Seljuks and the Ayyubids celebrating the conquest of the city he and his brothers were granted the *iqṭā*'s of Aksaray and Eyüphisar in central Anatolia. In Ibn Bībī's version, the sultan gave Rukn al-Dīn Jahānshāh a signet ring symbolising forgiveness (*angushtarī-yi amān*), robes of vassalage (*khil'a*), gold and a special horse. Conspicuous by its absence from Ibn Bībī's chronicle is any account of 'Alā' al-Dīn Kayqubād's marriage to 'Iṣmat al-Dunyā wa 'l-Dīn or of his murder of Rukn al-Dīn Jahānshāh, an event recorded by a majority of historians. Quite the opposite, in fact: Ibn Bībī paints the end of the suppression of this rebellion in a rosy light, which is not reflected in other sources and is contradicted by the inscriptional record.[13]

When not considered with the wisdom of hindsight, the Seljuk mini-dynasty of Erzurum can be seen as the only legitimate Anatolian Seljuk rival to the dynasty based in Konya, and not as just a lesser Anatolian state waiting to be swallowed up, like the Danishmendids and the Mengüjekids. A Seljuk dynast backed by the power of the Khwarazmian army must have been viewed as more than the usual kind of threat by 'Alā' al-Dīn Kayqubād. Accounts of the aftermath of Yassı Çimen by contemporaneous chroniclers make clear that there was personal enmity between 'Alā' al-Dīn Kayqubād and Rukn al-Dīn Jahānshāh, an enmity that predated Jahānshāh's decision to become a vassal of the Khwārazmshāh Jalāl al-Dīn.

Contemporary historians offered varying accounts of the aftermath of the Battle of Yassı Çimen and the fate of Rukn al-Dīn

Jahānshāh, which are summarised here: Ibn Wāṣil reports that 'Alā' al-Dīn Kayqubād captured and imprisoned Rukn al-Dīn Jahānshāh after Yassı Çimen and, taking him to Erzurum, took that city and all of his strongholds, and imprisoned and then killed him in one of them.[14] The Khwarazmian historian Nasawī relates that Jalāl al-Dīn Khwārazmshāh had offered Rukn al-Dīn Jahānshāh territories near Harput – presumably to add to his present realm – in return for his fealty. He reports that after the Battle of Yassı Çimen, 'Alā' al-Dīn Kayqubād tied his cousin to a mule and subsequently killed him brutally.[15] Ibn al-Athīr, writing in Mosul, attributes the military alliance between al-Malik al-Ashraf and 'Alā' al-Dīn Kayqubād leading to the Battle of Yassı Çimen to the latter's fear of the consequences of Rukn al-Dīn's swearing fealty to Jalāl al-Dīn Khwārazmshāh.[16] Ibn al-Athīr agrees with Nasawī in that he writes that Jalāl al-Dīn Khwārazmshāh had promised Rukn al-Dīn Jahānshāh some of the territories of his cousin 'Alā' al-Dīn Kayqubād as a reward for joining forces with him. He states that there was deep-seated enmity (*'adāwa mustaḥkama*) between the two, but without attributing this to Rukn al-Dīn Jahānshāh's refusal to marry his sister to 'Alā' al-Dīn Kayqubād as al-Ḥamawī and Bar Hebraeus do. Ibn al-Athīr's account of the aftermath of the battle is much the same as that of Ibn Wāṣil, except that he does not report that Rukn al-Dīn Jahānshāh was killed: he writes that he was captured at the battle, brought to 'Alā' al-Dīn Kayqubād and that they went to Erzurum, where he gave up all of his wealth and lands to the latter.

Al-Ḥamawī reports a detail that among these authors otherwise only Nasawī gives, which is that after the Battle of Yassı Çimen, Rukn al-Dīn Jahānshāh (and in al-Ḥamawī, his brother and brother-in-law) were tied to mules (used to transport bales of hay) and taken to Erzurum in this manner unbecoming to their station.[17] He also reports that that city resisted most fiercely for the three days preceding its surrender. Unlike Nasawī, he records not the killing of Rukn al-Dīn Jahānshāh but the guarantee of his safety, which Bar Hebraeus also reports. Al-Ḥamawī is the only author besides Bar Hebraeus to report that Rukn al-Dīn Jahānshāh had tried to prevent the marriage of 'Alā' al-Dīn Kayqubād to his sister. He places this wedding before the departure of the Ayyubid forces from Erzurum.

Like other authors, Bar Hebraeus states that Rukn al-Dīn Jahānshāh was taken prison after the Battle of Yassı Çimen. He agrees with Ibn Bībī and other authors in that 'Alā' al-Dīn Kayqubād and the Ayyubid al-Ashraf then went to Erzurum. He, too, reports that they attacked it before the inhabitants came to terms, one of which was that Rukn al-Dīn Jahānshāh not be killed. What follows is that part of his narrative that most directly bears on the topic of this chapter:

> And there was in it the sister of the lord of 'Arzân ar-Rûm, whom for a very long time the Sultan had longed to take to wife, but her brother would not permit it. And when the Sultan had taken her, he rejoiced over her more than over the victory which had come to him. But after a short time, when she asked the Sultan to release her brother from the prisoners, he was angry with her and destroyed her, and he also sent and drowned her brother in the sea.[18]

So, even though the causation is different, Bar Hebraeus, too, reports the death of Rukn al-Dīn Jahānshāh.

Conquering a city, killing its ruler, your cousin, and marrying his sister: this is the stuff of Greek tragedy, but in the medieval world dynastic marriage was common and was used to seal an alliance and/or a military conquest. Indeed, as we see in the case of Saladin and Nūr al-Dīn b. Zangī, marrying your dead predecessor's wife was also a way of acquiring legitimation. We see the connection between conquest and marriage in all three of 'Alā' al-Dīn Kayqubād's known weddings: to Māhparī in connection with the surrender of Kalonoros/Alanya, al-Malika al-'Ādilīya to seal an alliance with the Ayyubids, and, here, with 'Iṣmat al-Dunyā wa 'l-Dīn after the capitulation of Erzurum. If Bar Hebraeus' interpretation is correct, 'Alā al-Dīn Kayqubād had wanted to marry 'Iṣmat al-Dunyā wa 'l-Dīn previously, presumably as a way of gaining control of the territories of this mini-Seljuk dynasty in northeast Anatolia and the southern Caucasus, and eliminating any rival claimants to the legitimacy of the Seljuk state based at Konya. 'Alā' al-Dīn Kayqubād's enmity towards Rukn al-Dīn Jahānshāh may have stemmed from his cousin's refusal to agree to this.

If my interpretation of the Uluborlu inscription is correct, we can posit that after 'Alā' al-Dīn Kayqubād killed her brother or brothers and married her, 'Iṣmat al-Dunyā wa'l-Dīn, for reasons unknown to us but perhaps related to the circumstances of her marriage, lived out at least part of her husband's reign in or around Uluborlu, a region conquered by their mutual grandfather. However, her revenge on 'Alā' al-Dīn Kayqubād may have constituted the proverbial 'dish best eaten cold', in the form of her support for Ghiyāth al-Dīn Kaykhusraw II, whom she must have known when he was a child growing up in Erzincan: rather than solely the amir Sa'd al-Dīn Köpek, who plays the 'heavy' in Ibn Bībī's account of these events, is it possible that she and Māhparī Khātūn (Ghiyāth al-Dīn Kaykhusraw II's mother) joined in plotting with the new sultan against the Ayyubid queen, mother of the heir apparent, who herself was garrotted, and her progeny killed or exiled? This may have led to Ibn Bībī to take his own sort of revenge on 'Iṣmat al-Dunyā wa'l-Dīn, decades later. However, Ibn Bībī may alternatively have written her out of his history due to her association with the events that took place in Erzurum after Yassı Çimen.[19]

The inscriptional record returns to shed more light on the battle for succession and rule of the Seljuk sultanate. The daughters of al-Malika al-'Ādilīya built a tomb tower for their mother in Kayseri in 1247, a full ten years after her death, and, more significantly, after the death of Ghiyāth al-Dīn Kaykhusraw II. The inscription on this tomb tower makes no mention of the long-dead queen's dynastic connection with the Seljuks, only with the Ayyūbids; likewise it attributes to her the royal title of 'Iṣmat al-Dunyā wa 'l-Dīn. Like Sultan Ghiyāth al-Dīn Kaykhusraw II's mother Māhparī Khātūn, al-Malika al-'Ādilīya is also buried in Kayseri, in a tomb tower in the middle of the mosque, madrasa and bath complex that she built there. The inscription on her tomb, built after her son's death, like that of 'Iṣmat al-Dunyā wa 'l-Dīn, emphasises her learning, and also the fact that she paid for the tomb with her own money (although here this statement is innovatively, if awkwardly incorporated into the list of her attributes).[20]

J.M. Rogers, in an article on a dynasty that ruled in territory adjacent to Erzurum in the period examined here, had the following to say about the female members of its ruling family:

> The Mxargrdzeli ladies differed in fact little from their Muslim contemporaries – the Seljuk Queens, the Qarā-Khīṭāī viragoes of Kirmān, or the Mamlūk ladies: they were of similar character and temperament and were much inclined to be unscrupulous in the means they used to get their own way. Such similarities in such different societies certainly deserve consideration, and it might be useful to supplement the meagre historical information available by some anthropology.[21]

In the slice of Seljuk history presented here, the science of neither the study of men (anthropology) nor women has been employed to examine the wives of 'Alā' al-Dīn Kayqubād: Māhparī, al-Malika al-'Ādilīya and now 'Iṣmat al-Dunyā wa 'l-Dīn; the task of examining the workings of the Seljuk harem has fallen to Rustam Shukurov in his contribution to this volume. Instead, this chapter has concentrated on traditional dynastic and military history. These wives, whatever their actual characters, are all lauded in their inscriptions for their learning, leaving open to investigation that aspect of Seljuk culture: the virtue inherent in their names reinforced by Islamic learning, and only ceding to the vanity of royalty in the inscriptions of civic monuments like the Kırkgöz Han. In examining inscriptions in Tokat that bear royal women's names from later in the thirteenth century, Sara Wolper has commented on the role that women patrons played in ensuring continuity and legitimacy during the turbulent Mongol era. Inscriptions *and* chronicles combine to show sultanic wives playing subordinate but certainly important roles as insurers of dynastic continuity, expansion and alliance through marriage and motherhood, as historical actors themselves actively involved in dynastic succession and architectural patronage.[22]

I have tried here to use inscriptions to argue for a correction of the cut of Ibn Bībī's biases, especially in his 'dressing' of Seljuk wives for presentation to the historical public. Like many of their contemporaries, the Seljuks were no strangers to the practice of *damnatio memoriae*, chiselling out individual lines, names and sometimes entire inscriptions in a manner similar to excision by chroniclers. It is perhaps not coincidental that no inscriptions of Mughīth al-Dīn Tughrulshāh and Rukn al-Dīn Jahānshāh survive from Erzurum, and that they are only found in more remote locations like İspir and Bayburt. Two of the principal surviving medieval Islamic monuments of Erzurum, the Çifte Minareli Madrasa and the Mausoleum of Saltuk, are both devoid of foundation inscriptions where these should, by rights, exist. Lest it fall to someone else to point out, a chisel, too, could have been included in the title of this chapter.

Notes

1. I would like to thank editors Andrew Peacock and Sara Nur Yıldız, conference participants Gary Leiser, Oya Pancaroğlu and Rustam Shukurov, and the Uluborlu Municipality and Museum for their assistance.
2. Halil Edhem, 'Anadolu'da İslami Kitabeler', *Tarih-i Osmani Encümeni Mecmuası*, 27 (1330 [1912]), pp. 148–9; Osman Turan, *Selçuklular Zamanında Türkiye: Siyasi Tarih Alp Arslan'dan Osman Gazi'ye (1071–1328)* (Istanbul: Turan Neşriyat Yurdu, 1971), p. 394 note 78.
3. J. M. Rogers, 'Waqf and patronage in Seljuk Anatolia: the epigraphic evidence', *Anatolian Studies* 26 (1976), p. 74.
4. Edhem, 'İslami Kitabeler', pp. 148–9; see Said Demirdal, *Bütünüyle Uluborlu* (Istanbul: Karadeniz Matbaası ve Acar Matbaası, 1968), p. 86 for the arrangement of lines, and the information that the mosque burned down in AH 1327 (1910). I am grateful to Kayhan Dörtlük for this reference. In the Arabic text given here, certain orthographic peculiarities of the Seljuk scribes have been corrected.
5. İsmail Hakkı Uzunçarşılı, *Osmanlı Devleti Teşkilatına Medhal* (Istanbul: Maarif Matbaası, 1941), p. 66.

6. Scott Redford, 'The inscription of the Kırkgöz Hanı and the problem of textual transmission in Seljuk Anatolia', *Adalya* 12 (2009), pp. 351–2.
7. See ibid., p. 353 for a full translation of this inscription.
8. Ibn Bībī, *al-Awāmir al-'alā'īya fī 'l-umur al-'alā'īya,* facsimile edition published by Adnan Sadık Erzi as Ibn-i Bībī, *El-Evāmirü 'l-'Alā'iyye fī l-umūri 'l-'Alā'iyye* (Ankara: Türk Tarih Kurumu, 1956), pp. 472–3. For the Uluborlu inscription, see Demirdal, *Uluborlu*, p. 88; more recently, Nermin Şaman Doğan, 'Eski Uluborlu'daki Hamam ve Çeşmeler', *Vakıflar Dergisi* 28 (2004), p. 270.
9. Edhem, 'İslami Kitabeler', p. 151.
10. For the İspir inscription, see Ibrahim Hakkı Konyalı, *Abideleri ve Kitabeleri ile Erzurum Tarihi* (Istanbul: Ercan Matbaası, 1960), pp. 508–9 with photographs and a transcription and translation of the three-line inscription in what he calls both the Çarşı Camii and the Tuğrulşah Camii. The amir who erected the mosque (called a *masjid* in the inscription) was one (___) al-Dīn Atābak Erdemshāh. The inscription was destroyed in restoration work in the 1960s. For the dinar/dirham, see Şevki Nezihi Aykut, *Türkiye Selçuklu Sikkeleri* (Istanbul: n.p., 2000), p. 136, for examples, see pp. 257–68. For the Bayburt castle inscriptions of 1213, see Etienne Combe et al., *Répertoire chronologique d'épigraphie arabe* (Cairo: IFAO, 1931–91, 18 vols), x, pp. 94–7, nos. 3735–9 (with no. 3739, the main inscription, having the longest genealogy) and Abdurrahim Şerif Beygu, *Erzurum Tarihi, Anıtları, Kitabeleri* (Istanbul: Bozkurt Basımevi, 1936), pp. 241–3. In addition to these publications, information given here is based on my current research on the inscriptions of Bayburt citadel.
11. Yāqūt, *Mu'jam al-buldān* (Beirut: Dār Ṣādir, 1993), i, pp. 150–1. Yāqūt's description of the king as just constitutes another coincidence of stone and paper: as noted above, the main inscriptions of Bayburt mention him as wise and just.
12. Ibn Bībī, *al-Awāmir al-'alā'īya*, pp. 363–4. For the Georgian side of this story, which I regretfully have to neglect here, see

A.C.S. Peacock, 'Georgia and the Anatolian Turks in the 12th and 13th Centuries', *Anatolian Studies* 56 (2006), pp. 127–46.

13. Ibn Bībī, *al-Awāmir al-'alā'īya*, p. 410 for Erzurum, pp. 483–4 for the marriage of Ghiyāth al-Dīn Kaykhusraw to his cousin. See also Peacock, 'Georgia', p. 140.
14. Ibn Wāṣil, *Mufarrij al-kurūb fi akhbār banī Ayyūb*, ed. Jamāl al-Dīn al-Shayyāl and Ḥasanayn Muḥammad Rabī' (Cairo: Maṭba'at Dār al-Kutub, 1953–75, 5 vols), iv, p. 300.
15. al-Nasawī, *Sīrat al-Sulṭān Jalāl al-Dīn Mankubartī*, ed. O. Houdas (Paris: Ernest LeRoux, 1891), pp. 206–7.
16. Ibn al-Athīr, *al-Kāmil fī 'l-tārīkh*, ed. C. Tornberg (Beirut: Dār Ṣādir, 1965–7), xii, pp. 489–91.
17. al-Ḥamawī, *al-Tārīkh al-manṣūrī*, ed. Abū'l- 'Īd Dūdū (Damascus: Maṭba'at al-Ḥijāz, 1981), pp. 211–2.
18. Bar Hebraeus, *The Chronography of Gregory Abu'l Faraj*, trans. E.A.W. Budge (London: Oxford University Press, 1932), i, pp. 395–6.
19. For the tomb tower of al-Malika al-'Ādilīya, erected by her daughters ten years after her death, see Ahmet Akşit, 'Melike-i Adiliye Kümbetinde Selçuklu Devri Saltanat Mücadelesine Dair İzler', *Türkiyat Araştırmaları Dergisi* 11 (2002), pp. 239–45. I am grateful to Suzan Yalman for this reference. For the inscription itself, see Halil Edhem, *Kayseri Şehri* (Istanbul: Matbaa-i Orhaniye, 1334/1916), p. 86.
20. See ibid., pp. 67–8 for the text of this inscription. In it, she is styled, at the end of a list of many other titles, *ṣāḥibat al-ma'rūfa al-mutaṣaddiqa bi 'l-māl ulūf Ṣafwat al-Dunyā wa 'l-Dīn Māh Barī Khātūn*, '... possessor of knowledge, almsgiver of wealth [in] millions, Quintessence of the World and of Religion, Māhparī Khātūn ...'. The unusual use of the word *ulūf* here seems in order to create a (strained) rhyme with the word *ma'rūfa*.
21. J.M. Rogers, 'The Mxargrdzelis between East and West', *Bedi Kartlisa* 34 (1976), p. 321.
22. See Ethel Sara Wolper, *Cities and Saints. Sufism and the Transformation of Urban Space in Medieval Anatolia* (University

Park, Penn.: Pennsylvania State University Press, 2003), pp. 82–91 (Chapter 6, entitled 'Women as Guarantors of Familial Lines. Dervish Lodges and Gender Representation in Pre-Ottoman Anatolia'). I am grateful to Professor Wolper for corresponding with me on the matter of female patronage.

PART THREE

SUFIS AT COURT AND IN SOCIETY

CHAPTER SEVEN

IN THE PROXIMITY OF SULṬANS: MAJD AL-DĪN ISḤĀQ, IBN ʿARABĪ AND THE SELJUK COURT

Sara Nur Yıldız and Haşim Şahin

> The Prophet Muḥammad said, 'The worst of religious scholars (*ʿulamāʾ*) is he who visits those in power (*umarāʾ*); the best of those in power (*umarāʾ*) is he who visits religious scholars (*ʿulamāʾ*).
>
> *Fīhī mā fīhī*, Mawlānā Jalāl al-Dīn Rūmī[1]

Very little is known of the Muslim religious elite of Seljuk Anatolia. In part, this is because, unlike most of the rest of the Islamic world, Anatolia lacked a substantial class of *ʿulamāʾ*. As Claude Cahen has noted, elsewhere such scholars were commemorated in biographical dictionaries (*ṭabaqāt*), but an *ʿālim* who died in Anatolia was likely to be forgotten by his peers and posterity.[2] Yet, while we have no Anatolian *ṭabaqāt*, on occasion other sources such as Ibn Bībī's dynastic history allow us insight, albeit partial and unsatisfactory, into the careers of Anatolia's perhaps rather few religious scholars, especially when they had dealings with the court and political elite. In this chapter, we use such evidence to examine two major figures in the religious life of early thirteenth-century Anatolia, Majd al-Dīn Isḥāq and Ibn ʿArabī, and their relationship with one another on the one hand and with the Seljuk sultans on the other. This in turn allows us to contextualise Ibn ʿArabī's middle years, when he dispensed spiritual advice to Seljuk sultans, and allows us to understand better his subsequent influence in Anatolia.

Majd al-Dīn Isḥāq b. Muḥammad b. Yūsuf of Malatya[3] (d. c.1215–20),[4] was an influential figure at the Seljuk court as shaykh and advisor to two Seljuk sultans, Ghiyāth al-Dīn Kaykhusraw I (r. 1192–6, 1205–11), and his son and successor, ʿIzz al-Dīn Kaykāʾūs I (1211–19). In addition to his intimacy with sultans, Majd al-Dīn Isḥāq is known for his friendship with the great Sufi theorist and visionary, Muḥyī al-Dīn Ibn al-ʿArabī (1165–1240). He was also the father of Ṣadr al-Dīn Muḥammad al-Qūnawī (d. 1274), Ibn ʿArabī's main disciple and interpreter. Despite his proximity to renowned individuals and rulers, little is actually known about Majd al-Dīn Isḥāq himself.[5]

We thus begin by tracing Shaykh Majd al-Dīn Isḥāq in Ibn Bībī's Persian history of the Rūm Seljuks, *al-Awāmir al-ʿalāʾīya*. Ibn Bībī's text contains a letter composed by Kaykhusraw I in the form of a Persian *mathnawī* (verse in rhymed couplets) and addressed to his spiritual guide and advisor, the shaykh. This *mathnawī* describes the sultan's longing for Majd al-Dīn Isḥāq to return to the Seljuk court and join him in the rule of his realm. We explore the context and possible motives behind Kaykhusraw I's summoning of the shaykh in light of the sultan's difficulties in regaining his throne. Although Ibn Bībī's text containing the sultan's letter is the most extensive source on Majd al-Dīn Isḥāq and his relationship to the Seljuk sultans, this information is nevertheless sparse. Most striking is Ibn Bībī's silence on Majd al-Dīn Isḥāq's association with Ibn ʿArabī. It was through Majd al-Dīn Isḥāq that Ibn ʿArabī entered the orbit of the Seljuk court at Konya, and Ibn ʿArabī seems to have made Malatya, where Majd al-Dīn was serving as tutor to the Seljuk prince Kaykā'ūs b. Ghiyāth al-Dīn Kaykhusraw I, his own base on the rare times when he was not travelling, especially on and off during the years 1212–23. Both Ibn 'Arabī and Majd al-Dīn continued to serve 'Izz al-Dīn Kaykā'ūs I in an advisory capacity after he took the throne in 1211. We thus examine in this chapter how these two men mutually shaped each other's lives, networks and spiritual pursuits. Naturally there is unequal treatment of these two peers; indeed, the emphasis lies on the 'Great Master' Ibn 'Arabī, whose considerable spiritual fame spread throughout the Islamic world and whose prolific and voluminous writings have had a profound impact on Sufism.

The final section of the chapter focuses on the two shaykhs' relationships to political power, relying primarily on the evidence left behind by Ibn 'Arabī. Ibn 'Arabī aimed to transcend the corrupting influence of worldly gain while restraining the excesses of worldly power and guiding Muslim rulers in their role as God's representatives on earth through a strict adherence to the *sharī'a*. Ibn 'Arabī's spiritual claims to be the 'Seal of the Muhammadan Saints' (*khatm al-wilāya al-Muḥammadīya*) required involvement with the world through the practice of spiritual political advice (*al-naṣīḥa al-siyāsīya al-ilāhīya*).[6] We conclude by reflecting on the place of Majd al-Dīn and Ibn 'Arabī in the Seljuk court of the early thirteenth century and in Anatolian society more generally.[7]

Summoning the Shaykh: Kaykhusraw I's Verse Epistle to Majd al-Dīn

According to Ibn Bībī, Majd al-Dīn Isḥāq was highly regarded among the Seljuk political elite, *'ulamā'* and Sufi circles. Although we do not know when or how he first entered the orbit of the Seljuk court, the shaykh served as Ghiyāth al-Dīn Kaykhusraw I's spiritual advisor. Majd al-Dīn Isḥāq first appears in Ibn Bībī's narrative following Kaykhusraw I's return from exile and his second accession to the throne in 1205, as the addressee of a letter penned by the sultan in verse. In this letter, Kaykhusraw I urges Majd al-Dīn Isḥāq, who was living in Syria at the time, to return to the Seljuk court in Konya now that the sultan's days of exile were over and he was back on the throne. Ibn Bībī claims to have directly transcribed the document of 35 couplets from the sultan's own handwriting – thus providing us with the only known example of verse from the pen of a Seljuk sultan.[8]

Directly addressing Majd al-Dīn Isḥāq, the Seljuk sultan's *mathnawī* begins with lavish praise of the shaykh's virtues, referring to his exemplary nature, unblemished character, heavenly purity and his angel-like soul. Majd al-Dīn is described as saint-like as well as a firm upholder of the *sunna* (the correct Islamic path): *ay wālī-yi sīrat! ay bānī-yi sunnat!*[9] The laudatory introductory section concludes with blessings, exhorting Majd al-Dīn Isḥāq's soul to 'remain eternal upon Judgement Day' and his affairs to stay safe from the 'hand of calamity'. The poem then turns to the sultan's own story of hardship and affliction, paralleling Ibn Bībī's account of Kaykhusraw's difficult years of exile (1196–1205). The *mathnawī* compares the sultan's destiny to that of Jam (Jamshīd), the legendary Iranian hero, who, having lost divine fortune, was forced into exile. The poem makes reference to his wanderings far and wide, from Syria and Armenia to the Byzantine court at Constantinople where he found refuge, and alludes to his adventures and battles during these difficult times.[10]

A little more than halfway through the *mathnawī*, with line 18, the poem shifts to a triumphal tone, noting that when the 'wheel of fortune' turned in the sultan's favour and 'the grace of God revealed His beauty', the sultan received divine visions with instructions for the correct path to take. Just as Ibn Bībī's account describes the succession of events culminating with the sultan's arrival at the Byzantine–Seljuk frontier in order to return to Konya to claim his throne, the poem likewise narrates the sultan's decisive action toward the 'place of raiders' (*janāb-i ālamān*).[11] The Seljuk frontier lords, the *mathnawī* continues, rallied around the sultan and presented their support with letters and salutations, referring to him as the 'Rightly Guided One' (*mahdī*). A sea journey across the Marmara thus brought the sultan south to the Mediterranean coast, from where he made his way to the inland western Seljuk outpost at Burghulu (Uluborlu).

With the assistance of the Lord, the poem explains, the sultan overcame all opposition and put the realm back under his authority. With this final note of victory, the sultan ends his letter by recalling Majd al-Dīn back to the Seljuk court, promising him great rewards and a place by his side as co-ruler:

> The land is in submission to me and you.
> My good name and your desire [will reign] in the world.
>
> Those who seek virtue
> all gather in the embrace of my rule.
>
> Make haste! The time has come for you to seek your rightful place here.
>
> If your head is dirtied with dust (as the result of grief), come wash it here.

The initial reference in the epistle to Majd al-Dīn as 'the crown of the companions of the fraternal assembly' (*tāj-i aṣḥāb-i majlis-i akhawī*) may be read in two ways. First, it may be understood as a rhetorical device referring to Majd al-Dīn's spiritual brotherhood with the sultan. Another reading – a more speculative one – takes *akhawī* to mean 'brotherly' in the sense of the fraternal orders of the *akhī*, thus associating Majd al-Dīn with a prominent position in the *futuwwa*, or the ranks of the spiritual brotherhood. Majd al-Dīn's association with the *futuwwa*, however, remains obscure, and is only hinted at by Ibn Bībī in the context of Kaykā'ūs I's induction into the caliphal *futuwwa* in 1215. Following the poem embedded in his text, Ibn Bībī picks up the historical narrative by stating that after years of separation, Majd al-Dīn Isḥāq hurried back to Konya to be reunited with his beloved student and patron, Kaykhusraw I.[12] With additional rhetorical embellishments, Ibn Bībī emphasises their intimacy in terms which blur the distinction of rank and power with the likening of the joyful reunion between shaykh and sultan in Konya to the following couplet by Ḥallāj: 'I am He whom I love and He whom I love is I / We are like two souls in single body'.[13] Indeed, in this verse epistle we see the reversal of roles between the sultan and his servitor, with the sultan as supplicant and the shaykh as recipient of praise. It is striking how the sultan grants the shaykh an authority equal to that of his own, as we see in line 33: 'The land is in submission to you and me / My good name and your desire [will reign] in the world' (*mamlakat rām-i mā wa rām-i shumā-st / dar jahān nām-i mā wa kām-i shumā-st*). Thus, although the sultan takes the role of the chosen instrument of God to rule the land and make it prosper, in accordance with the conventions of panegyric verse,[14] the shaykh is nevertheless elevated to a position akin to that of a ruler. Kaykhusraw I's letter not only reaffirms the role of rulership and its relationship with the divine but, uniquely, grants a legitimate space for the religious shaykh to take an equal footing with the sultan in the rule of the state.

Majd al-Dīn Isḥāq: A Shaykh for Kaykhusraw I's Political Woes?

Why was, as one may conclude from this *mathnawī*, Kaykhusraw I so anxious to reunite with his shaykh and to rule jointly as equals? Aside from rhetorical exaggeration, part and parcel of the laudatory genre of praise poetry, one needs to situate Kaykhusraw's anxiety in the context of the grave difficulties that faced him upon his return to Konya in 1205. Kaykhusraw I's second enthronement was not without opposition. In fact, the population refused to surrender the city to him, preferring the reign of the young son of Kaykhusraw I's late brother, Rukn al-Dīn Sulaymānshāh.[15] In addition to their loyalties to Rukn al-Dīn Sulaymānshāh and his immediate family, their resistance may have also been partially due to a fatwa supposedly issued by a certain Qāḍī al-Tirmidhī.[16] The fatwa declared Kaykhusraw ineligible for the Seljuk throne as a result of his close relations with infidels and his having engaged in activities contrary to the *sharīʿa* while residing in Byzantium.[17] His wrath thus aroused by this fatwa, Kaykhusraw I had the qadi executed. Ibn Bībī tells us, however, that the qadi had been set up by enemies, and the fatwa had been the result of foul play. The unjust execution of Qāḍī al-Tirmidhī, an ascetic and pious religious figure greatly revered in the city – praised by Ibn Bībī as the 'Abū'l-Layth al-Samarqandī of his time'[18] – caused quite a public stir. In fact, this injustice was believed to have been the reason for a three-year-long famine brought on by inclement weather conditions that were responsible for bringing about the deaths of many. We are told that it was only when the sultan learned of the truth of the matter and righted the wrongs committed against the qadi, with the conspirators confessing and the sultan compensating the qadi's family, that the famine came to an end.[19]

Despite Kaykhusraw's forced entry into the city and the initial resistance towards the sultan's re-enthronement, Ibn Bībī's account plays down the sultan's unpopularity among the Muslim population of Konya. The possible source of this unpopularity may have been his close personal ties with Byzantine Christians, and his reputation for un-Islamic behaviour while in Byzantium, as the fatwa indicated. The betrothal of the sultan's daughter to a Christian, the Byzantine noble Manuel Komnenos Mavrozomes, as well as the integration of Mavrozomes' large Christian household with the Seljuk imperial household, may have been controversial among the piety-minded, even if it was common for members of the Anatolian Seljuk dynastic family to intermarry with Byzantines.[20]

The vows of loyalty taken in the name of Sulaymānshāh's young son, Rukn al-Dīn Qılıch Arslan III, may have also made the people of Konya reluctant to switch sides. This precarious position, with the legitimacy of his claim over the Seljuk sultanate in question, especially following the fatwa and the controversial execution of the popular Qāḍī al-Tirmidhī (an unfortunate decision apparently made in haste), may have made Kaykhusraw I anxious for the counsel and spiritual guidance of his shaykh Majd al-Dīn Isḥāq, if not for *barakāt* (blessings) for a prosperous reign. His summons to the shaykh in the form of the *mathnawī* may have indeed been a response to this deepening crisis of political legitimacy, an attempt to shore up his position through his association with the highly respected and influential shaykh, Majd al-Dīn Isḥāq.

The Conquest of Sinop and the Seljuk Embassy to Baghdad

Due to the lack of sources, it is impossible to know how much influence Majd al-Dīn Isḥāq wielded over Kaykhusraw I. His sway over ʿIzz al-Dīn Kaykāʾūs I, however, is more evident. Majd al-Dīn Isḥāq emerges in Ibn Bībī's narrative for one last time in 1215 as leader of the sultan's embassy to the caliph al-Nāṣir li-Dīn Allāh (1185–1225),[21] following Kaykāʾūs I's conquest of the Komnenian port of Sinop on 1 November 1214.[22] Ibn Bībī's narrative of the Seljuk mission and the induction of Kaykāʾūs I into the caliphal *futuwwa*, however, presents several difficulties. The section is prefaced by a seemingly irrelevant hunting anecdote regarding Malik Ashraf, presumably al-Malik al-Ashraf Mūsā b. ʿĀdil I, who, at the time, was the Ayyubid governor of the Diyar Mudar,[23] and concludes rather inconsistently with a *futuwwa-nāma* issued to the sultan by the caliph dated to 1212, two years before the conquest of Sinop. Osman Turan's solution to this chronological dilemma was to reorder the sequence of events as presented by Ibn Bībī. Rather than present the Seljuk embassy to the caliph, headed by Majd al-Dīn, as a way of announcing the Seljuk sultan's victory to the caliph as well as requesting the caliphal *futuwwa* trousers, as Ibn Bībī does, Turan places the embassy right after the sultan's ascension to the throne and dates it to 1212, matching the date on the *futuwwa-nāma*. Thus, according to Turan, the embassy led by Majd al-Dīn was aimed at announcing the sultan's accession in 1211 rather than his victory at Sinop in 1214.[24]

Although it is not immediately apparent, the brief anecdote about the Ayyubid prince al-Ashraf which prefaces Ibn Bībī's account of the Seljuk embassy to the caliph – and which Ibn Bībī leaves mysteriously unexplained – is highly significant in the context of *futuwwa* regional politics. Ibn Bībī recounts that the Seljuk sultan was informed that al-Malik al-Ashraf sent many generous gifts to the caliph al-Nāṣir li-Dīn Allāh after having killed a whooping crane (*kulang*) with a crossbow while hunting. The caliph reciprocated with an embassy delivering valuable gifts to the Ayyubid prince.[25]

Following this anecdote, and the list of gifts that the caliph sent al-Malik al-Ashraf, Ibn Bībī tells us, 'When the sultan of Rūm conquered Sinop, thus bringing it into the orbit of the Islamic world, where the *sharīʿa* was now put into effect, he offered prayers to the leader of the Islamic world, the caliph'.[26] One subtle detail in Ibn Bībī's account, however, provides a clue to the anecdote's narrative message. By telling us that al-Malik al-Ashraf pronounced the caliph's name while hunting the crane with the crossbow, Ibn Bībī alludes to the Ayyubid prince's induction into the caliph's courtly *futuwwa*, for such a pronouncement was required for *futuwwa* members whenever engaged in such hunting activities.[27] By prefacing the story of Kaykāʾūs I's induction into the caliphal *futuwwa* with the episode of al-Malik al-Ashraf's crane, Ibn Bībī may have been showing up the Ayyubids. In contrast to al-Malik al-Ashraf's hunting success with his downing of a crane, an occasion which he celebrated through an elaborate gift-exchange with the caliph, Kaykāʾūs I was victor over a much more significant prey: with the conquest of Sinop, the sultan brought an important trading emporium into the *Dār al-Islām*. This conquest, the highlight of Kaykāʾūs I's career, earned him prestige throughout the Islamic world. It likewise helped consolidate Kaykāʾūs I's shaky hold over the throne: he had, after all, only defeated his rival to the throne – his younger brother (and future sultan) ʿAlāʾ al-Dīn Kayqubād, the *malik* of Tokat – a few months before, in March 1214.[28] Thus, in parallel with the Ayyubid prince's gesture to the caliph, the Seljuk sultan likewise offered prayers to al-Nāṣir and sent an embassy to Baghdad loaded with gifts and jewels, headed by the shaykh Majd al-Dīn Isḥāq.[29] The gifts the sultan sent to the caliph reflect the variety of international goods passing through Sinop:[30] precious jewels; golden jewel-studded crosses (*chalīphā-yi zarrīn-i muraṣṣaʿ*); silver vessels; sumptuous furnishings and textiles from all over the world;[31] valuable horses and livestock;[32] and slaves, both male (*ghulām*) and female (*kanīz*). This extravaganza of gifts sent with the news of the conquest of Sinop thus reflected the economic ramifications of the sultan's seizure of an important trade emporium.[33]

In addition to announcing the sultan's victory, and safely delivering these precious gifts, Majd al-Dīn was charged with requesting the trousers (*sarāwīl*) that symbolised admission to the courtly *futuwwa* headed by the caliph. He was received with honour and presented with a host of valuable gifts in return.[34] Upon his departure for his country, the caliph presented Majd al-Dīn with the following items to bequeath to the sultan: a belt of *muruwwa* (representing the virtuous qualities of a mature man), which he stripped off his own body, as well as the trousers of righteousness and the *futuwwa* letter, the contents of which Ibn Bībī reproduces in full.[35] The caliph also bestowed upon 'Izz al-Dīn Kaykā'ūs the honorific title, *al-sulṭān al-ghālib*.

According to Stephen Hirtenstein, Majd al-Dīn Isḥāq, as a leading figure in the Abbasid caliph's reorganisation of the *futuwwa*, was given the task of introducing these reforms into Anatolia.[36] However, it is curious that Kaykhusraw I was never initiated into the *futuwwa* when it was newly organised under caliphal authority in 1207,[37] especially if his spiritual advisor, Majd al-Dīn, were indeed a high-ranking leader of the *futuwwa*. Rather, it was his son, Kaykā'ūs I, who sought membership in the caliphal *futuwwa*. Kaykā'ūs I, however, did not approach the caliph until he achieved what was perhaps his greatest military victory, the conquest of Sinop in 1214. In contrast, the Ayyubid princes were immediately inducted into the Nasirean *futuwwa* through diplomatic missions led by Shihāb al-Dīn Abū Ḥafṣ 'Umar al-Suhrawardī (d. 1234) in 1207–8.[38] Perhaps Kaykā'ūs I's desire to join the caliphal *futuwwa* was motivated in part by the intensifying rivalry with the Ayyubid princes of the Jazira.[39]

Finally, how do we reconcile the 1212 date of the *futuwwa* letter issued by the caliph with the progression of events as narrated by Ibn Bībī? If we disregard the possibility of being a copyist's mistake, this discrepancy may be tentatively explained by the outbreak of the succession struggle over the Seljuk throne, when 'Alā' al-Dīn Kayqubād challenged his older brother's claim to the throne. Kaykā'ūs I finally defeated his fraternal rival with great difficulty in 1214,[40] a few months before the conquest of Sinop. The succession struggle destabilised the Seljuk realm, as manifested by the Christian rebellion in Antalya between 1212 and 1214.[41] Did this struggle delay Kaykā'ūs

I from sending an embassy to the caliph in order to request initiation into the *futuwwa*? Was the letter composed and dated in anticipation of Kaykā'ūs I's sending an embassy, only to remain unclaimed for a few years until the sultan was able to firmly establish his rule, bring an end to his brother's claims to the throne, and bring stability to his realm? Indeed, as was the practice, the caliph would have hesitated to hastily recognise the sultanate of an individual in the midst of a succession struggle, the outcome of which was not certain.

The Shaykh of Sultans and Shaykh of Shaykhs: Majd al-Dīn and Ibn 'Arabī in Anatolia

That Majd al-Dīn Isḥāq was highly regarded at the caliphal court is clear from the long series of honorifics granted him in Caliph al-Nāṣir's *futuwwat-nāma*, as the document appears embedded in Ibn Bībī's text: 'the Learned Pious Shaykh' (*al-shaykh al-ajall al-'ālim al-'ābid al-wāri'*), 'the Star of Islam' (*najm al-Islām*), 'the Glory of the Community' (*fakhr al-ṭā'ifa*), 'the Beauty of Divine Truth' (*jamāl al-ḥaqīqa*) and 'the Pillar of the Gnostics' (*'umdat al-'ārifīn*).[42] He is also designated the 'Shaykh of the World' (*shaykh-i 'ālam*) and the 'Exemplar of the Universe' (*pīshwā-yi āfāq*).[43] Majd al-Din's wider reputation and influence among his peers and the general populace is perhaps reflected in the titles given to him by Ibn Bībī: 'the Exemplar of the Horizons' (*muqtadā-yi āfāq*)[44] and 'the Leader of Different Nations' (*qidwat al-ṭawā'if*), honorifics suggesting that the shaykh's wide influence and authority transcended Seljuk political borders and was recognised in different communities. The designation 'the Exemplar of the Devotees' (*uswat al-'ubbād*) may indicate that Majd al-Dīn belonged to a select group of Sufi masters. Perhaps most intriguing, however, is the honorific *sharaf al-awtād*,[45] 'the Glory of the Pegs', which associates Majd al-Dīn with the 'tent-pegs' or the 'cosmic tent-posts' (*awtād*; sing., *watad*), i.e. mystics high in the saintly hierarchy. The eleventh-century Sufi thinker al-Qushayrī considered that the peg kept the universe stable.[46] Ibn 'Arabī further developed this saintly hierarchy in his *al-Futūḥāt al-makkīya*, stating that at any given time, 'the universe is supported by one Pole, two

Imams, four Pegs, seven Substitutes, and so on.'[47] According to Ibn 'Arabī, the four *awtād* were the spiritual guardians who assumed 'the role of stabilizing the faith of the believers and ensuring the constant flow of God's grace and inspirations.'[48] Ibn 'Arabī claimed to be one of the four *awtād* of his time.[49] Is the honorific *sharaf al-awtād* a conscious association of Majd al-Dīn Isḥāq with the great mystic?

Rather curiously, Ibn Bībī refrains from directly referring to to Ibn 'Arabī's well-known association with Majd al-Dīn. Ibn 'Arabī himself referred to Majd al-Dīn Isḥāq as his 'righteous companion'.[50] Majd al-Dīn first became acquainted with Ibn 'Arabī when, based in Damascus, Majd al-Dīn led a group of Anatolian pilgrims from Konya and Malatya to perform the hajj in August 1203.[51] Notations in various copies of his works make it possible to locate Ibn 'Arabī's whereabouts on certain dates; this allows us to reconstruct a rough chronology of Ibn 'Arabī's and Majd al-Dīn's relationship.[52] Ibn 'Arabī notes in his *Rūḥ al-quds*, a work begun in Mecca in December 1203, that he had 17 aspirants (*murīd*), one of whom was Majd al-Dīn.[53] One may thus assume that Majd al-Dīn most likely became acquainted with Ibn 'Arabī around the period of the hajj in August, and joined his circle of adepts around this time. In the following years, Majd al-Dīn appears to be constantly in the presence of the great master as a disciple as well as intimate companion. Analysis of the *samā's* (reading certificates placed at the end of a work) issued by Ibn 'Arabī reveals Majd al-Dīn as one of two regular auditors of these sessions (the other being Ibn 'Arabī's son-in-law, Muḥammad b. Sa'd al-Dīn b. Baranqush b. Qamar al-Dimishqī).[54] Majd al-Dīn, however, was more than just a disciple of the shaykh. As Ibn 'Arabī explained to Majd al-Dīn's son – his principal disciple, Ṣadr al-Dīn Muḥammad al-Qūnawī – before he left Spain for his eastward journey, he had a divinely inspired vision telling him that his principal companions would be Majd al-Dīn Isḥāq and Ṣadr al-Dīn.[55] Indeed, Ibn 'Arabī regarded the father and son as essential to his mission as the 'Seal of the Saints' to preserve and spread the true teachings of the Prophet as ordained by the Divinity.[56]

When Majd al-Dīn prepared to return to Konya in 1205, he invited Ibn 'Arabī to accompany him to the Seljuk court. After passing briefly through Baghdad, they stopped for around a month in Mosul where Ibn 'Arabī acquainted himself with the local scholarly community, attracted new followers and held auditions of his works.[57] Ibn 'Arabī's travel was combined with teaching, reading his works in public and meeting other Sufis and noteworthy religious figures. A note dating from 29 Ramadan 601/20 May 1205 in a work in progress at the time, the *Rūḥ al-quds*, indicates that Majd al-Dīn was among Ibn 'Arabī's nine students in Mosul.[58] From Mosul they travelled to Malatya, arriving there in June or July, and then onto Konya, where they were received by the newly enthroned Kaykhusraw I.[59]

Despite the sultan's exhortations to join him in ruling the realm, Majd al-Dīn Isḥāq did not take up a high post in the administration or remain in Konya at the sultan's side. Rather, he departed soon afterwards for his home town of Malatya to serve as guardian and tutor to 'Izz al-Dīn Kaykā'ūs, the prince-governor of Malatya.[60] As Ibn 'Arabī informs us, the sultan loaded Majd al-Dīn and Ibn 'Arabī with gifts as they headed for Malatya as part of the entourage of the Seljuk prince.[61] Ibn Bībī makes no further mention of Majd al-Dīn Isḥāq during Kaykhusraw I's reign. While Majd al-Dīn remained in Malatya, Ibn 'Arabī resumed his travelling in 1206,[62] heading first for Hebron and then Cairo.[63] He was, however, forced to flee Cairo in 1207, it seems, as a result of a controversy over his doctrines.[64] After stopping over in Mecca, he returned to Anatolia, passing through Malatya in the winter in 607/1211; he notes in one of his works that the winter was so cold that the Euphrates froze over.[65] He appeared in Konya soon afterwards, arriving sometime around 'Izz al-Dīn Kaykā'ūs' enthronement in July 1211.[66]

While Stephen Hirtenstein has described Ibn 'Arabī's three-year Meccan period as the 'fulcrum of his earthly existence',[67] the subsequent 20 years were spent for the most part travelling back and forth between Mecca, Jerusalem, Egypt, Syria and Anatolia. His ambulatory lifestyle was no obstacle to literary production, and during this time he produced hundreds of works.[68] Amidst this constant travel, it may be estimated that Ibn 'Arabī spent a total of five or six years in Malatya from late 1205/early 1206 to 1222. Indeed, it seems that Malatya served as his base, especially towards the latter half of this period from 1215 onwards. Ibn 'Arabī was present in Malatya some time in 613/1216–17, as the record of reading of the *Tāj al-rasā'il* indicates.[69] His son's birth in 618/1221,[70] as well as the death of his constant companion Badr al-Ḥabashī[71] in Malatya strengthens this supposition. Situated in the upper Euphrates valley on the frontier between Seljuk Anatolia and Ayyubid Syria, Malatya must have served as a convenient base for constant travel between the Arab lands and the Seljuk centres of Konya and Kayseri. Other reasons for his prolonged stay in Anatolia, as Addas points out, were his close relations with Kaykā'ūs I as well as his domestic responsibilities. Indeed, following Majd al-Dīn's death, possibly in 612/1215–16, Ibn 'Arabī married Majd al-Dīn's widow and took on the responsibility of educating Majd al-Dīn's young son, Ṣadr al-Dīn.[72] In 1222–3, during the early years of 'Alā' al-Dīn Kayqubād I's reign, Ibn 'Arabī left Anatolia for Damascus.[73]

One may presume that it was through Majd al-Dīn Isḥāq that Ibn 'Arabī became acquainted with members of certain elite circles of religious scholars and shaykhs in Baghdad and Konya, including the renowned 'Umar al-Suhrawardī (d. 1234) and his wide-ranging network of disciples spreading the Suhrawardīya, particulary in the east. For instance, Ibn 'Arabī met the Suhrawardīya shaykh, Awḥad al-Dīn al-Kirmānī in Konya upon his arrival in 1205.[74] He likewise made the acquaintance of other eminent Iranian Sufis affiliated with the Suhrawardīya and/or caliphal *futuwwa*, such as Abū Ja'far Muḥammad al-Barzā'ī and Shaykh Nāṣir al-Dīn Mahmud Akhī Evren.[75] As a result of these contacts, Ibn 'Arabī's work may have begun to immediately circulate in cities such as Konya, Kayseri and Mosul, at least among certain elite circles, as a surviving *majmū'a* dating from 602/1205–6 indicates. The *majmū'a* includes works composed in Mecca and Mosul such as *al-Tanazzulāt al-mawṣiliyya fī asrār al-ṭahārāt wa 'l-ṣalawāt wa 'l-ayyām al-aṣliyya*,[76] *Kitāb ḥilyat al-abdāl*, *Tāj al-tarārajim fī ishārāt al-'ilm wa laṭā'if al-fahm* and *Kitāb al-shawāhid*.[77]

Guiding 'Izz al-Dīn Kaykā'ūs I: Ibn 'Arabī's Spiritual *Naṣīḥa* (Counsel)

Through Majd al-Dīn Isḥāq, Ibn 'Arabī not only gained entry into the world of the intellectual, religious and spiritual elite of Anatolia, but also that of the politically powerful, a situation which brought its own moral perils. With a line of verse in a letter to Majd al-Dīn, Ibn 'Arabī warned his friend to be aware of the danger of pride while in the service of rulers: 'Oh Ishāq, listen to some useful advice from your brother: may you not be proud for your proximity to sultans.'[78] Ibn 'Arabī regarded delusion and pride as the main obstacles to union with the Divine Self, and thus association with power and wealth, combined with the rewards of service, posed a danger to spiritual development. One did not have to remain in the administrative capital or take a position in the imperial *dīwān*, however, to influence the powerful. As tutor to the royal prince, Majd al-Dīn had the chance to shape the spiritual and intellectual development of the heir to the Seljuk throne. Ibn 'Arabī was also on intimate terms with Kaykā'ūs during these years as a spiritual guide and teacher.[79]

Could Sufi shaykhs and aspirants accommodate both worldly concerns and spiritual goals? Earlier in his career, Ibn 'Arabī did not attempt to do so. Rather, he avoided all political rulers and rejected their gifts, no matter how humble. As Addas points out, Ibn 'Arabī exhibited 'a guarded and even critical attitude with regard to the Almohad authorities', whom he regarded as corrupt.[80] His attitude to political power during this period is well illustrated by his anecdote of how, while in Ceuta, Spain, in 1193, he rejected the food sent to him by the sultan at the risk of putting himself in danger. In fact, a Sufi at the *zāwīya* where he was staying had denounced him before the sultan's vizier for having done so. Warned by a fellow shaykh of the precarious position he was putting himself in, Ibn 'Arabī nonetheless nonchalantly discounted the danger.[81]

Although Ibn 'Arabī continued to stress the precept 'do not approach the gates of the sultan' for his disciples, as seen in works such as the *Kitāb al-kunh* and the *Rūḥ al-quds*,[82] his own interactions with rulers changed noticeably after his pilgrimage to Mecca.[83]

Rather than avoid those wielding worldly power, Ibn 'Arabī began to dispense spiritual counsel to them. This change in his approach to those in power – accommodation without spiritual corruption – came about with his new understanding of his obligation to God as revealed through dreams and visions.

In a short treatise, *Risālat al-mubashshirāt* (Epistle of Good Tidings) dealing with 18 of his visionary dreams, Ibn 'Arabī describes one of his most transformative visions.[84] In this vision, which he had while circumambulating the Ka'ba in Mecca, Ibn 'Arabī was reproached by the Lord to admonish His servants, for earlier that evening Ibn 'Arabī had resolved to 'concern myself with my own soul, to forget about all the other people and their condition'.[85] As a result this vision, Ibn 'Arabī gained new insight into the Prophetic hadith included in Muslim's *Ṣaḥīḥ*: 'The Prophet said, "Religion is admonishment (*naṣīḥa*) for God, for the leaders of the Muslims, and for the common people among them".' Through this vision at the Ka'ba, Ibn 'Arabī realised that part of his mission on earth was to offer counsel (*naṣīḥa*), not only to the spiritual elite but to men of all ranks and stations – to all servants of God – according to God's law.[86] Even while under the patronage of Kaykā'ūs I, Ibn 'Arabī never abandoned his practice of shunning wealth and material rewards granted through political favour. One anecdote relates how, while in Konya, Ibn 'Arabī gave a poor man a villa bestowed upon him by Kaykā'ūs I, for the luxurious residence supposedly worth around 100,000 dirhams was apparently of no use to the shaykh.[87]

A letter to the sultan from Ibn 'Arabī incorporated into his masterpiece, *al-Futūḥāt al-makkīya* (The Meccan Revelations) demonstrates how Ibn 'Arabī exercised the spiritual obligation of guiding his charge, Kaykā'ūs I.[88] Here Ibn 'Arabī discusses how he counselled the sultan as a 'father who prays on his behalf' (*wāliduhu al-dā'ī lahu Muḥammad b. al-'Arabī*). After explaining that it was incumbent upon him to offer the sultan his religious inheritance (*al-waṣīya al-dīnīya*) and divine political counsel (*al-naṣīḥa al-siyāsīya al-ilāhīya*), Ibn 'Arabī cites the same well-known Prophetic hadith, 'religion is counsel' (*al-dīn al-naṣīḥa*) to which he gave such importance in his *Risālat al-mubashshirāt*.[89] Ibn 'Arabī's long preface concludes by reminding the sultan of his divinely appointed duties, pointing out that God had entrusted him with His commands as well as with rule over His servants.[90] He thus exhorts the sultan, as the shadow of God on earth, to rule justly and to ensure that His servants are protected from oppression. The letter then deals specifically with the Pact of 'Umar,[91] a set of regulations imposed on non-Muslim populations and, in this case, Christians under Muslim rule. Ibn 'Arabī's discussion of the Pact of 'Umar takes the form of a warning, pointing out that the greatest affliction for Muslims and Islam is the pealing of church bells – an open manifestation of disbelief – and the appeal of *shirk* (polytheism) in Muslim lands. Ibn 'Arabī deplores the abandoning of the *dhimmī* regulations as first imposed by Caliph 'Umar al-Khattāb. He then enumerates the regulations, stating that Christians were not to build or repair churches, monasteries or other Christian buildings. They were not to mount horses nor equip themselves with weapons. Their titles were not to be similar to that of Muslim ones. Nor could they use seals in Arabic, or sell alcoholic drinks. They were to be distinguished from Muslims in their clothing, footwear and headgear, and were to shave the front of their heads, and wear the *zunnār*, or distinctive belt, around their waists. They were not to expose their crosses or other religious symbols while going down roads used by Muslims, nor to bury their dead in the vicinity of Muslim graveyards. They were to ring their church bell only once, and they were not to bring too much attention to their religious ceremonies through excessive noise or visual display.[92]

The discussion of the enforcement of the *dhimmī* regulations seems to be directly related to the sultan's struggle to quell the Christian rebellion in Antalya, breaking out in 1212, the year the letter was written. Ibn 'Arabī's letter openly expresses a fear of Christian influence, if not dominance, over Muslims, in both belief and practice, and the resulting neglect of the Qur'an, the basis of religion. Ibn 'Arabī's attitude towards Christians, or rather, Christian dominance, should be understood in accordance with his self-proclaimed role of reviving Islam in face of Christian expansion into Muslims lands, during a time when Crusades in both Spain and the Levantine coastal region posed a real threat to Muslim sovereignty.[93] Muslim communities under Christian rule suffered the indignity of similar regulations.[94]

This discussion of *dhimmī* regulation is followed by a poetic piece of 17 lines directly addressing Kaykā'ūs I, in which Ibn 'Arabī plays upon the former's titles and names. In the first half of the poem, Ibn 'Arabī urges the sultan, in accordance with his *laqab* 'Izz al-Dīn, to honour Islam and not allow the religion to fall into disrepute, but rather to assure the triumph of Islam and have it return to its former days of glory. Embedded in the second half of the poem are oblique references to two troublesome aspects of the sultan's rule.[95] In the first, Ibn 'Arabī exhorts a show of mercy to two enemies, an obscure reference which Mahmud Erol Kılıç relates to the Seljuk sultan's unsuccessful military conflict with the Ayyubid ruler of the Jazira, al-Ashraf Mūsā.[96] The second, equally obscure, reference is to that of a vizier who was bringing great harm upon religion with his transgressions. Kılıç believes that the vizier referred to here is Sayf al-Dīn Ayaba *chasnīgīr*,[97] the Seljuk commander-in-chief who wielded an inordinate amount of power under Kaykā'ūs I.[98] Ibn 'Arabī challenges the sultan: how can you call yourself 'al-Ghālib' (the Vanquisher) when you cannot control him [the vizier]? Ibn 'Arabī concludes his poem by stressing that his advice was not like that of others, for his right to counsel the sultan was based on his divinely appointed mission to protect the religion, the world and the sultan himself.[99]

Other evidence points to a relationship involving regular correspondence between Ibn 'Arabī and Kaykā'ūs I. For instance, during Ramadan 612/1215 while in Sivas, the shaykh wrote a letter to the sultan immediately after having had a significant dream. Interpreting the dream as foretelling the sultan's reconquest of Antalya during the Christian rebellion, Ibn 'Arabī reported the details of the dream in his letter, including how he saw the sultan in the midst of the siege, setting up siege machines along the city's wall. He saw stones being hauled over the city walls, and an enemy commander die. Sure enough, by the end of Ramadan, the sultan seized the city, some 20 days after Ibn 'Arabī's dream.[100] In this instance at least, there was a fortunate coincidence between the sultan's worldly concerns of territorial expansion and Ibn 'Arabī's spiritual ones of defending the *umma*.

Conclusion

The case of Ibn 'Arabī and his companion and disciple, Majd al-Dīn Isḥāq, problematises the notion that a fusion between politics and religion brought about a strict division among the religious scholarly class, with one group advocating estrangement from the state in order to avoid being corrupted by power and the other seeking cooperation with it for worldly gain.[101] In early thirteenth-century Anatolia, still doubtless an overwhelmingly Christian society, both *'ulamā'* and political elites needed each other. For the sultan, association with men like Majd al-Dīn and Ibn 'Arabī and membership in the *futuwwa* offered the opportunity to burnish their Islamic credentials. These credentials, given the Christian-influenced Greek-speaking nature of the sultan's court described by Rustam Shukurov in an earlier chapter, must often have been in dire need of burnishing, and neighbouring rulers too on occasion taunted the Anatolian Seljuks for their pacific attitude towards their Christian subjects and neighbours.[102] Crises of rule caused by internal political strife and revolt, as seen by the reaction of Konya to Kaykhusraw I's return as sultan in 1205 and the revolt of Antalya in 1212–14, must only have exacerbated this sultanic need for religiously sanctioned legitimacy.

Of course, there was nothing particularly exceptional about this: throughout the Muslim world rulers often sought legitimation through the *'ulamā'*. In the Mamluk sultanate, slightly later in the thirteenth century, research has revealed similar examples of the *'ulamā'* acting as spiritual guides for sultans.[103] Yet as far as we can tell from the case of Anatolia, it was less that the sultans sought the approbation of a particular class or category of men, the *'ulamā'*, but rather that they relied on specific individuals, as in the case of Ibn 'Arabī and Majd al-Dīn – both of whom themselves were linked by ties of friendship and marriage. The difference was probably that in Anatolia there was not much of an *'ulamā'* group to speak of: there were some qadis here and there in the main towns, to be sure, but there were hardly the substantial swathes of society who would define themselves, at least at some times and for some purposes, as *'ulamā'*, as there were in lands such as Syria and Egypt. The relatively few examples from early thirteenth-century Anatolia of madrasas, the classic Islamic institution for *'ulamā'* career-development, is strong evidence of this.[104] So, instead of appealing to a group, the sultans sought to win the support of a handful of religiously influential figures.

At the same time, the very lack of a strong *'ulamā'* presence in Anatolia may well have been a major part of its attraction for Ibn 'Arabī. After having realised his true calling, beginning in 1200 and culminating during the hajj at Mecca, Ibn 'Arabī needed a safe haven, for his audacious spiritual claims to be 'The Seal of Saints' were sure to bring him enemies, especially (but far from exclusively) among scholarly circles hostile to Sufi practices and mystical thought. Majd al-Dīn, with his contacts as the Seljuk court, was able to offer Ibn 'Arabī such security. Anatolia offered Ibn 'Arabī a chance to enlarge his circle of followers and develop new networks within the religiously interested elite, among whom his works soon began to circulate. Furthermore, the absence of a class of *'ulamā'* meant that Ibn 'Arabī could propagate his claims to sainthood without fear of the persecution that had seen him forced to flee Cairo.[105] In this sense, Anatolia's very lack of Islamic infrastructure may have contributed to the spread of al-Shaykh al-Akbar's ideas and at the same time made him politically useful as a distinguished representative of the faith from the furthest west rather than the distinct liability he would have been to rulers elsewhere in the Muslim world.

Notes

1. Mawlānā Jalāl al-Dīn Muḥammad, *Kitāb-i fīhi mā fīhi*, ed. Badī' al-Zamān Furūzanfar (Tehran: Intishārāt-i Nigāh, 1387 sh./2008 [3rd edition]), p. 15. This and all translations into English belong to the authors unless otherwise specified.

2. Claude Cahen, *La Turquie pré-ottomane* (Istanbul: Institut Français des Etudes Anatoliennes, 1988), p. 210.
3. *Das Biographische Lexikon des Ṣalāḥaddīn Ḫalīl Ibn Aibak Aṣ-Ṣafadī*, ed. Sven Dedering (Wiesbaden: Franz Steiner Verlag, 1974), ii, p. 200. Information on Majd al-Dīn Isḥāq is found under the entry for his son Ṣadr al-Dīn. Ibn Bībī refers to his full name as Majd al-Dīn Isḥāq b. Yūsuf b. 'Alī: Ibn Bībī, *al-Awāmir al-'alā'īya fī 'l-umūr al-'alā'īya*, facsimile edition prepared by Adnan Sadık Erzi as İbn-i Bībī, *el-Evāmirü'l-'Alā'iyye fī'l-Umūri'l-'Alā'iyye* (Ankara: Türk Tarih Kurumu, 1956), p. 157.
4. We have no solid evidence regarding the date of Majd al-Dīn Isḥāq's death. Mahmud Erol Kılıç dates it at 1215 based on the supposition that around this time Ibn 'Arabī took on the responsibility of caring for his wife, whom he apparently married, and his son, Ṣadr al-Dīn Muḥammad. See Mahmud Erol Kılıç, 'İbnu'l-Arabî'nin 1. İzzeddîn Kaykâvus'a Yazdığı Mektubun Işığında Dönemin Dînî ve Siyâsî Tarihine Bakış', in Osman Eravşar (ed.), *I. Uluslararası Selçuklu Kültür ve Medeniyeti Kongresi. Bildiriler* (Konya: Selçuk Üniversitesi Yayını, 2001), ii, p. 17 note 18.
5. The most detailed information on Majd al-Dīn Isḥāq to date may be found in Haşim Şahin's doctoral thesis, 'Osmanlı Devletinin Kuruluş Döneminde Dinî Zümreler (1299–1402)' (PhD Dissertation, Marmara University, 2007), pp. 47–9, and Claude Addas, *Ibn 'Arabī, ou la quête du soufre rouge* (Paris: Gallimard, 1986), translated by Peter Kingsley as *Quest for the Red Sulphur: The Life of Ibn 'Arabī* (Cambridge: Islamic Texts Society, 1993), pp. 225–7.
6. For more on Ibn 'Arabī's self-conception as the Seal of the Saints, see the seminal studies by Michel Chodkiewicz, *Les sceaux des Saints: prophétie et saintité dans la doctrine d'Ibn Arabî* (Paris: Gallimard, 1986) and Addas, *Quest for the Red Sulphur*, especially pp. 218 ff. Also consult the more recent study by Gerald T. Elmore, *Islamic Sainthood in the Fullness of Time: Ibn al-'Arabi's Book of the Fabulous Gryphon* (Leiden: E.J. Brill, 1999), based on his doctoral thesis (Yale University, 1995).

7. The question of Ibn 'Arabī's subsequent reception in Anatolia has yet to be examined in detail. Alexander D. Knysh's extensive study of the afterlife of Ibn 'Arabī's works, primarily through the later biographical traditions and religious polemics up to the sixteenth century, focuses exclusively on the Arab lands without touching upon Anatolia or the Ottoman period (Alexander D. Knysh, *Ibn 'Arabī in the Later Islamic Tradition: The Making of a Polemical Image in Medieval Islam* [Albany, N.Y.: SUNY Press, 1999]).
8. Ibn Bībī, *al-Awāmir al-'alā'īya*, p. 91.
9. Ibid.
10. For more on the sultan's dual with the Frankish knight, see Dmitri Korobeinikov, 'A sultan in Constantinople: the feasts of Ghiyāth al-Dīn Kay-Khusraw I', in Leslie Brubaker and Kallirroe Linardou (eds), *Eat, Drink and Be Merry (Luke 12:19). Food and Wine in Byzantium. In Honour of Professor A. A. M. Bryer* (Aldershot and Burlington, Vermont: Ashgate, 2007), pp. 98–100.
11. According to Mürsel Öztürk, the Turkish translator of Ibn Bībī's Persian unabridged text, *ālamān* means 'the Germans who came to Anatolia with the Crusaders' (Ibn Bībī, *El-Evamirü'l-Ala'iye fi'l-umuri'l-Ala'iye (Selçuk name)*, (p. vii)] trans. Mürsel Öztürk (Ankara: Kültür Bakanlığı, 1996, 2 vols), ii, p.112 note 347. For the meaning of *ālamān* as 'raider', see Gerhard Doerfer, *Türkische und mongolische Elemente in Neupersischen, unter besonderer Berücksichtigung älterer neupersicher Geschichtsquellen, vor allem der Mongolen- und Timuridenzeit* (Wiesbaden: Steiner, 1963–75, 4 vols), ii, p. 119, entry no. 541–2. We are grateful to Ferenc Csirkes for helping us establish the more probable meaning of this word as raider.
12. Ibn Bībī, *al-Awāmir al-'alā'īya*, p. 93.
13. Ibid.: *Anā man ahwā wa man ahwā anā, naḥnu rūḥān jallalna badan*. For the identification of this couplet as verse from Ḥallāj, see Kılıç, 'İbnu'l-Arabî'nin 1. İzzeddîn Kaykâvus'a Yazdığı Mektubu', p. 16.
14. Cf. the comments of Stefan Sperl on the ritualistic function of panegyric poetry at court: Stefan Sperl, 'Islamic kingship and

Arabic panegyric poetry in the early 9th century', *Journal of Arabic Literature 8* (1977), especially pp. 21, 23, 33.

15. Bar Hebraeus, *The Chronography of Gregory Abu'l-Faraj*, trans. Ernest A. Wallis Budge (London: Oxford University Press, 1932), i, p. 360; Ibn Bībī, *al-Awāmir al-'alā'īya*, p. 85.
16. Ibn Bībī, *al-Awāmir al-'alā'īya*, pp. 94–5.
17. Ibid., p. 94.
18. Abū Layth al-Samarqandī (d. 983 or 993) was an eminent Transoxanian Hanafi jurist renowned for his fatwas. His *Kitāb fatāwā al-nawāzil* was one of the earliest fatwa collections, with fatwas issued by a wide range of Hanafi jurists. See Muhammad Khalid Masud, Brinkley Messick and David S. Powers, 'Muftis, fatwas, and Islamic legal interpretation', in idem, (eds), *Islamic Legal Interpretation. Muftis and their Fatwas* (Cambridge, Mass.: Harvard University Press, 1996), p.10; Wael Hallaq, 'From fatwās to furū': growth and change in Islamic substantive law', *Islamic Law and Society* 1, no. 1 (1994), pp. 39, 43.
19. Ibn Bībī, *al-Awāmir al-'alā'īya*, p. 94; Osman Turan, *Selçuklular Zamanında Türkiye: Siyasi Tarih Alp Arslan'dan Osman Gazi'ye, 1071–1318* (Istanbul: Turan Neşriyatı Yurdu, 1971), p. 276. Egypt was devastated by famine and plague in 1201–2, as was Ṭā'if, outside Mecca, in 1203 (Addas, *Quest for the Red Sulphur*, pp. 194, 217).
20. For the Seljuk dual identity as a result of constant interaction and intermarriage with the Byzantines and other neighbouring Christian rulers, see Rustam Shukurov's contribution to this volume. For an overview of Kaykhusraw I's close family ties and relations with Byzantine Christians, primarily the result of his period of exile in Byzantium, and in particular the role the Mavrozomes nobles came to play in the Seljuk realm, see S.N. Yıldız, 'Manuel Komnenos Mavrozomes and his descendants at the Seljuk court: the formation of a Christian Seljuk-Komnenian elite', in Stefan Leder (ed.), *Crossroads between Latin Europe and the Near East: Corollaries of the Frankish Presence in the Eastern*

Mediterranean (12th–14th centuries) (Würzburg: Ergon Verlag, 2011), pp. 55–77.

21. For more on the caliph, see Angelika Hartmann, *An-Nasir li-Din Allah (1180–1225): Politik, Religion, und Kultur in der spaten Abbasidenzeit* (Berlin: Walter de Gruyter, 1975), and Qamar al-Huda, 'The prince of diplomacy: Shaykh 'Umar al-Suhrawardī's revolution for Sufism, futuwwa groups, and politics under Caliph al-Nāṣir', *Journal of the History of Sufism 3* (2001), pp. 257–78.
22. For more on the Seljuk conquest of Sinop, see Turan, *Selçuklular Zamanında Türkiye*, pp. 302–7; Scott Redford, 'Sinop in the summer of 1215: the beginning of Anatolian Seljuk architecture', *Ancient Civilizations from Scythia to Siberia 16* (2010), pp. 124 ff; Andrew C. S. Peacock, 'Sinop: a frontier city in Seljuq and Mongol Anatolia', *Ancient Civilizations from Scythia to Siberia 16* (2010), p. 105. Peacock points out that the Seljuks were motivated to take Sinop following the expulsion of the city's Muslim merchants from Constantinople in the Fourth Crusade, and as a result of Trebizond's attempt to monopolise Black Sea trade, 'which had dire implications for the economy of Seljuq Anatolia'.
23. The Malik Ashraf mentioned by Ibn Bībī was the Ayyubid prince al-Ashraf Mūsā Abū 'l-Fatḥ al-Muẓẓafar al-Dīn (d. 1237) who was installed as governor of the Jazira (northern Mesopotamia) based in Harran, in 1201 by his father Sultan al-'Adīl I. He took possession of Damascus in 1229. See Stephen Humphries, *From Saladin to the Mongols. The Ayyubids of Damascus, 1193–1260* (Albany, N.Y.: State University of New York Press, 1977), pp. 127–31, 383. For the conflict breaking out between al-Ashraf and Kaykā'ūs I, see Turan, *Selçuklular Zamanında Türkiye*, pp. 317–18.
24. Turan, *Selçuklular Zamanında Türkiye*, pp. 297–9.
25. Ibn Bībī, *al-Awāmir al-'alā'īya*, p. 155.
26. Ibid.
27. For the pronouncing of the caliph's name while engaged in hunting with the crossbow and other such activities, see Deodaat Anne Breebaart, 'The Development and Structure of the Turkish

Futuwah Guilds' (PhD Dissertation, Princeton University, 1961), p. 58.

28. For more on this succession struggle, see Scott Redford and Gary Leiser, *Victory Inscribed. The Seljuk Fetihname on the Citadel Walls of Antalya, Turkey/Taşa Yazılan Zafer. Antalya İçkale Surlarındaki Selçuklu Fetihnamesi* (Antalya: Suna-İnan Kıraç Akdeniz Medeniyetleri Araştırma Enstitüsü, 2008), p. 95.
29. Ibn Bībī, *al-Awāmir al-'alā'īya*, pp. 154–5.
30. Ibid., p. 155.
31. Among these furnishing and textiles were thrones covered in Rūmī brocade (*takht-hā-yi zar-baft*), satin embroidered with jewels (*aṭlas-i ma'danī*), Russian linen (*kattān-i rūsī*), finely woven woollen broadcloth (*saqirlāt bi-'amal-i bināt*) and Cypriot carpets (*bisāṭ-hā-yi qibrisī*) (Ibn Bībī, *al-Awāmir al-'alā'īya*, p. 155).
32. Horses, both geldings and Arabian stallions (*asbān-i igdīsh u tāzī*), sure-footed mules (*astarān-i rahwār*), Bactrian camels (*shuturān-i Bukhtī*) (Ibn Bībī, *al-Awāmir al-'alā'īya*, p. 155).
33. For Sinop as an important trade emporium, see the classic study by Walter Leaf, 'The commerce of Sinope', *The Journal of Hellenic Studies 36* (1916), pp. 1–15; but see too the comments in Peacock, 'Sinop'.
34. Ibn Bībī, *al-Awāmir al-'alā'īya*, p. 155.
35. Ibid., p. 156.
36. Stephen Hirtenstein, *The unlimited mercifier: The spiritual life and thought of Ibn 'Arabī* (Oxford and Ashland, Oreg.: Anqa Publishing and White Cloud Press, 1999), p. 173. Hirtenstein unfortunately neglects to cite his sources for this. Mikâil Bayram, on the other hand, claims to have uncovered the role Awḥad al-Dīn played in the caliph's reorganisation of the *futuwwa* (Mikâil Bayram, *Şeyh Evhadü'd-Din Hâmid El-Kirmânî ve Menâkıb-Nâmesi* [Istanbul: Kardelen Yayınları, c.2005], p. xiii). He claims that Shaykh Awḥad al-Dīn had been sent to Anatolia by the caliph as the *shaykh al-shuyūkh* in order to set in place the framework of the *futuwwa*. Awḥad al-Dīn Kirmānī's anonymous *manāqib* reveals that during this period Ibn Arabi entrusted Sadr al-Dīn's education to his constant companion, Shaykh Awḥad al-Dīn Kirmānī.

Ṣadr al-Dīn Muḥammad al-Qūnawī had spent two years in Shiraz as Awḥad's companion and in his service (Addas, *Quest for the Red Sulphur*, p. 229). Awḥad al-Dīn had long been in the service of the caliph; for instance, in 1210–15 he was sent as al-Nāṣir's envoy to Azerbaijan at the court of the Atabeg Özbeg in order to negotiate peace between the him and the amir of Hamadan (Bayram, *Şeyh Evhadü'd-Din Hâmid El-Kirmânî ve Menâkıb-Nâmesi*, p.11). According to Weischer, Awḥad al-Dīn died in Baghdad in 1238 having lived his final days in the city, where he was honoured by the Abbasid caliph al-Mustanṣir (B.M. Weischer, 'Kirmānī, Awḥad al-Dīn Ḥāmid b. Abi'l-Fakhr', *EI2*, v, p. 166).

37. al-Huda, 'The prince of diplomacy', p. 263. Paul Kahle, 'Ein Futuwwa-Erlass des Kalifen en-Nâṣir aus dem Jahre 604 (1207)', in Ernst F. Weidner (ed.), *Aus fünf Jahrtausenden morgenländischer Kultur: Festschrift Max Freiherrn von Oppenheim zum 70. Geburtstage* (1933; reprint, Osnabrück: Biblio-Verlag, 1967), pp. 52–8.
38. The best overview of Shihāb al-Dīn Abū Ḥafṣ 'Umar al-Suhrawardī is Erik S. Ohlander, *Sufism in an Age of Transition. 'Umar al-Suhrawardī and the Rise of the Islamic Mystical Brotherhoods* (Leiden and Boston: Brill, 2008), pp. 94ff. See also al-Huda, 'The prince of diplomacy'.
39. While this question warrants further investigation, it falls outside the purview of this chapter.
40. Turan dates the end of the succession struggle to 1213 rather than 1214 (Turan, *Selçuklular Zamanında Türkiye*, pp. 301–2).
41. For an extensive study on Kaykā'ūs I's reconquest of Antalya, see Redford and Leiser, *Victory Inscribed.*
42. Ibn Bībī, *al-Awāmir al-'alā'īya*, p. 157.
43. Ibid., p.155.
44. Ibid., p. 25.
45. Ibid., p. 93.
46. Abū 'l-Qāsim al-Qushayrī, *Al-Qushayri's Epistle on Sufism*, trans. Alexander D. Knysh (Reading, UK: Garnet, 2007), p. 26.

47. William Chittick, *The Self-Disclosure of God. Principles of Ibn 'Arabī's Cosmology* (Albany, N.Y.: State University of New York Press, 1998), p. 144.
48. Samer Akkach, *Cosmology and Architecture in Premodern Islam. An Architectural Reading of Mystical Ideas* (Albany, N.Y.: State University of New York Press, 2005), p. 186.
49. The other three *awtād* were the Maghrebi Shaykh 'Abd al-'Azīz al-Mahdawī, Mahdawī's servant Ibn al-Murābit and Ibn 'Arabī's inseparable companion and faithful friend of 20 years, the Ethiopian Badr al-Dīn Ḥabashī. Ibn 'Arabī wrote: 'We were the four pillars supporting the being of the universe and the Perfect Man' (Addas, *Quest for the Red Sulphur*, p. 179). For more on Ḥabashī, see Addas, *Quest for the Red Sulphur*, p. 160.
50. This description comes from his reference to Ṣadr al-Dīn al-Qūnawī specifically as 'the son of my late, righteous companion, Majd al-Dīn Isḥāq ibn Muḥammad al-Qūnawī'. See Gerald Elmore, 'Ṣadr al-Dīn al-Qūnawī's personal study-list of books by Ibn al-'Arabī', *Journal of Near Eastern Studies* 56, no. 3 (1997), p. 166.
51. Ibid., p. 178. Although Addas dates their acquaintance at 1204, Kılıç provides evidence that Majd al-Dīn was a disciple of Ibn 'Arabī as early as 1203 (Kılıç, 'İbnu'l-Arabî'nin 1. İzzeddîn Kaykâvus'a Yazdığı Mektubu', p. 17; Addas, *Quest for the Red Sulphur*, p. 226).
52. Much of the groundwork on this has been done by Osman Yahya, *Histoire et Classification de l'Oeuvre d'Ibn 'Arabī* (Damascus: Institut français du Damas, 1964), ii, pp. 448, 486.
53. Kılıç, 'İbnu'l-Arabî'nin 1. İzzeddîn Kaykâvus'a Yazdığı Mektubu', p. 17.
54. Addas, *Quest for the Red Sulphur*, pp. 221, 224–5.
55. Ibid., p. 111.
56. Addas explains that, as the 'Seal of the Saints', Ibn 'Arabī realised that he had been sent by God 'to preserve the Sacred Law'. Thus, more specifically, as the 'Seal of the Muhammad Sainthood' he was the source of all sainthood, just as Muḥammad had been the

source of all prophecy: 'The Seal, *khatm*, is not simply someone who terminates a series; he is the inviolable seal or 'stamp' preserving a treasure's integrity' (Addas, *Quest for the Red Sulphur*, pp. 199–200).

57. Mosul was an important centre of the speculative sciences in the thirteenth century. It was home to the famous logician and mathematician, Kamāl al-Dīn Mūsā ibn Yūnus al-Mawṣilī (1156–1242), the professor at the Kamāliyya Madrasa attached to the Mosque of amīr Zayn al-Dīn in Mosul. See Shawkat Toorawa, 'A portrait of 'Abd al-Laṭīf al-Baghdādī's education and instruction', in Joseph Lowry, Devin J. Stewart and Shawkat M. Toorawa (eds), *Law and Education in Medieval Islam. Studies in Memory of George Makdisi* (Cambridge: E.J.W. Gibb Memorial Trust, 2004), p. 101.
58. Kılıç, 'İbnu'l-Arabî'nin 1. İzzeddîn Kaykâvus'a Yazdığı Mektubu', p. 17.
59. Ahmet Ateş, 'Ibn al-'Arabī', *EI*[2], iii, p. 708.
60. Ibn Bībī, *al-Awāmir al-'alā'īya*, p. 93; Kılıç, 'İbnu'l-Arabî'nin 1. İzzeddîn Kaykâvus'a Yazdığı Mektubu', p. 17; Turan, *Selçuklular Zamanında Türkiye*, p. 293. Turan points out that the Mamluk author Ibn Wāṣil refers to Majd al-Dīn as royal tutor to the prince. Mikâil Bayram's claim that Majd al-Dīn was sent to the Abbasid caliph to inform him of Kaykhusraw I's recovery of the Seljuk throne in 1205 is completely wrong and cannot be substantiated by any of the sources, including Ibn Bībī (*al-Awāmir al-'alā'īya*, pp. 90–5), whom he cites as his evidence. See Bayram, *Şeyh Evhadü'd-Din Hâmid El-Kirmânî ve Menâkıb-Nâmesi*, p. 13; idem, 'Anadolu Selçukluları Zamanında Kayseri'de Evhadî Dervişler', in Ali Aktan, Ramazan Tosun and Ayhan Öztürk (eds), *III. Kayseri ve Yöresi Tarih Sempozyumu Bildirileri, 06–07 Nisan 2000* (Kayseri: Erciyes Üniversitesi, 2000), p. 44 note 4.
61. Kılıç, 'Ibnu'l-Arabî'nin 1. İzzeddîn Kaykâvus'a Yazdığı Mektubu', p. 17. Kılıç bases this on Ibn 'Arabī 's *al-Futūḥāt al-makkīya*, (Cairo: Dār al-Kutub al-'Arabīyah al-Kubrā, 1329/1911), iii, pp. 126, 255.

62. Addas, *Quest for the Red Sulphur*, p. 3. Addas points out that Ibn 'Arabī completed his *Risālat al-anwār* in Konya in 1205, as stated explicitly by the author himself at the end of the text, not in 607/1210 as has been commonly believed.
63. Ibid., p. 3.
64. Seyyed Hossein Nasr, *Three Muslim Sages: Avicenna, Suhrawardī, Ibn 'Arabī* (Cambridge, Mass.: Harvard University Press, 1964, p. 96.
65. As Ibn 'Arabī recorded in his *al-Futūhāt*, iii, p. 459.
66. Addas, *Quest for the Red Sulphur*, p. 227; Turan, *Selçuklular Zamanında Türkiye*, p. 294.
67. Ibn 'Arabi, *The Four Pillars of Spiritual Transformation: the Adornment of the Spiritually Transformed*, trans. Stephen Hirtenstein (Oxford: Anqa, 2008), p. 4.
68. Gerald Thomas Elmore, 'The Fabulous Gryphon ('Anqā' Mughrib) on the Seal of the Saints and the Sun Rising in the West: An Early, Maghribine Work by Ibn al-'Arabī' (PhD Dissertation, Yale University, 1995), p. 164.
69. Addas, *Quest for the Red Sulphur*, p. 222.
70. Ateş, 'Ibn al-'Arabī', p. 708.
71. A freed Ethiopian slave, Badr al-Ḥabashī was Ibn 'Arabī's faithful companion from Fez to Malatya, and never left his master's side during all his travels. Addas describes him as Ibn 'Arabī's 'discreet and silent shadow' (Addas, *Quest for the Red Sulphur*, pp.160–1).
72. Addas, *Quest for the Red Sulphur*, p. 227; Kılıç, 'İbnu'l-Arabî'nin 1. İzzeddîn Kaykâvus'a Yazdığı Mektubu', pp. 17–18.
73. For a detailed overview of Ibn 'Arabī's Damascene years, see Chapter 10 of Addas, *Quest for the Red Sulphur*.
74. Addas, *Quest for the Red Sulphur*, p. 229. This is noted in a copy of Ibn 'Arabī's *Kitāb al-amr*. Awḥad al-Dīn al-Kirmānī was a disciple of the Suhrawardī shaykh, Rukn al-Dīn Abū 'l-Ghanā'im Muḥammad al-Sujasī, who received the mantle from his shaykh Quṭb al-Dīn Abharī (d. 1181–2), one of Abū'l-Najīb

Suhrawardī's disciples. See Weischer, 'Kirmānī', p. 166; Bayram, *Şeyh Evhadü'd-Din Hâmid El-Kirmânî ve Menâkıb-Nâmesi*, p. 7.

75. Bayram, *Şeyh Evhadü'd-Din Hâmid el-Kirmânî ve Menâkıb-Nâmesi*, p. 13 note 56. Ibn 'Arabī composed the work *Rawḍat al-murīdīn* (MS Süleymaniye, no. 1028, Kayseri, Raşid Ef. Ktp. no. 215000) in Konya.
76. Only chapter four of the five chapters of the *Tanazzulāt al-mawṣiliyya*, a work on the inner significance of religious duties, is included the *majmū'a* (Ateş, 'Ibn al-'Arabī', p. 709).
77. Ateş, 'Ibn al-'Arabī', p. 709. The *majmū'a* survives as MS Konya, Yusuf Ağa 4868.
78. The source of this anecdote is Ibn 'Arabi's *Muhaḍarat al-abrār* (MS Konya, Yusufağa Ktp., no. 546, f. 145a–145b); quoted and references provided by Bayram, *Şeyh Evhadü'd-Din Hâmid El-Kirmânî ve Menâkıb-Nâmesi*, p. 13 note 54; Mikâil Bayram, 'Selçuklular Zamanında Anadolu'da Bazı Yöreler Arasındaki Farklı Kültürel Yapınlanma ve Siyasî Boyutları', *Selçuk Üniversitesi Türkiyat Araştırmaları Dergisi* (1994), p. 83.
79. Kılıç, 'İbnu'l-Arabî'nin 1. İzzeddîn Kaykâvus'a Yazdığı Mektubu', p. 18. Although Kılıç admits that it is difficult to know how much influence Ibn 'Arabi exercised on Kaykā'ūs I, the Seljuk prince appears to have regarded Ibn 'Arabi as a *murīd*.
80. Addas, *Quest for the Red Sulphur*, pp. 165–6.
81. Ibid.
82. Ibid., p. 167.
83. Ibid.
84. For an in-depth discussion on Ibn 'Arabī's mission of *naṣīḥa*, see Addas, *Quest for the Red Sulphur*, Chapter 9, 'Counsel My Servants', pp. 218–44. Also consult the introduction to Ibn 'Arabī, *Contemplation of the Holy Mysteries and the Rising of the Divine Lights*, trans. Cecilia Twinch and Pablo Beneito (Oxford: Anqa Publishing, 2001).
85. James W. Morris, 'Some dreams of Ibn 'Arabī (from his *Risālat al-Mubashshirāt*)', *Newsletter of the Muhyiddīn Ibn 'Arabī Society* (1993), p. 2.
86. Ibid.

87. Kılıç, 'İbnu'l-Arabī'nin 1. İzzeddīn Kaykâvus'a Yazdığı Mektubu', p. 18. This story is taken from the *Kitāb nafḥ al-ṭīb min ghuṣn al-Andalus al-rātib* (Sweet Scent from the Tender Bough of al-Andalus), the Arabic history of Islamic Spain by Abū 'l-'Abbās Aḥmad b. Muḥammad al-Maqqarī (1591–1632).
88. Ibn 'Arabī worked on *al-Futūḥāt al-makkīya* over a period of almost 30 years, completing it in 1231. Consisting of over 2,500 printed pages in six sections subdivided into 50 chapters, *al-Futūḥāt al-makkīya* provides a full exposition of his Sufi doctrine through the 'openings' (*futūḥāt*) of the 'door to the unseen world' (Ateş, 'Ibn al-'Arabī', iii, p. 709).
89. Ibn 'Arabī, *al-Futūḥāt al-makkīya* (Bulaq: Dār al-Ṭibā'a al-Bāhira, 1257/1857–8), iv, p. 604. 'The inheritance of a religious nature' (*al-waṣīya al-dīnīya*) is explained by Ibn 'Arabī's view of his almost unique role on earth. After a vision of his nightly ascension to the heavens where he went before the Lord, experienced in 1198 in Fez, Ibn 'Arabī came to the realisation, following his union with God, that he had returned to the world. He was among the few spiritually gifted able to return and function among the worldly after such an experience, and thus was among those belonging to the category of 'knowing-heir' (*al-'ālim al-wārith*), those saints 'sent back to created beings for the sake of directing and guiding them'. See Addas, *Quest for the Red Sulphur*, p. 154.
90. Ibn 'Arabī, *al-Futūḥāt*, p. 604; Kılıç, 'İbnu'l-Arabî'nin 1. İzzeddîn Kaykâvus'a Yazdığı Mektubu', pp. 20–1. Kılıç offers a Turkish translation of the entire letter.
91. The law of the *dhimmī*, first appearing in a document known as the Pact of 'Umar, was supposedly a bilateral contract according to which non-Muslims in Muslim lands agreed to follow a host of regulations in return for protection. These regulations consist of both restrictions on public display and on the expression of their religious rituals, as well as the imposition of dress and behavioural codes distinguishing non-Muslims from Muslims. The classic treatment of the Pact of 'Umar is A. S. Tritton's *The Caliphs and the Non-Muslim Subjects: A Critical*

Study of the Pact of Umar (Oxford: Oxford University Press, 1930). For the most thorough updated account of these regulations, see chapter 4 of Mark R. Cohen's *Under the Crescent and Cross: The Jews in the Middle Ages* (Princeton: Princeton University Press, 1994).

92. Ibn 'Arabī, *al-Futūḥāt*, pp. 604–5; Kılıç, 'İbnu'l-Arabînin 1. İzzeddîn Kaykâvus'a Yazdığı Mektubu', pp. 20–1.
93. See Addas, *Quest for the Red Sulphur*, p. 235.
94. For restrictions imposed on Muslims in Christian lands, see Nora Berend, 'Medieval Patterns of Social Exclusion and Integration: the regulation of non-Christian clothing in thirteenth-century Hungary', *Revue Mabillon 8* (1997), pp. 155–76; Olivia Remie Constable, 'Regulating religious noise: the Council of Vienne, the mosque call and Muslim pilgrimage in the late medieval Mediterranean world', *Medieval Encounters 16* (2010), pp. 64–95. See also Elena Lourie's seminal studies, collected and published as *Crusade and Colonisation: Muslims, Christians and Jews in Medieval Aragon* (Aldershot: Variorum, 1990).
95. Ibn 'Arabī, *al-Futūḥāt*, iv, p. 605; Kılıç, 'İbnu'l-Arabî'nin 1. İzzeddîn Kaykâvus'a Yazdığı Mektubu', p. 23.
96. For information on al-Ashraf, see footnote 23.
97. Sayf al-Dīn Ayaba *chasnīgīr* (the 'food-taster'), also known as Sayf al-Dīn Qızıl Bey, was the amir of Ankara, and the *beglerbeg* (commander-in-chief of the imperial armies) under Kaykā'ūs I. He was killed by Kayqubād soon after he came to power, presumably because he threatened the young sultan's authority.
98. Kılıç, 'İbnu'l-Arabī'nin 1. İzzeddīn Kaykâvus'a Yazdığı Mektubu', p. 24 note 42.
99. Ibn 'Arabī, *al-Futūḥāt*, 605; Kılıç, 'İbnu'l-Arabî'nin 1. İzzeddîn Kaykâvus'a Yazdığı Mektubu', p. 23.
100. Kılıç bases his discussion of this dream on Ibn 'Arabī's *Kitāb muḥāḍarāt al-abrār wa musāmarāt al-akhyār* (Damascus: Dār al-Yaqẓah al-'Arabīyah, 1968), vii, p. 241 (Kılıç, 'İbnu'l-Arabî'nin 1. İzzeddîn Kaykâvus'a Yazdığı Mektubu', p. 18).
101. Yaacov Lev, 'Symbiotic relations: ulama and the Mamluk sultans', *Mamluk Studies Review* 13, no. 1 (2009), p. 7.

102. Michel Balivet, *Romanie Byzantine et Pays de Rûm Turc: Histoire d'un espace d'imbrication gréco-turque* (Istanbul: Isis, 1994), p. 84.
103. Lev, 'Symbiotic relations: ulama and the Mamluk sultans', pp. 1–26.
104. Gary Leiser, 'The madrasah and the Islamization of Anatolia before the Ottomans', in Joseph Lowry, Devin Stewart and Shawkat M. Toowara (eds), *Law and Education in Medieval Islam: Studies in Memory of George Makdisi* (Cambridge: Gibb Memorial Series, 2004), pp. 174–91.
105. Wilferd Madelung claims that, during his lifetime, Ibn 'Arabī was not a controversial figure, for not only was he a strict observer of *sunna* and known for his exemplary conduct, but also his teaching was restricted mostly to a small group of intimate followers. It was only with the widespread propagation of his ideas following his death that polemical disputes arose regarding Ibn 'Arabī's teachings. Madelung, however, does not take into consideration events such as Ibn 'Arabī's being forced to flee Cairo in 1206. How controversial Ibn 'Arabī was during his lifetime needs to be more closely reviewed (Wilferd Madelung, review of Alexander D. Knysh's *Ibn 'Arabī in the Later Islamic Tradition*, in the *Journal of the American Oriental Society* 120, no. 4 [2000], p. 682).

CHAPTER EIGHT

SUFIS AND THE SELJUK COURT IN MONGOL ANATOLIA: POLITICS AND PATRONAGE IN THE WORKS OF JALĀL AL-DĪN RŪMĪ AND SULṬĀN WALAD

A.C.S. Peacock

According to Aflākī's *Manāqib al-'arifīn*, our major hagiographical source for thirteenth- and early fourteenth-century Anatolian Sufism, the fall of the Seljuk dynasty was caused by Sultan Rukn al-Dīn Qılıch Arslan IV (d. 1266) offending the great Sufi saint Jalāl al-Dīn Rūmī (d. 1273). Aflākī records that 'the destruction of the courtyard of their royal power' was brought about because the sultan, who had become a disciple of Rūmī, then accepted his rival Shaykh Bābā-yi Marandī as his spiritual master. Rūmī stormed off in a jealous fury. Shortly afterwards, contrary to Rūmī's advice, the sultan went to confront the invading Mongols, but was strangled near Aksaray, calling vainly on Rūmī as he died.[1]

The story is of course rooted not in historical fact, but in Aflākī's aim to demonstrate Rūmī's immense spiritual power. Indeed, the *Manāqib al-'ārifīn* – a hagiography of Rūmī, Rūmī's spiritual guides and his successors, written between roughly 1318 and the 1350s – was commissioned by Rūmī's grandson. The latter, known as Ulu 'Ārif Chelebi, was himself one of Aflākī's's spiritual guides.[2] The end of a dynasty being caused by the ruler rebuffing a saint is a standard theme in hagiographies. Aflākī asserts that the end of the Ilkhanid dynasty was caused by the Ilkhan Abū Sa'īd's vizier mistreating Mevlevi dervishes, including another of Aflākī's spiritual masters, Chelebī Amīr 'Ābid.[3] Aflākī even attributes to Rūmī a claim that his father, Bahā' al-Dīn, had himself brought down the Khwarazmian dynasty by invoking God, who sent the Mongols as vengeance for the Khwārazmshāh's mistreatment of the saint.[4]

Holy men did not use their powers solely to punish errant rulers. For instance, the *Manāqib* of Awḥad al-Dīn Kirmānī (d. 1238),[5] written in the late thirteenth century, credits him with bringing 'Alā' al-Dīn Kayqubād I to the throne. According to Aflākī, the Mongols' agreement to the accession of 'Alā' al-Dīn Farāmarz to the Seljuk throne in Konya was obtained by a disciple of Rūmī's, Majd al-Dīn the *atabeg*. As a result, the sultan 'rendered many forms of service to Sulṭān Walad and Chelebī 'Ārif, as well as to the noble disciples.'[6] Men of state frequently appear in Aflākī as humble disciples of the saint. For instance, the Parwāna Mu'īn al-Dīn Sulaymān, who was the effective ruler of Anatolia on behalf of the Mongols between 1256 and 1277, features prominently in the *Manāqib al-'ārifīn* as a follower of Rūmī. Aflākī underlines his subordinate status to Rūmī:

> Sulṭān Walad said, 'One day Mu'īn al-Dīn the Parwāna came to visit Mawlānā. I informed my father and I sat for a long time with the Parwāna. The Parwāna sat waiting and I occupied myself with presenting apologies because Mawlānā had many times given instructions that, "I have my own business and ecstatic states and immersions in God. The amirs and friends cannot see me any time. They should busy themselves

with their own affairs and those of the people; we will go and see them."'[7]

Modern readers are likely to regard the extravagant claims for saintly power made by authors like Aflākī with scepticism. Recent studies have, however, highlighted that elsewhere in the Islamic world, in Morocco and in India for instance, saints were profoundly involved in political life, and their claims to possess *wilāya* (authority) were widely accepted by political elites.[8] Research on the Great Seljuk empire also points to a close association between leading statesmen and Sufi saints.[9] Yet studies on religion in Seljuk Anatolia tend to be divorced from the political and historical context, while political historians have rarely devoted much attention to those whom they see as purely religious figures. Rūmī provides a prime example of this phenomenon. Unquestionably the best-known figure of medieval Anatolia to the outside world, the subject of almost endless studies, translations and popularisations, his career is largely avoided by political historians. Neither Osman Turan nor Claude Cahen grants him more than a few passing references in their *magnum opuses* on Seljuk Anatolia. Conversely, despite the vast volume of Rūmī scholarship, few scholars have gone beyond the superficial in trying to establish the nature of Rūmī's links with the later thirteenth-century Anatolian elite, or indeed to explore his work in its contemporary historical context. The best effort to date is undoubtedly that of Franklin Lewis in his survey of Rūmī's life, works and legacy, but the author mainly restricts himself to summarising the main facts regarding names and dates of Rūmī's political contacts.[10]

A detailed study of Rūmī and Sufism in the historical context of medieval Anatolia is thus a desideratum for future scholarship, and not one that a short chapter such as this can hope to offer. Here I simply wish to offer some reflections on the relations between Sufis and the elite of late Seljuk Anatolia through drawing on two sources that have been neglected to date: the letters of Rūmī, and the poems of his son Sulṭān Walad. The latter also became a leading Sufi and played a prominent role in establishing the Mevlevi Sufi order, which was to remain a major force in Anatolian Islam until the twentieth century.

These works present a very different picture of relations between Sufis and statesmen from that of Aflākī. In contrast to Aflākī's depiction of all-powerful saints humbling sultans, the works consulted here show Rūmī and Sulṭān Walad's reliance on elite patronage. Although Aflākī does occasionally allude to the petitions to rulers that they made on behalf of their followers,[11] these sources allow us to document in some detail the nature of the patronage. This discord between the image presented by Aflākī and that of the primary sources used here may be one reason why the latter have been neglected. For instance, despite the wealth of pertinent information contained in Rūmī's correspondence, even Abdülbaki Gölpınarlı, unquestionably Turkey's most notable Rūmī scholar, does not refer to them once in his discussion of Rūmī's relationship with the ruling elites – despite the fact he himself translated the letters into Turkish.[12]

Viewing the saints as supplicants to temporal power offers a new perspective on the relationship between holy men and the elite. It has become a common refrain in scholarship that rulers found Sufis to be useful allies in their search for legitimacy. As Lewis puts it, while admitting that some of the political elite were genuinely pious,

> Sultans and men of state found it useful to support religious scholars and pious men of various bents for political reasons. By founding law colleges, patronizing religious scholars, associating with popular preachers and saints, they could gain the respect of various sections of society and earn some kind of religious or spiritual legitimation for their rule.[13]

The underlying assumption is that Sufi saints had a certain mass popularity which, with their support, could somehow attach itself to political leaders. Yet, it is far from certain that every Sufi who was patronised by elite groups had a wide popular following: as we shall see, even Rūmī and his followers did not meet with universal acceptance. Rather, rulers and statesmen perceived saints, or at least certain saints, as possessing *wilāya*, power, in both this world and the next, a desire to reap the benefits of which was a significant factor in ruling elites' association with Sufis.[14]

Associating with rulers was, however, by no means an obvious step for a saint. Traditions warned against the dangers of proximity to rulers; perhaps the most famous of all Sufis, Abū Ḥāmid Ghazzālī, had taken a vow against attending sultans in person or accepting from them any money.[15] While Aflākī makes no attempt to gloss over the close relationship between Anatolian holy men and the political elite, he is at pains to emphasise the saints' lack of interest in material favours. Yet a very different view emerges from the letters of Rūmī and the poems of Sulṭān Walad, which show how holy men relied on rulers to give them and their followers pensions, tax exemptions and endowments (*waqf*s). In what follows, I shall analyse how political elites and Sufis sought a mutually beneficial relationship in late Seljuk Anatolia.

Rūmī's Relations with the Seljuk Elite as Reflected in his Letters

The addressees of most of Rūmī's letters are members of the ruling elite of Anatolia.[16] None of the letters is precisely dated, and in quite a few instances the addressee can only be inferred from his titulature as no precise name is given. Often the addressee is identified only by a later editor, and it is far from certain how reliable such attributions may be. Nonetheless, the broad outlines are clear enough: the Parwāna was a particularly important correspondent, but there are also missives addressed to the sultan; Tawfiq Subḥānī, the most recent editor of the text, identifies this with Sultan 'Izz al-Dīn Kaykā'ūs II (r. 1246–62).[17] Others are addressed to Fakhr al-Dīn 'Alī Ṣāḥib 'Aṭā, who held the senior offices of *amīr-dād, malik al-umarā'* and *nā'ib al-salṭana*, and who acted as vizier from 1260 until his death in 1288; Amīn al-Dīn Mīkā'īl (d. 1277), who held the posts of *nā'ib al-salṭana* and *malik al-umarā' wa'l-nuwwāb*; and the qadi of Konya, Sirāj al-Dīn al-Urmawī (d. 1283).[18] A few letters are also addressed to Jalāl al-Dīn, identified by the editor as Jalāl al-Dīn Qaratay,[19] who was *atabeg* to 'Izz al-Dīn Kaykā'ūs II and the main power in Konya between 1249 and c.1254. While this is certainly credible, Jalāl al-Dīn is a common *laqab* and it is possible that the letters refer to some other, less famous amir. Even where the precise identity of the recipients is obscure, it is usually possible to identify them as amirs, sultans or bureaucrats through their titulature. Letters directed to members of Rūmī's own circle do exist – to his son, Sulṭān Walad, for instance, or his disciple Ṣalāḥ al-Dīn – but these are very much in the minority. The letters must date largely from the 1250s or late 1240s up to Rūmī's death in 1273. This was an especially traumatic period in Seljuk history, as Anatolia struggled to come to terms with the Mongol invasion and occupation in the wake of the disastrous defeat of Ghiyāth al-Dīn Kaykhusraw II's army at Kösedağ in 1243. After a campaign by Baiju in 1256, Anatolia was more firmly incorporated into the Mongol empire in the Middle East, the Ilkhanate, with the Anatolian political elite, including the sultans, surviving only as servants of their Mongol masters.[20]

The relationship between rulers and Sufis that emerges from the letters is rather more balanced than that in the hagiographies. Where Aflākī goes to some pains to illustrate the saints' lack of interest in the prizes of this world,[21] the letters make it quite clear that the elite were expected to extend their patronage and protection to needy members of Rūmī's circle. Indeed, perhaps the majority of letters are essentially those of recommendation: Rūmī starts with a formulaic expression of desire to see the addressee, who is usually given his full titles; the Parwāna, for instance, is often referred to by his Turko-Mongol title, *ulugh-qutlugh*, and titles such as *malik al-wuzurā'* are almost invariably applied to ministers, while sultans are referred to by sobriquets such as Fakhr-i Āl-i Dā'ūd (Glory of the House of David), alluding to their shared lineage with Chaghrı Beg, known as Dā'ūd, the ancestor of most of the Great Seljuk sultans, as well as their claim to descent from the Biblical David.[22] There is none of the disdain for worldly offices that some mystics showed. 'Ayn al-Quḍāt al-Hamadānī (d. 1131), for instance, frequently berated his *murīd*, the *mustawfī* 'Azīz al-Dīn, for his involvement in the Great Seljuk state,[23] but in Rūmī's letters the admonitory tone is generally absent. However, unlike 'Ayn al-Quḍāt, Rūmī was seeking specific favours from his addressee.

After Rūmī's greetings, the candidate for patronage is introduced, with comments as to how deserving and religious he is; then the specific request is made. The letter concludes with a reminder to the addressee of the eternal rewards his generosity will bring. Many of the requests are for stipends or loans,[24] but others are direct appeals for commercial or financial privileges for members of Rūmī's circle. One letter to the Parwāna introduces *fakhr al-tujjār*, 'the glory of the merchants', Shihāb al-Dīn, who was apparently engaged in trade with Sivas and for whom Rūmī asks for an exemption from customs tolls (*bāj*).[25] Another letter, to Fakhr al-Dīn 'Alī, refers to the exemption of a number of Rūmī's associates from government levies (*muṭālabāt* and *muṣādarāt*) and requests the privilege be extended to others of his circle.[26] Various letters request the investigation of cases of *muṣādara* – state expropriation of property[27] – and on one occasion Rūmī asks the Parwāna to assist Ḥusām al-Dīn who overspent on rebuilding the wall of an abandoned garden.[28] In another, the Parwāna is asked to assist the heirs of Ṣalāḥ al-Dīn, who had purchased a garden for 500 dirhams but had fallen into arrears with the payments.[29]

Rūmī refers to himself repeatedly in the letters as an intercessor (*shafī'*). Through his position he sought to secure worldly advancement for relatives and associates. One letter, to Sultan 'Izz al-Dīn Kaykā'ūs II, mentions one Shams al-Dīn and his son who had previously served the sultan; evidently they had difficulty finding new positions, or as Rūmī artfully puts it, 'someone who has experienced your generosity cannot then set himself up with another monarch'.[30] The pair wish to return to the sultan's service but cannot say so out of shame, which is why it falls to Rūmī to intercede in order to ask that they be employed again. A letter to the Parwāna refers to the misdeeds (*bad-khidmatī*) of one Niẓām al-Dīn,[31] and asks for him to be reinstated. An unnamed amir is addressed, recommending the abilities of Niẓām al-Dīn, son of Ṣalāḥ al-Dīn.[32] A letter to the Parwāna's father, Muhadhdhab al-Dīn (d. c.1243/4) requests for employment for one Shams al-Dīn,[33] and one to Amīn al-Dīn Mīkā'īl, the *nā'ib al-salṭana*, asks him to find suitable employment for Shams al-Din Muḥammad, on the grounds that his father was one of Rūmī's disciples.[34] Other letters to the Parwāna also beg him to find a job for Shams al-Dīn because, as Rūmī puts it, 'he desires, one way or another, to be honoured by serving this court' (*arzū-yi ān ast kih bih wasīla az wasā'il bih khidmatī-yi ān bārgāh musharraf shawad*).[35] Rūmī's intercessions also frequently aimed to secure the forgiveness of various associates of his, some of whom seem to have been embroiled in political disputes. A letter to Fakhr al-Dīn 'Alī raises the case of Najm al-Dīn b. Khurram b. Chāwush, imprisoned for some kind of involvement in civil disturbances (*ātish-i fitna*).[36] Rūmī writes to the Parwāna relaying the gratitude of the sons of one Sayf al-Dīn, whose pardoning had allowed them to start a new life.[37] A certain Karīm al-Dīn Maḥmūd had been accused on account of greed for, presumably, some unspecified financial offence; the Parwāna is asked to issue a decree (*yarlıgh*) exonerating him.[38]

Rūmī also interceded for his clients with the Anatolian elite to ward off the worst excesses of the Mongols. It was suggested by Gölpınarlı, largely on the basis of Rūmī's poetry, that he was unconcerned with the Mongol invasion, quoting a verse to the effect that as dervishes have no money they have nothing to lose from the pillaging with which the Mongols were associated.[39] According to Gölpınarlı, Rūmī realised that after the initial upheaval the world would settle down, reinvigorated by the new energy of the Mongols. This reading of Rūmī's verse of course fits well with the widespread perception of the Sufi as unconcerned with the things of this world. A similarly other-worldly view of the Mongols is reflected in the *Manāqib al-'ārifīn*, itself begun under Ilkhanid rule, in which Aflākī also attempts to link the Mongols to Islam and to Rūmī. For instance, an anecdote attributed to Rūmī states that the Mongol ruler Hülegü had successfully conquered Baghdad in 1258 because he and his men had fasted and prayed for three days beforehand, whereas the caliph's arrogance led to his downfall.[40] Thus the Mongols, even if not technically Muslims, are depicted as acting in a more *muslim* way than the leader of the *umma*, thus justifying their victory. Equally, Aflākī depicts Mongols such as Baiju, the general who led the devastating occupation of 1256, and Geikhatu, governor of Anatolia in the late thirteenth century before he became Ilkhan, as recognising Rūmī's spiritual powers.[41] Aflākī is thus far from hostile to the Mongols, and this perspective may have influenced Gölpınarlı's treatment.

In fact, Rūmī's correspondence reveals him as anything but sanguine. A letter to the Parwāna complains bitterly of the Mongols, with their incessant demands for loans and camels.[42] A missive to Amīn al-Dīn Mīkā'īl is even stronger; Rūmī writes that, 'since this group (i.e. the Mongols) have gained power over us, fear has prevailed; if it has abated for a moment, it is like a viper reposing in a house, sleeping in a corner.'[43] The letter then goes on to allude to the security problems in Konya in the absence of Amīn al-Dīn Mīkā'īl, which were presumably caused by the Mongol soldiery: houses were broken into in the night, women and children killed, and property stolen. Rumours swept the town, for every day a new piece of bad news came and people were slaughtered like cattle. Both this letter and that to the Parwāna are pleas for help and protection from the Mongols. Elsewhere, in *Fīhi mā fīhi*, Rūmī directly criticises the Parwāna for his links with the Mongols.[44]

The letters thus indicate the reliance of Rūmī and his circle on the elite for protection, money and employment. Association with Rūmī could evidently confer on his followers worldly benefits, such as tax breaks and positions at court, as well as spiritual ones. Yet, how did Fakhr al-Dīn 'Alī, the Parwāna and other members of this elite profit in turn from their association with the Sufis? It was probably not simply a question of Rūmī's popularity 'rubbing off' on his patrons, for there are indications in the letters that the popularity of these proto-Mevlevis was rather less than Aflākī would have us believe. In one communication we read of a mother and her son who had embraced the way of the dervishes, only for the son to be turned out of the house by his disgusted father.[45] Even more telling is an evidently exasperated letter from Rūmī to a vizier, possibly Fakhr al-Dīn 'Alī, referring to a clash between Rūmī's followers and another group – perhaps rival dervishes – who had complained to the vizier; the vizier is enjoined to look at both groups, and, Rūmī believes, he will soon see who is more dangerous to public order.[46] The final sentence of the letter suggests that the vizier had forbidden Rūmī and his associates to gather outside the town, while the situation within it was intolerable. Other letters to the Parwāna refer to jealousy aroused by the privileges given to dervishes,[47] and to the hostility Rūmī himself faced from 'the envious'.[48] Indeed, even the Parwāna's own associates did not always treat Sufis with much regard. In one letter, Rūmī complains to the Parwāna that his men (*jamā'atī az muta'allaqān-i shumā*) have occupied a *zāwīya* 'and disturbed men of good works'; he asks the Parwāna to tell his henchmen not to harm the dervishes and not to stay there.[49] Another letter addressed to the sultan, probably 'Izz al-Dīn Kaykā'ūs II, begs him to end the 'oppression and hostility' that Rūmī's disciple Ḥusām al-Dīn had suffered at the hands of an unnamed governor (*wālī*).[50] Correspondence addressed to Nūr al-Dīn Jibrā'īl b. Jājā (Cacaoğlu) – who endowed a famous *waqf* in Kırşehir – suggests an angry dispute between this amir and Rūmī's disciple Niẓām al-Dīn.[51] Whatever truth lies behind cases like these, of which we know nothing other than passing allusions, it is clear that Rūmī and his circle were far from universally admired or popular – another reason why we should be wary of regarding Rūmī through the rose-tinted eyes of Aflākī.

Popularity or legitimacy was thus not necessarily to be gained by associating oneself with a specific group of Sufis. In fact, Rūmī is perfectly explicit in his letters about why politicians should support him. The benefit they receive is *du'ā-yi dawlat*, a phrase which crops up in almost every letter and which we may roughly translate as meaning 'praying for your prosperity'. To give one extreme example, Rūmī requests a tax exemption for some dervishes 'because they have been preoccupied with praying [for your prosperity] which has kept them from earning a living'.[52] A request to Majd al-Dīn asking for Kamāl al-Dīn's exemption from taxes is explained by the fact that Kamāl al-Dīn had become too preoccupied with the afterlife, which had resulted in his financial problems; if these were solved then he could devote himself to 'praying for your prosperity'.[53] Fakhr al-Dīn 'Alī, asked to extend the tax privileges he has already granted, is assured that 'our disciples (*jamā'at-i yārān-i mā*), since they have been freed from concern about taxes and expropriations in these difficult days by your efforts, have been preoccupied with praying for you'.[54] Nor were these prayers always bland supplications for the soul of the patron. An unnamed amir is recommended one Bahā' al-Dīn as the object of his patronage. If he grants him a madrasa, people would pray for the amir, which would be 'a reason for the continuation of your prosperity, happiness and the crushing of your enemies'.[55] A letter to an amir named Niẓām al-Mulk even more explicitly links the patron's charity, the resulting prayers and worldly success: Niẓām al-Mulk had taken such good care of dervishes and the poor, it was said, that their prayers had been accepted by God, which gave Niẓām al-Mulk the victory on the occasion of which this congratulatory letter was written.[56]

From the correspondence, Rūmī emerges as the pivot of a system of patronage whereby his followers benefited from the protection and favour of the elite in return for the spiritual blessings that could be conferred by their prayers. Although this may contradict the common view of Sufi saints as concerned with the divine to the exclusion of more worldly affairs – an image strengthened by Gölpınarlı's influential biography – Rūmī's behaviour was probably not atypical of at least some Sufi saints. While the surviving correspondence of many famous Sufi figures, such as Sanā'ī and 'Ayn al-Quḍāt al-Hamadānī, tends to consist of elevated admonitions to the elite, the corpus of letters of the fifteenth-century Central Asian Naqshbandī Khwāja 'Ubaydallāh Aḥrār and his associates bears many similarities to Rūmī's. Consisting largely of petitions, the Khwāja Aḥrār correspondence indicates that this saint too played a crucial role in mediating patronage relationships between his followers and the Timurid court, on which they relied for material support, protection, appointment to office, tax relief, *waqf* and property.[57]

Sulṭān Walad: Poetry and Patronage

Rūmī's efforts to secure elite patronage were continued by his son Sulṭān Walad. As with the father, this is a subject that the hagiographies treat only selectively. Aflākī depicts Sulṭān Walad as instrumental in converting to Islam the Mongol commander in Anatolia, Irenjin Noyan, and of exerting great influence over the Ilkhan Ghazan's (r. 1295–1304) deputy, Oposhgha Nogayan, who became a disciple.[58] The conversion of Mongols is doubtless intended to be read as a miracle, affirming Sulṭān Walad's credentials as his father's successor. However, a rather different picture of Sulṭān Walad's links with the political elite emerges from the poems, largely in Persian, collected in his *Dīwān*.[59] The poetic quality of the *Dīwān* is generally judged to be rather low, and thus it has attracted little scholarly attention. Indeed, these poems have been almost entirely ignored since F. Nafız Uzluk published a summary of their contents in the introduction to his edition of Sulṭān Walad's *Dīwān* in 1941.[60] Yet, since many of its poems are addressed to senior officials of the late Seljuk state it is a source of great importance for our theme.

The recipients are in some cases the same as Rūmī's patrons: there is a *qaṣīda* addressed to the Parwāna,[61] one to Fakhr al-Dīn 'Alī[62] and one to Majd al-Dīn Muḥammad.[63] The Seljuk family itself features prominently among the dedicatees, with several poems addressed to Ghiyāth al-Dīn Mas'ūd II (r. c.1284–96, 1303–8), usually considered the last Seljuk sultan,[64] and others to Seljuk women, such as Rukn al-Dīn Qılıch Arslān IV's wife Gumāj Khātūn and his daughter Saljūq Khātūn.[65] Gurjī Khātūn, said by Aflākī to have been a devotee of Rūmī's,[66] is also mentioned warmly in a poem addressed to one Ḥusām al-Dīn, a notable of Kayseri where she was apparently living.[67] Reflecting the growing importance of the urban fraternities in the late thirteenth century, several poems address leading *akhī*s. One, for example, is a plea to the akhī Amīr Aḥmad of Bayburt (who also features prominently in Aflākī) to visit Konya and pay his respects at Rūmī's grave.[68] Only one elite Mongol family features in the *Dīwān*, in a poem that is dedicated to Samaghar Noyan, his wife Qultaq, his son 'Arab and his daughter Nawuqī.[69] Although these Mongol names differ from those given in the *Manāqib al-'ārifīn*, the poem does at least confirm that Aflākī's tale of Sulṭān Walad's links with senior Mongols is correct. Samaghar was a Tatar who had served Hülegü as his *ataqchi* (squire) and subsequently rose to become governor of Anatolia, probably from the early 1270s, if not earlier, until c.1296.[70]

As one might expect, much of Sulṭān Walad's poetry is of thoroughly mystical inspiration – many of the *ghazal*s seem to have been written expressly as counterparts to Rūmī's own verses – but those addressed to men of the state tend to be more secular in tone. Far from adopting the lyrical, mystical tone of Rūmī's great works like the *Dīwān-i Shams-i Tabrīzī*, some of Sulṭān Walad's poems are worldly panegyrics that aim to achieve the traditional ambition of court poets, that of netting the author a suitable financial reward in return for praising and glorifying his patron. A good example is one of the poems addressed to sultan Ghiyāth al-Dīn Mas'ūd II:

> You are the pivot of life and the world, O dear being; you were the purpose of the creation of the whole world,
>
> Life, were it even in heaven, would be hell if you were not present
>
> ...
>
> I have two requirements of your Majesty, that you should do what is customary for your family [to do].
>
> A pension was settled on us by your grandfather and father; such a son as you should give a hundred such [pensions].
>
> Fourteen of our lord [Rūmī]'s disciples (*'āshiqān*) were exempted and relieved of government tax by that generous king.
>
> In your epoch, O king, it should be so, such that everyone profits without loss from your generosity.
>
> Instruct the *ṣāḥib* [*-dīwān*] to do this, so that everyone may sincerely say his heart is at rest ...[71]

A poem to Tāj al-Dīn, the *za'īm al-jaysh* (commander of the army) is equally explicit in requesting this amir's assistance in restoring to Sulṭān Walad and his followers a *waqf* that had been unjustly taken from them. After an introduction comparing Tāj al-Dīn to stock heroes of Perso-Islamic culture (in beauty like Joseph, chivalry [*jawānmardī*] like Ḥātim Ṭayyi, bravery like 'Alī b. Abī Ṭālib and justice like Anūshirwān), Sulṭān Walad begs,

> I pray to you every evening and morning to bestow on me that village called Kara Arslan.[72]

> It is certain, there is no doubt, that Badr al-Dīn Gawhartash[73] made it a *waqf* for this group who pray for him (*bikarda būd waqf ānrā barīn jam'-i du'ā gūyān*).
>
> Najīb seized it from him [to finance] fighting on the frontier (*barā-yi jang-i sīnūrī*), but just two days later he saw his recompense from God for that.
>
> O lord, protect the religious scholars (*faqīhān*) in this respect: make flourishing a charitable donation that was destroyed by his oppression ...[74]

As befits a man whose father had so strongly criticised the Mongols, Sulṭān Walad adopts a somewhat surprised tone in his panegyric to Samaghar:

> Although in body you are a Mongol, in wisdom you are deeply versed; you are an enemy of devils and ghouls, our lord, do not forget us.[75]

Sulṭān Walad's dependence on the Mongol order is strikingly suggested by the *radīf* in Turkish, by this time probably the main language of the Mongol armies, which occurs at the end of every line of this otherwise Persian poem: *beğimiz bizi unutma*, 'our lord, do not forget us'. Indeed, Samaghar's generosity was held up as an example to Ghiyāth al-Dīn Mas'ūd II, who is asked in the poem cited above (p. 218) to restore his forefathers' favour to the dervishes 'especially seeing as Samaghar has written an order concerning this need [of ours] and [thereby] has cleansed away rust from our hearts' (*khuṣūṣ chūnkih Samāqār ham darīn ḥājjat binibisht al-tamghā waz sīna zang zidūd*).[76]

Sulṭān Walad's closeness to the Seljuk elite is illustrated by a *qaṣīda* written to commemorate the entry of the sultan into Konya on 25 Rabī' II 680/13 August 1281. It was perhaps written on the occasion of Ghiyāth al-Dīn Mas'ūd's accession to the throne, and extravagantly praises the sultan and the leading amirs of Konya. The stock epithets of panegyric are pulled out in order to praise him: the sultan resembles Rustam in his courage, Anūshirwān in justice, the amirs are like stars, and the sultan like the moon.[77] Sulṭān Walad also seems to have had links with a newly arisen beylik of western Anatolia, the Germiyanid dynasty of Kütahya, founded in the last two decades of the thirteenth century. The story related by a much later Mevlevi writer, Esrar Dede (d. 1796), that Sulṭān Walad's daughter Muṭṭahara Khātūn married the Germiyanid Sulaymānshāh and gave birth to a daughter, Dawlat Khātūn, who herself married the Ottoman sultan Yıldırım Bayezid,[78] is probably a later fiction, although it is itself instructive that even so many generations later authors were seeking to link rulers and Sufi lineages. Clearer evidence of some kind of association between Sulṭān Walad and the Germiyanids comes in the form of a poem in the *Dīwān* praising Kütahya's natural beauty, its gardens and rivers, and its strong fortress,[79] while Aflākī also records that a gift of a basin of white marble was sent to Sulṭān Walad from Kütahya.[80]

Conclusion

The relationship between Sufis and the elite was rather more equal than the hagiographies would lead us to believe. Rūmī and his circle needed the financial support of statesmen, as well as their protection from rival Sufi groups and other enemies. Amirs, viziers and rulers needed the Sufis less to lend their rule legitimacy, but rather through the latter's prayers and spiritual power to ensure their continued prosperity and success, in this world as much as the next. The role of court patronage in spreading Sufism and broadening the appeal of groups like the Mevlevis through the provision of financial incentives is a subject that needs further research.

The willingness of Sulṭān Walad to write panegyric poetry and Rūmī to seek preferment at court for his disciples may contrast with our image of 'saintly' behaviour, even though, as the later example of Khwāja 'Ubaydallāh Aḥrār suggests, this kind of engagement with patronage networks on the part of holy men may have been fairly common. I do not intend to suggest that Sufism was shorn of devotional content, nor that its devotees were motivated purely by the things of this world. Yet Rūmī too seems to have felt the need to explain himself. The question of relations between Sufis and sultans features prominently in his Discourses, the *Fīhi mā fīhi*. Indeed, it cannot be a coincidence that the opening chapter of this work is devoted to justifying saints' associations with rulers. He writes:

> If the saints seek status and exalted position in this world, they do so because people are unable to perceive their exaltedness. They want to ensnare worldly people with the trap of this world and fall into the snare of the next world. Similarly, the Prophet conquered Mecca and the surrounding countries, not because he needed them, but in order to bestow light on all ... The saints deceive men in order to give to them, not in order to take anything from them.[81]

Notes

1. Shams al-Dīn Aḥmad al-Aflāki, *Manāqib al-'ārifīn*, published as Şams al-Dīn Aḥmed al-Aflākī al-'Ārifī, *Manāḳib al-'Ārifīn*, ed. Tahsin Yazıcı (Ankara: Türk Tarih Kurumu, 1976, 2 vols) (henceforth: Aflākī, *Manāqib*), i, 3: 60–61, pp. 146–7; Shams al-Dīn Aḥmad-e Aflākī, *Feats of the Knowers of God* (Manāqeb al-'arefīn), trans. John O'Kane (Leiden: Brill, 2002), 3: 60–61, pp. 102–4 (henceforth: *Feats*).
2. Aflākī, *Manāqib*, i, p. 4; *Feats*, p. 3. On Aflākī and his work, see Franklin D. Lewis, *Rūmī, Past and Present, East and West: The life, teachings and poetry of Jalāl al-Din Rūmī* (Oxford: Oneworld, 2008), pp. 249–60.
3. Aflākī, *Manāqib*, ii, 9: 4, p. 980; *Feats*, 9: 4, pp. 686–7.
4. Aflākī, *Manāqib*, ii, 9: 5, pp. 981–2; 9: 6, p. 985; *Feats* 9: 5, pp. 687–8; 9: 6, p. 690.
5. *Manāqib-i Awḥad al-Dīn Ḥamīd ibn Abī 'l-Fakhr-i Kirmānī*, ed. Badī' al-Zamān Furūzanfar (Tehran: Bāngah-i Tarjuma wa Nashr-i Kitāb, 1347/1969). Mikâil Bayram has published a study of the work, accompanied by a Turkish translation of the text: *Şeyh Evhadü'd-Din Hâmid El-Kirmânî ve Menâkıb-Namesi* (Istanbul: Kardelen Yayınevi, c. 2005).
6. Aflākī, *Manāqib*, i, 8: 20, p. 849; *Feats*, 8: 20, p. 593.

7. Aflākī, *Manāqib*, i, 3: 214, p. 299; *Feats*, 3: 216, p. 207 (spelling modified).
8. Vincent J. Cornell, *Realm of the Saint: Power and Authority in Moroccan Sufism* (Austin, Tex.: University of Texas Press, 1998); Carl W. Ernst, *Eternal Garden: Mysticism, History and Politics at a South Asian Sufi Center* (Albany, N.Y.: SUNY Press, 1992).
9. Omid Safi, *The Politics of Knowledge in Premodern Islam: Negotiating Ideology and Religious Inquiry* (Chapel Hill, N.C.: The University of North Carolina Press, 2006).
10. Lewis, *Rūmī, Past and Present, East and West*, pp. 123–8, 275–84.
11. Aflākī, *Manāqib*, i, 3: 125, p. 217; *Feats*, 3: 126, 127, pp. 150–1.
12. Abdülbaki Gölpınarlı, *Mevlânâ Celâleddin: Hayatı, Eserleri, Felsefesi* (Istanbul: İnkilap, 1999), pp. 218–24. For the Turkish translation of the letters, see Abdülbaki Gölpınarlı, *Mevlânâ Celâleddin: Mektupları* (Istanbul: İnkilap, 1963).
13. Lewis, *Rūmī, Past and Present, East and West*, p. 126; cf. Safi, *The Politics of Knowledge*, pp. 126, 128–9.
14. Safi, *The Politics of Knowledge*, p. 156.
15. Jonathon A.C. Brown, 'The last days of al-Ghazzālī and the tripartite division of the Sufi world: Abū Ḥāmid al-Ghazzālī's letter to the Seljuq vizier and commentary', *Muslim World* 96, no. 1 (2006), p. 95.
16. The original text of the letters has been published twice: *Maktūbāt-i Mawlānā Jalāl al-Dīn/Mevlânânın Mektubları*, ed. Ahmed Remzi Akyürek (Istanbul: Sebat Basımevi, 1937) and *Maktūbāt-i Mawlānā Jalāl al-Dīn Rūmī*, ed. Tawfiq H. Subḥānī (Tehran: Nashr-i Dānishgāhī, 1371). Reference here is made to the more accessible Tehran edition (henceforth: *Maktūbāt*).
17. *Maktūbāt*, pp. 59–61, no. 1; pp. 107–11, no. 38, 39. It is not entirely clear why no letters seem to have been written to the ill-fated Rukn al-Dīn Qılıch Arslan IV, whom Aflākī tells us was a devotee of Rūmī; perhaps his very limited power as, essentially,

a puppet of the Parwāna, meant that he was excluded from the correspondence.

18. On Sirāj al-Dīn's career and relations with Rūmī, see Louise Marlow, 'A thirteenth-century scholar in the eastern Mediterranean: Sirāj al-Dīn Urmavī, jurist, logician, diplomat', *al-Masāq* 22, no. 3 (2010), pp. 279–313.
19. *Maktūbāt*, p. 91, no. 23; pp. 165–6, no. 73; pp. 218–9, p. 126.
20. For an overview of the period, see Charles Melville, 'Anatolia under the Mongols', in Kate Fleet (ed.), *The Cambridge History of Turkey*, i: *Byzantium to Turkey, 1071–1453* (Cambridge: Cambridge University Press, 2009), pp. 51–101.
21. Aflākī, *Manāqib*, i, 3: 37, pp. 118–19; 3: 204, pp. 292–3; 3: 224, p. 308; *Feats*, 3: 37, pp. 84–5; 3: 206, pp. 202–3; 3: 266, pp. 234–5.
22. In the Great Seljuk empire, descent from Chaghrı seems to have been regarded as a requirement for succession to the sultanate from the beginning of the twelfth century, as collateral lines such as the Seljuks of Kirman were excluded from eligibility for the sultanate. This is discussed further in A.C.S. Peacock, *The Great Seljuk Empire* (Edinburgh: Edinburgh University Press, 2015), pp. 131–3.
23. Safi, *The Politics of Knowledge*, pp. 185–9.
24. *Maktūbāt*, p. 78, no. 12; p. 98, no. 29; pp. 141–2, no. 63; pp. 196–7, no. 108.
25. Ibid., p. 95, no. 26.
26. Ibid., pp. 104–5, no. 36.
27. Ibid., p. 91, no. 23; p. 231, no. 135.
28. Ibid., p. 80, no. 15.
29. Ibid., pp. 165–6, no. 83.
30. Ibid., p. 109, no. 39.
31. Ibid., p. 114, no. 43.
32. Ibid., p. 117, no. 25.
33. Ibid., pp. 203–4, no. 113.
34. Ibid., p. 83, no. 18.
35. Ibid., p. 187, no. 101.

36. Ibid., p. 76, no 10.
37. Ibid., p. 81, no. 16.
38. Ibid., p. 126, no. 51.
39. Gölpınarlı, *Mevlana Celaleddin: Hayatı, Eserleri*, pp. 220–1.
40. Aflākī, *Manāqib*, i, 3: 113, pp. 204–05; *Feats*, 3: 113, pp. 140–1.
41. Aflākī, *Manāqib*, i, 3: 167, pp. 259–60; 3: 2, pp. 331–3; *Feats*, 3: 170, p. 180; 3: 257, pp. 229–31.
42. *Maktūbāt*, p. 113, no. 42.
43. Ibid., p. 139, no. 61.
44. Mawlānā Jalāl al-Dīn Muḥammad, *Kitāb-i Fīhi Mā Fīhi,* ed. Badīʿ al-Zamān Furūzanfar (Tehran: Intishārāt-i Nigāh, 1387, 3rd edition), pp. 19–20; *Signs of the Unseen: The Discourses of Jalaluddin Rūmī*, trans. W.M. Thackston (Boston, Mass.: Shambhala, 1994), p. 5.
45. *Maktūbāt*, p. 140, no. 62.
46. Ibid., p. 127, no. 52.
47. Ibid., p. 169, no. 87.
48. Ibid., p. 227, no. 132.
49. Ibid., p. 164, no. 82.
50. Ibid., p. 163, no. 80.
51. Ibid., p. 94, no. 25; p. 128, no. 53.
52. Ibid., p. 169, no. 87.
53. Ibid., p. 82, no. 17.
54. Ibid., p. 104.
55. Ibid., p. 112, no. 41.
56. Ibid., p. 240, no. 144.
57. See Jo Ann Gross and Asom Urubayev, *The Letters of Khwāja ʿUbayd Allāh Aḥrār and his Associates* (Leiden: Brill, 2002), especially pp. 23–56.
58. Aflākī, *Manāqib*, ii, 2, 7: 12, p. 797; 7: 29, pp. 818–19; *Feats*, 7: 12, pp. 556–8; 7: 29, p. 571.
59. *Divanı Sultan Veled*, ed. F. Nafız Uzluk (Istanbul: Uzluk Basımevi, 1941; Anadolu Selçukileri Gününde Mevlevi Bitikleri 3). The Tehran edition was unavailable to me: *Dīwān-i Sulṭān Walad*

Bahā' al-Dīn Muḥammad-i Balkhī, ed. Sa'īd Nafīsī (Tehran: Kitābfurūshī-yi Rūdakī, 1338/1959).

60. *Divan*, ed. Uzluk, Introduction, pp. 41–92.
61. Ibid., p. 201.
62. Ibid., p. 182.
63. Ibid., p. 143.
64. Ibid., pp. 131–3, 144, 247, 466–8. On the end of the Seljuks, see A.C.S. Peacock, 'Seljuq legitimacy in Islamic history', in Christian Lange and Songül Mecit (eds), *The Seljuqs: Politics, Society and Culture* (Edinburgh: Edinburgh University Press, 2011), pp. 79–95.
65. *Divan*, pp. 251, 253. Gumāj Khātūn is also mentioned as a disciple of Rūmī by Aflākī, *Manāqib*, i, 3: 285, p. 335; *Feats*, 3: 260, p. 232.
66. Aflākī, *Manāqib*, i, 3: 171, pp. 262–3; 3: 371, pp. 425–6; *Feats*, 3: 173, p. 182; 3: 373, p. 292.
67. *Divan*, p. 453.
68. Ibid., pp. 150, 370.
69. Ibid., p. 306. 'Arab Noyan, son of Samaghar, is identified by Aflākī as governor of Sivas and a devoted disciple of Chelebi Amir 'Ārif (*Manāqib*, ii, 8: 23, p. 855; *Feats*, 8: 23, p. 597).
70. On Samaghar, mentioned as one of the witnesses of Nūr al-Dīn b. Jājā's *waqfiya* at Kırşehir, see Ahmet Temir, *Kırşehir Emiri Nur el-Din'in 1272 Tarihli Arapça-Moğolca Vakfiyesi* (Ankara: Türk Tarih Kurumu, 1959), pp. 206–8; idem, 'Anadolu Ilhanli Valilerinden Samağar Noyan', in *60. Doğum Yılı Münasebetiyle Fuad Köprülü Armağan/ Mélanges Fuad Köprülü* (Istanbul: Ankara Dil ve Tarih-Coğrafyası Fakültesi, 1953), pp. 495–500.
71. *Divan*, pp. 131–2.
72. Identified by Uzluk, *Divan*, Introduction, p. 63 as a village near Konya.
73. Badr al-Dīn Gawhartash was a senior amir who had been *lala* (*atabeg*) to 'Alā' al-Dīn Kayqubād I. See Osman Turan, *Selçuklular Zamanında Türkiye: Siyasi Tarih Alp Arslan'dan Osman*

Gazi'ye (1071–1328) (Istanbul: Turan Neşriyat Yurdu, 1971), pp. 325, 520.

74. *Divan*, p. 226. Samaghar is also praised by Āqsarā'ī for his justice, see *Musāmarat al-akbār*, edited by Osman Turan as Aksaraylı Kerîmüddin Mahmud oğlu, *Müsameret ül-ahbâr: Moğollar Zamanında Türkiye Selçukluları Tarihi* (Ankara: Türk Tarih Kurumu, 1944), p. 104.
75. *Divan*, p. 306.
76. Ibid., p. 133.
77. Ibid., pp. 224–6.
78. Esrar Dede, *Tezkire-i Şuarâ-yı Mevleviyye*, ed. İlhan Genç (Ankara: Atatürk Kültür Merkezi Başkanlığı, 2000), pp. 137, 325–6; Mustafa Çetin Varlık, *Germiyan-oğulları Tarihi (1300–1429)* (Ankara: Ankara Ünversitesi Yayınları, 1974), p. 64.
79. *Divan*, p. 550.
80. Aflākī, *Manāqib*, 8: 52, p. 906; *Feats*, 8: 52, p. 633.
81. Mawlānā Jalāl al-Dīn Muḥammad, *Kitāb-i Fīhi Mā Fīhi*, pp. 38–9; translation from Rūmī, *Signs of the Unseen*, p. 27 (trans. Thackston).

CHAPTER NINE

FUTUWWA IN THIRTEENTH-CENTURY RŪM AND ARMENIA: REFORM MOVEMENTS AND THE MANAGING OF MULTIPLE ALLEGIANCES ON THE SELJUK PERIPHERY[1]

Rachel Goshgarian

> May our brothers be peace-loving in this world; may they take pleasure in speaking with and listening to men from every nation, such that they become wise from every nation, grow and gain wisdom.[2]

In one of the two thirteenth-century Armenian-language *futuwwa* constitutions compiled by the priest–poet Yovhannēs Erznkacʻi (1230–93), members of an urban lay confraternity are encouraged to be open to knowledge from all nations. It was a rather astonishing statement, given the resistance of the Armenian Church to Islamic institutions and practices. Indeed, Yovhannēs composed several constitutions which were very similar to *futuwwa* codes written around the same time in various cities in Anatolia in Arabic, Persian and Turkish for Muslim urban confraternities. This chapter will attempt to show that Armenian *futuwwa* texts were the product of interaction with *futuwwa* treatises composed in Anatolia, especially the works of Shihāb al-Dīn 'Umar al-Suhrawardī (1144–1234), as well as those written in the tradition he pioneered.[3] I suggest that these Armenian works were penned as part of the Armenian Church's attempt to restructure its own institutions in the face of a fear of 'corruption' by Islamic social and religious institutions. In this context, I examine the intellectual and political environment of thirteenth-century Erzincan, the city where Yovhannēs lived, with its competing currents of Armenian resistance to the acknowledgement of Mengüjekid and Seljuk political hegemony, its openness to Persian linguistic and literary influence, and the political and societal instability that accompanied Mongol overlordship. These regional currents underlay the recognition of the need to reform local Armenian institutions (including urban confraternities) as well as an impetus for the development of a new Armenicised Islamicate literary text speaking to the broader Anatolian trend of civic self-governance in a period of great political upheaval.

Futuwwa: *Crystallisation and Development*

Futuwwa was a moral code that crystallised in an Islamic context around the notion of an 'ideal man'. By the eighth century, *futuwwa* had transformed into a philosophy of conduct associated with specific moral and behavioural qualities and linked to a communal life led by groups of men in various cities of the Islamicate world.[4] While the earliest treatises on *futuwwa* from the eleventh century place the code within the spiritual framework associated with Islamic mysticism, in time, worldly concerns and regulations became central. The chapter on *futuwwa* embedded in the epistle of Abū 'l-Qāsim 'Abd al-Karīm al-Qushayrī (d. 1072), known as the *Risālat al-Qushayrī*, indicates that *futuwwa* encompasses a set of moral ideals and practices that can be acquired. Qushayrī's text represents a turning point in the development of *futuwwa*, which, until he composed this work, had been firmly embedded within the context of mysticism. Qushayrī was the first to stipulate that *futuwwa* is a set of actions and not necessarily of beliefs, and was also the first to comment on a connection between *futuwwa* and the marketplace, a link that persisted and eventually became an essential part of the code by the twelfth century.[5]

By the twelfth century, Islamic scholars and chroniclers, especially in Baghdad, began criticising the activities of members of the urban brotherhoods (called *'ayyārūn* or *fityān*, sing. *fatā*) who used codes of *futuwwa* as constitutions for their organisations. Some Islamic scholars censured the 'unorthodox' nature of the code itself, while others accused members of the brotherhoods of not abiding by *futuwwa* codes and indulging in physical combat. In his *Talbīs Iblīs* (or, the 'Devil's Deception'), the twelfth-century Hanbali jurist of Baghdad, Abū 'l-Faraj Ibn al-Jawzī (1115–1201), attacked both the concept of *futuwwa* and the activities of the *'ayyārūn* who claim to adhere to it.[6] In particular, he condemned the proclivity for violence exhibited by members of *futuwwa* brotherhoods.[7] It is within this environment of *futuwwa* activity and criticism of the most basic foundations of the code – and of the actions of those pretending to abide by it – that *futuwwa* experienced a rebirth and redirection due to the reforms of the supreme leader of the Islamic world, the caliph himself.

At the time of the accession of the 22-year-old caliph al-Nāṣir li-Dīn Allāh in 1180, *futuwwa* was a widespread urban phenomenon throughout the Islamic world. Still, the verdict was not in on whether or not it was legitimately Islamic. For this reason in particular, the caliph's participation in – and eventual leadership of – *futuwwa* is widely considered to be a decisive moment in its development, as well as a clear statement of the caliph's ultimate interests.[8] Al-Nāṣir was invested in the *futuwwa* in 1182, just two years after his elevation to the caliphate. In 1207, 25 years after his investiture, the caliph subordinated it to his authority and began distributing the garments, primarily the *sarāwīl,* or *futuwwa* trousers, to the Ayyubid rulers as an initiation rite into the newly reorganised caliphal *futuwwa*.[9] These activities were part of an overarching plan of the caliph's not only to reform *futuwwa* but to renovate the entire organisational structure of the caliphate and to realign all entities with himself and the capital of the caliphate, the city of Baghdad.[10] According to Ibn Wāṣil's history, the *Mufarrij al-kurūb*, the caliph sent letters in 1218 to the kings of the frontier regions (*mulūk al-aṭrāf*) requesting that they drink from the cup of *futuwwa* and wear its trousers (*sarāwīl*), and thus become members (*intimā'uhum ilayhi*) of the pyramid-like structure of what has come to be known as 'courtly' *futuwwa*. Ibn Wāṣil writes that after receiving the letters, the kings drank from the cup and donned the trousers.[11]

The two centuries following this institutional revision represent a period of active *futuwwa* code-writing that was inspired both by caliphal interest in the moral code and in controlling the organisations that adhered to it. While the caliph's reform was intended to permeate the aristocracy of the Islamic world, the caliphal *futuwwa* movement seems to have left its greatest influence in Anatolia. This was most likely the result of the promotion of the reorganised *futuwwa* by Shihāb al-Dīn 'Umar al-Suhrawardī in the early thirteenth century. Over the course of that century *futuwwa* developed into a significant means of civic self-government, as institutional hierarchies became blurred and a myriad of people and polities competed for power and prestige under Mongol overlordship.

The caliph al-Nāṣir li-Dīn Allāh showed an active interest in Anatolia. He was married to the daughter of the Seljuk sultan Qılıch Arslan II (r. 1156–92), Saljuq Khātūn (d. 1188/9),[12] and it seems that the Seljuk elites were responsive to the caliph's reformed programme of *futuwwa*. According to Ibn Bībī, in 1214, just after the Seljuk conquest of Sinop, the Seljuk sultan 'Izz al-Dīn Kaykā'ūs I (r. 1211–19) sent Shaykh Majd al-Dīn Isḥāq[13] to Baghdad with exquisite gifts and a request to join the caliphal *futuwwa*. The belt of *muruwwa*, the 'trousers of justice' (the *sarāwīl* of *futuwwa*) along with the book of *futuwwa* by Ibn al-Mi'mār (d. 1244) were given to Majd al-Dīn to present to the sultan.[14]

The caliph's dispatch of the famed mystic and orator, Shihāb al-Dīn ʻUmar al-Suhrawardī, to the region in 1221 as his spiritual and political envoy indicates his concern for the development of *futuwwa* in this frontier region of the Islamic world. Suhrawardī was a prolific scholar whose training at the Niẓamīya in Baghdad had developed him into one of the most effective orators in Baghdad. He was made director of the Sufi lodges of the city of Baghdad and also acted as a diplomat in the service of the caliph, not only in Anatolia but also in Ayyubid Egypt as well as in Bukhara, at the court of the Khwārazmshāhs. The relationship between the caliph and Suhrawardī was not without friction. At one point, the caliph had Suhrawardī's position revoked and forbade him from speaking in public. His mission to Anatolia in 1221 came after this period of cooling off. One of Suhrawardī's tasks in the region was to bestow the caliphal *manshūr* (diploma of appointment) upon the newly enthroned sultan, ʻAlā' al-Dīn Kayqubād I, as well as to initiate the sultan and members of the political elite into the Suhrawardī *ṭarīqa*. Unlike his elder brother ʻIzz al-Dīn Kaykā'ūs I, however, Kayqubād appears to have not been initiated into the caliphal *futuwwa*.[15]

The Futuwwa *of Suhrawardī and After*

Suhrawardī's influence in Anatolia was great and long-lasting, as Ibn Bībī, writing in late thirteenth century, suggests in his description of Suhrawardī's 1221 visit to the Seljuk capital:

> While the shaykh [Suhrawardī] stayed in Konya, the sultan sought to visit him repeatedly. All the elite and commoners of the land of Rūm, especially the inhabitants of Konya, young and old, nobles and *akhīs*, gained the honour of wearing the shaykh's *khirqa* of *tabarruk* and *irāda*.[16] Everyone received his due portion of the shaykh's magnificent powers in the *sunna*, the *ṭarīqa*, the *sharīʻa* and the *ḥaqīqa*. To this day, the fruits of that happiness [of his visit] still remain.[17]

Once in Anatolia, Suhrawardī seems to have pursued a programme organisationally distinct from the *futuwwa* espoused by Caliph al-Nāṣir.[18] Nonetheless, loyalty to the caliphate remained a fundamental part of his conception of *futuwwa*, and his first treatise on the subject describes it as a part of Sufism which in turn was fundamentally associated with the caliphate.[19] This association between Sufism and *futuwwa* is emphasised by Suhrawardī, who points out that the garments donned by members of the *futuwwa* were similar to the clothing of dervishes: 'The clothing of Sufism (*taṣawwuf*) is the cloak (*khirqa*) and the clothing of *futuwwa* is the trouser; since the under-garment (*zīr-jāma*) and the trouser is part of the cloak, so *futuwwa* is part of the Sufi way.'[20] Suhrawardī also insists on the wearing of the *sarāwīl* by members of *futuwwa* as an indication of their abstinence from fornication, and the importance of buildings associated with *futuwwa* organisations to house travellers, just as those of the dervishes did.[21]

After Suhrawardī, at least three Islamic treatises on *futuwwa* were composed in Anatolia.[22] The lengthiest was penned in Persian by Mawlānā Nāṣirī in Tokat in 1290.[23] Another was composed in Arabic by Ilyāsoğlu Naqqāsh Aḥmad of Harput and dedicated to Abū 'l-Ḥassan 'Alī, son of Caliph al-Mustanṣir (r. 1226–42). The first Turkish-language treatise on *futuwwa* was composed by Yahyā b. Chūbān Fatā al-Burghāzī in the early fourteenth century. Each of these works shows allegiance to Suhrawardī's code although divergences are also present, and especially prevalent in Burghāzī's work.

Like Suhrawardī, all three authors describe either basic tenets or certain stipulations of *futuwwa* according to the metaphor of opening and closing certain parts of the human body. Both Naqqāsh and Burghāzī explain that the *fatā* must keep his eyes, mouth and hands closed from forbidden things, shameful speech and physical harm.[24] While all three texts insist that faith is the basis of *futuwwa*, they vary in the extent to which they assert the relationship between *futuwwa* and the *sharī'a*.[25] The texts of both Nāṣirī and Naqqāsh organise the hierarchies of *futuwwa* in a bipartite fashion according to the relationship between master and novice, just as Suhrawardī insists in his treatises, in emulation of the hierarchy of a Sufi lodge.[26] Burghāzī's text, however, suggests a novelty: a tripartite organisation of the confraternities associated with *futuwwa*.[27] All three works emphasise the importance of girding the garments of the order, which variously symbolise the heavy responsibility of *futuwwa*, the initiation of the novice and the *futuwwa*-member's commitment to chastity.[28] Like Suhrawardī's texts, all three treatises place importance upon table manners and behaviour while in the presence of fellow *futuwwa* members.

While each work is unique, the treatise composed by Burghāzī is most distinct from the others with its insistence upon the pressing need for the reform of *futuwwa*. Burghāzī links falsities associated with *futuwwa* to bravery and heroics (*alplık* and *bahadırlık*).[29] Indeed, he explains that his decision to compose the text was influenced by what he saw as the corruption of *futuwwa*:

> In the place of obedience, they behaved mischievously; in the place of education and correctness, they placed shamelessness. Even more, they put ignorance on the name of *futuwwa* ... I saw that the *akhīs* sitting at the door of *futuwwa* had no *futuwwa-nāma* (moral constitution), so I decided that I would write a book on *futuwwa*.[30]

Considering these three texts were composed between 50 and 100 years after the texts of Suhrawardī, it is clear that the shaykh did have a lasting influence in the region – and specifically on the composition of *futuwwa* texts in Anatolia. As has been shown by Erik Ohlander and noted above, the form of *futuwwa* propagated by Suhrawardī was, in fact, distinct from that promulgated by the caliph himself (although Suhrawardī's texts most likely would not have been composed had the caliph not shown such a great interest in the institution). Each text is somewhat divergent from the prescriptions articulated by Suhrawardī – whether in its expression of the relationship between *futuwwa* and the caliphate, its organisational structure or the level of importance placed on descriptions of the house of *futuwwa*. Nevertheless, most of the fundamental concerns of the treatises echo the *futuwwa* ideology of Suhrawardī, with great importance given to the centrality of faith, the master–novice relationship, the girding as a symbol of chastity, and table manners, as well as in their description of behaviour and morals in the context of the human body.

In his treatises, Suhrawardī encouraged a *khānaqāh*-centred, urban-based, spiritual and social community of interdependent men linked by the master–novice relationship and not necessarily connected either to the Seljuk sultanate or to the caliphate. It is perhaps because the sort of communal brotherhood envisioned by Suhrawardī encouraged, on the one hand, a prescribed way of life and, on the other, allowed members of a *futuwwa* community independence from other forms of social control – whether from the Seljuk sultanate or the caliphate – that his particular constitutions had such resonance amongst city-dwellers in Anatolia, a region whose inhabitants found themselves navigating a grid of confused and overlapping power hierarchies, especially during the period of Mongol domination of the region. What is perhaps most surprising is that the concerns and prescriptions present in Suhrawardī's discourses on *futuwwa* are also echoed in the two Armenian *futuwwa* treatises composed by the priest-poet Yovhannēs Erznkac'i.

Christians and Futuwwa

There is some evidence that in the early thirteenth century the *ahl al-dhimma* (Christians, Jews and Sabaeans) could participate on a limited basis in the caliphal *futuwwa*, as Ibn al-Mi'mār's treatise on *futuwwa* indicates.[31] In Anatolia, however, at least during the late thirteenth and early fourteenth centuries, non-Muslims were not meant to participate in institution, as the treatises by Nāṣirī and Burghāzī indicate. In fact, Nāṣirī stipulates that non-Muslims may not even enter buildings associated with *futuwwa.*[32] Burghāzī, in his list of those who are not admissible into the fold of *futuwwa*, ranks non-Muslims first, before mischief-makers, astrologers, those guilty of crimes and liars.[33] He explains that non-Muslims cannot participate in *futuwwa* because they are 'blind to the true faith'.[34]

Nevertheless, the existence of Christian *futuwwa*-like organisations stretches back to the early twelfth century, well before the caliphal reform; evidence of Armenian participation in *futuwwa*-like brotherhoods is provided by the chronicle of Matthew of Edessa (d. c.1136), with this description of an episode that took place in the city of Antioch in the 1120s:

> On the day of *barekendan* (Arm., the Sunday immediately preceding the start of *mec pahk'*, or Lent) of the same year, a caravan carrying salted fish (Arm., *tarex*) came to the city of Antioch from the East.[35] The people belonging to this caravan had set themselves up in the marketplace and were drinking and making merry. When the townspeople heard the sounds of their dancing and singing, all the men of the city pounced upon them and beat them to a pulp, after which they began to throw them out of the city. Now the men of this caravan were 80 in number and they had truncheons and were resolute in purpose. So when their leader (*manktawagn noc'a*)[36] cried out to them, in their drunken condition they fell upon the townspeople, pursuing them from the Gate of *Sevodn* (Arm., black foot) to the Church of Saint Peter, they put all the townspeople to flight and broke the skulls and bones of many. Finally, the Antiochenes swore by the cross and the Gospels that they would never bother them again. So, after peace was re-established, the caravan returned to its place of origin.[37]

Based on the terminology used, the trade-related interests of the group and the violence ascribed to them, scholarship has suggested that this event proves the existence of Armenian urban confraternities engaged with *futuwwa* in the region of Van/Ahlat as early as the first half of the twelfth century.[38] Still, from 1120 until the late thirteenth century there are no extant textual references to anything resembling a *futuwwa*-based association in an Armenian context.[39] Although Seta Dadoyan has suggested that the caliphal reform influenced the development of the Armenian code,[40] it was not specifically the *caliphal* re-appropriation of *futuwwa* but rather the impact of the Persian-language writings of the caliphal *envoy* to the region, Shihāb al-Dīn al-Suhrawardī, that shaped the development of *futuwwa* in Anatolia, and also amongst the Persian-proficient members of the Armenian brotherhood of Erzincan. At the same time, an Armenian concern with institutional reform in the wake of the establishment of Islamic institutions and social patterns of organisation in the region added impetus for the creation of moral codes for Armenian (Christian) lay confraternities.[41]

The two Armenian texts written in the late thirteenth century by the priest-poet Yovhannēs Erznkacʻi are quite different from each other, although they were most probably composed within five years of one another. Yovhannēs Erznkacʻi 'Pluz' (the moniker 'Pluz' suggests that he was either blue-eyed or short), a native of Erznka/Erzincan, studied at the monastery of St Minas on Mount Sepuh (Keşiş Dağları, outside of Erzincan) and in other monastic complexes in the same region,[42] and later at the monastery of St Andrew in Kayan Berd,[43] founded by Vartan Arewelcʻi (1198–1271). It was probably while at St Andrew (around 1260) that the young Yovhannēs, with a great interest in things Islamic, translated the 'Epistles of the Brethren of Purity' (*Rasāʼil Ikhwān al-ṣafā*), a popular Arabic Neoplatonic text.[44] It appears that the hierarchical brotherhood described in the *Rasāʼil* made an impression on Yovhannēs, as suggested by his composition of the two *futuwwa* texts some 20 years later.

Yovhannēs travelled widely between 1272 and 1280. He visited Jerusalem and studied at the seat of the Armenian *catholicos* at Hṛomgla (Rūm Kale), as well as at the monastery at Kayan Berd. While in the kingdom of Georgia, he composed 'On the Movement of the Celestial Bodies' for a local Armenian noble.[45] In the 1280s Yovhannēs returned to the monastery of his youth, Surb Minas, and composed a commentary on *The Art of Grammar* of Dionysios Thrax and also wrote poetry and advice (*xratakan*) literature 'for the common folk' (Arm., *xratkʻ hasarakacʻ*), priests, Armenian princes and members of the brotherhood of Erznka.[46] Yovhannēs' work, as reflected in his great body of advice literature, shows wide-ranging cultural interests and a deep concern for people of various stations.[47]

While the two *futuwwa*-like treatises he composed are distinct from one another, together they embody many of the concepts associated with Suhrawardī's version of *futuwwa*. The first of his treatises is titled *Sahman ew kanonkʻ miabanutʻean ełbarcʻ* ('Constitution and

Rules of the Association of Brothers'). This constitution is divided into two general parts: a description of the various sorts of brotherhood, and a selection of practical and moral rules for members of the association. The work is framed around adherence to Christianity, and filled with quotations from the Gospels. In the first section of the text, Yovhannēs defines four kinds of brotherhoods – those which exist between: (1) all of God's creations; (2) those born of the same parents; (3) those who are baptised into Christianity; (4) the members of the association for whom the constitution is written. He particularly emphasises that not only is this brotherhood not new, but that it is specifically befitting Christianity. The three goals of the fourth brotherhood are to encourage honest conduct, to share profit and to preserve worldly customs in the name of Christ.[48] This text, composed at the same time as Mawlānā Nāṣirī of Tokat's Persian-language treatise, is the first Anatolian constitution explicitly to link this sort of brotherhood with trade and communal living based on profit-making.

Yovhannēs Erznkac'i explains moral actions vis-à-vis the body, although he does not use the Suhrawardic method of prescribing 'opening' or 'closing' of certain body parts:

> Keep the mouth, which is the confessor in the name of God and communicative, holy from offensive words and from all improper talk, and do not use the tongue that God created for the work of Satan. Fortify your senses by means of the fear of God: the eye, from indecent looks; the ear, from evil and sinful advice; the hand, from robbing and stealing and beating; and the leg/foot, from the sin of running from committed sin. But do [behave] in this way: by means of the eyes, see God's beautiful creations; by means of the mouth, bless the Creator; by means of the ear, hear His orders; by means of the hands, do well in prayer and in work and in the blessing of the poor, and purify the heart from evil advice.[49]

Although Yovhannēs specifies that the aforementioned rules are directed particularly at the brothers of the association, he maintains that they should be followed by all Christians. This section is followed by a second set of rules that are specific only to the brotherhood: keeping brothers from engaging in violent acts, helping a brother decide against sin, helping a brother with little money, helping a brother who has fallen ill and burying a brother who has expired.[50] The text also encourages the brothers to behave in a hospitable manner to foreigners.

Yovhannēs's second *futuwwa* constitution is entitled *Krkin kanonk' ew xratk' tłayahasak mankanc' ašxarhakanac'* ('Again Rules and Advice for Worldly Pubescent Youths'). Quite distinct from the previous set of rules, this treatise focuses on the origins of the practice of brotherhood and presents requirements for those who wish to join as well as progress within the association. Yovhannēs, like the authors of the Muslim *futuwwa* constitutions, suggests that there are certain sorts of people who must be excluded from the association.

In his explanation of who is allowed to participate in such an organisation, Yovhannēs stipulates that youthfulness (here, *mankut'iwn*, i.e. *futuwwa*) consists of courage, honesty and benevolence. The leader of the youths (*manktawag*) must be knowledgeable of the Holy Scriptures, pure of deed (as people learn best by example), generous towards others and obedient to the rules of the Church.[51] Yovhannēs also explores the Christian origins of the brotherhood, insisting that its practice originated with Jesus Christ and the Holy Apostles; this could, in fact, be a subtle indication of the author's aversion to admitting the similarity of Armenian ('Christian') *mankut'iwn* to ('Islamic') *futuwwa*.

This treatise, like Islamic texts on *futuwwa*, centres the brotherhood in the master–novice relationship. Yovhannēs explains that the leaders of the youths are called *manktawag* (Arm., leader of the youth) and that their novices are called simply *manuk* (pl., *manukk'* and *mankti*). Once a youth is assigned a master, however, he is called *vordegīr* (Arm., adopted) and is then given the belt (Arm., *gawti*). Indeed, this suggests that the Armenian brotherhoods of Erzincan were also organised according to a tripartite structure similar to that proposed by Burghāzī, who wrote his text after Yovhannēs. Yovhannēs likewise distinguishes the different classes of belts: the belt of baptism (in the obligatory colours of red and white), and those donned by priests, by ascetics, by the soldiery (Arm., *zinvorakan*) and by travellers.[52] A final category of belt belongs to the members of the brotherhood; as a symbol of the corporation, this belt 'brings holiness and binds the great dragon's desire.'[53] Thus, the significance of the belt in the Armenian context mirrors that of the *libās al-futuwwa* (*futuwwa* garments) in contemporary Arabic, Persian and Turkish texts. It is both a symbol of courage and an indicator of chastity. The Armenian texts, however, make no mention of the trousers so consistently associated with *futuwwa*, thus distinguishing Armenian brotherhood members from their Muslim counterparts. Despite these differences, there can be no doubt that the Armenian (Christian) codes, like contemporary *futuwwa* treatises, were developed in an Anatolian urban environment inspired by the texts of Suhrawardī and also by an overarching local concern with civic government in the face of competition between various political hierarchies. To understand the processes by which the Islamic idea of *futuwwa* could be translated to a Christian context, we must turn to examine the city of Erzincan, Yovhannēs' home town and the place of composition of these works.

Erzincan and Muslim–Christian Cultural Exchange

Erzincan was one of the largest cities in thirteenth-century Anatolia, after Konya, Sivas and Antalya. A largely Armenian metropolis, Erzincan was a centre of fabric production, as is attested by the Venetian traveller Marco Polo, who visited it in the second half of the thirteenth century.

> [Armenia Major] is an extensive province, at the entrance of which is a city named Arzingan (Erzincan), where there is a manufacture of very fine cotton cloth called bombazines, as well as many other curious fabrics, which it would be tedious to enumerate.[54]

In his geography, the *Mu'jam al-buldān* (compiled around 1224–8), Yāqūt al-Ḥamawī describes Erzincan thus:

> Erzincan is one of Armenia's most beautiful, famous, pleasant, active and populated cities, which lies between Rūm and Ahlat and near Erzurum. The locals call the city *Erzinka*. The majority of the population is Armenian. There are also Muslims, who are the local elite (*a'yān ahlihā*). Wine drinking and inappropriate behaviour are open and widespread. I do not know of anyone of note from this city.[55]

It should come as no surprise that an Arabic-speaking Muslim traveller to Erzincan might not have come into contact with (or might refrain from elaborating on) the active Armenian, Christian intellectual life of the city.[56] During the thirteenth century, the region of Erzincan had several active monasteries (with scriptoria), including those at Avag, Lusavorič, Surb Kirakos, Surb Minas, Surb P'rkič and Tirašēn. Because of its geographical position, its importance as a city of trade, and perhaps simply due to the fact that there were so many Armenians and Armenian monasteries there, Erzincan was an important Armenian intellectual centre in the thirteenth century.

Indeed, the colophons of Armenian manuscripts produced in Erzincan suggest that Muslim power may have been more limited than Yāqūt indicates.[57] The structural elements of colophons give clues regarding local power structures. Colophons are often organised in the following way: after the author refers to himself with self-deprecating terms (such as 'the bad servant,' 'the sin-filled deacon' and 'the unworthy priest'), he names the monastery in which he wrote or copied the manuscript and lists the names of the representatives of the eclesiastical and political hierarchy to which he was subject in ascending order, including fellow priests, bishop, Armenian prince or king, Armenian *catholicos* and, sometimes, foreign overlord. On occasion the order is reversed, with a mention of the king first, the Armenian *catholicos* and then the church leaders in descending hierarchical order). It appears from the structure of the colophons and the placement of any foreign ruler *after* all Armenian constituents that Armenian scribes included the name of a non-Armenian ruler in the colophon if and when Armenians were subservient to that foreign ruler. In the case of the Armenian manuscripts completed around Erzincan, no non-Armenian rulers are mentioned until the Mongols.[58] For example, a colophon composed in Erzincan in 1280 (approximately 40 years after the Mongols had entered the region) explains:

> This was written in the mother city of Erznka, under the protection of the church of the Holy Saviour, which was built by the lord Sargis, the worthy bishop and his devoted son, Baron John. It was written in the year 1280, during the kingship of Levon the Kind (Levon II, 1270–89), son of Het'um (1226–70), and under the catholicate of Yakob, and during the episcoposate of Nersēs, grandson of Sargis, and his God-loving brother Grigoris and under the sovereignty of Abgha Khan (1284–2), son of Hulagu (1217–65).[59]

Although the Mengüjekids ostensibly ruled over the region from the seat of Erzincan for much of the twelfth century until 'Alā' al-Din Kayqubād annexed the city to the Seljuk state in 1228[60] (another branch of the Mengüjekids survived in Divriği until 1277),[61] their presence in Erzincan is rarely noted in contemporary Armenian sources. There seems to be a unique reference in the chronicle of Smbat the Constable (1208–76) to a certain Lord of Erznka/Erzincan (*tērn Eznkayin*), Vahram Shah (i.e. Fakhr al-Dīn Bahrāmshāh), the Mengüjekid ally of the Seljuk Rukn al-Dīn Sulaymānshāh who was captured by the Georgians in 1201/1202.[62] Thus the Armenian population of Erzincan seem to have considered the Mengüjekid ruler Bahrāmshāh nothing more than a lord – the Armenian source uses the term *tēr*, which is comparable to *baron*, the title given to the Armenian leader of Erzincan, whereas the Seljuk Rukn al-Dīn is called a *sultan*.

The dearth of references to the Mengüjekids in the Armenian sources is curious. This could be an indication of an Armenian reluctance to place importance on the family of Mengüjek in Erzincan, but it might also be an indicator of the Muslim dynasty's relative insignificance in the eyes of local Armenian authors. As suggested by the colophon of 1280 cited above, an alternative focus of political allegiance for the Armenian population of Erzincan was the kingdom of Cilicia. This is confirmed by another work by Yovhannēs Erznkac'i, the author of our two Armenian *futuwwa* treatises, who also composed around 1289 or 1290 a text entitled *Letter to the princes of the region of Ekełeac'* (Erzincan) addressed to the Armenian royal family of Cilicia.[63] In his letter, Yovhannēs seems to be requesting strengthened ties with the kingdom of Cilicia, and he criticises Armenian 'princes' (*išxank'*) for leaving the Armenians 'without leaders in the region' and 'forced to abide by laws that are not theirs'. This text, with its lamentation of the lack of Christian leadership in the face of the development of an Islamic social fabric, and during the beginning of Mongol overlordship in the region, is reminiscent of the reformative spirit of the law code of Mxit'ar Goš (1130–1213) and that of the Cilician Smbat the Constable, which will be discussed further below. However, despite Yovhannēs' search for a Christian overlord, the encyclical is permeated by Islamicate themes. With its admonition against wine drinking and exhortations to just rule and hard work, it should be considered within the context of late medieval Anatolia's fascination with advice literature, or 'mirrors for princes'. The heyday of the genre in the Islamicate world is generally considered the second half of the eleventh century,[64] but such works enjoyed a remarkable degree of popularity in Anatolia during the thirteenth and fourteenth centuries and were one of the most popular literary genres in the region during this period.[65]

An appreciation of Islamicate literature can be observed in the works of other Armenian authors from Erzincan. Of the three most celebrated Armenian poets of the thirteenth century, two – Kostandin Erznkac'i and Yovhannēs Erznkac'i – hailed from Erzincan. Their works suggest that interfaith or intercultural interaction in Anatolia during this period did not simply result in marketplace exchanges of words, foods and textiles, but also in the inter-permeation of themes and ideas thanks to a multilingual environment within which overarching social needs created links between people, sometimes regardless of the faith(s) they practised or the language(s) they spoke.

Born in Erzincan, Kostandin Erznkac'i most probably received his education in the nearby monastery of Tirašēn, although it is thought that he was never ordained, and left its walls to live a more worldly life.[66] Writing in a vernacular style, Kostandin was the first poet to incorporate into Armenian verse the mystical imagery of the 'Rose and Nightingale'[67] as used by contemporary Persian poets like Farīd ad-Dīn 'Aṭṭār (d. 1221) and Sa'dī (d. 1283). K'iwrtian has suggested that it was Kostandin's distance from monastic life that allowed his work to blossom in a way that was distinct from the body of poetry composed by his religiously minded contemporaries.[68] The lyrical aspect of his poetry suggests that his work was intended to be both read and heard,[69] as is confirmed by references to conversations with 'brothers' (Arm., *ełbayrk'*). Theo Van Lint has suggested that the reference to these brothers indicates that Kostandin Erznkac'i was a member of an Armenian *futuwwa* brotherhood. For instance, Kostandin composed a work for a certain Baron Amiṛ P'olin, in which he refers to the baron as 'our honoured and beloved brother' (Arm., *mer parcanac' ełbayr ew sireli*).[70] It is most probable that Baron Amiṛ was a member of the same brotherhood that enjoyed Kostandin's worldly poetry. Still, the title used to refer to him indicates that he was a layman and not a priest. Kostandin speaks to the worldly standing of this Baron Amiṛ, and writes:

> I know that not everyone can learn from the Scriptures.
>
> Therefore, I have written this, that you may hear it from me.[71]

As Van Lint suggests, this would indicate that the beloved 'brother' of Kostandin was not a religious man. Kostandin's poetry was so popular that many became jealous of him: 'Some speak evil of me out of envy, saying: "How can he recite such a poem, as he has not had much tuition from a *vardapet* (Arm., a learned priest)?"'[72] Still, there is an important Christian-oriented undertone to the poetry of Kostandin; two poems of his collection admonish 'deceivers' and 'ignorant ones' who lead good Christians astray.[73]

The poet's lay brothers in the confraternity shared an intimate knowledge of Persian literary culture, as is clear from the beginning of this poem by Kostantin:

> A man was seated and recited the *Shāhnāma* aloud. The brothers asked me, recite for us a poem in the manner (Arm., *jayn*) of the *Shāhnāma*. I composed this poem. Read it in the manner of the *Shāhnāma*.[74]

This one sentence indicates that some Armenians living in Erzincan – specifically, those who participated in Kostandin's brotherhood – were sufficiently aware of Persian culture to know the specific metre of the *Shāhnāma*. However, this interest in Persian literature in the region of Erzincan was not, by any means, limited to members of the Armenian brotherhood. The famed Persian poet Niẓāmī of Ganja (c.1141–1209) dedicated his late twelfth-century poem the *Makhzan al-asrār* to Fakhr al-Dīn Bahrāmshāh, the Mengüjekid lord of Erzincan.

A poem composed by T'oros of Taron further strengthens this impression of a shared Islamicate culture in Erzincan.[75] The poem depicts the earthquake of 1287 that devastated Erzincan, and is made up of 14 four-lined stanzas, of which ten lines were composed in Armeno-Turkish (Turkish with Armenian letters, or *hayataṛ t'urk'erēn*).[76] Scholars have suggested that Armenians began writing Turkish with Armenian letters in the fourteenth century,[77] but this poem's ten Turkish lines suggest that the practice began even earlier, in the late thirteenth century. The Armeno-Turkish section of the original poem and the same portion of the text both transliterated into modern Turkish and translated into English are given below.

Պարոնն զիւր ֆաղաֆն ձգեց,
Մինչ ի Բաբերթ գնաց *չափառ*,[78]
Պուկիւն վէրէմ սանղայ խէպար,
Տէկիլ ստախուռլայ ու հաֆպար:

Հախտան կէլտի պիզէ զաւալ.
Էրզընկայ օլտի տէրպէտէր.
Պեյլէ զաւալ կեւրմէմիշ իտիմ.
Հիչ կեօրունմէզ չարսուպազար:

Պուկիւն նազուկ իկիթլեր.
Տամլար ալթընտայ նէչէ վար.
Կալմատի կանճուն ւ արաստա.
Հիչ կէւրունմէզ չարսու պազար։[79]

Bugün vereyim sana haber
Değil estağfurullah ve ekber.

Haktan geldi bize zeval
Erzincan oldu derbeder
Böyle zeval görmemiş idim
Hiç görünmez çarşı pazar.

Bügün nazik yiğitler
Damlar altında nice var
Kalmadı gancin ve arasta
Hiç görünmez çarşı pazar.

The baron left his city
And ran as far as Bayburt, saying:
'Today let me give you the news,
Say "May the Lord protect us, God is great"

A calamity has come to us from God,
Erzincan has been levelled.
Never have I seen such destruction,
Nothing is left of the market and bazaar

Today the brave and decent lads[80] –
So many of them lay under roofs.
Nothing remains of the markets' treasuries and storehouses,
Nothing is left of the market and bazaar.'

The above composition reminds one of Andalusian *muwashshaḥ*, short poems meant to be sung, while its use of Turkish is an example of mixed-language 'macaronic poetry' (*mulamma'āt*), a discursive strategy likewise used by Kostandin's contemporary Jalāl al-Dīn Rūmī, who incorporated Arabic, Armenian, Greek and Turkish verses in his extensive Persian poetic corpus.[81] The poem by T'oros is also filled with borrowed terms from Persian, and the use of these languages may perhaps be explained by a desire to impress his audience or simply to express himself in a way that might be understood by a specific Persian- and Turkish-familiar audience. That these verses constitute the first evidence of the existence of Armeno-Turkish and that the poem was composed about the city of Erzincan suggest that there was something unique about the cultural atmosphere in the city. And the fact that the text's Turkish lines represent a verbal announcement made by an Armenian lord from Erzincan suggests that this noble in fact spoke Turkish as he shared the news of the earthquake's devastation.

It would seem that linguistic plurality and interfaith interaction were part and parcel of everyday life in Erzincan. We can thus venture that concepts related to *futuwwa* were not transmitted to an Armenian audience via the Seljuk elite, but rather by the literature associated with *futuwwa* itself, composed by mystics such as Suhrawardī. In a city like Erzincan it seems likely that the kind of civic self-government offered by *futuwwa* codes would have been attractive for locals attempting to maintain a sense of stability in a city and region that was both an educational and a mercantile hub. Still, the Armenian Church's 'management of multiplicities' was not necessarily one that encouraged openness to the enormous cultural and social changes that were taking place in the region. In fact, from the mid twelfth century the Church began a reform movement that was meant to limit the extent to which new institutions influenced the Armenian (Christian) populations living outside the Armenian kingdom of Cilicia.

Armenian Reform Movements

Like Burghāzī, Yovhannēs also explains the impetus behind the composition of his code in the context of a need for institutional reform:

> We saw, in the world, a practice that by means of tradition has remained amongst those men of men, who are called *manktawag*

> (leader of the youth) and they call the youths their adopted sons and bestow upon them the girdle. And there was no possibility that this [tradition] be removed from the realm, for the practice was ancient, and those who employed this practice were considered sweet and attractive. But their practice was corporeal and worldly and ignorant. So, we hoped to write them advice and show them the way, such that the practice would become enlightened by means of knowledge and wisdom and rules, and untainted by evil, and by means of the testimony of the Holy Scriptures and not by means of incorrect knowledge.[82]

Yovhannēs' text suggests that the need for a reform of the Armenian brotherhoods was at least partly informed by a concern on the part of the Church that the organisations were not operating according to Christian ideals, but rather according to worldly concerns.

Just as the caliph's reform of *futuwwa* was part of an overarching plan to strengthen and recentralise the caliphate, so were the Armenian constitutions composed for lay confraternities based on *futuwwa* (Arm., *mankut'iwn*) one aspect of a larger concern with Armenian institutional reform in the late medieval period. Waves of migrations and the development of new (Islamic) institutions created a concern amongst Armenian intellectuals that led to a reform movement. As James Russell has shown, the twelfth-century Armenian *catholicos* Nersēs Šnorhali (1102–73) developed new poetic styles and composed much of his work (including his 'Lamentation on the City of Edessa') as a means of bringing Armenians back to the Christian fold and ensuring their understanding of, and dedication to, the Church.[83] David of Gancak (b. c.1070 in Gancak, or Ganja, in modern-day Azerbaijan) wrote a series of canonical statutes, *Kanonakan Xratk'* (Canonical Advice).[84] His work became partially absorbed into the late twelfth-century law code of Mxit'ar Goš, a text that was used as the basis for many centuries of Armenian legal practice from Van to Poland. The *Kanonakan Xratk'* offers specific guidelines on food consumption vis-à-vis unavoidable contact with Muslim neighbours:

> One shall not eat bread handled by an infidel (*aylazg*) nor drink wine or water tasted by them. Priests shall not drink anything left over by them or which their hand has touched, and this shall not be used as a holy offering. If there be a large quantity, it shall be used outside, and if there is but a little, it shall be poured away. Likewise milk and whey (*t'an*), these shall also be poured away. If they should take meat, cheese or oil, that which has been handled shall be cut out and the rest washed and eaten. One shall not eat anything given by them — bread, cheese, meat, vegetables, grapes, and wine — except for those [fruits] which are in shells [or rinds]: walnuts, pomegranates, and melons, etc., and those things which are used to heal the body, apart from *theriaca* and other filthy (*piłc*) drugs.[85]

Mxit'ar Goš was the first to compose a law code for the Armenian population living outside of the kingdom of Cilicia. Writing in Getik (near Ičevan in the modern Republic of Armenia) in 1184, Mxit'ar enumerates 12 reasons for the creation of such a code, among them being that without a code Armenians would make use of readily available channels of 'recourse to foreigners'.[86] Mxit'ar's text depicts a fear of corruption through contact with Muslims, on either an institutional and personal level.[87] Forbidding Armenians from frequenting the courts of 'non-believers', Mxit'ar pronounces the superiority of the Christian code:

> It is necessary to use the superior and compassionate code … so it is not right for a Christian to go to the court of those who are so distant in justice … we see many of the believers rushing there, when they see that by going to the foreigners our case is carried out victoriously; and if it turns out well among the believers according to their desires, they then go to them. But it is not right for the sake of avarice and victory for believers to go to the unbelievers, but to the believers, even if by law the case is lost.[88]

Mxit'ar Goš's code was an attempt to offer Armenians living within a developing Islamicate society the possibility of government and regulation by Armenian laws rather than Islamic ones.[89] His work speaks of the urgent need for reform of the most fundamental and significant of Armenian institutions during this time period, the Armenian Church, which had an important role in both regulating and representing Armenians living under non-Armenian rule.[90] In fact, 60 of the 250 chapters of Goš' code deal directly with regulations concerning clergy and church property, and many of the remaining chapters are related to activities performed by clergy members (baptism, divorce, marriage, etc.). For example, Goš criticises Armenian monasteries for allowing non-religious types to reside in them and disapproves of them for behaving much in the way that dervish or *futuwwa* lodges operated during this time period:

> Some nobles and mounted riders, when they arrive at villages which are situated in the region of a monastery, do not dismount at the village, but some with their wives and female servants lodge at the monastery, and in this way trample on the canon of the fathers. With minstrels (Arm., *gusank'*) and singing girls they feast in the house of holiness and worship, which is horrible for Christians to hear, let alone see ... So let the priests of the monasteries recall these above-mentioned canons in the ears of such persons. If they pay heed and lodge in the village, it is good. But if they persist in the same stubbornness, such persons likewise will be far from our blessing and will receive vengeance from the saints. For 'monastery' means a resting place of the saints and a lodging for bishops and priests and monks, and the poor. But nobles and cavalry, inasmuch as they are called men and women, must with great awe pray and join in prayer and worship, as it is fitting in the house of God. This legislative statute is clear to all.[91]

Goš's code underwent two editions within the century after it was composed, in order to take into account various sociopolitical changes. The second and third editions suggest that the code was, in fact, used already in the thirteenth century.[92] In fact, the code became so relevant that by the fourteenth century the elder brother of the Cilician king Het'um I, Smbat the Constable, had already translated and adapted it for use in the Armenian kingdom of Cilicia, an area of the region that was *not* under Islamic control or law.[93]

Conclusion

The Armenian Church's apprehension concerning the prevalence of secular interests coupled with a perceived necessity for reorganisation in the face of the establishment of Islamic institutions seems to have created the impetus behind the composition of the treatises on the brotherhoods at Erzincan. These Armenian *futuwwa* texts were composed within the context of an Armenian reluctance to acknowledge non-Armenian, non-Mongol power hierarchies, and a certain local openness to Persian forms of literature and the Turkish language. It seems quite clear that there existed in the city of Erzincan and in its surrounding Armenian monastic complexes an environment amenable to cultural permeation in spite of an obvious resistance to non-Armenian political presence. Given the closeness of the Armenian texts to those composed both by Suhrawardī and by other Anatolian Muslim authors, it can only be assumed that these organisations were established, or reformed, with a certain degree of influence from similar treatises composed with a Muslim audience in mind. In fact, despite Erzincan's location on the peripheries of the Seljuk sultanate, Suhrawardī's voice echoes quite consistently in the Armenian *futuwwa* texts composed there. This suggests that the activities taking place at the Seljuk capital in Konya had great resonance throughout Anatolia, and even beyond the central cultural and societal sphere of the sultanate itself. The similarities between the Armenian texts and the Arabic, Persian and Turkish texts composed around the same time elsewhere suggest that individuals living in Anatolian cities during this period experienced a new interest in civic self-governance. At the same time, these Armenian texts also fit into the framework of the Armenian Church's concern with institutional reform – due to a fear of Islamic 'corruption' – during the long thirteenth century. It seems quite fitting, in fact, given the complicated web of political, religious and cultural hierarchies that existed in the region, that an Armenian attempt at institutional reform and, indeed, at managing multiple identities in the city of Erzincan should, on the one hand, incorporate themes and organisational patterns that were being used in a regional Islamicate (and political) context and, on the other hand, articulate them within the framework of Armenian Christianity and under the banner of the Armenian Church. This is aptly demonstrated by a poem written by Yovhannēs Erznkac'i, embedded in his second treatise on *futuwwa*:

You consider yourself a traveller
But you stray from your path
You love the name of *mankut'iwn* (*futuwwa*)
But lack the fairness of the *manuk* (*akhī*).
This path is thin and narrow,
You close your eyes and walk along it;
Sweet is the name of *mankut'iwn* (*futuwwa*),
But you stand bitter and unpleasant.
I will call you a traveller when
You know the rules of the path;
You were born and came to this world,
Tell me, where do you come from?
You have come to a strange country,
Show me, how will you stay?
When you die and are buried in the ground,
Tell me, where will you go?[94]

Notes

1. I would like to thank Robert Bedrosian, Cemal Kafadar, Scott Redford, James Russell, Suzan Yalman and the editors of this volume for their comments and suggestions on this chapter while it was being written.
2. E. Pałtasaryan, *Hovhannes Erznkac'i ev nra xratakan arjakə* ('Hovhannes of Erzincan and His Advice Literature') (Yerevan: Armenian Academy of Sciences, 1977), p. 227.

3. See Angelika Hartmann, 'al-Suhrawardī, Shihāb al-Dīn 'Umar', *EI*², ix, pp. 778–81.
4. For an introduction to *futuwwa* studies, see Claude Cahen and Franz Taeschner, 'Futuwwa', *EI*², ii, pp. 961–9; Claude Cahen, 'Mouvements populaires et autonomisme urbain dans l'Asie musulmane du moyen âge', *Arabica* 5 (1958), pp. 225–50; *Arabica* 6 (1959), pp. 25–56, 233–65; D.A. Breebaart, 'The *Fütüvvet-nāme-i kebīr*: a manual on Turkish guilds', *Journal of the Economic and Social History of the Orient* 15, nos. 1–2 (1972), pp. 203–15; Franz Taeschner, 'Akhī', *EI*², i, pp. 321–3; idem, *Zünfte und Bruderschaften im Islam: Texte zur Geschichte der Futuwwa* (Zurich: Artemis-Verlag, 1979).
5. Al-Qushayrī, *Risāla al-Qushayrī*, ed. Muḥammad Amīn 'Amrān (Cairo: Maṭba'at Muṣṭafa al-Bābī al-Halabī, 1940), p. 114.
6. Ibn al-Jawzī, *Talbīs Iblīs*, ed. Khayr al-Dīn 'Alī (Beirut: Dār al-Wa'ī al-'Arabī, 1970), p. 444.
7. Ibid.
8. Franz Taeschner, 'Die islamischen Futuwwabünde, das Problem ihrer Entstehung und die Grundlinien ihrer Geschichte', *Zeitschrift der Deutschen Morgenländischen Gesellschaft* 87 (1934), pp. 6–49.
9. Erik S. Ohlander, *Sufism in an Age of Transition: 'Umar al-Suhrawardī and the Rise of the Islamic Mystical Brotherhoods* (Boston and Leiden: Brill, 2008), p. 96.
10. Ibid., pp. 20–7.
11. Ibn Wāṣil, *Mufarrij al-kurūb fī akhbār banī Ayyūb*, ed. Jamāl al-Dīn al-Shayyāl and Ḥasanayn Muḥammad Rabī' (Cairo: Maṭba'at Dār al-Kutub, 1953–75, 5 vols), iii, pp. 206–7.
12. To the best of my knowledge, the lone contemporary reference to this marriage is offered by Ibn al-Athīr who writes in his section on deaths for 1188/9: 'Saljuqa Khatun, daughter of Qilij Arslān and wife of the Caliph. Previously she was the wife of Nūr al-Dīn Muḥammad ibn Qarā Arslān, the lord of Ḥiṣn (Kayfā). After his death, she married the caliph, who had a great love for her, which was manifest to everyone. He built a mausoleum over her town on the West Bank and alongside the mausoleum his celebrated

hospice in al-Ramla.' *The Chronicle of Ibn al-Athir for the Crusading Period from al-kāmil fī 'l tārīkh*, trans. D.S. Richards (Aldershot: Ashgate, 2006–8, 3 vols), ii, p. 358.

13. For more on Majd al-Dīn Isḥāq, see Chapter Seven in this volume by Sara Nur Yıldız and Haşim Şahin, 'In the Proximity of Sultans: Majd al-Dīn Isḥāq, Ibn 'Arabī and the Seljuk Court'.
14. Ibn Bībī, *al-Awāmir al-'alā'īya fī 'l-umūr al-'alā'īya*, facsimile edition published by Adnan Sadık Erzi as İbn-i Bībī, *El Evāmirü'l-Alā'iye fī'l-Umūri'l-Alā'iye* (Ankara: Türk Tarih Kurumu, 1956), pp. 154–60.
15. Ibid., pp. 232–3. Despite his rich description of the symbols of sovereignty sent by the caliph and the associated rituals, including the ritual of initiation undergone by the sultan as a disciple to Suhrawardī, Ibn Bībī is significantly silent about the sultan's initiation into the caliphal *futuwwa*, suggesting that he did not actually don the *sarāwīl*.
16. These two different types of *khirqa* seem to have corresponded to two different types of *futuwwa*-member, the *qawlī* and the *sayfī*. The former had a tangential relationship with a master, the latter a direct one. See Shihāb al-Dīn 'Umar Suhrawardī, *Futuwwat-nāma*, in M. Ṣarrāf (ed.), *Rasā'il-i jawānmardī: mushtamil bar haft futuwwat-nāma* (Tehran: Anjuman-i Īrānshināsī-i Farānsa, 2001), pp. 94–5, 101, 109, 110, 125–6.
17. Ibn Bībī, *al-Awāmir al-'alā'īya*, p. 233.
18. Ohlander, *Sufism*, pp. 272–3.
19. Suhrawardī, *Idālat al-'iyān*, MS Bursa Ulu Cami 1597, fol. 89a, cited in Ohlander, *Sufism*, p. 279.
20. Suhrawardī, *Futuwwat-nāma*, p. 94. See also introduction by Henri Corbin, ibid., p. 42.
21. Ibid., pp. 94–5, 109–10, 125–6.
22. See Breebaart, 'The *Fütüvvet-nāme-i kebīr*', pp. 203–15. Many Anatolian *futuwwa* treatises were first published and studied by Abdülbaki Gölpınarlı. See his 'İslam ve Türk illerinde fütüvvet teşkilâtı ve kaynakları', *İktisat Fakültesi Mecmuası* 11, nos. 1–4 (1949–50), pp. 23–354; idem, 'Burgazi ve fütüvvet-namesi', *İktisat*

Fakültesi Mecmuası 15, nos. 1–4 (1953–4), pp. 76–154; idem, 'Şeyh Seyyid Ghaybioğlu Şeyh Seyyid Hüseyn'in fütüvvet-namesi', *İktisat Fakültesi Mecmuası* 17, no. 1–4 (1955–6), pp. 27–126; idem, 'Fütüvvet-name-i Sultani ve fütüvvet hakkında bazı notlar', *İktisat Fakültesi Mecmuası* 17, no. 1–4 (1955–6), pp. 127–44.

23. Taeschner has deduced that although the text was composed in Tokat, the author was most likely a native of Sivas: Franz Taeschner, *Der anatolischen Dichter Nāṣirī (um 1300) und sein Futuvvetnāme* (Leipzig: Brockhaus, 1944), p. 3.
24. Gölpınarlı, 'İslam ve Türk', pp. 215–6; idem, 'Burgazi', p. 125.
25. Gölpınarlı, 'İslam ve Türk', p. 209; idem, 'Burgazi', p. 111.
26. Ohlander, *Sufism*, pp. 286–8.
27. Ibid., pp. 115–6.
28. Taeschner, *Nāṣirī*, p. 209; Gölpınarlı, 'İslam ve Türk,' pp. 222–4; idem, 'Burgazi', p. 124.
29. A similar criticism of *futuwwa* as being too closely linked with militaristic behaviour is echoed in the '*Kerāmāt* of Akhī Evren', a text composed in the early fourteenth century by Ahmed Gülşehri. Franz Taeschner, *Gülschehrīs Mesnevī auf Akhī Evren, den Heiligen von Kirschehir und Patron der türkische Zünfte* (Wiesbaden: Steiner, 1955), p. 14.
30. Gölpınarlı, 'Burgazi,' pp. 112–3.
31. Ibn al-Mi'mār, *Kitāb al-futuwwa*, ed. Muṣṭafā Jawād (Baghdad: Maktabat al-Muthanna, 1960), pp. 167, 175.
32. Taeschner, *Nāṣirī*, p. 10.
33. Gölpınarlı, 'Burgazi', p. 121.
34. Ibid.
35. It has generally been assumed in Armenian scholarship that the caravan came from Van. See V. Grigoryan, 'Arevmtyan Ukrainayi Haykakan Gałut'neri Ktričvorac' Ełbayrut'yunneri Masin' ('Concerning the brotherhoods of the braves of the Armenian communities of western Ukraine'), *Patma-banasirakan Handēs* (Yerevan) 2, no. 21 (1963), pp. 115–6.
36. The term *manktawag* means 'elder of the youths'. The term is used in the constitutions of the Armenian brotherhoods composed in

the late thirteenth century, and is a synonym for *akhī* or *fatā*. See L. Xačik'yan, '1280 T'vakanin Erznkayum kazmakerpvac ełbayrut'yunnə' ('The Brotherhood organised in Erzinjan in 1280'), *Tełekagir* (Yerevan) 12 (1951), p. 208.

37. *Armenia and the Crusades Tenth to Twelfth Centuries: the Chronicle of Matthew of Edessa*, trans. Ara Edmond Dosturian (Lanham, Md.: NAASR and University Press of America, 1993), pp. 148–9; Matt'eos Uṙhayec'i, *Žamanakagrut'iwn*, ed. M. Melik-Adamian and N. Ter-Mik'aelyan (Vałaršapat: Vałaršapat, 1898), p. 226.
38. Dickran Kouymjian, 'The Canons dated 1280 of the Armenian *akhī*-type brotherhood of Erzinjan', *Actes du XXIXe Congrès International des Orientalistes* (Paris: L'Asiathèque, 1975), part I, ii, pp. 107–5.
39. That there are no references to this sort of organisation in Armenian texts for over 150 years is not necessarily an indication that they were completely absent in the region during this period. It could be that there was a reluctance in the sources to mention such organisations, or that their popularity had temporarily waned.
40. Seta Dadoyan, 'A case study for redefining Armenian-Christian cultural identity in the framework of Near Eastern urbanism – 13th century: the Nāṣirī *futuwwa* literature and the brotherhood poetry of Yovhannēs and Kostandin Erzěnkac'i (texts and contexts)', in J.J. Van Ginkel, H.L. Murre-van den Berg, and T.M. Van Lint (eds), *Redefining Christian Identity: Cultural Interaction in the Middle East Since the Rise of Islam* (Leiden: Brill, 2005), pp. 237–64; eadem, 'The Constitution of the brotherhood of Erzinjān (1280): an Armenization of the *futuwwa* reform project and literature of Abbasid Caliph al-Nāṣir li-Dīn Allāh', *Revue des Études Arméniennes* 29 (2004), pp. 117–65.
41. James Russell has shown that similar sorts of confraternities existed in Armenia in a pre-Christian context. In fact, he suggests that the pre-Christian, Iranian substrata, linked to the practices of Mithraic cults in Anatolia, were preserved within the context of late medieval *futuwwa*-type confraternities. He was also the

first to propose that the thirteenth-century *futuwwa*-type constitutions of the brotherhood of the city of Erzincan were part of a wider church-inspired institutional reform. James R. Russell, 'On Mithraism and freemasonry', *Heredom: the Transactions of the Scottish Rite Research Society* 4 (1995), pp. 269–86; idem, 'Medieval Armenian fraternities', *Transactions of the American Lodge of Research, F. & A.M.* 22 (1993), pp. 28–37.

42. An entry in the 'Anonymous Chronicle of Sivas' from the year 1268 reads: 'In the year 1268, Ter Hakob became Kat'ołikos and Pluz from Erznka became Vardapet.' V.A. Hakobyan (ed.) *Manr Žamanakagrut'iwnner XIII-XVIII dd* ('Lesser Chronicles of the Thirteenth through Eighteenth Centuries') (Yerevan: Armenian Academy of Sciences, 1956), ii, p. 156. Bałdasaryan suggests that if Yovhannēs did not become a priest until 1268, then the 1268 inscription that makes mention of the *sargawag* (Arm., deacon) Yovhannēs most probably refers to the same person. A colophon from the year 1266 reads: 'In the city of Ekełeac' (the region of Erzincan), with the blessings of the Holy Saviour, from *sargawag* (deacon) Yovhannēs in the year 1266.' Cited in Pałtasaryan, *Hovhannes*, pp. 23–4 and in H. K'iwrtean, *Eriza ew Ekeleac Gawaṛ* (Venice: San Lazzaro, 1953), p. 118. K'iwrtian found a reference to this manuscript and its colophon in the Index of Manuscripts from Karin (Erzurum) printed in the journal *Ejmiacin* in 1863,w vol. 1, p. 78. Later, he located the actual manuscript itself, number 561, at Ejmiacin in Armenia. K'iwrtian has suggested that it is the first extant manuscript composed in the hand of Yovhannēs.

43. It remains unknown where exactly this monastery and fortress were located, although it was probably situated either in the province of Lori or Tavuš (in the modern Republic of Armenia).

44. Seta Barsoumian-Dadoyan, *Hay-Arabakan mšakut'ayin haraberut'eanc patmut'enēn, 13 daṙ: Yovhannēs Pluz Erznkac'ii 'i Tačkac' imastasirac'' ə ew imastasirakan arjekə Islamakan ałbiwrnerun loysin dak* ('From the History of Armenian–Arab Cultural Relations, Thirteenth Century: Yovhannēs Pluz Erznkac'i's

"From the Wisdom of the Muslims" and his Intellectual Prose Under the Light of the Islamic Sources') (Beirut: Self-published, 1991), pp. 21–46.

45. On this text, see Yovhannēs Erznkac'i, *On the Movements of the Celestial Bodies*, ed. Lusik Step'anyan, Aram T'opjyan, and Thomas Samuelian (Yerevan: Matenadaran, 2001), p. 11.
46. Armenuhi Srapyan, *Hovhannes Erznkac'i Pluz* (Yerevan: Nairi, 1993), p. 44. The texts he authored include: Compilation of Commentary on Grammar; On the Movements of the Celestial Bodies; On the Muslim Philosophers; Admonition to All Christians, Priests and Laity According to the Canons of the Holy Apostles; Statutes and Constitution of the Congregation of Brothers; Admonitions for Corporeal Life in the World According to Wisdom; and Against the Tondrakians. See Pałtasaryan, *Hovhannes*, especially pp. 26–7.
47. Pałtasaryan, *Hovhannes*, pp. 26–7.
48. Ibid., pp. 223–4.
49. Ibid., p. 225.
50. Ibid., pp. 226–7.
51. Ibid., p. 232.
52. Ibid., pp. 234–5.
53. Ibid., p. 236.
54. *The Travels of Marco Polo* [The Venetian], ed. Manuel Komroff (New York: Horace Liveright, 1926), p. 25.
55. Yāqūt al-Ḥamawī, *Mu'jam al-buldān* (Beirut: Dār Ṣādir, 1993), i, p. 150.
56. The criticism of the moral and religious welfare of the region was a topic on the mind of Najm al-Dīn Rāzī (d. 1256), a Sufi and scholar originally from Rayy, whilst he was living in Erzincan. In the introduction to his *Marzūmāt-i asadī*, composed in Erzincan, Rāzī criticised the Muslims of Rūm for their lack of religious interest, and singles out those of Erzincan for their 'vileness'. Cited in Najm al-Dīn Rāzī, *The Path of God's Bondsmen from Origin to Return*, trans. Hamed Algar (North Haledon, N.J.: Islamic Publication International, 1980), pp. 12–13.

57. On Armenian colophons as a historical source, see Avedis K. Sanjian, *Colophons of Armenian Maunscripts, 1301 – 1480* (Cambridge, Mass.: Harvard University Press, 1969), pp. vii-xv; A.S. Mat'evosyan, *Hayeren Ceragreri Hišatakaranner, ŽG dar* ('Colophons of Armenian Manuscripts of the Thirteenth Century') (Yerevan: Armenian Academy of Sciences, 1984), pp. 6–11; L.S. Xačikean, *ŽE dari Hayeren Ceřagreri Hišatakaranner* ('Colophons of Armenian Manuscripts of the Fifteenth Century') (Yerevan: Armenian Academy of Sciences, 1955), vol. i, pp. v-lxvi.
58. To the best of my knowledge, no foreign rulers are mentioned in this manner in any thirteenth-century Armenian colophons composed in Anatolia until the arrival of the Mongols.
59. Mat'evosyan, *Hayeren Ceřagreri Hišatakaranner*, p. 508
60. See Necdet Sakaoğlu, *Türk Anadolu'da Mengücekoğulları* (Istanbul: Yapi Kredi, 2005), especially pp. 101–9.
61. See the chapter by Oya Pancaroğlu in this volume and eadem, 'The Mosque-Hospital Complex in Divriği: A History of Relations and Transitions', *Anadolu ve Çevresinde Ortaçağ* 1 (2009), pp. 169–98.
62. Smpat Sparapet, *Taregirk'* (Venice: San Lazzaro, 1956), pp. 212–13; Gérard Dédéyan (ed.), *La Chronique Attribuée au Connétable Smbat* (Paris: Librarie Orentaliste Paul Guenther, 1980), pp. 82–3.
63. Pałtasaryan, *Hovhannes*, p. 83.
64. E.I.J. Rosenthal, *Political Thought in Medieval Islam: an Introductory Outline* (Cambridge: Cambridge University Press, 1968), pp. 68–9; C.E. Bosworth, 'Administrative Literature', in M.J.L. Young et al. (eds), *The Cambridge History of Arabic Literature: Religion, Learning and Science in the 'Abbasid Period* (Cambridge: Cambridge University Press, 1990), pp. 165–7.
65. During the thirteenth and fourteenth centuries, different forms of advice literature were produced throughout Anatolia in various languages. Najm al-Dīn al-Razī composed the Persian-language *Mirṣād al-'ibād min al-mabdā' ilā al-ma'ād* in the early thirteenth century as a book of advice for those embarked on the path of mysticism. The *Qabūsnāma* was adapted from Persian into Turkish in

the early fourteenth century just around the time the *Garīb-nāme*, a work offering both spiritual and practical advice for people in all stations of life, was composed in Turkish by 'Aşık Paşa Veli (1271–1332). Aḥmad al-Zanjānī also composed *al-Laṭā'if al-'alā'īya*, an Arabic 'mirror for princes' dedicated to Sultan 'Ala' al-Dīn Kayqubād I. See H. Hüseyin Adalıoğlu, *Sultana Öğütler* (Istanbul: Yedi Tepe, 2005). For another example of this literature from the thirteenth-century Seljuk court, see Charles-Henri de Fouchécour, 'Hadayeq al-Siyar: un Mirroir de Princes de la cour de Qonya au VIIe-XIIIe siècles', *Studia Iranica* 1/2 (1972), pp. 219–28. The comparatively large amount of advice literature composed in the region suggests that the political and cultural turbulence of the period created a certain demand for guidance in the form of advice. Advice literature was not uniquely popular amongst Muslims in the region. Armenuhi Srapyan has noted that during the thirteenth and fourteenth centuries, almost all Armenian poets, including Frik (d. c.1300), Kostandin Erznkac'i (d. c.1336) and Yovhannēs Erznkac'i (d. c.1293]), favoured the advice (Arm., *xratakan*) genre of literature (Srapyan, *Hovhannes Erznkac'i Pluz*, pp. 136–7).

66. Theo van Lint, 'Kostandin of Erznka: An Armenian Religious Poet of the XIIIth-XIVth Century' (PhD Dissertation, University of Leiden, 1996), pp. 8–9.

67. 'The nightingale is the soul-bird *par excellence*, since the rose is a reflection of God's glory, or of the face of the beloved ... The adventure of rose and nightingale, so often recalled by Rumi (and even more later by mystical and non-mystical poets) is, together with that of moth and candle, a particularly fitting symbol of the story of eternal love.' Annemarie Schimmel, *The Triumphal Sun: a Study of the Works of Jalālodin Rumi* (Albany, N.Y.: SUNY Press, 1993), p. 115. See also James Russell, *Yovhannēs T'kuranc'i and the Medieval Armenian Lyric Tradition* (Atlanta, Ga.: Scholars Press, 1987), p. 6: 'Armenian lyric poetry in the Middle Ages came out of the pre-Islamic Iranian tradition of minstrelsy that Arsacid Armenia shared. But to these very archaic origins were added the innovations of a Christian culture, and, often, an "Islamic"

aesthetic (itself again largely Iranian and drawing upon images of gardens, wine, and lovers which antedated and frequently opposed Islam).'

68. K'iwrtean, *Eriza ew Ekeleac Gawaṛ*, p. 154.
69. Van Lint, 'Kostandin', p. 20.
70. Ibid., p. 23.
71. Ibid., p. 25.
72. Ibid., p. 189.
73. Ibid., pp. 172–8.
74. Ibid., pp. 253, 257.
75. The author was a well-known manuscript illustrator of the late thirteenth and early fourteenth centuries who spent much of his life at the Armenian monastery at Glajor (approximately 200 miles due east of Erzurum). While we know of another T'oros of Taron who lived in the late thirteenth-early fourteenth century and was a deacon, it would seem that this poem was most likely composed by the manuscript illustrator and author as he was a peripatetic priest and would have had more of a possibility of visiting the cities of Erzincan and Bayburt and of knowing Turkish.
76. Hasmik Stepanyan has edited two catalogues of materials composed in *hayataṛ t'urk'erēn* (Armeno-Turkish). The first is a collection of the major published works in Armeno-Turkish: *Ermeni Harflı Türkçe Kitaplar ve Süreli Yayınlar Bibliyografyası, 1727–1968* (Istanbul: Turkuaz, 2005). The second lists manuscripts composed in Armeno-Turkish that are currently housed either at the Mesrop Mašdoc' Manuscript Repository in Yerevan, Armenia, or in the Library of the Mother See of Holy Etchmiadzin in Armenia: *C'uc'ak Hayerēn Jeṛagreri Hayatar T'urkerēn niwt'eri ew Hayataṛ T'urkerēn Jeṛagreri* ('Catalogue of Materials and Manuscripts Written in Armeno-Turkish') (Yerevan: National Academy of Sciences, 2008).
77. Rober Koptaş's article 'Ermeni Harfleriyle Türkçe' ('Turkish with Armenian Letters'), article no. 125 dated 19 March 19 2003 in *Hyetert*, offers a wonderful basic history and historiography of the Armeno-Turkish phenomenon.

78. The first line of the couplet is Armenian, not Turkish.
79. Manuscript #85, Mxit'arean Manuscript Repository at San Lazzaro, Venice. Personal manuscript collection of H. K'iwrtean, *Taɫaran*, 1681. See K'iwrtean, *Eriza ew Ekeleac Gawaṛ*, pp.139–41.
80. The Turkish term '*yiğit*', meaning 'brave youth', is frequently associated with *futuwwa*-based Turkish-language confraternities from the early fourteenth century. In fact, in Burghāzī's *futuwwa* treatise, he writes that the *yiğit* is the most junior member of a *futuwwa* brotherhood, a full member being called *akhī* and the shaykh being the most advanced member. Gölpınarlı, 'Burgazi', p. 111. Ahmed Gülşehrī (d. c.1317) inserted a chapter on *futuwwa* into his early fourteenth-century Turkish translation of Farīd al-Dīn 'Aṭṭār's twelfth-century Persian mystical book of poems known as *Manṭiq al-ṭayr* ('Conference of the Birds'). In this chapter, he also uses the term *yiğit* in reference to junior members of *futuwwa* associations. See Aziz Merhan (ed.), *Die 'Vogelgespräche' Gülşehrīs und die Anfänge der türkischen Literatur* (Göttingen, 2003; *Materiala Turcica*, Beiheft 15), p. 226. Given that the term is used in relation to the marketplace of Erzincan and that we know there were Armenian *futuwwa*-based associations in Erzincan in 1280, 13 years after this poem was composed, and that the Armenian *futuwwa* treatise indicates a link between confraternity members and the marketplace, it seems quite possible that the reference here to *yiğit*s is a direct reference to members of a *futuwwa* brotherhood, whether Armenian, Turkish or Persian-speaking, Christian or Muslim.
81. For a discussion on the multilingual poetry of Rūmī and the terms 'macaronic' and '*mulamma'āt*', see Nargis Virani, '"I am the Nightingale of the Merciful". Macaronic or Upside-Down?: The *Mulamma'āt* of Jalāl al-Dīn Rūmī' (PhD Dissertation, Harvard University, 1999).
82. Paɫtasaryan, *Hovhannes*, p. 231.
83. James R. Russell, 'The credal poem *hawatov xostovanim*', in Van Ginkel et al., *Redefining Christian Identity*, pp. 185–236. Russell shows (p. 232) that in the introduction to the poem, the author

laments those who have been influenced by Muslims and explains that he has composed the 'Confession of Faith' such that all can understand the basic tenets of Christianity.

84. The 'Canonical Advice' (*Kanonakan Xratk'*) of David was translated and edited by Charles Dowsett as *The Penitential of David of Ganjak* (Louvain: Secretariat du Corpus SCO, 1961). Prior to Dowsett's translation, the text was studied by Ł. Ališan in 'The Ancient Faith, or Pagan Religion, of the Armenians' (*Hin hawatk' kam het'anosakan kr̄ōnk' hayoc'* [Venice: San Lazzaro, 1910]), and by A. Aprahamyan (trans., ed., *'Tawit' Alvka ordu kanonagirk'*, in *Eǰmiacin* [Eǰmiacin 1952], pp. 48–67, and *Eǰmiacin* [Eǰmiacin 1953], pp. 56–63), who recognised its importance in the development of Armenian law.

85. Dowsett, *Penitential*, p. 14. The original Armenian title for the section is 'Concerning Muslims who hold our food' (Arm., *vasn aylazgoy zkerakur mer əmbṛnē*). Aprahamyan, *'Tawit'*, p. 57.

86. Mxit'ar Goš, *Girk' Datastani*, ed. Xosrov T'orosyan (Yerevan: Armenian Academy of Sciences, 1975), p. 3. See also *The Lawcode of Mxit'ar Goš*, transl. and ed. by Robert W. Thomson (Amsterdam: Rodopi 2000), p. 72.

87. Mxit'ar Goš, *Girk' Datastani*, p. viii; Thomson, *Lawcode,* pp. 47, 72.

88. Mxit'ar Goš, *Girk' Datastani*, p. 22; Thomson, *Lawcode*, pp. 101–2.

89. Thomson, *Lawcode*, p. 47.

90. Mxit'ar Goš, *Girk' Datastani*, pp. i-cxviii; Thomson, *Lawcode*, pp. 71–5. The importance of the Armenian Church as a body both controlling Armenian populations and advocating for their rights to independence under the Church was established clearly within the framework of the Byzantine empire. See Nina Garsoian, *Armenia Between Byzantium and the Sasanians* (London: Variorum Reprints, 1985) and Nina Garsoian, Thomas Mathews and Robert Thomson (eds), *East of Byzantium: Syria and Armenia in the Formative Period* (Washington, D.C.: Dumbarton Oaks, 1982). The means by which 'minority' issues were negotiated in Byzantium has been addressed in Hélène Ahrweiler and Angeliki

Laiou (eds), *Studies on the Internal Diaspora of the Byzantine Empire* (Washington, D.C.: Dumbarton Oaks, 1998).

91. Thomson, *Lawcode*, pp. 254–5.
92. Mxit'ar Goš, *Girk' Datastani*, pp. xxxi-43.
93. Smbat Sparapet, *Datastanagirk'*, ed. A.G. Kalstean (Yerevan: Armenian State Publishing House, 1958), pp. 195–200. The condition of Armenians living in Cilicia was distinct from that of those living outside of it.
94. Pałtasaryan, *Hovhannes*, pp. 236–7.

CHAPTER TEN

CONCLUSION: RESEARCH ON THE SELJUKS OF ANATOLIA: SOME COMMENTS ON THE STATE OF THE ART

Gary Leiser

This volume, *The Seljuks of Anatolia*, represents a benchmark in the study of the Seljuks of Anatolia. It arose from the first workshop devoted to the history of this subject and, to my knowledge, consists of the first collection of scholarly articles devoted to a specific theme within this field. Furthermore, the sophistication of the articles, covering many aspects of the main theme, and the fact that they were contributed by scholars from many countries are striking evidence that the history of the Seljuks of Anatolia has truly attracted broad interest and has become recognised as a distinct object of research, in many disciplines, within Islamic or Middle Eastern studies in general. This is a far cry from the first attempt at a scholarly account of the Seljuks of Anatolia, M.Th. Houtsma's article, 'Over de geschiedenis der Seldjuken van Klein Azië',[1] in Dutch (!) published in 1893. It was only 20 pages long. This subject was not properly taken up again until M.F. Köprülü published 'Selçukiler zamanında Anadoluda Türk medeniyyeti' in Ottoman Turkish in 1916.[2] Clearly marginalised, this field was not opened to a wide audience until the appearance of Claude Cahen's *Pre-Ottoman Turkey* in 1968. In an important sense, the history of the Seljuks of Anatolia is a relatively new subject.

As a 'new' subject, many basic questions about it remain unanswered. Scholars now know the political history of the Seljuks in some detail, but their religious, economic and social history in particular is largely unexplored – hence the rationale for the present volume. Indeed, it is enough to describe Seljuk Anatolia 'as problem' in the German sense to provoke intriguing questions, for it was like no other part of the contemporary Muslim world. It seemed to be full of anomalies. Seljuk Anatolia was regarded by contemporary Muslim sources, both within and without the region, as part of *Dār al-Islām*, the Abode of Islam. However, throughout the Seljuk period, the majority of the population was Christian. To what extent was the Seljuk elite of Turkish nomadic origins, thus constituting an alien element of rulership over the population? Indeed, the ethnic composition of this minority Muslim ruling group remains unclear. Moreover, the degree of the Islamisation of the Turkish nomads is problematic. They were probably not far removed from shamanism. For the population as a whole, the most important language was Greek. As Rustam Shukurov has pointed out in his chapter, even many of the Seljuk rulers were the product of mixed marriages and spoke Greek. Persian was the literary language of the court but was otherwise not widely spoken. There were probably even fewer speakers of Arabic. This language was generally confined to the study of the religious sciences, which may have been rudimentary; the composition of certain documents; inscriptions; and coinage. Turkish was not yet a written language. There were some Turkish poets but Turkish was not a language of high culture or administration. With respect to military alliances, political marriages and places of refuge, the Seljuks gravitated more toward Christian Constantinople than the Muslim south or east.

Nevertheless, under Seljuk rule Anatolia began a cultural transformation – one that would take several centuries – in which a large Greek-speaking Christian region within the *Dār al-Islām* would become predominantly Turkish speaking and Muslim. In my view, the most important question for the student of the history of the Seljuks of Anatolia to try to answer is 'How did this happen?'[3] The answer will certainly be multifaceted, and one may need to compare this transformation with others. The Arab invasion of Byzantine Syria, which ultimately led to its Arabisation and Islamisation, easily comes to mind, as does the Christian reconquest of the Iberian Peninsula, or al-Andalus, which resulted in a transformation 'in the other direction'. Were many of the dynamics of these transformations the same? In Syria, for example, many Byzantine institutions remained intact, Greek remained an important language and conversion to Islam was slow. The faith of the invading Arab tribes was relatively new and the level of Arabic literacy among their rulers was low, although, like the Turks, they had poets to inspire them.

In Anatolia, the gradual conversion of the Christian population has been attributed, in large measure, to the missionary work of Sufis or Muslim mystics. Indeed, Seljuk Anatolia seems to have been especially conducive to Sufism. It flourished there to an extent not found in contemporary Syria and Egypt. Why was this the case? As Sufi lodges spread throughout the country, under what circumstances were institutions of Islamic orthodoxy, such as mosques and madrasas, established and how did they function? And how was Islamic law brought to bear on the Muslim population? It is curious to me that the cities that the Seljuks used as their capitals, Konya and Kayseri, seem to have had no major centre of orthodox, that is, Sunni instruction. There was no al-Azhar as in Cairo, Umayyad Mosque as in Damascus or Great Mosque as in Aleppo (rebuilt by Nūr al-Dīn, d. 1174). Furthermore, the distinction in function between Sufi lodge and madrasa was sometimes vague.[4] Why did the Seljuk sultans not take a greater interest in the promotion of Sunnism? Despite their lofty titles, such as 'the Might of the Brilliant Religious Community, Helper of the Shining Nation of Islam, the Manifestation of the Word of God Most High, the Guardian of the Religious Community and

This World,'[5] they seem to have been somewhat tepid as promoters of the orthodox faith. Were they not concerned by the spread of 'heterodox' beliefs?

Between the eighth and tenth centuries, Muslims travelled continuously and fairly intensively from al-Andalus to the Islamic east – Alexandria, Mecca and Medina – and back for the sake of learning, that is, religious instruction. This was critical for the spread and maintenance of Islam in al-Andalus. Was there similar travel from Seljuk Anatolia to centres of learning to the south – Aleppo, Damascus, and of course the Holy Cities? It is worthy of mention that in 1204 Ibn 'Arabī met in Mecca a number of pilgrims from Konya and Malatya. They were led by Majd al-Dīn Isḥāq, the father of the renowned Sufi Ṣadr al-Dīn al-Qūnawī. Ibn 'Arabī went to Anatolia with Majd al-Dīn. Later, Ṣadr al-Dīn became Ibn 'Arabī's disciple and adopted son.[6] The travel of Muslims from Anatolia to centres of religious instruction in Persian- or Arabic-speaking lands, and their return, needs to be investigated. If the majority of Muslims in Anatolia spoke only Turkish and were nomadic, then the number who went 'abroad' for study must have been small. Related to this is the fact that, for the period in question, the *ṭabaqāt* works, that is, the biographical dictionaries of jurists, or *fuqahā'*, have almost no entries for men from Anatolia. All of this would suggest that, apart from Muslim religious scholars from abroad who were attracted to the Seljuk court or who fled to Anatolia from the Khwarazmians or Mongols, Islam may have evolved in Anatolia in some isolation, albeit within the *Dār al-Islām*! If so, this could help explain the remarkable religious syncretism that occurred there.

Anatolia was certainly not, however, isolated from the Muslim world in other respects. It was traversed by many major trade routes that connected Constantinople with the Silk Road and Syria. Another important route running from the Black Sea to the Mediterranean linked the Crimea with Alexandria. Here we may note that the most monumental structures of the Seljuk rulers were not mosques but caravanserais. How much of this trade was simply in transit? The major cities and fairs of Seljuk Anatolia certainly attracted merchants from throughout the Middle East and Europe. Did they come more to buy or sell? Anatolia was known for some products, such as alum, that were not found elsewhere, and others, such as textiles, that were held in high regard. Anatolia was a rich and fertile region. Did these merchants bring goods that Anatolia lacked? Did they otherwise contribute to the local culture? A full account of the economic history of Seljuk Anatolia remains to be written. This account should include not only trade goods but also services, which are rarely discussed.[7] The strength and complexity of the economy has important implications not only for international trade of course, but also for such things as relations with neighbouring states, infrastructure, taxes, coinage, the fluorescence of the arts and perhaps even the general health of the population, since trade included food products and *materia medica* (although much of it was of dubious efficacy). With regard to health, or at least nutrition, one wonders if the people in Anatolia lived better or longer than those in other regions because of its varied agricultural abundance (fruits, vegetables and grains), animal products and fish (for instance, fish from Lake Van were dried and exported, and life on the Black Sea revolved around fishing for anchovies).[8]

Perhaps the most fascinating aspect of the period in question is social life in the broadest sense. It is best to think of Seljuk Anatolia as a kind of 'salad', a region with a unique mixture of religions and ethnic groups. This made the cultural evolution of Anatolia noticeably different from that of other regions of the Muslim world. Here we have Greeks and Armenians (and some Georgians) who practised different forms of Christianity and Turks (including distinct tribes and new arrivals from Central Asia in the army of the Khwārazmshāh), Kurds and some Persians, Arabs and Mongols practising different forms of Islam, or shamanism in the case of some Turks and Mongols, Laz (when and how did they become Muslims?), a scattering of Jews and no doubt resident merchant communities that included many Europeans. These groups were all acculturated to each other, a process the intensity of which depended on local conditions. During the two centuries of Seljuk political domination, they continuously exchanged customs and rituals, religious beliefs, forms of administration and taxation, stories and legends, music and dance, crafts, food, women and words. As Shukurov suggests in his chapter, bilingualism among Greeks, Armenians and Turks was probably much more common than we realise. As some scholars have mentioned, the 'eclectic', if not bizarre, decoration of the renowned hospital at Divriği might well symbolise this mixture. We know that people from various backgrounds, religious and ethnic, could participate in the construction of religious (e.g. mosques) and non-religious structures (e.g. caravanserais, hospitals).

Tracing acculturation can be challenging, but perhaps asking certain questions will help. What proportion of the whole population was rural or urban? What proportion was settled or nomadic? What was the density of the population, settled or nomadic, in various parts of the region? How large were the cities? How were the cities bound to their satellite villages? To what extent did members of different religious or ethnic groups live in separate quarters in the cities, or share space? Were most villages composed of one group? Did certain groups dominate certain crafts or monopolise certain products? The symbiotic relationship between town and country, nomad and villager, among many farmers and craftsmen, or even between saint and supplicant, contributed naturally to acculturation. Understanding how acculturation took place can be especially revealing. By this means we can learn how different groups interacted and behaved.[9]

Finally, before turning to sources I would like to comment on one other dimension of the history of the Seljuks of Anatolia that warrants additional research: that is their political and military relations with the Muslim states of Egypt and Syria, Iraq and further east. As I have done above, scholars usually emphasise that the Seljuks tended to gravitate to the west, or Byzantium, rather than to the south and east, in their political and military relations. We should not forget, however, that Seljuk ambitions included expansion toward the east which sometimes resulted in complicated diplomacy and conflict with neighbouring Muslim powers, above all the Ayyubids in Egypt and Syria and the Ayyubid line in Diyarbakır, which also controlled Mayyāfāriqīn (Silvan), Jabal Sinjār, Ḥisn Kayfā (Hasankeyf), Ahlat and other towns. Relations with the Ayyubids were often hostile, such as when they contested territory in the Jazira, but they quickly changed when faced with a common threat, such as the Khwārazmshāh or the Mongols. In 1234, al-Malik al-Kāmil, the Ayyubid sultan of Egypt and Syria, carried out a disastrous invasion of Anatolia in response to 'Alā' al-Dīn Kayqubād I's capture of Ahlat the previous year. Al-Kāmil hoped, in fact, to expand his realm well into Anatolia, but he fell victim to the Seljuk sultan's military tactics and ability to play the Ayyubid princes against each other.[10] In peaceful times there were marriage alliances, exchanges of envoys and continuous trade. The Seljuk sultan 'Izz al-Dīn Kaykā'ūs I even corresponded with Jalāl al-Dīn Ḥasan III (r. 1210–21), the ruler of the Nizari Isma'ilis headquartered at Alamut in Iran. Among other things, he described to him the Seljuk armies' reconquest of Antalya from the Christians in 1216.[11] This suggests that the Seljuks of Anatolia were in contact with, and were informed about, Muslim rulers well beyond their immediate neighbours. In short, further investigation of the Seljuks' relations with the states to the south and east are needed in order to place the Seljuk sultanate in its proper political context and to show the extent to which it was integrated into the wider Muslim world.

The key, of course, to shedding light on the issues that I have mentioned here, as well as on those raised in the chapters in this volume, is the sources. Students of the history of the Seljuks of Anatolia have long lamented the paucity of contemporary narratives describing this history. And the narratives that we have are virtually all in Persian. The dearth of narratives no doubt resulted from the facts that Turkish was not yet a literary language and that the audience of Persian speakers was very small. The few narratives, in any language, may also be an indicator of the small size of the Turkish element in Anatolia and of the small number of urban Turks, who were more likely to be literate. In other words, the number and type of narratives that we have are probably a reasonable reflection of the size and nature of the audience. The lack of narratives may tell us something, but we have to be careful.

While exploiting the narratives that we have, the authors of the present volume have been extremely resourceful in extracting information on various aspects of Seljuk history and culture from non-narrative sources, such as titulature, inscriptions, art and architecture. The amount of information that can be gleaned simply from the recovery of the name of one of the wives of a Seljuk sultan, as Scott Redford has done in his chapter, is remarkable. Our authors have also re-emphasised the need to expand our vision to include sources in non-Muslim languages, primarily Greek and Armenian, not the least because Christians were the majority of the population under Seljuk rule. If we add Latin and Syriac, we have more, and more diverse, sources on the Seljuks than is generally recognised. Making them accessible will take work.

Many well-known sources need to be reviewed and even corrected, as is the case with a number of inscriptions. Some published literary sources may also need to be revised. We now have a facsimile digital edition of the unique Syriac manuscript of Michael the Syrian's *Chronicle*,[12] which should be compared with J.C. Chabot's French translation. The latter, published in Paris between 1899 and 1910, was made under somewhat dubious circumstances. The many contemporary Arabic literary sources in our possession have not been fully explored. D.S. Richards' recent translation of Ibn al-Athīr's *al-Kāmil* for the years 491–629/1097–1231 now makes most of that work's coverage of the Seljuks readily accessible to English readers,[13] but some works still hold surprises. The *History of the Patriarchs of the Egyptian Church*, written by various authors – some contemporaneous with the Seljuks – over many centuries, contains, somewhat unexpectedly, what is apparently the earliest known account in Arabic of the Battle of Manzikert. It also contains an unknown description of Alp Arslan's siege of Edessa prior to that battle.[14] The extensive coinage of the Seljuks, quite literally a treasure trove of material on political and economic history, needs much more attention.[15] Furthermore, we have abundant art and architectural remains that await analysis. In short, we have many different sources, and in some cases an abundance of sources, that are comparable to those for some of the most studied regions of the medieval Muslim world. All information is valuable. Much can be extrapolated from a few facts, and one cannot predict how they may help flesh out certain subjects or answer future questions.

Finally, let me say a few words about a poorly known and poorly exploited source whose importance should not be underestimated for the history of the Seljuks of Anatolia: *waqf* documents or *waqfiyyas*. A *waqf* was a pious endowment that was established for the public good or for the benefit of one's family. In either case, the endowment usually consisted of various kinds of property. The revenue that it generated was to be used in perpetuity for a specific purpose. In Anatolia, as in other parts of the Muslim world, *waqfs* were used to construct and maintain religious and non-religious institutions and facilities, chiefly mosques, madrasas, Sufi convents or hospices, soup kitchens, hospitals, bridges, fountains and irrigation systems. The documents that were drawn up for these endowments were highly detailed. They usually began with honorifics concerning the founder followed by the purpose of the endowment; a delineation of its properties; an explanation of the function of the endowed institution; a description of its staff, services provided, salaries and expenses, and oversight; and its relationship to the founder's family. The property used to endow a large institution, such as a mosque, could be very extensive. It could include a large number of villages – everything in them, and all their agricultural lands – and many shops and other revenue-generating centres, such as warehouses, in the cities. All of this is clearly spelled out.

The importance of *waqf* documents for the study of social and economic history has long been recognised. But what has not been properly appreciated is that we have a very large cache of such documents from Seljuk Anatolia. Many decades ago, Mehmet Altay Köymen examined 49 of them in various places.[16] Indeed, some of the oldest surviving *waqfīyas* in the Muslim world are from the period of the Seljuk sultanate. Moreover, Nicolas Trépanier has recently analysed another 35 from fourteenth-century Anatolia, which are also relevant in many respects to the preceding Seljuk period.[17] As Köymen noted, these documents can be used for many purposes, including the study of ethnicity, religious and social relations, toponomy, onomastic and economic development. We could easily add demography, agriculture and the professions. In a study that is in press, I have shown how, during the Seljuk period, *waqfs* often included Christian villages and lands that generated funds to support Muslim institutions, particularly religious institutions. Thus, by contributing monetarily to these institutions, Christians contributed, albeit involuntarily, to their own cultural transformation, that is, Islamisation. In other words, the *waqf* was used as a mechanism for the Islamisation of Anatolia.[18] This is only one example of the kind of ore that can be mined from this rich vein of material.

These documents have the potential to tell us more about life in Seljuk Anatolia than any other type of source. A proper economic history, in particular, of this period cannot be written without them. In order to exploit fully these documents, they must, of course, be accessible. Osman Turan first published three of them, among the oldest, in the late 1940s.[19] Since then, others have been published from time to time in *Vakıflar Dergisi*. While most of these publications include a Turkish translation, few include a critical edition of the Arabic text (in some cases an unreadable facsimile is provided), and none include a translation into a western language. The last deficiency is important because these documents, once readily available, will, for many reasons, undoubtedly attract the attention of scholars working on other regions and periods of the Muslim world.

Therefore, to my mind, one of the most urgent tasks for students of the history of Seljuk Anatolia is to publish a corpus of these *waqfīyas*, perhaps modelled on the old *Répertoire chronologique d'épigraphie arabe*, that includes the Arabic text, a Turkish translation and a translation into a western language. This would have to be a long-term project undertaken and funded by a major university or research institute. But publishing these documents systematically and making them accessible to a wide audience is absolutely critical to an understanding of the history of Seljuk Anatolia. Turkish scholars have made a good start in this direction, but the bulk of the work remains to be done.

In sum, the chapters in the present volume address a specific theme of the history of the Seljuk sultanate for the first time. In the course of this, they present new sources and new interpretations of old sources, thus adding to our knowledge and understanding of this subject. Furthermore, these chapters show new avenues of research. My comments are intended to be complementary, re-emphasising both areas of future research and the richness of our sources. As suggested by this volume, we clearly have the skills and resources to describe, in great detail, life in one of the most fascinating regions of the medieval Muslim world.

Notes

1. In *Verslagen en Mededeelingen der koninklijke Akademie van Wetenschappen, Afdeeling Letterkunde*, 3rd series, 9 (1893), pp. 133–53.
2. Trans. Gary Leiser as 'Turkish civilization in Anatolia in the Seljuk period', *Mésogeios* 9–10 (2000), pp. 37–82.
3. The pioneering study of this question is, of course, Speros Vryonis, Jr., *The Decline of Medieval Hellenism in Asia Minor and the Process of Islamization, from the Eleventh through the Fifteenth Century* (Berkeley, Calif.: University of California Press, 1971). This work has been recently reissued in a revised edition with a new introduction (N.Y.: greekworks.com, 2011).
4. We can note here Ethel Sara Wolper, *Cities and Saints: Sufism and the Transformation of Urban Space in Medieval Anatolia* (University Park, Penn.: Pennsylvania State University Press, 2003), which shows a gradual displacement of madrasas by Sufi lodges.
5. These were among the titles of 'Izz al-Dīn Kaykā'ūs I. See Scott Redford and Gary Leiser, *Victory Inscribed. The Seljuk* Fetiḥnāme *on the Citadel Walls of Antalya, Turkey/Taşa Yazılan Zafer. Antalya İçkale Surlarındaki Selçuklu Fetihnamesi* (Antalya: Suna-İnan Kıraç Akdeniz Medeniyetleri Araştırma Enstitüsü, 2008), p. 111.
6. See the chapter by Sara Nur Yıldız and Haşim Şahin, pp. 184–6 above.
7. One can get an idea of the diverse services that were provided in Erdoğan Merçil's *Türkiye Selçukluları'nda meslekler* (Ankara: Türk Tarih Kurumu, 2000).
8. For an innovative study regarding food, see Nicolas Trépanier, *Foodways and Daily Life in Medieval Anatolia: a new social history* (Austin: University of Texas Press, 2014). This study is also relevant to earlier centuries.
9. Michel Balivet has done some recent work on cultural exchange. See for example his 'Entre Byzance et Konya: l'intercirculation

des idées et des hommes au temps des Seldjoukides', *Mésogeios*, 25–26 (2005), pp. 171–207.

10. This campaign is described in detail in the *History of the Patriarchs of the Egyptian Church* and Ibn Wāṣil's *Mufarrij al-kurūb*. For these and other accounts, see Gary Leiser, 'The *History of the Patriarchs of the Egyptian Church* as a Source for the History of the Seljuks of Anatolia', in Yasir Suleiman (ed.), *Living Islamic History: Studies in Honour of Professor Carole Hillenbrand* (Edinburgh: Edinburgh University Press, 2010), pp. 116–21.
11. See Wheeler M. Thackston, ''Izz al-Dīn Kai-Kā'ūs' Letter to Jalāl al-Dīn Nawmusalmān', Appendix I in Redford and Leiser, *Victory Inscribed*, pp. 141–2.
12. *The Edessa-Aleppo Syriac Codex of the Chronicle of Michael the Great*, ed. Gregorios Yuhanna Ibrahim (Piscataway, N.J.: Gorgias Press, 2009).
13. *The Chronicle of Ibn al-Athir for the Crusading Period from* al-Kamil fi'l-Ta'rikh (Aldershot: Ashgate, 2005–8, 3 vols).
14. See Leiser, 'The *History of the Patriarchs*', pp. 112–3 and 108–12 respectively.
15. We now have Yılmaz İzmirlier's very impressive catalogue *Anadolu Selçuklu paraları* (Istanbul: n.p., 2009), for which scholars will be grateful.
16. Mehmet Altay Köymen, 'Selçuklu devri kaynakları vakfiyeler', in Aldo Gallotta (ed.), *Studi Preottomani e Ottomani* (Naples: Istituto Universitario Orientale, 1976), pp. 153–63.
17. See note 8 above.
18. 'The *waqf* as an instrument of cultural transformation in Seljuk Anatolia', forthcoming in *The Turkish Presence in the Islamic World*, the proceedings from the 2010 Levi Della Vida Conference honouring C.E. Bosworth, ed. Ismail Poonawala.
19. Osman Turan, 'Selçuk devri vakfiyeleri: I. Şemseddin Altun-Aba, vakfiyesi ve hayatı', *Belleten* 11 (1947), pp. 197–235; idem, 'Selçuk devri vakfiyeleri: II. Mübarizeddin Er-Tokuş ve vakfiyesi', *Belleten* 11 (1947), pp. 415–29; idem, 'Selçuk devri vakfiyeleri: III. Celâleddin Karatay, vakıfları ve vakfiyeleri', *Belleten* 12 (1948), pp. 17–158.

GENEALOGICAL TABLE OF SELJUK SULTANS OF ANATOLIA

- 1. Qılıch Arslan I b. Sulaymān b. Qutlumush b. Arslan Isrā'īl b. Saljuq (1092–1107?)
  - 2. Rukn al-Dīn Mas'ūd I (1115–1156)
    - 3. 'Izz al-Dīn Qılıch Arslan II (1156–1192)
      - 4. Ghiyāth al-Dīn Kaykhusraw I (1192–1196, 1205–1211)
        - 6. 'Izz al-Dīn Kaykā'ūs I (1211–1219)
        - 7. 'Alā' al-Dīn Kayqubād I (1219–1237)
          - 8. Ghiyāth al-Dīn Kaykhusraw II (1237–1246)
            - 9. 'Izz al-Dīn Kaykā'ūs II (1246–1261)
              - Farāmurz
                - 13. 'Alā' al-Dīn Kayqubād III (1298–1303)
              - 12. Ghiyāth al-Dīn Mas'ūd II (1282–1298; 1303–1308)
            - 10. Rukn al-Dīn Qılıch Arslan IV (1249; 1259–1265)
              - 11. Ghiyāth al-Dīn Kaykhusraw III (1265–1284)
            - 'Alā' al-Dīn Kayqubād II (never asserted power as sultan)
      - 5. Rukn al-Dīn Sulaymanshāh (1196–1205)

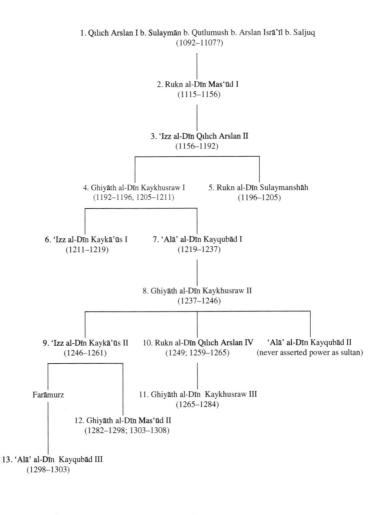

GLOSSARY OF TERMS

(terms are Arabic unless otherwise designated)

adab (pl. *ādāb*)	1) good upbringing, refinement. (2) equivalent to *humanitas*, the sum of knowledge which constitutes urbane culture as distinct from *'ilm*, or religious learning; includes poetry, belles-lettres and history writing.; the plural form can also refer to the various accomplishments of refinement or of a particular field of learning.
adīb	he who excells in *adab*; belletrist.
akhī	someone with full membership in a *futuwwa* brotherhood.
amir (pl. umara')	military commander.
al-amīr al-isfahsālār	military commander-in-chief; Arabicised form of the Middle Persian military title, *spah-salar* (or *spah-badh*).
amīr-dād or *amīr-i dād*	constable or marshal; military official responsible for keeping order among the political elite and for seizing and detaining officials or commanders accused of wrongdoing.

atabeg	(T, ata = father) guardian of a royal prince, in the Anatolian context; usually a commander ruling a province jointly with his royal charge, and specifically in charge of his household, even after the prince's accession to the throne.
bāj	(P) a general term for tax of different kinds, including tribute but especially customs dues and road tolls during the Mongol period.
baraka (pl. *barakāt*)	blessing or divine beneficent force bringing prosperity and well-being; prophets and saints in particular emanated divinely implanted *baraka*.
bargāh	(P) imperial court of the sultanate.
beylik	(T) Turkish principality in Anatolia emerging at the end of the thirteenth century or the fourteenth century.
chashnīgīr	(P) food taster; a palace post usually held by an imperial *ghulām*; even when promoted out of palace service into the ranks of the military as commander, a former *chashnīgīr* often retained this title as a symbol of prestige.
Dār al-Islām	'Land of Islam', i.e. where the law of Islam prevails.
dhimmī; *ahl al-dhimma*	non-Muslim communities which are members of revealed religions in the *Dār al-Islām* considered protected on the basis of submission and the payment of *jizya*, or poll tax.
dinar	Islamic gold unit of currency equivalent to the Byzantine *solidus*, with a weight standard ranging from 4.25 to 4.55 grammes.

dirham	the silver unit of currency in the Islamic world during the classical period; anywhere from 10 to 50 dirham comprised a dinar.
dīwān	(1) imperial council headed by the head vizier, and consisting of the core highest-ranking state officials. (2) collection of poems.
faqīh (pl. *fuqahā*)	specialist in *fiqh*, or Islamic jurisprudence.
fatā (pl. *fityān*)	'young man', equivalent to the Persian *jawānmard*; often used in the context of the *futuwwa*.
fatwa	legal advice or opinion on a point of law issued by a jurisconsult, jurist or cleric.
futuwwa	'manliness'; corporate group or brotherhood linked to guild organisations. In the latter usage, the *futuwwa* were characterised by a high level of communal solidarity and a strict moral code, and organised according to a strict hierarchy. The term *libās al-futuwwa* refers to the specific clothing donned by initiates, especially the trousers.
futuwwat-nāma	(1) treatise on *futuwwa* organisation. (2) initiation document drawn up by the caliph as part of the induction process into the caliphal *futuwwa*.
ghazal	lyric love poetry.
ghulām	'young man'; of servile or slave status, *ghulām*s were usually war captives who, trained as palace attendants or guards, manned the sultan's personal entourage and rose through the military or administrative ranks.

hadith	Prophetic tradition: reported account of what the Prophet Muḥammad said or did, considered second in authority to the Qur'an in Islamic law; *ḥadīth qudsī* (sacred tradition) represents God's words revealed through visions, dreams or inspiration.
ḥājib	chamberlain; the superintendent of the palace, who controlled access to the ruler and was concerned with court ceremonial.
ḥaqīqa	literally, 'truth' or 'reality'; mystical sense, 'Divine reality'.
iqṭāʿ	revenue grant to military or administrative officials based on land and other taxes of a designated territorial unit.
jāmiʿ	(T. cami) congregational mosque.
khānqāh or *khānaqāh*	(P) dervish hospice; building designed for Sufi rituals and communal life as well as for sheltering individual mystics, often accompanied by funerary buildings or tombs.
khatchkar	(Arm.) cross.
khilʿa(t)	robe of honor denoting vassalage, these garments were presented by rulers as a special token of distinction.
khirqa	'cloak', 'robe'; in a Sufi context, the *khirqa* was conferred upon initiation as a symbol of status as a formal disciple of a shaykh: the *khirqa* of *irāda* (robe of free will) is the habit of aspiration, indicating a serious commitment to the spiritual path, whereas the *khirqa* of *tabarruk* (robe of benediction) is merely that of affiliation with a shaykh.
kyr, or *kyra*	(Gk.) sir, or lady.
lālā	(P) tutor of a royal prince.

laqab — honorific title or sobriquet, often formed by a compound with *dīn* (faith).

madrasa — religious college, or school of higher education, focused on Islamic law.

majlis — the assembly at which intellectual or entertaining activities are pursued (from the Arabic root of 'to sit down', and, by extension, 'to hold a session'); *majlis-i bazmī* (wine symposium) refers to an intimate convivial assembly with wine, music and the recitation of poetry.

majmū'a — compilation of more than one work bound together in a single manuscript.

malik (fem., *malika*) — based on the Semitic root signifying 'possession', and, by extension, 'government' or 'rule', in the Rūm Seljuk context it means royal possessor of an autonomous appanage as lord or prince subject to a supreme sovereign.

malik al-umarā' — commander-in-chief, equivalent to the Turkish *beglerbeg* and the Arabo-Persian *al-amīr al-isfahsālār*.

manāqib — (plural of *manqaba*), 'deeds' or 'achievements', designates a genre of laudatory biographical literature (for a ruler) and hagiographical works (for a religious figure) by which the deeds constitute miraculous acts (*karamāt*).

mankut'iwn — (Arm.) *futuwwa*, religious brotherhood guild.

manshūr — certificate or diploma of appointment.

masjid — (T. mescit) mosque for daily, private worship; any place of worship for the ritual prayer (i.e. performance of the *ṣalāt*).

mathnawī	verse in rhyming couplets independently strung together with no limits in length, thus an ideal form for a narrative or didactic content.
mihrab	prayer niche in a mosque which shows the direction of the *qibla*, the prayer direction facing Mecca.
minbar	mosque pulpit from which sermons were delivered.
muḥtasib	'enforcer of religious law', an official appointed from among the ranks of the *'ulamā'* who, in addition to supervising the markets, was entrusted with controlling the moral behavior of the community.
munādama	the post of the *nadīm*, or boon companion.
muqarnas	decorative vaulting system based on the replication of units arranged in tiers and applied on different parts of a building including domes, minarets, columns and portals.
murīd	aspirant, novice or initiate of a Sufi order under the supervision of a shaykh.
muruwwa	the qualities of the mature man, as opposed to those of the *fatā*, or young man.
muṣādara (pl. *muṣādarāt*)	confiscation; disgorging an official of part of his wealth based on the suspicion of ill-gained income; extracting money or seizing valuable goods or land from a dismissed official.
Muslim's *Ṣaḥīḥ*	the most authoritative of sound collections of hadith (together with that

	of Bukhārī compiled by Muslim (d. 261/875).
mustawfī	administrative official in charge of financial accounts.
muṭālaba (pl. *muṭālabāt*)	same as *muṣādara*.
nadīm (pl. *nudāma'*)	boon companion.
nā'ib (pl. *nuwwāb*)	deputy (short form for the sultan's deputy), in charge of overall administration of the realm.
nā'ib al-salṭana	the sultan's deputy, one of the highest officials at the Seljuk court.
pādishāh, *pādshāh*	(P) monarch, sovereign.
qadi	magistrate or religious judge and administrator.
qaṣīda	a poem of at least seven, but often more, verses ending in a monorhyme and conventionally consisting of three parts with a prologue (*nasīb*), the narration of a journey (*raḥīl*), and culminating in the third section of the panegyric.
qutlugh, as in *qutlugh atabeg*	(T) title meaning 'auspicious'.
radīf	recurring rhyming element in a poem.
ṣāḥib-diwān	chief financial minister.
sarāwīl	*futuwwa* trousers; in the caliphal *futuwwa*, ceremonial trousers were presented upon being granted full membership.
shafī'	spiritual intercession by a saint or one 'close to God'.
shāhanshāh	'the shah of shahs', a Persian royal title traceable to the Achaemenid kings and extinct with the Sasanians but revived in the tenth century.
sunna	'way or manner of acting', 'custom'; the normative practice of the Prophet

	Muḥammad and his Companions, which forms the major basis for Islamic law.
ṭabaqāt	'layers of things of the same sort', 'classes'; biographical compilations or dictionaries of groups of people according to geographical location, profession or other such different classes or groupings.
ṭarīqa (pl. *ṭuruq*)	'path' or 'way': (1) the way to the Divine reality based a set of stages of mystical development. (2) religious brotherhood or mystical order; Sufi adherents following the 'path' of a particular shaykh, or Sufi master.
'ulamā'	(plural of *'ālim*) religious learned class responsible for the transmission and interpretation of religious knowledge, and fulfilling religious functions in the community, such as qadis, preachers, *imāms*, *faqīhs*, madrasa teachers and *muftīs*.
ulugh-qutlugh	(T) title meaning 'the great and fortunate one'.
umma	'people', 'community'; community of Muslims.
vardapet	(Arm.) learned priest.
waqf	pious endowment established for the public good (*khayr*) or for the benefit of one's family.
waqfiya	document drawn up for a pious endowment, or *waqf*, specifying the parameters of the *waqf*, such as how the property was to be used by whom, description of staff, services provided, salaries, income, expenses, oversight

and relationship to the founder's family.

yarlıgh — (Mongol.) decree.

yiğit — (T) 'brave youth'; according to Burghāzī's *futuwwa* treatise, the *yiğit* is the most junior member of a *futuwwa* brotherhood.

zāwiya — a lodge for devotees of a Sufi brotherhood; it also accommodated travellers; it often consisted of cells arranged around a courtyard, and was often built in conjunction with the tomb of its founder.

SELECT BIBLIOGRAPHY

Primary sources

Acropolites, *Georgii Acropolitae Opera*, edited by A. Heisenberg and P. Wirth (Stuttgart: In aedibus B.G. Teubneri, 1978, 2 vols); English translation by Ruth Macrides as George Akropolites, *The History* (Oxford: Oxford University Press, 2007).

Aflākī, *Manāqib al-ʻārifīn*, edited by Tahsin Yazıcı as Şams al-Dīn Ahmad al-Aflākī al-ʻĀrifī, *Manāḳib al-ʻĀrifīn (Metin)* (Ankara: Türk Tarih Kurumu, 1959–61, 2 vols); English translation by John O'Kane as Shams al-Dīn Aḥmad-e Aflākī, *Feats of the Knowers of God (Manāqeb al-ʻarefīn)* (Leiden: Brill, 2002).

Anadolu Selçukluları Devleti Tarihi III: *Histoire des Seljoukides d'Asie Mineure par un anonyme*, fascimile and Turkish translation by Feridun Nâfiz Uzluk (Ankara: Örnek Matbaası, 1952; Anadolu Selçukluları Gününde Mevlevi Bitikleri 5); edited by Nādira Jalālī as *Tārīkh-i āl-i Saljūq dar Ānāṭūlī* (Tehran: Mīrāth-i Maktūb, 1999).

Āqsarāʼī, *Musāmarat al-akhbār*, edited by Osman Turan as Aksaraylı Kerîmüddin Mahmud oğlu, *Müsameret ül-ahbâr: Moğollar zamanında Türkiye Selçukluları Tarihi* (Ankara: Türk Tarih Kurumu, 1944); German translation by Fikret Işıltan as *Die Seldschuken-Geschichte des Akserayi* (Leipzig: Harrassowitz, 1943); Turkish translation by Mürsel Öztürk as Kerimüddin Mahmud-i Aksarayî, *Müsâmeretü 'l-Ahbâr* (Ankara: Türk Tarih Kurumu, 2000).

Attaleiates, Michael, *Historia*, edited and translated by I. Pérez Martín (Madrid: Consejo Superior de Investigaciones Científicas, 2002).

Bar Hebraeus, *The Chronography of Gregory Abu'l-Faraj*, translated by Ernest A. Wallis Budge (London: Oxford University Press, 1932).

Combe, Étienne, Jean Sauvaget, and Gaston Wiet et al. (eds), *Répertoire chronologique d'épigraphie arabe* [=*RCEA*] (Cairo: Institut Français d'Archéologie Orientale, 1931–91, 18 vols).

Gülschehrīs Mesnevī auf Akhī Evren, den Heiligen von Kirschehir und Patron der türkische Zünfte, edited by Franz Taeschner (Wiesbaden: Steiner, 1955).

Ibn al-Athīr, 'Izz al-Dīn, *al-Kāmil fī al-tārīkh* (Beirut: Dār Ṣādir, 1965–7, 13 vols); partial translation by D.S. Richards, *The Chronicle of Ibn al-Athir for the Crusading Period from al-Kamil fi 'l-Ta'rikh* (Aldershot: Ashgate, 2006–10; 3 vols); idem, *The Annals of the Saljuq Turks. Selections from al-Kāmil fī 'l-Tārīkh of 'Izz al-Dīn Ibn al-Athīr* (London: RoutledgeCurzon, 2002).

Ibn Bībī, *al-Awāmir al-'alā'īya fi 'l-umūr al-'alā'īya*, facsimile edition of the full text in MS Aya Sofya 2985 prepared by Adnan Sadık Erzi as İbn-i Bībī, *El-Evāmirü'l-'Alā'iyye fī 'l-Umūri'l-'Alā'iyye* (Ankara: Türk Tarih Kurumu, 1956); partial edition by Necati Lugal and Adnan Sadık Erzi as İbn-i Bībī, *El-Evāmirü'l-'Alā'iyye fī 'l-Umūri'l-'Alā'iyye. I Cild (II Kılıç Arslan'ın Vefâtından I 'Ala'ü'd-Dīn Keykubâd'ın Cülûsuna Kadar)* (Ankara: Ankara Üniversitesi İlahiyat Fakültesi Yayınları, 1957; no more published); Turkish translation based on the full text by Mürsel Öztürk as İbn-i Bībī, *El-Evāmirü'l-'Alā'iyye fī 'l-Umūri'l-'Alā'iyye* (Ankara: Kültür Bakanlığı, 1996, 2 vols). Abridged version of text edited by M. Th. Houtsma as *Histoire des Seldjoucides d'Asie Mineure, d'après l'abrégé du Seldjouknāmeh d'Ibn-Bībī: texte persan* (Leiden: E.J. Brill, 1902; Recueil de textes relatifs à l'histoire des Seldjoucides, 4); German translation from the abridged version, with some additions by H. Duda as *Die Seltschukengeschichte des Ibn Bibi* (Copenhagen: Munksgaard, 1959).

Ibn Sa'īd, *Kitāb al-jughrāfīya*, edited by Ismā'īl al-'Arabī (Beirut: al-Maktab al-Tijārī, 1970).

Ibn Wāṣil, *Mufarrij al-kurūb fī akhbār banī Ayyūb*, edited by Jamāl al-Dīn al-Shayyāl (Cairo: Maṭba'at Dār al-Kutub, 1972).

İstanbul'un fethinden önce yazılmış tarihî takvimler, edited by Osman Turan (Ankara: Türk Tarih Kurumu, 1954).

Manāqib-i Awḥad al-Dīn Ḥamīd ibn Abī 'l-Fakhr-i Kirmānī, edited by Badī' al-Zamān Furūzanfar (Tehran: Bungāh-i Tarjuma wa Nashr-i Kitab, 1969); Turkish translation and study by Mikâil Bayram as *Şeyh Evhadü'd-Din Hâmid El-Kirmânî ve Menâkıb-Namesi* (Istanbul: Kardelen Yayınevi, 2005).

Matthew of Edessa, *Armenia and the Crusades, Tenth to Twelfth Centuries: The Chronicle of Matthew of Edessa*, translated by Ara Edmond Dosturian (Lanham, Md.: NAASR, 1993).

Michael the Syrian, *Chronicle*, edited and translated by J.B. Chabot as Michel le Syrien, *Chronique* (Paris: Ernest Leroux, 1899–1910); facsimile edition prepared by Gregorios Yuhanna Ibrahim with text summary by Sebastian

Brock, *The Edessa-Aleppo Syriac Codex of Michael the Great* (Piscataway, N.J.: Gorgias Press, 2009; Texts and Translations of the Chronicle of Michael the Great, edited by G. Kiraz, vol. i).

al-Nasawī, Shihāb al-Dīn Muḥammad, *Sīrat al-sulṭān Jalāl al-Dīn Mankubartī*, edited and translated by O. Houdas as *Histoire du sultan Djelal ed-Din Mankobirti, prince du Kharezm* (Paris: Ernest LeRoux, 1891–5, 2 vols); edited with a Russian translation by Z. M. Buniatov as *Zhizneopisanie sultana Jalal ad-Dina Mankburny* (Moscow: Vostochnaia literatura, 1996).

Nicetas Choniates, *Historia*, ed. J.A. van Dieten, (Berlin and New York: De Gruyter, 1975; 2 vols); translated by Harry J. Magoulias, *O City of Byzantium: Annals of Niketas Choniates* (Detroit, Mich.: Wayne State University Press, 1984).

Rāwandī, Muḥammad ibn 'Alī, *Raḥāt al-ṣudūr wa-āyat al-surūr*, edited by Muhammad Iqbal (Leiden: E. J. Brill, 1921); Turkish translation by Ahmed Ateş as Muhammed b. 'Ali b. Süleyman er-Râvendi, *Râhat-üs-sudûr ve Âyet-üs-sürûr (Gönüllerin Rahatı ve Sevinç Alâmeti* (Ankara: Türk Tarih Kurumu, 1960).

Rūmī, Jalāl al-Dīn, *Maktūbāt-i Mawlānā Jalāl al-Dīn/Mevlânânın Mektubları*, edited by Ahmed Remzi Akyürek (Istanbul: Sebat Basımevi, 1937; Anadolu Selçukileri Gününde Mevlevi Bitikleri 2); edited by Tawfiq H. Subḥānī, *Maktūbāt-i Mawlānā Jalāl al-Dīn Rūmī* (Tehran: Nashr-i Dānishgāhī, 1371); Turkish translation by Abdülbaki Gölpınarlı, *Mevlânâ Celâleddin: Mektupları* (Istanbul: İnkilap, 1963).

—, *Kitāb-i fīhi mā fīhi,* edited by Badī' al-Zamān Furūzanfar (Tehran: Intishārāt-i Nigāh, 1387sh./2008 [3rd edition]); translated by W.M. Thackston as *Signs of the Unseen: The Discourses of Jalaluddin Rūmī* (Boston, Mass.: Shambhala, 1994).

Sibṭ b. al-Jawzī, *Mir'āt al-zamān fī tārīkh al-a'yān*, selections edited by Ali Sevim as Sıbt İbnü'l-Cevzî, *Mir'âtü'z-zeman fî Tarihi'l-âyân, Selçuklularla ilgili bölümler* (Ankara: Dil ve Tarih Coğrafyası Fakültesi, 1968); revised and augmented edition by Ali Sevim in *Belgeler* 14, no. 18 (1989–92); Turkish translation by Ali Sevim as Sıbt İbnü'l-Cevzî, *Mir'âtü'z-zeman fî Tarihi'l-âyân* (Ankara: Türk Tarih Kurumu, 2011).

Simon de Saint-Quentin, *Histoire des Tartares*, edited by Jean Richard (Paris: Paul Geuthner, 1965).

Smbat the Constable, *Chronicle*, edited and translated by Gérard Dédéyan as *La Chronique Attribuée au Connétable Smbat* (Paris: Librarie Orentaliste Paul Geuthner, 1980).

Sulṭān Walad, *Dīwān* edited by F. Nafız Uzluk as *Divanı Sultan Veled* (Istanbul: Uzluk Basımevi, 1941; Anadolu Selçukileri Gününde Mevlevi Bitikleri 3).

Turan, Osman, *Türkiye Selçukluları Hakkında Resmî Vesikalar* (Ankara: Türk Tarih Kurumu, 1958).

Secondary Literature

Acun, Hakkı (ed.), *Anadolu Selçuklu Dönemi Kervansarayları* (Ankara: Kültür ve Turizm Bakanlığı Yayınları, 2007).

Akşit, Ahmet, 'Melike-i Adiliye Kümbetinde Selçuklu Devri Saltanat Mücadelesine Dair İzler', *Türkiyat Araştırmaları Dergisi* 11 (2002), pp. 239–45.

Aykut, Şevki Nezihi, *Türkiye Selçuklu Sikkeleri* (Istanbul: n.p., 2000).

Bakırer, Ömür, *Onüç ve Ondördüncü Yüzyıllarda Anadolu Mihrablari* (Ankara: Türk Tarih Kurumu, 1976).

Balivet, Michel, *Romanie byzantine et pays de Rûm turc: Histoire d'un espace d'imbrication gréco-turque* (Istanbul: Isis, 1994).

—, 'Entre Byzance et Konya: l'intercirculation des idées et des hommes au temps des Seldjoukides', in Gary Leiser (ed.), *Les Seldjoukides d'Anatolie* (*Mésogeios* 25–26 [2005]), pp. 171–207.

Bates, Ülkü, 'The Anatolian mausoleum of the twelfth, thirteenth and fourteenth centuries' (PhD Dissertation, University of Michigan, 1970).

Berchem, Max van and Halil Edhem, *Matériaux pour un Corpus Inscriptionum Arabicorum, Troisième partie, Asie Mineure, Tome premier, Siwas, Diwrigi* (Cairo: Institut Français d'Archéologie Orientale, 1917).

Berchem, Max van and Josef Strzygowski, *Amida* (Heidelberg: Carl Winter, 1910).

Boran, Ali, *Anadolu'daki İç Kale Cami ve Mescidleri* (Ankara: Türk Tarih Kurumu, 2001).

Brand, Charles, 'The Turkish element in Byzantium, 11th-12th centuries', *Dumbarton Oaks Papers* 43 (1989), pp. 1–25.

Breebaart, Deodaat Anne, 'The Development and Structure of the Turkish Futuwah Guilds' (PhD Dissertation, Princeton University, 1961).

—, 'The *Fütüvvet-nāme-i kebīr*: a manual on Turkish guilds', *Journal of the Economic and Social History of the Orient* 15, nos. 1–2 (1972), pp. 203–15.

Cahen, Claude, *Pre-Ottoman Turkey: a general survey of the material and spiritual culture and history, c. 1071–1330* (London: Sidgwick and Jones, 1968).

—, *La Turquie pré-ottomane* (Istanbul: Institut Français d'Études Anatoliennes, 1988).

Clauson, Gerard, *An Etymological Dictionary of Pre-Thirteenth-Century Turkish* (Oxford: Clarendon Press, 1972).

Dadoyan, Seta, 'The Constitution of the brotherhood of Erzinjān (1280): an Armenization of the *futuwwa* reform project and literature of Abbasid Caliph al-Nāṣir li-Dīn Allāh', *Revue des Études Arméniennes* 29 (2004), pp. 117–65.

—, 'A case study for redefining Armenian-Christian cultural identity in the framework of Near Eastern urbanism— 13th century: the Nāṣirī *futuwwa* literature and the brotherhood poetry of Yovhannēs and Kostandin Erzĕnkac'i (texts and contexts)', in J.J. Van Ginkel, H.L. Murre-van den Berg, and

T.M. Van Lint (eds), *Redefining Christian Identity: Cultural Interaction in the Middle East Since the Rise of Islam* (Leiden: Brill, 2005), pp. 237–64.

Delilbaşı, M., 'Greek as a diplomatic language in the Turkish chancery', in N.G. Moschonas (ed.), Η επικοινωνία στο Βυζάντιο: πρακτικά του Β Διεθνούς Συμποσίου, *4–6* Οκτωβρίου *1990* (Athens: Κέντρο Βυζαντινών Ερευνών, 1993), pp. 145–53.

Doerfer, Gerhard, *Türkische und mongolische Elemente im Neupersischen* (Wiesbaden: Franz Steiner Verlag, 1963–75, 4 vols).

Eastmond, Antony, 'Gender and patronage between Christianity and Islam in the thirteenth century', in *First International Sevgi Gönül Byzantine Studies Symposium* (Istanbul: Vehbi Koç Vakfı, 2010), pp. 78–88.

Edhem, Halil, 'Anadolu'da İslami Kitabeler', *Tarih-i Osmani Encümeni Mecmuası*, 27 (1330 [1912]), pp. 134–58.

Fouchécour, Charles-Henri de, 'Hadayeq al-Siyar: un Mirroir de Princes de la cour de Qonya au VIIe-XIIIe siècles', *Studia Iranica* 1, no. 2 (1972), pp. 219–28.

Fuess, Albrecht and Hartung, Jan Peter (eds), *Court Cultures in the Muslim World: Seventh to nineteenth centuries* (London: Routledge, 2011).

Gölpınarlı, Abdülbâki, 'İslam ve Türk illerinde fütüvvet teşkilâtı ve kaynakları', *İktisat Fakültesi Mecmuası* 11, nos. 1–4 (1949–50), pp. 23–354.

—, 'Burgazi ve fütüvvet-namesi', *İktisat Fakültesi Mecmuası* 15, nos. 1–4 (1953–4), pp. 76–154.

—, 'Şeyh Seyyid Gaybi oğlu Şeyh Seyyid Hüseyn'in fütüvvet-namesi', *İktisat Fakültesi Mecmuası* 17, nos. 1–4 (1955–6), pp. 27–126.

—, 'Fütüvvet-name-i Sultani ve fütüvvet hakkında bazı notlar', *İktisat Fakültesi Mecmuası* 17, nos. 1–4 (1955–6), pp. 127–44.

—, *Mevlânâ Celâleddin: Hayatı, Eserleri, Felsefesi* (Istanbul: İnkilap, 1999).

Hasluck, F.W., *Christianity and Islam under the Sultans* (Oxford: Oxford University Press, 1929, 2 vols).

Hillenbrand, Carole, *The Crusades: Islamic Perspectives* (New York: Routledge, 2000).

—, *Turkish Myth and Muslim Symbol: The Battle of Manzikert* (Edinburgh: Edinburgh University Press, 2007).

Hopwood, Keith, 'Nomads or bandits? The pastoralist/sedentarist interface in Anatolia', in A. Bryer and M. Ursinus (eds), *Manzikert to Lepanto. The Byzantine World and the Turks 1071–1571* [*Byzantinische Forschungen* 16 (1991)], pp. 179–94.

—, 'Peoples, territories, and states: The formation of the Begliks of pre-Ottoman Turkey', in C.E. Farah (ed.), *Decision Making and Change in the Ottoman Empire* (Kirksville, Mo.: Truman State University Press, 1993) pp. 129–38.

Houtsma, M.Th., 'Over de geschiedenis der Seldjuken van Klein Azië', *Verslagen en Mededeelingen der koninklijke Akademie van Wetenschappen, Afdeeling Letterkunde*, 3rd Series, 9 (1893), pp. 133–53.

Huda, Qamar al-, 'The Prince of Diplomacy: Shaykh 'Umar al-Suhrawardī's revolution for Sufism, *futuwwa* groups, and politics under Caliph al-Nâsir', *Journal of the History of Sufism* 3 (2001), pp. 257–78.

İzmilier, Yılmaz, *Anadolu Selçuklu Paraları* (Istanbul: n.p., 2009).

Kafadar, Cemal, 'A Rome of one's own: cultural geography and identity in the lands of Rum', in Sibel Bozdoğan and Gülru Necipoğlu (eds), *History and Ideology: Architectural Heritage of the 'Lands of Rum'* [*Muqarnas* 24 (2007)], pp. 10–8.

Karamağaralı, Beyhan, *Ahlat Mezartaşları* (Ankara: Selçuklu Tarih ve Medeniyeti Ensitüsü, 1972).

Khanikoff, N., 'Les inscriptions musulmanes du Caucase', *Journal Asiatique* 20 (August 1862), pp. 57–155.

Kılıç, Mahmud Erol, 'İbnu'l-Arabī'nin 1. İzzeddīn Kaykâvus'a Yazdığı Mektubun Işığında Dönemin Dini ve Siyasi Tarihine Bakış', in Osman Eravşar (ed.), *I. Uluslararası Selçuklu Kültür ve Medeniyeti Kongresi. Bildiriler* (Konya: Selçuk Üniversitesi Yayını, 2001), ii, pp. 11–28.

Konyalı, İbrahim Hakkı, *Âbideleri ve Kitabeleri ile Niğde, Aksaray Tarihi* (Istanbul: Fatih Yayınevi, 1974).

Korobeinikov, D.A., 'A sultan in Constantinople: the feasts of Ghiyāth al-Dīn Kay-Khusraw I', in Leslie Brubaker and K. Linardou (eds), *Eat, Drink, and be Merry (Luke 12:19): Food and Wine in Byzantium. In Honour of Professor A.A.M. Bryer* (London: Ashgate, 2007), pp. 93–108.

—, 'Raiders and neighbours: the Turks (1040–1304)', in Jonathan Shepard (ed.), *The Cambridge History of the Byzantine Empire, c. 500–1492* (Cambridge: Cambridge University Press, 2008), pp. 692–730.

—, 'A Greek Orthodox Armenian in the Seljukid service: the colophon of Basil of Melitina', in Rustam Shukurov (ed.), *Mare et litora. Essays presented to S. Karpov for his 60th birthday* (Moscow: Indrik, 2009), pp. 709–24.

Kouymjian, Dickran, 'The Canons dated 1280 of the Armenian *akhī*-type brotherhood of Erzinjan', in *Actes du XXIXe Congrès International des Orientalistes* (Paris: L'Asiathèque, 1975), part I, ii, pp. 107–15.

Köymen, Mehmet Altay, 'Selçuklu devri kaynakları vakfiyeler', in Aldo Gallotta (ed.), *Studi Preottomani e Ottomani* (Naples: Istituto Universitario Orientale, 1976), pp. 153–63.

Kuban, Doğan, *Divriği Mucizesi: Selçuklu Çağında İslam Bezeme Sanatı Üzerine Bir Deneme* (Istanbul: Yapı Kredi Yayınları, 1997).

Kucur, Sadi S. 'Vekîl-i Hâsslık ve Selçuklu Saraylarında Üstâdü'd-dârlık', *Türk Kültürü İncelemeleri Dergisi* 14 (2006), pp. 1–10.

—, 'Nāib-i saltanat', *Türkiye Diyanet Vakfı İslam Ansiklopedisi*, xxxii (2006), pp. 313–4.

Kunt, İ. Metin, 'Turks in the Ottoman Imperial Palace', in Jeroen Duindam, Tülay Artan and Metin Kunt (eds), *Royal Courts in Dynastic States and Empires: A Global Perspective* (Leiden: Brill, 2011), pp. 289–312.

Lampros, S., ''Η Ἑλληνικὴ ὡς ἐπίσημος γλῶσσα τῶν Σουλτάνων', Νέος Ἑλληνομνήμων 5 (1908), pp. 40–78.

Laurent, V., 'Une famille turque au service de Byzance. Les Mélikès', *Byzantinische Zeitschrift* 49 (1956), pp. 349–68.

—, 'Note additionnelle. L'inscription de l'église Saint-Georges de Bélisérama', *Revue des études byzantines* 26 (1968), pp. 367–71.

Leiser, Gary, 'The madrasah and the Islamization of Anatolia before the Ottomans', in Joseph Lowry, Devin Stewart and Shawkat M. Toowara (eds), *Law and Education in Medieval Islam: Studies in Memory of George Makdisi* (Cambridge: Gibb Memorial Series, 2004), pp. 174–91.

—, (ed.), *Les Seldjoukides d'Anatolie* (*Mésogeios* 25–26 [2005]).

—, 'The *History of the Patriarchs of the Egyptian Church* as a source for the history of the Seljuks of Anatolia', in Yasir Suleiman (ed.), *Living Islamic History: Studies in Honour of Professor Carole Hillenbrand* (Edinburgh: Edinburgh University Press, 2010), pp. 116–21.

—, 'The *waqf* as an instrument of cultural transformation in Seljuk Anatolia', in Ismail Poonawala (ed.), *The Turkish Presence in the Islamic World, the proceedings from the 2010 Levi Della Vida Conference honoring C.E. Bosworth* (forthcoming).

Lewis, Franklin D., *Rūmī, Past and Present, East and West: The life, teachings and poetry of Jalâl al-Din Rūmī* (Oxford: Oneworld, 2008).

Marlow, Louise, 'A thirteenth-century scholar in the eastern Mediterranean: Sirāj al-Dīn Urmavī, jurist, logician, diplomat', *al-Masāq* 22, no. 3 (2010), pp. 279–313.

Martin, M.E., 'The Venetian-Seljuk treaty of 1220', *English Historical Review* 95 (1980), pp. 321–3.

Meinecke, Michael, *Fayencedekorationen seldschukischer Sakralbauten in Kleinasien* (Tübingen: Wasmuth, 1976).

Meisami, Julie Scott, 'Rāvandī's *Rāḥat al-ṣudūr*: history or hybrid?', *Edebiyat* n.s. 5 (1992), pp. 181–215.

Melioranskii, P.I., 'Sel'dzhukname kak istochnik dlya istorii Vizantii XII-XIII vv', *Vizantiiskii Vremennik 1* (1894), pp. 613–40.

Melville, Charles, 'The early Persian historiography of Anatolia', in Judith Pfeiffer, Sholeh A. Quinn and Ernest Tucker (eds), *History and historiography of post-Mongol Asia and the Middle East: studies in honor of John E. Woods* (Wiesbaden: Harrassowitz, 2006), pp. 135–66.

—, 'Anatolia under the Mongols', in Kate Fleet (ed.), *The Cambridge History of Turkey*, i: *Byzantium to Turkey, 1071–1453* (Cambridge: Cambridge University Press, 2009), pp. 51–101.

Merçil, Erdoğan, *Türkiye Selçukluları'nda meslekler* (Ankara: Türk Tarih Kurumu, 2000).

Ocak, Ahmet Yaşar, 'Social, cultural and intellectual life, 1071–1453', in Kate Fleet (ed.), *The Cambridge History of Turkey*, i: *Byzantium to Turkey, 1071–1453* (Cambridge: Cambridge University Press, 2009), pp. 353–422.

Ohlander, Erik S., *Sufism in an Age of Transition: 'Umar al-Suhrawardī and the Rise of the Islamic Mystical Brotherhoods* (Leiden: Brill, 2008).

Önkal, Hakkı, *Anadolu Selçuklu Türbeleri* (Ankara: Atatürk Kültür, Dil ve Tarih Yüksek Kurumu, 1996).

Oral, Zeki, 'Anadolu'da san'at değeri olan ahşap minberler, kitabeleri ve tarihçeleri', *Vakıflar Dergisi* 5 (1962), pp. 23–77.

Pancaroğlu, Oya, 'Caves, borderlands and configurations of sacred topography in medieval Anatolia', in Gary Leiser (ed.), *Les Seljoukides d'Anatolie* (*Mésogeios* 25–26 [2005]), pp. 249–82.

—, 'The mosque-hospital complex in Divriği: a history of relations and transitions', *Anadolu ve Çevresinde Ortaçağ* 3 (2009), pp. 169–98.

Peacock, A.C.S., 'Ahmad of Niğde's *al-Walad al-Shafīq* and the Seljuk past', *Anatolian Studies* 54 (2004), pp. 95–104.

—, 'Georgia and the Anatolian Turks in the 12th and 13th centuries', *Anatolian Studies* 56 (2006), pp. 127–46.

—, 'Sinop: a frontier city in Seljuq and Mongol Anatolia', *Ancient Civilizations from Scythia to Siberia* 16 (2010), pp. 103–24.

—, 'Seljuq legitimacy in Islamic history', in Christian Lange and Songül Mecit (eds), *The Seljuqs: History, Politics and Culture* (Edinburgh: Edinburgh University Press, 2011), pp. 79–95.

Redford, Scott, 'Thirteenth-century Rūm Seljuq palaces and palace imagery', *Ars Orientalis* 23 (1994), pp. 215–32.

—, *Landscape and the State in Medieval Anatolia: Seljuk Gardens and Pavilions of Alanya, Turkey* (Oxford: Archeopress, 2000).

—, 'The inscription of the Kırkgöz Hanı and the problem of textual transmission in Seljuk Anatolia', *Adalya* 12 (2009), pp. 347–59.

—, 'Sinop in the summer of 1215: the beginning of Anatolian Seljuk architecture', *Ancient Civilizations from Scythia to Siberia* 16 (2010), pp. 125–38.

Redford, Scott and Gary Leiser, *Victory Inscribed. The Seljuk* Fetiḥnāme *on the Citadel Walls of Antalya, Turkey/Taşa Yazılan Zafer. Antalya İçkale Surlarındaki Selçuklu Fetihnamesi* (Antalya: Suna-İnan Kıraç Akdeniz Medeniyetleri Araştırma Enstitüsü, 2008).

Rogers, J. M., 'Waqf and patronage in Seljuk Anatolia: the epigraphic evidence', *Anatolian Studies* 26 (1976), pp. 69–103.

Russell, James, 'Medieval Armenian fraternities', *Transactions of the American Lodge of Research, F. & A.M.* 22 (1993), pp. 28–37.

Sakaoğlu, Necdet, *Türk Anadolu'da Mengücekoğulları* (Istanbul: Yapı Kredi Yayınları, 2005).

Shukurov, Rustam, 'Turkoman and Byzantine self-identity. Some reflections on the logic of title-making in twelfth- and thirteenth-century Anatolia', in Antony Eastmond (ed.), *Eastern Approaches to Byzantium* (Aldershot: Ashgate, 2001), pp. 259–76.

—, 'Iagupy: tiurskaya familiia na vizantiiskoi sluzhbe', in G. G. Litavrin (ed.), *Vizantiiskie Ocherki* (St Petersburg: Aleteia, 2006), pp. 205–29.

—, 'Semeistvo 'Izz al-Dina Kai-Kavusa II v Vizantii', *Vizantiiskii Vremennik* 67 (2008), pp. 89–116.

—, 'Tserkvi v tsitadeliakh Ispira i Bayburta: relikt garemnogo khristianstva?', in M.V. Bibikov (ed.), *Vizantiiskie ocherki* (St Petersburg: Aleteia, 2011), pp. 228–42.

Sinclair, T.A., *Eastern Turkey: An Architectural and Archaeological Survey* (London: Pindar Press, 1987–90, 4 vols).

Sümer, Faruk, *Selçuklular Devrinde Doğu Anadolu'da Türk Beylikleri* (Ankara: Türk Tarih Kurumu, 1990).

Taeschner, Franz, *Der anatolischen Dichter Nāṣirī (um 1300) und sein Futuvvetnāme* (Leipzig: Brockhaus, 1944).

—, *Zünfte und Bruderschaften im Islam: Texte zur Geschichte der Futuwwa* (Zurich: Artemis-Verlag, 1979).

Tekinalp, V.M., 'Palace churches of the Anatolian Seljuks: tolerance or necessity?', *Byzantine and Modern Greek Studies* 33, no. 2 (2009), pp. 148–67.

Temir, Ahmet, 'Anadolu İlhanlı Valilerinden Samağar Noyan', in 60. *Doğum Yılı Münasebetiyle Fuad Köprülü Armağanı/ Mélanges Fuad Köprülü* (Istanbul: Ankara Dil ve Tarih Coğrafyası Fakültesi, 1953), pp. 495–500.

—, *Kırşehir Emiri Nur el-Din'in 1272 Tarihli Arapça-Moğolca Vakfiyesi* (Ankara: Türk Tarih Kurumu, 1959).

Trépanier, Nicolas, *Foodways and Daily Life in Medieval Anatolia: a new social history* (Austin: University of Texas Press, 2014).

Turan, Osman, 'Selçuk devri vakfiyeleri: I. Şemseddin Altun-Aba, vakfiyesi ve hayatı', *Belleten* 11 (1947), pp. 197–235.

—, 'Selçuk devri vakfiyeleri: II. Mübârizeddin Er-Tokuş ve vakfiyesi', *Belleten 11* (1947), pp. 415–29.

—, 'Selçuk devri vakfiyeleri: III. Celâleddin Karatay, vakıfları ve vakfiyeleri', *Belleten* 12 (1948), pp. 17–158.

—, 'Les souverains seldjoukides et leurs sujets non-musulmans', *Studia Islamica* 1 (1953), pp. 65–100.

—, *Selcuklular Zamanında Türkiye: Siyasi Tarih Alp Arslan'dan Osman Gazi'ye (1071–1318)* (Istanbul: Turan Neşriyatı Yurdu, 1971).

—, *Doğu Anadolu Türk Devletleri Tarihi* (Istanbul: Turan Neşriyat Yurdu, 1973).

Vryonis, Speros, *The Decline of Medieval Hellenism in Asia Minor and the Process of Islamisation, from the Eleventh through the Fifteenth century* (Berkeley, Calif.: University of California Press, 1971).

—, 'Another note on the inscription of the Church of St George of Beliserama', *Byzantina* 9 (1977), pp. 11–22.

—, 'Byzantine and Turkish societies and their sources of manpower', in Speros Vryonis, *Studies on Byzantium, Seljuks, and Ottomans: Reprinted Studies* (Malibu. Calif.: Undena Publications, 1981), no. III, pp. 125–40.

Wolper, Ethel Sara, *Cities and Saints: Sufism and the Transformation of Urban Space in Medieval Anatolia* (University Park, Penn.: Pennsylvania State University Press, 2003).

Yalman, Suzan, 'Building the Sultanate of Rum: Memory, Urbanism and Mysticism in the Architectural Patronage of 'Ala al-Din Kayqubad, r. 1220–1237' (PhD Dissertation, Harvard University, 2011).

Yıldız, Sara Nur, 'Manuel Komnenos Mavrozomes and his descendants at the Seljuk court: the formation of a Christian Seljuk-Komnenian elite', in Stefan Leder (ed.), *Crossroads between Latin Europe and the Near East: Corollaries of the Frankish Presence in the Eastern Mediterranean (12th-14th centuries)* (Würzburg: Ergon Verlag, 2011), pp. 55–77.

Zhavoronkov, P.I., 'Nikeiskaia imperiia i Vostok', *Vizantiiskii Vremennik* 39 (1978), pp. 93–101.

INDEX

G

H

I

J

K

L

M

N

S

V

W

Y

Z